ECONOMIC HISTORY

AN ECONOMIC HISTORY OF THE UNITED STATES SINCE 1783

NORTH AMERICA

AN ECONOMIC HISTORY OF THE UNITED STATES SINCE 1783

PETER D'ALROY JONES

LONDON AND NEW YORK

First published in 1956
by Routledge & Kegan Paul Limited

Published 2010 by Routledge
2 Park Square, Milton Park, Abingdon, Oxfordshire OX14 4RN
711 Third Avenue, New York, NY 10017

First issued in paperback 2015

Routledge is an imprint of the Taylor and Francis Group, an informa business

© 1956 Peter d'Alroy Jones

All rights reserved. No part of this book may be reprinted or reproduced or utilized in any form or by any electronic, mechanical, or other means, now known or hereafter invented, including photocopying and recording, or in any information storage or retrieval system, without permission in writing from the publishers.

The publishers have made every effort to contact authors and copyright holders of the works reprinted in the *Economic History* series. This has not been possible in every case, however, and we would welcome correspondence from those individuals or organisations we have been unable to trace.

These reprints are taken from original copies of each book. In many cases the condition of these originals is not perfect. The publisher has gone to great lengths to ensure the quality of these reprints, but wishes to point out that certain characteristics of the original copies will, of necessity, be apparent in reprints thereof.

British Library Cataloguing in Publication Data
A CIP catalogue record for this book
is available from the British Library

An Economic History of the United States since 1783
ISBN 0-415-38000-6 (volume)
ISBN 0-415-37974-1 (subset)
ISBN 0-415-28619-0 (set)

Routledge Library Editions: Economic History

ISBN13: 978-0-415-75923-6 (pbk)
ISBN13: 978-0-415-38000-3 (hbk)

An Economic History of the United States
Since 1783

AN ECONOMIC HISTORY OF THE UNITED STATES SINCE 1783

by

PETER d'A. JONES

M.A. (*Manchester*), PH.D. (*London*)

Routledge & Kegan Paul

LONDON

*First published 1956
by Routledge & Kegan Paul Limited
Broadway House, Carter Lane, E.C.4.*

To
Margaret

CONTENTS

Preface ... vii

Part One. GROWTH AND CRISIS OF THE SECTIONAL STRUGGLE (1783–1861)

I Emergence of a Nation ... 3
II The Westward Movement and Agriculture ... 14
III Industry and Labour ... 32
IV Internal Improvements ... 44
V Trade and Finance ... 56
VI The Crisis: Civil War ... 76

Part Two. EMERGENCE OF AMERICAN CAPITALISM (1861–1917)

VII Industry and Combination ... 97
VIII The Westward Movement and Agriculture ... 119
IX Agrarian Unrest and Labour ... 136
X Immigration and Transportation ... 154
XI Trade and Finance ... 167
XII Social Criticism and Reform ... 190

Part Three. AMERICA AND THE WORLD ECONOMY (SINCE 1917)

XIII War and Prosperity ... 209
XIV Slump and New Deal ... 229
Epilogue: America and World Power ... 255
Note ... 263
Index ... 265

MAPS

Territorial Growth of the United States	5
Civil War, Alignment of States	91
The American Frontier	127
Specialization in Agriculture	139

PREFACE

HERE, in this Preface, I allow myself the luxury of the first person singular. This book was conceived in Manchester, planned in Brussels and written in its final form in London. While the original idea of writing it was solely mine, it would not have been finished perhaps but for the interest and encouragement of friends. Of these I must particularly thank Willis Hurst (just for being there); James F. S. Russell (for personal reasons, as well as for his careful reading of the early chapters and for giving me the benefit of his wide knowledge of railroad history); Robert Estall, of the Geography Department of L.S.E., who made the maps with characteristic competence and friendliness; Marcus Cunliffe for advice and encouragement on matters not closely related to the text of this book, but nevertheless essential to its completion; and, for their training in early life, Richard C. Smith and Tom S. Turner.

I thank Margaret Hateley-Jones for many intangibles, and for making it possible for me to begin the work in the first place, as well as for specific contributions throughout the text (such as the Statistical Analysis of the Election of 1860) and painstaking reading and checking. Miss Mary Gillatt was in charge of the typing and layout of the manuscript in its most crucial stages.

London,
August 1955

Note on the edition of 1964

The new edition is issued in direct response to continued demand for a book of this sort on the American economy. Books of greater dimensions and weightier claims are available; nevertheless, we have obeyed the dictates of our own market by making no basic alterations in this text beyond the elimination of one or two factual errors.

Northampton, Massachusetts,
February, 1964.

PART ONE

Growth and Crisis of the Sectional Struggle 1783–1861

I
EMERGENCE OF A NATION

Sectionalism and American economic history – Economic aspects of the Revolution; postwar reforms – The economic depression and radical agitation – The Federal Constitution of the United States.

IN 1787, for the first time in modern history, a political nation was 'made' by one single written act, or rather one body of acts—the American Constitution. But the State must always rest on Society, and a definite degree of social cohesion must precede political association. This necessity is tragically illustrated by the history of the United States between the end of the War of Independence (1783) and the end of the Civil War (1865). Seventy-eight years after the Treaty of Paris that terminated the war of the American colonists against the Mother Country, the new American nation disintegrated. The 'War Between the States' which ensued was the result of the disastrous failure of the political structure to maintain compatible within itself the swiftly-diverging social elements.

It is precisely these 'social elements' with which we are concerned in the first part of this economic history. From time to time the facts under review will be referred both forwards and backwards into the historical process, in order to reveal that growth of 'sectionalism' which culminated in bitter civil conflict. There was nothing 'inevitable' about this culmination however. This book is, of necessity, written in historical 'shorthand'; it deals with 'development' more than with historical 'reconstruction', with real or supposed 'trends' rather than with the *texture* of social and economic life at any given, distinct and recognizable period. This shorthand technique alone makes it possible to write a book of this type, fulfilling this definite need. But in order to derive the most benefit, the reader as well as the writer must remain alert throughout, to guard against certain insidious influences that are unfortunately inherent in the technique itself. Merely because it is possible for a general historian to examine the historical process with *ex post facto* knowledge and isolate trends of development, one cannot therefore assume that the trends he isolates were 'there', fixed, determined even before the events themselves took place that completed his retrospective picture. More simply, we can—with a greater or lesser degree of accuracy—decide what happened in the past; but we can never eliminate the boundless possibilities, the might-have-beens, bound up with every situation in the past. But with a book of this kind it is fatally easy to build up, unconsciously, a cast-iron framework for the complex facts of the story, a framework that can become part of our mental furniture for life. The framework then becomes a cage in which the mind is caught, and the very purpose of the historian is thus subverted. The Civil War was not 'inevitable', although we can examine the factors 'leading up to' its outbreak.

'Sectional' loyalties and economic groupings can be traced back to Colonial days at least. Parochialism was rife before the Revolution and cleavage existed between North and South, between individual states, and even between the coastlands and interior areas of each single state. The War of Independence moreover was accompanied by an internal 'American Revolution' engendered by these very facts. Many historians believe that the break away of the American colonies from the Mother Country was perhaps not unavoidable; it was precipitated not only by the dissatisfaction felt by the British Government itself and its sharp change in attitude after 1763, but also by the exigencies of the internal situation in the Colonies.

What was this situation? Briefly, there was an imprecise stratification of society between on the one hand the old colonial aristocracy of the 'seaboard' (landowners, merchants and slave owners backed by Church officials) and on the other the hardy small farmer of the 'back country'. This was especially true of South Carolina. The political supremacy of the colonial aristocracy was buttressed by the narrow basis of the franchise and the lack of representation for new areas opening up in the West. The backcountry Western element was less English in origin and also felt strong religious antipathy to the Eastern seaboard Anglican Church, to which it had taxes to pay and high marriage fees. Taxation generally was levied on polls and not on property, thus Westerners paid more than their share, in one sense. Moreover, the West had very poor roads and marketing facilities, and received no adequate supplies in its constant need for defence against Indians. It was the latter complaint which led to Bacon's Rebellion of 1676. Most of the grievances of Westerners, however, can be attributed to one basic factor: they constituted a *debtor* section. For instance they held out for the issue of paper money, which the creditor seaboard commercial sections always vigorously opposed.

Perhaps class consciousness was greatest in Pennsylvania in this

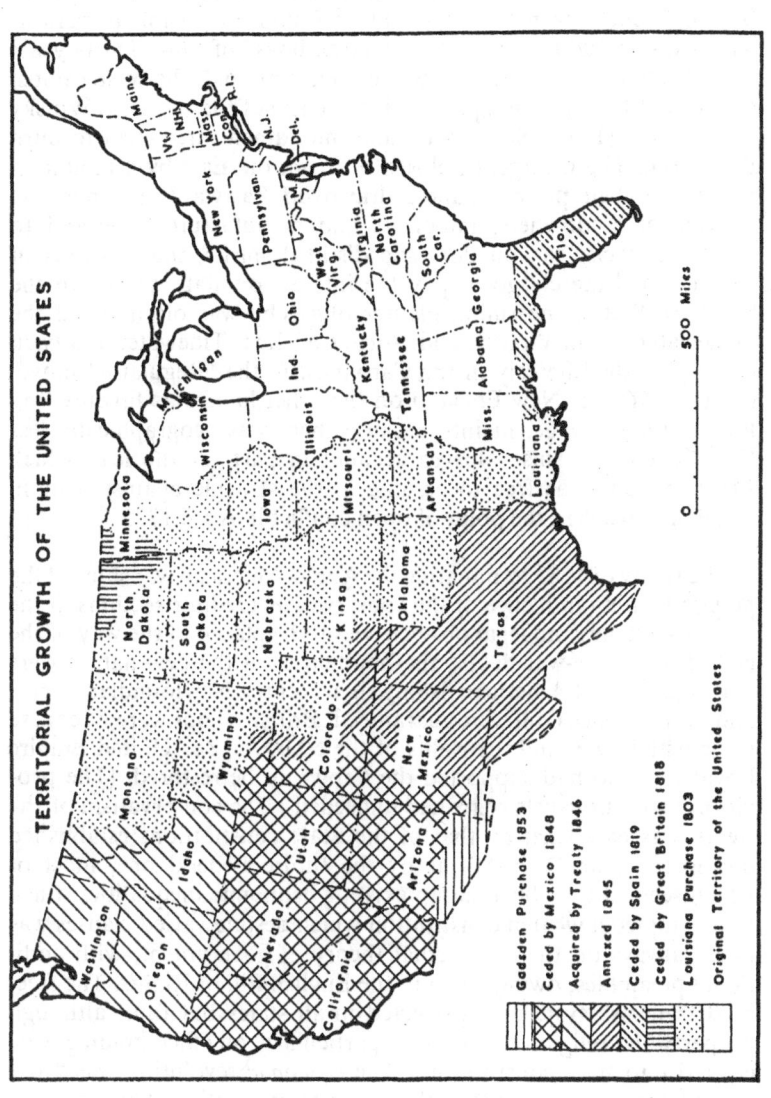

early period. Here the colonial aristocracy was more deeply rooted; the rich Quaker merchants and lawyers dominated the political scene and both Western farmers and urban proletariat were excluded by the freehold franchise. Discontent found expression in various outbreaks, including that of the ' Paxton boys ' of 1764. Thirty years later, when the young nation was eleven years old, the westernmost counties of Pennsylvania provided the centre of the so-called Whisky Insurrection (1794). Seven thousand militiamen threatened to burn Pittsburgh. The insurgents, closed off from the East by a mountain range and their paltry finances drawn off Eastwards to enter the pockets of landowners, importers and manufacturers, refused to accept an excise tax on domestic distilled spirits, the proceeds of which would merely go to pay the interest on state debts. In the Southern States, the ruling planter oligarchy was often called the 'Tidewater', as in Virginia and North Carolina. Tidewater and back country clashed fiercely in the Carolinas, in the 'Regulator' movement of 1768-71. New England on the other hand was favoured by less hostile cleavage, mainly because there was geographically less 'back country'. This helps to account in part for the lead which Massachusetts was free to assume in the struggle against Britain, which first reached the point of open conflict in April 1775.

The treaty of 1783 terminating the Anglo-American war showed the preponderating influence of the conservative, creditor sections in the former Colonies: no legal obstacle was to be placed in the way of the collection of pre-war debts; the boundaries of the new nation were left vague, whilst American fishing rights off the Newfoundland coast and St. Lawrence Gulf were guaranteed; British troops were of course to be withdrawn, and the rights of the 60,000 or so 'United Empire Loyalists' who had supported the Crown to be restored. (The provision about Loyalists remained unheeded.) The conservatism of the treaty was paralleled by that of the State constitutions established during the years 1776-80, as by the future Federal one, most of which seemed to rubber-stamp existing economic inequalities. Each state adopted a written constitution which despite varied clauses was based always on the contractual theory of government, with additional preambles, owing much to the English Bill of Rights. The freehold franchise system was rejected in all states but four, although property and religious restrictions particularly on office-holding were erected into state constitutions. The *economic* revolution was more radical, involving in the first place land redistribution. The estates of Loyalists were confiscated, with a loss of almost one million pounds sterling to the Penn family in Pennsylvania and a loss to Loyalists in New York amounting to an estimated total of $2½ million. This extensive policy was matched by striking legal changes: in the South primogeniture and entail were abolished by 1790. The regulations of the royal proclamation of 1763 were also suspended: an attempt to regularize relations with the American Indians, this proclamation had set aside the trans-Allegheny area as an Indian reservation. Governors had been forbidden to grant warrants for the survey of or patents for any lands within the region, all white settlers had to vacate the restricted zone, and all trading with Indians had to be licensed. While this was never meant by the Mother Country as a permanent check to westward migration the action had caused grave anxiety among pioneers and land speculators. The suspension of the proclamation together with that of the provisions of the Quebec Act of 1774 (extending the province of Quebec to the Ohio and recognizing the Catholic Church there) greatly facilitated further settlement. 'Quitrents' to the King and to proprietors were automatically wiped out in 1783, and all former Crown lands within the respective states were disposed of by the Legislatures themselves at very cheap prices. Thus was inaugurated a land policy which played a major rôle in American political development for over half a century, and reached a logical conclusion in the Homestead Act of 1862.

The redistribution of land was accompanied by the growth of religious freedom and the separation of Church and State. Also there was a movement towards penal reform sponsored by Jefferson, and prison conditions gradually improved. But promises of thorough governmental reforms in the interests of the back country came to nothing or very little, and the condition of the debtor sections failed to improve with the coming of peace and national independence.

The years 1783 to 1789 have become known to historians as the 'Critical Period'. The name largely belies the purely economic history of these years but is an accurate title from the social and political viewpoint. Business activity was continually enlarging its scope and commerce revived rapidly, despite the depression of 1785–9. By the time reluctant little Rhode Island ratified the Constitution (May 1790) a revival of prosperity had long begun in which the Federal Constitution was a central factor.

The stimulus and ravages of war were not significantly felt in agriculture, although the cast-iron plough appeared and various attempts to improve livestock were made. Indigo and rice cultivation were hindered to some extent in the South and the British commandeered crops and slaves in Virginia and the Carolinas during spasmodic raids (1778–81), but cotton cultivation was stimulated in the general quickening of economic processes, and tobacco production increased by almost one-third, 1774 to 1790. The non-importation agreement favourably affected wool production generally, and in the Middle Colonies where most of the campaigning took place the price of farm products was artificially raised by the ease with which British and French money flowed.

In these same battle areas however industry suffered heavily. In Virginia, the Carolinas, Georgia and New Jersey, British military forces sought to destroy manufacturing centres. The stimulus of wartime production tended to be limited to inland establishments removed from the risks and hazards of conflict. Interference with normal commerce forced the colonists to depend more upon home production, and in addition the war created special needs. Thus Congress exempted all ironworkers from military service and several states gave subsidies to the industry. Munitions were produced in small centres in Massachusetts, Pennsylvania and Connecticut, for instance the government armoury established at Springfield in 1778. The war aided in the growth of the textile and paper industries, and in the production of glass, pottery, leather and household utensils. V. S. Clark[1] has shown how the cutting-off of imports of English woollen cloth helped to popularize the use of domestic fabrics and hasten the transition of homespun manufactures into household industries organized by merchant employers and small entrepreneurs who supplied the commercial market.

The pace of industrial progress slackened considerably towards the end of the war however, and from the beginning there were several serious drawbacks. As many fishermen turned to privateering the fishing industry almost disappeared—which accounts for the clause in the Treaty of Paris (valiantly negotiated by John Adams) protecting American fishing rights. The slave trade also declined and labour remained quite scarce despite the impressment of Hessian and other prisoners of war into industry. Above all, the chaotic state of the currency formed a severe deterrent to industrial enterprise.

From 1781 to 1786 only half a million dollars were paid into the Treasury—whilst the National Debt at the war's end was nearly $7,900,000. The revenue barely covered administrative expenses; Morris, the Finance Minister of the Confederacy, resigned in despair in 1783. Meanwhile overdue interest on debt accumulated and continental securities fell in value. For four years after the war, state and federal finances were in anarchy. Hundreds of millions of dollars' worth of paper currency was issued by individual states and the central authority had negligible control. Partial or complete repudiation was inevitable. A severe post-war depression originating chiefly in the influx of European goods maiming the infant industries and the drain of specie from America was thus aggravated by the weakness of the Confederate Government and the unco-operative attitude of the States. The latter, in desperate efforts to attain commercial

[1] *History of Manufactures in the United States, Vol. I*, new ed. Washington, 1929.

protection, built up tariff barriers between themselves. Trade and boundary disputes ensued: New York and New Hampshire quarrelled about Vermont, which in turn was ready to secede to Canada; Maryland and Virginia disagreed about their boundary along the Potomac. During this transitional period the new nation had neither the benefits of national unity nor those of being part of 'a trading Empire'.

It was the currency famine, the roots of which went back beyond the Revolution, which led debtors to agitate for some kind of relief legislation from State legislatures. This relief could take the form of 'tender' Acts making land and goods at a fixed price a legal discharge, or it could constitute 'stay' laws which postponed debt collection. In its most disastrous form it legalized a policy of 'cheap money', as in Rhode Island. Creditors fled from this state sooner than accept worthless paper money as legal payment. At the depth of the depression in 1786 seven out of thirteen states issued paper money. In Massachusetts in that same bleak year, a small civil war erupted, Shays' Rebellion. Captain Daniel Shays, a Revolutionary veteran, organized a large body of distressed Western farmers to prevent by force the sitting of the courts. Under the Constitution 'rigged' by commercial interests so that 40 per cent of taxation fell on cattle and all but property owners were excluded from office-holding and the franchise, the courts had become clogged with suits for debt, and justice was slow and dealt by grasping lawyers. Loyal militia put down Shays' show of force and scattered the rebels into the hills of central Massachusetts during heavy snows. But it did not hearten conservatives enough, and this despairing call to violence on the part of debtor sections was by no means the last.

It is important to remember, however, that a year later, also in Massachusetts (Beverley), the first cotton factory in the United States was established. The Bank of North America had previously been set up in 1781, the Banks of Boston and New York in 1784. Throughout the decade of the 1780's bridges, canals and turnpike roads were constructed and exploitation of the West undertaken. Trade with France and Holland rose over pre-war limits, and while the Yankees lost the three-cornered trade, commercial relations with the Baltic and the Near and Far East were begun. The New England–China trade routes were firmly established during the last three years of the decade. The historian's tag 'the Criticial Period' has as usual no value unless he makes his framework of reference quite clear.

The Confederate Government drew whatever authority it possessed from the Articles of Confederation and Perpetual Union approved by the Continental Congress in 1777, and subsequently ratified by the several states. These Articles gave Congress the right to raise an army and navy, requisition troops and money, establish a post office, regulate coinage, weights and measures and borrow on the credit of the 'United States'. But they provided no real federal government strong and efficient enough to meet the pressing needs of a nation disunited by post-war depression and traditional sectionalism, beset by foreign governments and internal dissensions. In fact the Confederation was more like an international alliance than a government; its defects exemplified the unwillingness of Americans to institute any *new* external control, now that freedom over taxation and commerce had been wrested from the English Parliament by the states. The 'sovereignty, freedom and independence' of each state was to be firmly guaranteed; they had entered 'a firm league of friendship' only. Yet the preamble had talked of 'perpetual Union'. In fact each state had one vote in Congress whatever the number of its delegates; any amendment needed a *unanimous* decision; the states retained complete supervision of taxation and commerce; there was no provision whatsoever for a federal executive or judiciary, and finally, no *sanction* in any case for federal powers.

The Philadelphia Constitutional Convention which first met on 25 May 1787 was the off-shoot of more than one earlier attempt to reach some conclusions on the need for governmental reform. A group at Alexandria, Virginia, failed to agree on any plan in 1785 but the Annapolis Convention the following year not only passed a report urging immediate amendment of the Articles of Confederation but issued the call for the final Convention, which was to meet

'... for the sole and express purpose of revising the Articles of Confederation, and reporting to Congress and the several legislatures such alterations and provisions therein as shall, when agreed to in Congress and confirmed by the states, render the federal constitution adequate to the exigencies of government and the preservation of the Union.'

Political efficiency and national integrity were not the only factors however which lay behind the conservative agitation for a stronger federal government—as Charles A. Beard the distinguished American historian pointed out.[1] Alexander Hamilton, the outstanding 'Federalist' who laboured vigorously for the Constitution and whose economic ideas and policy no economic history can omit, stated clearly:

'The new Constitution has in favour of its success these circumstances. A very great weight of influence of the persons who framed it, particularly in the universal popularity of General Washington.

---

[1] *An Economic Interpretation of the Constitution of the United States* (New York, 1913).

The goodwill of the commercial interest throughout the states, which will give all its efforts to the establishment of a government capable of regulating, protecting, and extending the commerce of the Union. The goodwill of most men of property in the several states, who wish a government of the Union able to protect them against domestic violence, and the depredations which the democratic spirit is apt to make on property, and who are besides anxious for the respectability of the nation. The hopes of the creditors of the United States, that a general government possessing the means of doing it, will pay the debt of the Union.'[1]

In the debate of the Philadelphia Convention, the frictions of sectionalism found expression. The representatives of large states opposed the demands of small states for equal representation in the new government, on the grounds that power should be proportionate to population and wealth; the small states feared for the rights of minorities. Southern planters objected fiercely to any hint of the prohibition of slave traffic; Northern merchants wanted to abolish interstate tariff barriers and give Congress the power to retaliate against European commercial discriminations. Land speculators thought that Congress should be empowered to do more than virtually give land away: if a federal standing army were maintained for defence against the Indians, and if Great Britain and Spain could be induced by a strong American government to climb down on the respective questions of British troops in posts south of the Great Lakes and the free navigation of the Mississippi to its mouth, they would be assured of greater profits. Moreover, bond speculators, having bought state and federal securities at much less than face value, desired a federal government empowered to collect taxes directly and thus raise the market value of bonds to par. Full payment of debts to creditors could be more easily exacted if the states were not allowed to issue paper money and if there were Congressional control of bankruptcy laws. Basically, the aim of the creditor sections regarding the foreign debt was to prevent forcible intervention for its collection and at the same time to uphold public credit in order to extend the chances of favourable commercial treaties in the future.

However, the Constitution managed to resolve much of this confusion by subtle compromise. So, representation in the House of Representatives was to be based on population, whilst in the upper chamber the states were to be equally represented by two senators each. As a sop to the planters, slaves were to be counted as three-fifths in assessing the federal ratio for representation in the House, but on the other hand the slave trade (*not* slavery) was to be prohibited after 1808. Such compromise was only possible—and perhaps

[1] *Works of Alexander Hamilton*, ed. H. C. Lodge, New York, 1885-6. Vol. I.

only ever *is* possible—because the Convention members were all in agreement on fundamentals. They were all conservatives and property-owners. It was the pressing demands of the radicals that brought the addition of the later ten Amendments guaranteeing the Rights of Man. The Constitution itself was drawn up in 1787 by a group of conservative men, mainly lawyers, professors, teachers, investors or speculators. Of the thirty-nine who signed the document, no small farmers or artisans were present. About five-sixths of the members profited later by Hamilton's funding of the national debt, twenty-four were moneylenders, fifteen were shareholders and eleven were businessmen of one type or another. Moreover Beard has written:

'Four-fifths of the active, forceful leaders of the Convention helped to realize as a process of government, the paper Constitution they had drafted.'[1]

Yet how could this decided minority of wealthy men in a commercial and agricultural society overcome the heavy opposition of debtors, small farmers, mechanics and artisans, and radicals? They formed well-organized and strategically well-placed pressure-groups, concentrated in the urban areas on or near the coast, and represented in every state. Furthermore they had a valuable asset in the undemocratic restricted franchises of the period. Indeed it seems doubtful that ratification would have been accomplished without this, the division was so close in several states. In Daniel Shays' state the vote was 187:168, in New York 30:27 and in Virginia 89:79. It has been claimed that not more than one-sixth of the adult male population ratified the Constitution. It is too easy to disparage the document, however, to recognize it only, for instance, as the result of a Frenchman's[2] misinterpretation of the British Constitution of the eighteenth century, foisted by the American propertied and moneyed classes onto a proletarian majority. Its true worth is that it gave political stability to an emerging democracy. An English Revolution terminated in the military dictatorship of Cromwell; a French Revolution in the 'plebiscitary' military dictatorship of Napoleon I; a Russian Revolution in the semi-theocratic totalitarian state, which is a further and more powerful extension of the plebiscitary idea. The American Revolution resulted in the American Constitution. Only in this light can the real value of that Constitution be judged.

[1] *The Economic Origins of Jeffersonian Democracy* (New York, 1915).
[2] Montesquieu. This semi-satirical view exaggerates Montesquieu's influence and ignores the fact that the United States inherited working political institutions and established traditions from former Colonial governments.

SUGGESTED FURTHER READING

(These brief lists are added to each chapter to guide students in the preparation of essays and papers. They are, of course, very selective.)

BEARD, CHARLES A. *An Economic Interpretation of the Constitution of the United States* (New York, 1913).

EAST, R. A. *Business Enterprise in the American Revolutionary Era* (New York, 1938).

JAMESON, J. F. *The American Revolution Considered as a Social Movement* (Princeton, 1926).

II

THE WESTWARD MOVEMENT AND AGRICULTURE

Agriculture and the Westward Movement – Expansion before 1783; the Ordinance of 1787 and later legislation – The Old South-West: King Cotton; slavery; Southern crops – The Old North-West and the decline of Eastern agriculture; early mechanization and applied science – The Frontier Thesis and the politics of expansion.

THE United States of 1783 was a distinctly commercial and agricultural nation, and down to the Civil War agriculture remained dominant in the American economy—despite the fact that the beginnings of modern industrialism in the North had been considerable enough to make a grave contribution to the steady alienation of the Northern and Southern sections. It therefore seems logical, when faced with a series of financial, commercial, industrial and agricultural developments between 1783 and 1861, to begin with agriculture.

But it is quite impossible to study the history of American agriculture in the first half of the nineteenth century without constant and close reference to the Westward Movement. For in this period the two great changes which made themselves felt on American farming were: firstly, the rapid and vast expansion of the geographical area of cultivable land, and secondly, the coming of the first forms of scientific farming. This was a cheerful, confident, expansionist era in farming generally, in spite of the Southern depression which did not lift until about 1830. Ever-widening European and home demand and stimulated prices made it (but for the recurrent crises) a period of well-to-do farmers. Land values rose in the area known as the Old North-west, and after 1830 slaves also rose in value in the South. Labour was fairly scarce for industry as for agriculture, although the population was just about doubling each decade. This scarcity aggravated the wasteful tendencies of American farmers who 'used up' the soil quickly and then passed on to abundant virgin lands further

West. Also it stimulated the invention of labour-saving devices and machinery which were usually taken up with great alacrity and enthusiasm. But, even in the South to a large extent, the 'frontiersman' who moved ever-Westward from the ravaged areas of soil-erosion was primarily a land *speculator* and only secondly a farmer. His hope was to buy cheap land, hold it until the value rose, sell out and move on. The rapidity with which the West was 'opened' after 1783 forced many Eastern farmers, especially in New England, either to give up cultivation or to turn hastily from grain to dairy and fruit production. Even in the South the plantations of the Old South-west were soon to make the chill wind of competition blow upon the seaboard cotton and tobacco fields.

One of the most decisive factors in American economic life and development for three centuries was this existence of extensive un-occupied land. For a century after 1783 a leading question facing the American nation was the occupation and utilization of these vast Western territorial resources. In the words of Frederick Jackson Turner, the historian of the 'frontier':

'American history has been to a large degree the history of the Great West. The existence of an area of free land, its continuous recession, and the advance of American settlement Westward, explain American development.'[1]

This movement began in Colonial days among fur traders and missionaries, who later gave way to cattlemen, miners and farmers and eventually to capitalists determined on large-scale exploitation of the natural resources. There was no regularity about the stages of development of the 'frontier', but the Westward movement affected agriculture, industry, labour and transport, and the American Civil War was in part its outcome.

Some moves Westward had already taken place before America became an independent nation. Cortés first sailed to Mexico from Cuba in 1519 to establish a Spanish trading post. By 1521 he had become ruler of Mexico. Eighteen years later, Spanish expeditions began to explore the area later called New Mexico, discovering the Grand Canyon in 1540. Thus Spain gained a start of a century over the French and English colonists. By 1770, San Diego and Monterey and by 1776 San Franciso, were founded.

The French from 1699 onwards settled southwards from the Great Lakes and northwards from the Mexican Gulf, setting up various Mississippi posts including New Orleans, Fort Chartres and Vincennes. Slavery began on the upper Mississippi and after the mid-

[1] *The Frontier in American History* (1921).

eighteenth century exports from the interior of cereals, meat and copper were made through New Orleans. The French imported the first 'bluegrass' and white clover of Kentucky and began lead workings in Missouri.

The English settlers in the eighteenth century entered the Ohio valley, establishing settlements in Tennessee and Kentucky. The latter was reached in 1751 by way of the Cumberland Gap and in 1775 Daniel Boone made his famous 'Wilderness Road' trip to the Kentucky River. The plan for a new State—Transylvania—collapsed in 1777; the new territories were at first assimilated by existing states.

Land speculation arose almost simultaneously. The agitation of land monopolists under General Rufus Putnam and the Rev. Manasseh Cutler led in 1787 to the passing of the North-West Ordinance, which provided for the government of the area Northwest of the Ohio and for the abolition of slavery in this region. An act of 1785 had already instituted a rectangular survey of land into townships of thirty-six square miles, further divided into 'sections' of one square mile, one section of each township being put aside for educational purposes. The Ordinance established the 'Territorial' system whereby as soon as a newly settled area had a population of 5,000 free male adults, a local legislature could be formed regulated by a federal governor and composed of a legislative council, a house of representatives and a judiciary of federal judges. The 'Territory' thus set up could claim the right to enter the Union as a member state only when its population numbered 60,000 free residents.

The main questions facing the government concerning land were: In what size lots should it be sold? Should it be sold for revenue, or very cheaply to help pioneers and facilitate speedy settlement? Should it be sold for cash or on credit?

Generally the East opposed rapid Westward expansion because it caused a labour scarcity, depressed land values and presented the Eastern farmer with the competition of cheap Western produce. The West, as a debtor area, demanded a liberal land policy and laws became increasingly liberal as Western representatives entered Congress.

Three years later, the South-West Ordinance of 1790 provided for the organization of this area, but permitted slavery to be maintained as an economic institution. In 1792 Kentucky entered the Union as a fully fledged state and in 1798 the Mississippi Territory was organized. The smallest area of land allowed to be sold by the government was cut down to 320 acres (a half section) in 1800, to 160 acres in 1804 and to 80 acres in 1820. Also in that year the credit system inaugurated in 1796 was abolished as it had engendered much overexpansion and speculation, and the price of land lowered from

$2 to $1·25 an acre. Meanwhile the Louisiana Purchase of 1803 had doubled the size of the country. The land was bought for $15 million to control the river outlets for Western farm produce. But Western pressure was unrelenting. Two further concessions were demanded after 1820: the right of pre-emption[1] (legalized in 1841) and the actual donation of free land by the government to bona-fide settlers (legalized by the Homestead Act, 1862).

The two principal new areas of settlement were the 'Old North-west' and the 'Old South-west'. The former covered much the same ground as the modern states of the East North Central zone (Ohio, Indiana, Illinois, Michigan and Wisconsin); the latter covered the present East South Central zone (Kentucky, Tennessee, Mississippi, Alabama) and one West South Central zone state (Louisiana). The Old South-west was occupied at a later date than the Old North-west, although Kentucky (1792) and Tennessee (1796) were settled by backwoodsmen from the hill country areas of Virginia and the Carolinas in the eighteenth century. The War of 1812 and the invention of the cotton gin were two important factors in the migration to the South-west. It was 'land hunger' that sent the planters westwards from the Eastern fields to the rich black loams of Mississippi, Louisiana, Arkansas, Alabama and southern Georgia. Many plantation owners, ignorant of soil-conservation and modern techniques, had despoiled the formerly rich lands of the East by constant monoculture of cotton, and then simply moved out, with their slaves and household baggage, to begin once more on the virgin soils of the West. The Old South-west tried to become merely a reproduction of the Eastern plantation life, just as the Old North-west paralleled the economy of New England. The 'poor white' element, originally mainly Northern pioneers and yeomen who left marginal farms and trekked South in the hope of making a more substantial living with one or two slaves, were again pushed further West before the tide of successful planters. Ill-feeling had always existed between these 'crackers' or 'hill-billies' and their wealthier cousins, and with the wave of migration which established the Old South-west the poor whites were sent beyond the Mississippi, or north once more beyond the Ohio, or remained to eke out a precarious living on inferior soils whilst the rich plantation owners monopolized the fertile 'bottom' lands. As A. O. Craven has shown, however,[2] the numbers of poor whites probably never exceeded a few thousand.

[1] The right of any squatter then on the public lands to buy the land he occupied at a minimum price. The Act of 1841 said that any adult male could 'pre-empt' 160 acres of surveyed land, simply by erecting a 'dwelling' and making certain minimum 'improvements'.
[2] *The Coming of the Civil War* (New York, 1942).

The centre of cotton cultivation shifted therefore to the Mississippi valley and this change led to the removal of the Cherokee and Creek Indians to more Western reservations and to the ejection of Spain from Texas and Florida. Louisiana (1812), Mississippi (1817) and Alabama (1819) entered the Union in quick succession and the 'Cotton Kingdom' thus became established. In the first half of the century cotton replaced tobacco as the chief crop of large planters, who in Colonial days had relied on tobacco, indigo and rice. The exhaustion of the tobacco fields, the decline of indigo production and the greatly increased demand for cotton due to the innovations in textile machinery, together with the geographical shift and vast increase in cultivable area, explain this succession. In 1820 the cotton crop weighing 160 million pounds was the most valuable Southern interest; but by 1830 the crop had doubled, and by 1840 more than doubled again. In 1850 when 60 per cent of all American slaves were engaged in cotton production, it reached a thousand million, and in 1860 touched on 2,300 million pounds—two-thirds of the total value of United States exports.

Two chief types of cotton were grown in the South, long staple and short staple. The long staple cotton used in fine fabrics was restricted mainly to the sea islands of the coast of Georgia and South Carolina. It had been introduced from the Bahamas by Loyalist refugees in about 1786 and by the 1820's reached its peak of export production (an average of 11 million pounds a year sent abroad). The disadvantages of this 'sea island cotton' were the comparatively small yield per acre of only 150 pounds and the necessity for very skilled picking. It was not this, but the hardy short staple type cultivable in upland and interior regions that managed to succeed the declining indigo industry. This was not possible, however, until the technical difficulties of separating seed and cotton were solved by Eli Whitney's cotton gin.

Whitney, a Connecticut Yankee and Yale graduate who moved South in the hope of becoming a tutor, devised his crude but efficient invention at a plantation near Savannah, Georgia, in 1793. His machine replaced the work of ten men if hand-operated, and fifty men if used with horse-power. In March 1794 he took out a patent and expected to make a fortune from his monopoly: other inventors perfected his original ideas, however, and neither planters, entrepreneurs nor judges would regard his patent rights seriously. Cotton mills had already been introduced into the Northern states from England and with the ending of the 1812–14 War with that country these factories, despite the temporary postwar depression, began to thrive under tariff protection. The Industrial Revolution was well under way in Britain, where the growth of a mechanized cotton industry much preceded similar developments in other textiles. Thus

THE WESTWARD MOVEMENT AND AGRICULTURE 19

Southern planters were blessed with two expanding eager markets. The perfection by I. M. Singer in the 1850's of an earlier sewing machine by Elias Howe increased this voracious demand still further.

The improved gin enabled a man to work 350 pounds of cotton a day, whereas formerly this figure had been one pound. But a gang of slaves could cultivate much more than could be picked, and labour difficulties during cotton-picking time were severe. It was, and is still even now, not possible to mechanize entirely the gathering of cotton, for the bolls tend to ripen unevenly at different times. In the pre-Civil War years the cotton belt did not stretch as far as north Virginia, Kentucky, Maryland or Missouri because the crop needs 200 frost-free days during its lengthy growing season. The ravages of the boll-weevil (which dislikes frost even more) have altered this situation since.

Cotton cultivation was intimately bound up with slavery and the plantation system. This is not the place to attempt an analysis of the slavery issue in its many aspects, political, racial or moral. But as an economic and social institution slavery cannot escape our notice.

Cotton plantations, like the manors of feudal Britain, differed so widely in character and size as to make modern 'revisionist' scholars doubt the validity of generalizations altogether. It is first essential to agree with A. O. Craven and many others in dismissing the idea of an aristocratic 'cavalier' South in which huge plantations were predominant. About 50 per cent of the total cotton crop at least was grown by men employing anything from only one to five or six negroes and working alongside them: what Morison and Commager have called 'middle class plantations'.[1] Those who migrated to the Old South-west, although the poor whites fled before them, were mainly yeomen farmers, men 'on the make' searching for fresher, cheaper lands. Some had slaves; some had none. But each looked forward to the day when he would own a plantation and 'a parcel of negroes'. Some large planters also moved, but outside the famous 'Sugar Bowl' area where conditions fluctuated, only a few could build traditional Southern homes in the South-west. The Old South-west shared, despite profound differences, those buoyant, aggressive characteristics that were evidenced in the Old North-west. Professor Craven has explained this by saying that the region possessed all the 'Western' qualities, added to a 'Southern' base. In Georgia according to the 1850 Census there were only 1,900 cultivators describable as 'planters', but 81,000 'farmers'. The white population of the South in 1860 totalled over 8 million, but the number of slaveholders only 383,637. Less than 3 per cent of all Southern farms exceeded 500 acres in size. 'Such were two-thirds of the Southern peoples;' says Professor Craven, 'not squires, certainly not poor whites, but

[1] *Growth of the American Republic, Vol. I,* 1950 Edition.

rather middle-class Americans bent on getting on in a land of opportunity.' The great tragedy of what Americans call the *antebellum* South was that this majority failed to assert itself, but was driven by the attacks of Northern 'abolitionists' to a curious but fierce defence of slavery and the Southern aristocratic minority.

In 1619 a Dutch sea-captain sold a score of negroes to settlers in Virginia. There were no precedents in English law for slavery, but these and later importations were absorbed into a growing system of servitude based on old English apprenticeship and vagrancy laws. This system spread to all the Colonies and furnished probably the chief supply of Colonial labour for a century. The acute economic need for cheap labour, more even than the distinctive colouring of the Africans, provided what sanctions were called for in treating them quite separately. From 1670 onwards Virginia and other Colonies legally fixed the status of the negro as a slave. Due to geographical accident, slavery did not develop in the North on a large scale: the contrast between Northern family farms carved out of deciduous forests and the plantations which soon began to supplant other forms of organization in the South, were already apparent under British and French colonial rule. The majority of Northern slaves were in domestic service and were gradually freed. Slave-trading on the other hand prevailed in New Jersey and New York as late as the Missouri Compromise (1820) and Yankees had helped to supply slaves for the American market for decades. The continuation of traffic in slaves illegally after 1808 was only made possible through Northern capital and ships. What is more surprising still is that even *after* the Civil War itself Yankee ships and capital continued to trade in slaves with Brazil and other nations. Slavery was in origin a labour system, whose basis was economic.

For a brief period following the War of Independence slavery as an institution seemed in full decline and liberation a distinct possibility, simply because of the Southern economic depression. But unfortunately from one point of view, the crisis passed and in the boom which followed, as we have observed, Cotton became King and the question of plantation slavery was left over to be decided but not solved by civil conflict.

In an analysis of slavery it is helpful to keep a distinction between life on the plantations and the domestic slave trade. The conditions of plantation slavery differed greatly: on the larger plantations where the productivity aspect overshadowed the social one, the negro became a mere tool, slave trading was common and brutal treatment less restrained by peculiar traditions and customs. This E. F. Frazier has called 'industrial slavery'.[1] On other generally small plantations,

[1] *The Negro In The United States* (New York, 1949).

however, 'the lives of blacks and whites became intertwined in a system of social relationships', and conditions for the negro were definitely superior. This is to omit the fact that there were various grades of slave on each plantation: *house* servants who lived and worked close to the whites, assimilated their customs and considered themselves socially superior to the *field hands*, whose only contact with the whites was with the overseers. The latter were usually enlisted from the 'poor white trash' group or embittered small farmer class and were seldom up to the standards of the intelligent negroes. Plantation slavery was to be found chiefly in the Deep South, tobacco, corn, hemp, wheat and livestock not being best managed on a large scale like sugar cane, rice and cotton. Three slaves could till about fifty acres of hemp. The very word 'plantation' was almost obsolete in the 'border States'—Kentucky, Maryland and Missouri —by the 1850's. Out of economic necessity slaves generally received adequate housing, food and clothes and either fixed hours of work or 'stints' (set tasks). Perhaps the industrial proletariat and farmers of Canada and Great Britain had slightly better returns for their labour, but certainly peasants in Ireland were worse off economically. Although food was generally coarse and lacked variety this was probably no more true than it is now of Spain and Italy. Finally, the standards of life of the white farmers of the South who formed the majority of the population, were not very high. F. L. Olmsted, the Northern traveller who made a penetrating study of Southern life and institutions, commented generally on Southern destitution. Slaves, poor whites, overseers and yeomen farmers would wear coarse homespun cotton and cowhide, eat corn bread, salt pork and milk with vegetables only in season, and inhabit log houses commonly without windows. The negro usually worked no longer hours than the Iowa pioneer or the Northern 'wage-slave'. (Sugar plantations labouring sometimes eighteen hours a day were the worst.) Southerners in fact strenuously defended slavery against the industrial 'wage-slavery' where the factory hand was subjected to cyclical and technological unemployment and discarded when not needed. The Southern slave was kept with his family throughout the year, in and out of season.

The worst features of slavery were the domestic slave trade and the legal discriminations practised against negroes. The latter being mainly a racial problem still unsolved, we will concentrate on the former, mentioning only in passing that there were few laws against assaulting a slave, and even free negroes had little legal protection. The economic origins of the domestic slave trade lay in the decline of the Upper South and simultaneous growth of the cotton states. This led inevitably to a sale of slaves from Virginia, Maryland and North Carolina to Alabama, Mississippi, Texas and Louisiana. It cannot be denied too that slave breeding took place in Maryland,

Kentucky and Virginia, becoming a principal source of profit to many farmers and planters of the Upper South. The various incentives to indiscriminate breeding included the donation of land, separate cabins, cash bonuses, cheap clothes, rest—even freedom. Between 1840 and 1850 the Upper South 'exported' 180,000 slaves; in the following decade, 230,000. At an average price of $800 this represented a huge profit to traders, speculators and auctioneers. Despite the social opprobrium attached to the profession, it gave rise to a class of *nouveaux riches* such as the Gadsdens, Ryans and De Saussures of South Carolina. The trade was centred in the District of Columbia, Charleston, Savannah, Memphis and New Orleans.

In attempts to defend slavery, Southern leaders used arguments culled from Greek democracy, from the Bible and from pseudo-biology, John C. Calhoun eventually declaring slavery to be a 'positive good'. The economic arguments adduced in favour of slavery, besides the important 'wage-slavery' idea already mentioned, said that cotton production, the basis of the American economy, needed negro labour which was well adapted to this type of subtropical production. Slavery was the best administrative system to control negroes in such large numbers, and facilitated division of labour and various internal economies. The slaves were less poverty-stricken than Northern wage-slaves and a spirit of co-operation replaced in the South bitter industrial struggle and class war. But the economic arguments *against* slavery were much less flimsy. Slaves were highly expensive, and grew more than they could harvest; Southern capital became increasingly absorbed in slaves and lacked mobility, never being available to be ploughed back into existing enterprises or used to develop new industries and a less dangerous, more diversified economy. Added to this came the arguments of the Southern non-slaveholding whites who complained that wealth was being concentrated in fewer and fewer hands and would end in a complete political and social monopoly. This belief was on less sure ground historically.

Cotton was not the only Southern crop which depended on plantation slavery. Rice cultivation in Georgia and the Carolinas, which increased steadily until 1850, was a highly capitalized affair with concentrated slaveholdings amounting in some places to 700 slaves. On the Atlantic seaboard the peak of production was reached in the mid-century, and the ravages of the Civil War together with the competition from rice lands in Louisiana, Arkansas and Texas dealt this area a blow from which it never recovered. A series of storms culminating in the tropical holocaust of 1906 destroyed the remaining plantations on the seaboard, which were turned into game preserves for wealthy Northerners.[1]

[1] On this see Clement Eaton, *History of the Old South* (New York, 1949).

There is some controversy about the decline which is said to have occurred in tobacco cultivation with the War of 1812. The embargo, the war and foreign competition adversely affected the market and it is claimed that a recovery did not come about until after 1840. Tobacco production in 1839 totalled over 219 million pounds weight; in 1849 under 200 million pounds; in 1859 over 434 million pounds. After 1840 new species of leaf were introduced, improved curing methods initiated and fresh lands opened up. By that same year the yeoman farmers had moved back into the Tidewater areas, abandoned by tobacco planters because of soil erosion and because in the later period tobacco could be grown profitably on small farms. The planters moved to the Piedmont zones and crossed the mountains to Tennessee, Kentucky and Ohio, thus causing grave anxiety in Virginia and North Carolina besides incurring the risks of so-called overproduction. There can be little doubt that the miscalculations of scholars regarding production figures due to the change in weight of the 'hogshead' measure, has in the past confused this issue,[1] but the record tobacco production of the eighteenth century was achieved in the half-decade preceding the Revolution; then a decline occurred, followed by a revival in 1790–92. But in the years 1832–40 tobacco exports already exceeded the high level of the eighteenth century. Production doubled in Kentucky and Virginia, 1850–60, and trebled in North Carolina, the record year for exports being 1859. Prices dropped from 14·5 cents a pound in 1816 to 7·8 cents on the outbreak of civil war. At that time Virgina still headed the list of principal tobacco-producing states, followed in order of importance by Kentucky (the state with the most diversified agriculture of the South), Tennessee, Maryland, North Carolina, Ohio and Missouri; the United States formed the greatest tobacco-growing area in the world.

Two other crops of local importance were hemp and sugar cane. The former was centred mainly in Kentucky, although it had always been prized as a frontier zone crop because it supplied a coarse cloth which was in universal use. Hemp cultivation flourished especially for a brief period, 1826–8, because of the tariff and high prices, in the 'Bluegrass' area of Kentucky, in Central Tennessee and in Missouri. The outstanding American statesman, Henry Clay, who was married to a hemp industry heiress, was undoubtedly influenced by this background in his strong advocacy of tariff protection. In Louisiana the sugar-cane plantations were enabled to compete with West Indies sugar only because of the American tariff and the extreme fertility of the delta earth. The crop did manage to spread to Texas, but never became much of an economic success in Florida, Georgia or the Carolinas.

[1] See on this J. C. Robert, *The Tobacco Kingdom* (Durham, N. Carolina 1938) and Clement Eaton, op.cit.

It would be a serious limitation and misinterpretation of Southern economic life before the Civil War if these remarks omitted all mention of the crops grown by innumerable small yeomen farmers. Their main anxiety was food and subsistence, and their chief concern therefore grain; firstly corn, and if not corn, wheat. The latter was most prevalent in the Upper South. As for livestock, the Southern States (with well under half the total American population) possessed 90 per cent of the mules, 45 per cent of horses, 60 per cent of pigs, 52 per cent of oxen, over 50 per cent of poultry and 40 per cent of the dairy herds of the United States. These were mainly owned by the small farmers. Kentucky and Tennessee led the corn-producing states of the South, followed by Virginia, which incidentally led in Southern wheat production. At the very height of the boom of King Cotton on the other hand, the South had to import foodstuffs from states north beyond the Ohio.

Having considered the Old South-west, King Cotton and Southern agriculture generally, and the economic and social institution of slavery, let us turn to the Westward movement and agriculture in the Northern United States. Of the two chief new areas of settlement, the *Old North-west* was rapidly settled by Southern backwoodsmen driven northwards across the Ohio through the overwhelming competition of rich plantations, by migrants from the Middle States and New England, and later by Swiss, British and Germans fleeing from intolerable European conditions. Its geographic character was not unlike that of New England and perhaps as a consequence the agricultural pattern was the small self-sufficing farm. Population increased from a few thousands to nearly seven million between the enactment of the North-west Ordinance (1787) and the firing on Fort Sumter (1861),[1] and as early as 1803 Ohio became a State. Indiana (1816), Illinois (1818), Michigan (1837) and Wisconsin (1848) followed suit.

The immense potentialities of the Old North-west were not fully understood until the transportation revolution brought canals and railways, which opened the new area to Eastern and European markets. Agricultural developments were at first perhaps less spectacular than those in the South. Livestock assumed immediate importance, and later on, cereals. Once it was realized that the flat, treeless prairie possessed a soil ideal for grain crops, Indiana, Illinois and Wisconsin began to replace Tennessee and Kentucky as the centres of cereal cultivation. By 1859 the five states of the former North-west Territory presented the nation with almost half its wheat crop. Four obstacles to early farming had been the erroneous belief that a treeless prairie was infertile; the need for a new plough to supplant

[1] Population increases are shown in Table facing this page.

POPULATION INCREASES 1790–1860

STATE	1790	1800	1810	1830	1850	1860
Old North West (Now 'East North Central' States)						
Ohio	—	45,000	231,000	938,000	1,980,000	2,340,000
Indiana	—	5,600	24,500	343,000	988,000	1,350,000
Illinois	—	2,400	12,300	157,500	851,000	1,712,000
Michigan	—	2,700	4,700	32,000	397,700	1,184,000
Wisconsin	—	—	—	31,000 (1840)	305,000	776,000
Old South West (Now 'East South Central' States)						
Kentucky	74,000	221,000	406,000	688,000	982,000	1,156,000
Tennessee	36,000	106,000	262,000	682,000	1,003,000	1,110,000
Mississippi	—	8,900	40,000	137,000	606,000	791,000
Alabama	—	70,000	128,000 (1820)	310,000	772,000	964,000
(Now a 'West South Central' State)						
Louisiana	—	—	77,000	216,000	518,000	708,000

the old wooden one which was no match for the tough prairie sod; the lack of an adequate water supply, and the lack of efficient transportation. These difficulties were swiftly overcome with the constant pressure of expanding markets, due to the industrial revolution as a whole in Western Europe and to the British repeal of the Corn Laws (1846) in particular. The Southern States, as we have observed, had to import Northern foodstuffs as planters turned increasingly to specialized staples. The products of the Old North-west thus streamed eastwards by canal and rail and southwards by river-steamboat and rail after about 1825. Prior to the transport innovations cattle and pigs were driven east 'on the hoof'. Industries allied with agriculture —such as meat packing and flour milling—sprang up swiftly with the coming of canals and railways. After the settling of the Ohio valley, Cincinnati ('Porkopolis') became the meat packing and distributing centre for markets all over the globe. From about 1860 the centres became Chicago, Kansas City and Omaha. It remains of course a leading activity in the Middle West, together with its countless by-products: leather goods, glue, fertilizers, soap and fats. The milling industry flourished in Cincinnati, Louisville and St. Louis, and it is important to notice in this connection the political and economic tendency of the Mississippi. This was to build up a Western-Southern 'alliance' based on mutual need. The opening of the Erie Canal[1] and the cutting of lines of communication between North-east and North-west facilitated the movement of grain directly eastwards, which had a profound effect on the history of the sectional struggle and on the Civil War.

The cotton boom of the Old South-west and the extensive migration to the Old North-west contrasted sharply with the precarious position of Eastern agriculture during the same years. It has been shown how the Tidewater lands of the South-east were abandoned for the Piedmont, and how the depression of the Upper South forced Virginia planters into the dubious business of trading slaves to their more fortunate Southern cousins. In the middle seaboard states similar conditions, created by the growing competition of Western goods, were eased by the increase of the local market for foodstuffs: industries grew up in the Delaware and Hudson valleys and urban centres on the coast gradually expanded. Farming was more scientific and there was a high soil fertility. In New England, however, Western competition proved to be ruinous and the land was less fertile. The rapid urbanization and the growth of industry in this area alone saved the adaptable farmer, by providing a market for dairy produce and fruit. 'Truck farming' (called in Britain 'market gardening')[2] entirely dependent on local urban markets sprang up.

[1] Constructed 1817–25. See Chapter IV, below, pp. 48–9.
[2] There are of course important differences of scale and technique.

It might seem surprising that American agriculturists during the first half of the nineteenth century did not take up the ideas of scientific farming disseminated so much earlier in eighteenth-century England by Arthur Young, Tull, Bakewell, Coke of Holkham, and Townshend. This slow development in America is directly related with the superabundance of unoccupied Western land. Some idealists and progressive farmers such as Washington, Jefferson and Livingston, acting under the influence of the French pre-Revolutionary philosophers—the Physiocrats—used European methods of fertilization, crop-rotation and breeding. Henry Clay, another politician, introduced the first Herefords into America in 1817. Also some attempts were made at agricultural education, with societies and schools, farm journals, county fairs and the beginnings of government aid. But busy men like Washington sadly neglected their model farms for the calls of public life; 'Mount Vernon' was described only twenty-five years after Washington's death as a 'widespread and perfect agricultural ruin'. Although Jefferson's son-in-law first introduced contour ploughing to the Piedmont at 'Monticello', the place was valued at only $2,500 at his demise.

Labour shortage and an expanding market for foodstuffs made the farmer maintain a keen interest in labour-saving devices even though he largely ignored the benefits of conservation and scientific planning. In the words of Thomas Jefferson: 'In Europe the object is to make the most of their land, labour being abundant; here it is to make the most of our labour, land being abundant.' In the new century the wooden ploughs, hand scythes and grain cradles were replaced, through the innovations of men like Charles Newbold of New Jersey (who patented an iron plough in 1797), John Lane of Chicago (who first made the steel mouldboard in 1833) and James Oliver of Indiana (who invented the chilled-steel plough in 1869). The metal plough came into general use in the 1830's. Patents were taken out for mowers and reapers by William Manning (1831), Obed Hussey (1833) and Cyrus McCormick (1844), although the significant McCormick machines were not fully introduced until after the Civil War. Simultaneously the threshing machine replaced the hand flail and came into wide circulation by the mid-century. Hiram and John Pitts patented a portable thresher in 1836 and as mechanical threshing spread, much of it was performed by itinerant crews travelling about the countryside at harvest time. A workshop was set up at Racine, Wisconsin, in 1844 to manufacture mechanical threshers, which represented a labour-saving of two thirds over the old hand flails. Such improvements were little compared with the changes still to come after 1865. But in the first half of the century agriculture was triumphant and industry its servant; in the second half, this situation was exactly reversed.

·   ·   ·   ·   ·

This unusual phenomenon, the Westward Movement, which must lie at the back of our minds whenever we discuss or think about American economic and social development in the last century, has inevitably had its interpreters and its historians. Very recently a distinguished American scholar brought out a book which in effect applies the concept of the 'frontier' very widely in an interpretation of the history of Western Civilization itself.[1] The most famous historian of the American frontier, however, was undoubtedly Frederick Jackson Turner. Turner it was who introduced the *Frontier Thesis* into historiography. His works, particularly *The Frontier In American History*, are hailed as classics and very rapidly a 'Turner school' of historical scholarship grew up. Many points of his thesis have been severely criticized. Firstly the term 'frontier' is dismissed because it is said that Turner uses it with rather different meanings. Thus it is never certain whether he means a line, an area, a process of development or merely a state of mind. More confusing still is his use of 'West' and 'frontier' as interchangeable terms, for although the frontier was always 'West', the West was not always 'frontier'. Did Turner generalize too much about the frontier, considering that he knew only of American experience and nothing of Canada, Brazil and Australia? Turner's main contention was that the Western frontier life gave rise to democratic and radical ideas of reform and innovation; that this 'region of revolt' was the fortress of liberty. He characterized the movement as a 'westward marching army of individualistic liberty-loving democratic backwoodsmen' and greatly over-emphasized the desire for liberty among the migrants, largely ignoring their purely economic and selfish motives. In truth very few inventions came from the West and very few fresh political or social ideas. What time had the frontier pioneer for leisure or deep thought? Moreover, Turner in dealing with the pioneer farmer, omitted all those other characters and occupations which made up the movement—the land-grabber, miner, artisan and mill-owner. Rarely mentioning the rise of cities, Turner associated the rough independence of frontier farming life with the American democratic faith. In fact the frontier never gave the vote to Indians, negroes or women until its very end and the roots of American democracy are European. The concern for the 'Common Man' was largely a product of Eastern city life in the U.S.A. From the East came the anti-slavery movement, the demand for railroad control, prison reform, missionary enterprise and most political ideas. Even Henry George (1839–97) developed the ideas of his great book, *Progress and Poverty* (1879), not only in California on the Far Western mining frontier but also in New York City, where he experienced the distress of urban life in the late nineteenth century. The West copied the East, as Eastern

[1] W. P. Webb, *The Great Frontier* (Boston, 1952).

ideas were derived ultimately from Europe. Finally, the idea that the frontier was a 'safety valve' because dissatisfied Easterners moved West and expended their energies in frontier pioneering, has long since been discarded. The West was not mainly settled by unemployed factory workers moving in times of depression but on the contrary by farmers moving in times of prosperity. The frontier was merely one outlet for the many ambitions of an energetic and expanding nation.

However, even accepting these limitations, the importance of the frontier is undeniable. Westward expansion confined the greater part of American energy to internal development until about 1890. It is noticeable that American imperialism emerged soon after the official 'closing' of the frontier. Moreover the United States had no large amounts of goods or capital to spare for overseas investment and trade until the end of the century. Industrial developments and labour problems were probably slowed down by the mass migration beyond the Appalachians. America lagged behind Britain for many years in these aspects. The labour shortage caused by this movement accounts for the high rates of pay maintained in America throughout the period, which attracted immigrants from Europe on a vast scale. Finally, the expanding frontier gave many opportunities for discord between the rapidly-diverging Northern and Southern sections of American society.

How did the Westward Movement in particular present opportunities for friction between North and South? This has been hinted at already and implied several times. To understand it, a quantum of American political history is required. Briefly, the political importance of Westward expansion lies in its rôle as a focus of public opinion on the question of the legal and constitutional position of slavery. The positions secured for slavery in the new Western Territories was likely to determine its status when these became states. As the population and wealth of the South declined towards 1860, so did its numerical strength in Congress. This is the basis of the conflict over slavery in the Territories: a Territory which became a 'free' State added yet another two Sènators and a number of Representatives to Congress to represent Northern interests. The North wanted to ensure this, and the South to prevent it and develop territorially themselves in a westerly and southerly direction. By 1861 fifteen states had passed through the Territorial phase of development and finally been accepted into the Union. Only in the exceptional cases of Texas (1845) and California (1850) had this formative stage been omitted. The organization of new Territories was always likely to produce a crisis between South and North over the slavery issue. While Congress had no power to control slavery in any state, it did possess authority to do so in the 'maturing' Territorial phase of a state's evolution. Each time a new Territory was formed a Congressional crisis occurred.

This happened in 1819 when a Bill was presented to admit Missouri into the Union as a state. Tallmadge of New York introduced an amendment in the House of Representatives prohibiting any further introduction of slaves into Missouri and demanding freedom at the age of twenty-five for all slaves subsequently born in the state. The Bill passed the lower House and was rejected by the Senate. Congress dissolved in March and the question became an electoral issue. A national crisis ensued but in 1820 the *Missouri Compromise* was agreed to. Missouri was admitted as a slaveholding state but slavery was henceforth prohibited in the Louisiana Purchase, north of the line 36°30′. Maine was admitted in the North as a free state to maintain the balance between South and North, as twelve states each. The Compromise secured comparative agreement over the issue for thirty years.

A revolution of American cattlemen and cotton planters in Texas successfully overthrew Mexican domination in 1836 and in 1845 Texas was annexed to the American Union at its own request. This did not mark the end of American intervention in this area. By the *Treaty of Guadalupe Hidalgo* which terminated the U.S. war with Mexico (1846–8) immense stretches of territory were added to the Union: the Rio Grande became the acknowledged boundary of Texas, and the whole of 'New Mexico' and California were ceded in return for a payment to Mexico of $15 million and the recognition of Mexican claims against the U.S. Government amounting to $3,250,000. In terms of modern state boundaries the 'Mexican Cession' of 1848 included the western half of what is now New Mexico, western parts of Colorado and a south-western section of Wyoming, the whole of Utah, most of Arizona (excluding the southern section which was part of the Gadsden Purchase), the whole of Nevada and the whole of California.[1] The new expansion gave occasion for a further crisis over the status of slavery in the Territories. In 1850 the *Clay Compromise* made an uneasy settlement concerning slavery in the area of the Mexican Cession: New Mexico and Utah were to be organized as Territories free to enter the Union with or without slavery when their population was sufficiently numerous; California was admitted as a 'free' state; the Fugitive Slave Law was enacted to ensure the return to the South of runaway slaves, and the slave-trade was abolished in the District of Columbia.

[1] See the map. States in this area admitted into the Union at the following times: California (1850); Nevada (1864); Utah (1896); Colorado (1876. Formed by parts of the Mexican and Texan cessions and of the Louisiana Purchase); New Mexico (1912. Her Eastern half was formerly part of Texas); Arizona (1912).

Meanwhile the Westward movement had stretched to the northern Far West, to Oregon. An *Anglo-American treaty* of 1846 fixed the boundary between the U.S.A. and Canada at the 49th parallel, thus ceding to the former a vast area now comprising the states of Washington (admitted to statehood in 1889), Oregon (1859), Idaho (1890), and parts of Montana (1889) and Wyoming (1890). The administration of the 'Oregon Territory' (which included all the treaty area of 1846) was set up by Act of Congress in August, 1848.

The three years 1845-8 thus saw the addition to American territory of some 1,200,000 square miles. In 1853 the *Gadsden Purchase* of a small area of land from Mexico (now incorporated in Arizona and New Mexico) which lay on the easiest route for a Southern transcontinental railway, gave the United States its present continental boundaries.

SUGGESTED FURTHER READING

BILLINGTON, R. A. *Westward Expansion* (New York, 1949).
CRAVEN, A. O. *The Coming of the Civil War* (New York, 1942).
EATON, CLEMENT. *History of the Old South* (New York, 1949).
PHILLIPS, U. B. *Life and Labour in the Old South* (Boston, Mass. 1939).
TURNER, F. J. *The Frontier in American History* (New York, 1921).
—*The Significance of Sections in American History* (New ed., New York, 1950).

III

INDUSTRY AND LABOUR

Wars as a stimulus to industry; the decline and revival of manufacturing 1783–1815; the iron and textile industries; the factory system – Immigration before 1860 – 'Imported' social doctrines: Associationists and Owenites – The demands of Labour – Early trade societies and the law – Trends in the growth of Unions – The 1840's: general living standards; the Ten-Hours movement; wage levels to 1860 – Unionism in the 1850's.

BETWEEN the Peace of Ghent (1814) and the surrender of Lee to Grant at Appomattox courthouse (1865) the population of the U.S.A. increased almost four times. The volume of manufactured goods increased twelve times and their value multiplied by eight. Changes came about in industrial organization, scale and technique, and transportation developments facilitated increased mobility of the factors of production, increased specialization and sectionalization. More briefly, the 'Industrial Revolution' came to America.

The importance of war as a stimulus to this acceleration of economic activity cannot be overlooked. Three conflicts—the War of Independence, the War of 1812 and the Civil War—helped to hasten the processes of industrialization, mechanization and urbanization in America, and accentuated various existing social trends. But of course industrial developments were intimately bound up with road, canal, and rail developments and with the expansion of overseas trade. We have already surmised that the American Revolution afforded a well-defined impetus to manufacturing but that it did not last. The revival of commercial intercourse with Britain after 1783 ruined the infant American industries, and the first Tariff Act of the new government set up under the strengthened Federal Constitution (the Act of 4 July 1789) imposed only low duties, chiefly for revenue purposes, not for protection. This period of largely household industries ('usufacture') and village crafts has been styled the era of 'merchant capitalism'. A type of 'putting-out' system prevailed (e.g. in the linen, hosiery, lace and nail-making industries) until well on into the middle years of the century, operating side by side with the newer factory centres and transitional workshops. The Industrial Revolution was considerably less complete in America by 1860 than it was in England, although even in the latter country certain groups such as the hand-loom weavers persisted.

It was not until about 1807 that American industries began to 'hustle' and throw off their European masters. Despite various technical innovations in the textile industries the growth of domestic manufactures was quite slow up to that year. The scarcity and the high price of labour and capital, the abundance of land and increased agricultural and commercial activity, besides the dragging on of old Colonial habits, explain this tardiness. America as the foremost neutral nation during the Revolutionary and Napoleonic Wars, realized the great profits to be made out of agricultural goods and the carrying trade. There was a 'canalization' of economic effort, labour and capital, towards farming and commerce; merchant shipping tonnage multiplied sevenfold. Manufacturing stagnated and there was a flood of cheap imported goods.

Napoleon's 'Continental System' (the Berlin and Milan Decrees) and England's retaliatory Orders in Council led swiftly to Jefferson's Embargo Act (1807). The British and French manœuvres theoretically cut out neutral trading, and Jefferson hoped to solve the problem by applying economic sanctions, short of actual force. The Embargo Act prohibited American ships from sailing to European ports, and although a less stringent Non-Intercourse Act was passed in 1809, it is from 1807 that we can date the beginning of *national* industrial development. Finally the outbreak of the War of 1812 not only partly destroyed American foreign commerce and emphasized the switch of economic interests back to domestic manufacturing, but led once more to a hasty concern for the iron and textile industries arising from the needs of warfare.[1]

In view of these factors the growth of the factory system was more rapid in the years 1807-15. With the coming of peace in Europe was the post-1783 situation to be repeated? The answer is: partly. The economy was temporarily checked once more with the influx of European goods, as was the English economy by the influx of European grain (witness the fateful Corn Law of 1815). Few individual entrepreneurs survived the severity of this saturation of the American market. Imports leapt from $13 million worth (1814) to $147 million worth (1816). But the setback was acute rather than prolonged, and did not affect all industries (e.g. the 'agricultural industry' of flour-milling expanded rapidly in the years 1815-19 to meet the tremendous demand in Southern Europe for flour).

[1] See below, pp. 56-61.

Under the protection of federal tariffs (1816 and 1818) and encouraged by the abundance of cheap raw materials and fuel, the introduction of labour-saving devices, an ever-expanding home market and the expansion of world trade, an industrial revival soon got under way.

The output of iron increased twenty-fold during the first half of the nineteenth century. In the East the industry was second in importance only to cotton textiles. Yet these facts should not be taken at their face-value: the iron industry occupied an inferior position in the national economy which was predominantly agrarian. The total annual value of pig, bar and rolled iron produced in the United States reached, according to the Census of 1860, some $42 million. But that of leather exceeded $67 million in the same year —flour and grist mills produced a value of over $223 million —cotton mills of over $115 million. Agricultural predominance meant that flour-milling, leather tanning, meat-packing and the liquor trade would take up most of the national product of manufactures. Yet the developments which are to be seen in the metal industries before the Civil War are of prime significance: the Industrial Revolution when it came was based solidly on coal and iron, the distribution of which partly explains the decline of the Netherlands in the eighteenth century, the rise of industrial Britain and slightly later the rise of industrial America itself.

The transformation of the American iron industry seems from the British viewpoint to have taken place backwards. The earliest known method of smelting iron with coal instead of charcoal dates in English history (excluding the obscure attempts of Dud Dudley) from Abraham Darby's experiments in 1709. This step was the first in the revolutionizing of the English iron industry in later modern times; but the changeover from charcoal to coal had not taken place completely in the U.S.A. until the 1870's. Coal was cheaper and American entrepreneurs knew how to use it; but they had no great shortage of timber for fuel. The shortage of labour was the main American difficulty. So the 'puddling and rolling' processes were first in the stream of innovations. Devised by Cort in 1783–4 in Britain, they were introduced in Pennsylvania in 1816–17. Although it was made clear that a coal-mine in a six foot seam covering half an acre could replace the fuel ordinarily supplied for the ironmasters by two to five thousand acres of forest-land, the adoption of Cort's process using coal and saving labour, took place very slowly. Why should this method not become popular? Firstly, the product of the fairly crude, reverberatory puddling furnaces was inferior to that refined with charcoal and manipulated; secondly, it had to face the keen competition of a well-established British industry. These two stumbling-blocks vanished in the 1840's with the introduction of technical changes improving the quality of puddled iron, and the growth of a huge and insatiable domestic demand for iron products effected by the coming of the railroads. In the later '40's the first great mills were built, all using this method and all with blast furnaces burning coal. The use of coal had been delayed in the East because deposits there were non-bituminous. But even the West with its bituminous supplies admirably suited for making the coke needed in the Cort process, had been slow to change to coal, due mainly to inelasticity of demand.[1] By 1833 an American (F. W. Geisenheimer) had independently discovered a method which could make use of *anthracite* coal by way of a hot blast. In 1840 six furnaces smelted with anthracite coal; in 1856, one hundred and twenty-one. Kelly of Kentucky independently evolved in 1851 the Bessemer process of decarbonizing molten metal by forcing air through it. Anthracite smelting now surpassed charcoal smelting and was not in turn surpassed by bituminous smelting until about 1875.

The centralization of the iron industry was facilitated by coal, and iron manufacturing lost its rural character. Pennsylvania with the largest and finest anthracite coal deposits in the country was by 1860 producing over half the iron made and manufactured in the U.S.A., followed in order by Ohio and New Jersey. Total tonnage of American pig-iron was in that year almost a million. This was used to make agricultural implements (the value of which increased 160 per cent between 1850 and 1860); machinery and steam engines, and (since 1845 when they were first made in the U.S.A. instead of being wholly imported from Britain) heavy rails; small-arms, subsidized by the Federal Government from 1792; and such domestic implements as stoves. About 400,000 stoves were made in 1850.

In Britain the cotton industry was the most sensitive to the new spirit of the Industrial Revolution, and was the most 'advanced' branch of the national economy. The mechanization of woollen textiles was delayed by inadequate raw material supplies, technical difficulties, craft conservatism and inelasticity of demand. In the U.S.A. parallel differences existed between the two great textile industries, although underlying causes were not so similar. The Revolution came first to the cotton industry. Early attempts to establish factory production of woollens in America (e.g. that at Hartford, Connecticut, in 1788 mentioned in Alexander Hamilton's famous House of Representatives *Report on Manufactures*, 1791) dissolved in face of British competition, the poorer quality of American wool and the cheapness and abundance of cottons. The coarser cloths were made at home in individual farms; the finer cloths imported. The War of 1812 and the introduction of merino sheep helped to meet

[1] For further details about the coal industry see below, Chapter VII.

these obstacles and woollen factories increased in number from about 100 (1820) to almost 2,000 (1860). Farmhouse handlooms persisted in America as in Britain until late on in the nineteenth century. There was an overall increase in the production of woollens of 51 per cent in the 'ante-bellum' decade and their annual value in 1860 was about $40 million. The production of cotton and cotton goods in the same year was valued at over $115 million as we have seen, and there had been an increase in production of nearly 76 per cent during the decade. Cottons had thus already outstripped woollens, producing goods of nearly three times the value of woollens in that year.[1]

Throughout the 1780's attempts were being made to build carding and spinning machines, usually on English models adapted and altered by American inventors. The invention of Eli Whitney's cotton gin in 1793[2] necessitated developments in the manufacturing processes and encouraged the growth of spinning mills such as that one begun three years earlier in Pawtucket, Rhode Island, by Samuel Slater, an English immigrant. He had built from memory (in defiance of English laws seeking to confine technical innovations to that country) a water-frame of twenty-four spindles and two carding machines. Many mills failed, but in 1800 eight remained in production, doubling in number by 1804. The year 1814 witnessed the erection of several spinning and weaving factories, the latter using the new power looms, as at Waltham. Lowell, Lawrence, Manchester and Nashua—all on New England streams—followed suit. Almost simultaneously emigrants from New England spread the new industries into the Mohawk and Hudson valleys. By 1810 there were 269 cotton mills, twenty years later nearly 800, and by 1860 nearly 1,100. The cotton industry suffered a severe setback after the War of 1812 due to the flood of imports from Britain, but recovered in about ten years and was by the mid-twenties firmly established. It consumed almost 423 million pounds of raw cotton in 1860; in 1800 this figure had been merely 150,000 pounds. New England and especially Massachusetts, claimed the bulk of the cotton industry, although some experiments were made before 1860 to root the industry in the South—in Georgia, the Carolinas and elsewhere. Despite all this expansion, the Southern planters remained dependent to a large extent on their export market. Although the number of cotton spindles in the U.S.A. had leapt from under 20,000 (1800) to over 5,000,000 (1860) we must remember that the English mid-century figure stood at about 21,000,000.

[1] For these, as for preceding figures, advanced students should see the *Preliminary Report on the Eighth Census, 1860 (Washington, 1862)*.
[1] See Chapter II, above, pp. 18–19.

The greatest developments in American manufacturing were to come in the decades immediately after the Civil War, yet the rate of growth was astonishingly swift before 1860 and fundamental changes took place both in productive techniques and in industrial organization. The change-over to the factory system was an uneven, halting process, but in New England and the Middle Atlantic states this form was firmly established by 1860. It was not so in the South, where the competition of King Cotton and the slowness of transport developments retarded industrialization considerably.

The roots of the factory system went back at least to those large flour mills of late eighteenth-century merchant capitalism. The small textile yarn mills of early nineteenth-century New England did not lead directly, by their own expansion, towards mass production, integrated industrial processes and huge capital investments. Instead an unusual experiment made in Waltham, Massachusetts, in 1813-14 obviated this evolution. Francis Cabot Lowell of Boston (the founder of the Boston Manufacturing Company) together with several associates, took a huge financial risk by introducing at Waltham an integrated, standardized process of cotton cloth manufacture based on the power loom. The company began operating with a paid-in capital of $300,000, which was doubled within a decade. The factories which sprang up at Lowell (1822), Chicopee (1823) and elsewhere in Massachusetts, Maine and New Hampshire, were based on the 'Waltham plan'. That was: a unified management governing all the main processes of production from spinning to dyeing, in a single plant; a standardized product of fairly coarse weave requiring very little craft skill on the part of the factory hands; a single marketing agency; and finally (up to the middle 1840's) female labour drawn from farms and agricultural areas far and wide and housed in special dormitories. Until this type of labour was displaced by male immigrants and urban Americans the Waltham industrialists could claim themselves 'philanthropists'. Even before the rise of an urban proletariat, however, the Waltham plan had a seamy social side: model boarding-houses were a useful means of despotic control; the net wage of a factory girl for a seventy-five-hour week spent in a dangerous, noisy factory was but two dollars after stoppages for board; employers combined to fix wages and hours, and the 'blacklist' was a common weapon used against less docile 'operatives'. It is with the organizations of Labour for self-defence and social betterment that we must now deal.

During the first half of the nineteenth century, as we have seen, labour was scarce in the United States. Immigration before 1860 was small in comparison with the movement after that date and the type of labour organizations which dominated the scene were mainly small-scale craft unions and 'backwoods Utopias'—experimental Communities. We shall be questioning in the second part of this book why Socialism or the idea of an independent Labour party never struck root in America. The constant flood of immigration certainly delayed the growth of the labour movement time and again in ways both obvious and subtle. In the early period though, when England, Ireland and Germany were the main sources of immigrants and their numbers were relatively small, labour leaders were only beginning dimly to perceive the nature and complexities of the problem. During the 1820's less than 10,000 immigrants entered the U.S.A. per year. By the next decade the annual average reached 50,000—or half a million in the years 1830–40. Of these 74 per cent were Irish or German, the former predominating. In the decade 1840–50 the total was trebled becoming one and a half million, nearly half of whom were of Irish origin. The total U.S. population of 23 million in 1850 included a million Irish, mainly settled in the Northern Atlantic States, and half that number of Germans chiefly settled in the West and North. Emigration to the South was almost negligible. Irish immigration reached a peak immediately after the Great Famine of 1845–6; German immigration after the failure of the 1848 revolutions. Almost all the immigrants before 1860 originated in Northern Europe and more often than not became Jacksonian Democrats in politics. There was much social friction and street warfare, opposition to aliens being based mainly on economic and religious grounds.

Despite this cleavage it is nevertheless hardly surprising that foreign influences were soon at work on the American labour movement. In 1851, for instance, Joseph Weydemeyer, a German disciple of Karl Marx, arrived in the U.S.A. and founded a newspaper to spread Marxist ideas. Failing to gain any lasting support in this early period he eventually became a General in the Union Army in the Civil War. One early group advocating peaceful social reconstruction were the Associationists who operated generally under the influence of Charles Fourier the French socialist and were most active during the '40's and '50's. Albert Brisbane, Horace Greeley the outstanding editor, and other enthusiasts attempted at Brook Farm to increase the production of wealth through the application of 'natural' laws. In their zeal for productive efficiency however they tended often to relegate problems of just social distribution to a second place. They gained more publicity perhaps by their close connection with Ralph Waldo Emerson, the famous transcendentalist thinker, than through the notions they advocated: colonies of associated workers on the land, combining farming with manufacturing. Robert Owen, the 'father' of British Socialism, who was so active in the revolutionary period of British unionism in the 1830's, also made lecture tours in the United States and with his son Robert Dale Owen, founded a socialist community at New Harmony in Indiana. Owen believed that the increased productive powers of industrialized Man necessitated social and political reorganization; that co-operation should replace wasteful, overlapping and vicious competitive industry; and finally, that society should abandon large cities and solitary farms alike, and resolve itself into independent associations—communities uniting agricultural and industrial pursuits in an ideal balanced whole. Several Owenite and many other kinds of religious and social communities were established in the '30's and '40's but few managed to survive for very long.

Apart from the 'communitarians', labour and working-class leaders before the Civil War presented a multitude of demands, political, economic and social. They became mixed inevitably in the struggle for the extension of the franchise. Normally their aims in this respect did not include Negroes and only occasionally did they include women. They pressed for free and equal public education, the ten-hour day, the full legal recognition of the right to strike and bargain collectively, the payment of wages in cash and not in 'store goods', the institution of safety and health regulations in factories. In addition labour leaders often espoused other causes, according to their area of origin and local or other pressures, such as antimonopoly campaigns, the restriction of immigration, a national 'cheap land' policy and abolition of imprisonment for debt.

Professor Selig Perlman[1] divided the period up to 1862 into four sections for the purpose of labour history: the beginnings to about 1827; 1827 to 1832 when as well as the enlarged activities of craft unions, urban workers turned their attention chiefly to the political problems of franchise reform; 1833 to 1837, the years of what he called 'wild-cat prosperity' which saw a considerable price inflation ending in financial crisis and during which occurred the great wave of trade union growth; and finally 1837 to 1862 when the aggressive unionism of the '30's practically disappeared and the social scene was dominated by Utopian socialists, communitarians and the abolitionist and other issues which led to civil war.

Trade union growth was checked and hampered in the early period by the legal doctrine of 'conspiracy'. American jurisprudence assimilated the English common law doctrine developed in the Middle Ages, which asserted firstly that maximum wages could be legally fixed (Statutes had been enacted to do so since Edward III's day), and secondly that workers could, in effect, be compelled to work. This idea was legalised at the time of the Black Death in the Statute of Labourers, 1351. Thus if workers associated or took action to force a rise in wages above the average or standard in their particular occupation

[1] *History of Trade Unionism in the United States* (New York, 1922).

they were deemed guilty of a criminal conspiracy at Common Law. For instance, in 1806 in the *Commonwealth* v. *Pullis* case in Philadelphia,[1] a group of shoemakers were tried because in the words of the court:

'(They) were not content to work at the usual prices and rates for which they and other workmen and journeymen, in the same art and occupation used to work. . . . But contriving and intending unjustly and oppressively to increase and augment the prices usually paid them . . . did combine, conspire, confederate and unlawfully agree together that they would not work except at certain large prices and rates. . . .'

The men were found guilty of 'a combination to raise their wages'. A few years later the same decision was followed by a New York court in the case *People* v. *Melvin* (1809–10).

Despite this legal opposition, trade societies did exist, however, although no real labour 'movement' or feeling of solidarity extending beyond one single trade can be traced until 1827. Perhaps one of the earliest genuine strikes in America happened in 1786 when Philadelphia printers demanded a minimum wage of six dollars a week. Further strikes occurred in 1791, 1795, 1805, and 1807 but they left no permanent results and were piecemeal and local. The idea of a continuous organization meant to exist also between strikes and crises and not just as a temporary medium for dealing with one particular problem, was favoured in 1792 by the shoemakers of Philadelphia. They reorganized in 1794 and as the 'Federal Society of Journeymen Cordwainers' lasted until 1806. It was this society which ran in 1799 one of the first *organized* strikes, one that took nine or ten weeks to resolve. This group also probably inaugurated the 'closed shop' policy in America by attempting in 1794 to compel employers to hire only Union men. That same year saw the institution of the first 'Typographical Society' or union of New York printers, which managed to maintain a continuous existence for ten and a half years. By the 1830's the leading trades in Boston, New York, Baltimore, Philadelphia and elsewhere had societies of skilled artisans—bookbinders, printers, shoemakers, hatters, plumbers, ships' joiners, millwrights and glassmakers included.

Some years earlier for the first occasion workers in different trades had united to form a central labour organization: the 'Mechanics Union of Trade Associations' of Philadelphia (1827). Carpenters had struck for a ten-hour day and were almost immediately joined by bricklayers, glaziers and painters. The Association consequently

[1] For a fuller account of this trial students should see, if available, W. Nelles: 'The First American Labour Case' (*Yale Law Journal*, XLI, 1931, pp. 165–200).

formed came to include as many as fifteen different unions. After
this other central bodies sprang up in New York, Boston and leading
cities and the 1830's even saw the beginnings of *national* unions
among the shoemakers, comb makers, carpenters, printers and hand-
loom weavers. This wave of labour organization stimulated the first
labour incursion into politics (also facilitated by the wide extension
of the suffrage in the new and revised state constitutions).[1] The
Mechanics' Union of Trade Associations of Philadelphia, for instance, tendered suggestions to other unions that candidates representing working-class interests be nominated for election in 1828.
Their candidates were successful and with Jacksonian backing polled
2,400 votes in the city. Labour political parties were founded in about
fifteen states and many Labour newspapers commenced between
1828 and 1830. In New York in 1829, 6,000 votes out of 21,000 went
to Labour. This success was short-lived, however: the workers were
inexperienced in the political game and hotly divided in leadership
and aim. By 1833 the political movement had largely collapsed.
Unionization however proceeded at a quickening pace up to 1837.
The first national convention of labour representatives met in 1834.
Further growth of unions was stimulated by the economic boom and
price rise of 1835–7. The general prosperity favoured demands on the
part of Labour for a larger share of the national income, and in the
extension of union protection even female workers were reached in
some sectors. In 1853–4 a 'Female Society of Lynn and Vicinity
for the Protection and Promotion of Female Industry' was to be
found at Lynn, Massachusetts, among the shoe-binders. A 'Female
Union Association' in New York, a 'United Seamstresses' Society'
in Baltimore and what was probably the first federation of American
women workers in Philadelphia, were all established in 1835. The
severe depression of 1837 set back the trade union movement considerably, for not only did it close down factories and cause widespread unemployment but it also wiped out union treasuries. Local,
city and even national unions such as the National Trades Union
established in New York City in 1834 'went under' in 1837.

The decade of the eighteen-forties was one of such political, social,
economic and intellectual ferment as America had never experienced,
when almost every possible creed and eccentricity lived its brief
ephemeral life in a context of constant flux and change. Labour turned
to political and Utopian experiments on Fourierist, Owenite or other
communitarian lines, to land reform, the ten-hours movement and
producers' and consumers' co-operation. For instance, in 1845 the
Working Men's Protective Union was formed after the complete

[1] The Pennsylvania Constitution of 1790 had granted the franchise to
anyone who paid any kind of state or county tax, whatever its size. Massachusetts enfranchised the working class in 1820; New York in 1822.

failure of a strike movement for higher wages during the slight industrial revival of 1843–4. From modest beginnings this co-operative enterprise had grown until by October 1852 it embraced over 400 divisions, 167 of which had a capital of nearly $242,000 and annual sales amounting to about $1,700,000. A split occured in the organization in 1853 when a faction seceded to form the American Protective Union. This would not have impeded the development of working men's co-operatives, however, for in the fifteen years preceding the outbreak of the Civil War more than 800 distributive (consumers') co-operatives were founded. But the war almost eradicated the whole movement.

What of living standards generally in the 1840's? One observer, Miss Harriet Martineau, claimed in the mid-thirties that 'all the strikes she heard of' were on the question of hours, not wages.[1] In 1830 workmen commonly laboured twelve and a half hours a day. The agitation to reduce this average had begun in Jacksonian days and received wide support in the 1840's. President Van Buren in 1840 decreed a general ten-hour day for federal employees, despite strong conservative opposition. In October 1844 a 'New England Convention' at Boston strongly urged ten-hour legislation, and meetings continued regularly down to 1848. After agitation, walk-outs and political pressure brought to bear against state legislatures, several states enacted ten-hour laws, New Hampshire, Pennsylvania, Maine, New Jersey, Ohio and Rhode Island having done so by 1853. The legislation was badly formed on the whole and permissive rather than compulsory in character. After a decline in the late '40's the ten-hours movement revived after 1852 mainly under middle class and humanitarian auspices. Even the large textile mills in Lowell and elsewhere agreed to reduce hours to eleven a day in the '50's. The *idea* of the ten-hour day was widely accepted by 1860.

It is now agreed upon by economic historians that *real* wages underwent a general increase up to 1860 and that workers were enabled, when employed, to buy more from a wider choice of goods. The source generally used for this knowledge has been the *Aldrich Report*, or more strictly, the Senate report of the 52nd Congress (Second Session, 1893) on *Wholesale Prices, Wages and Transportation*. From the figures of this report A. Hansen built in 1925 an annual index of *real* wage rates which revealed an increase in real wages in the '20's, '30's and '40's with a decline in the '50's. The net increase from 1820 to 1860 was 13 per cent. Although his studies have been broadly supported by those of later scholars,[2] this question remains

[1] *Society in America*, 2 vols., (London, 1834–6).

[2] J. Kuczynski, *A Short History of Labour Conditions under Industrial Capitalism*, 3 vols., (London, 1943).

quite undecided as the data used for any given index are never satisfactory for this period. Moreover the general conclusion that real wages increased favourably during the period of the early Industrial Revolution in America takes but little account of technological or cyclical unemployment, as in the depressions which followed the panics of 1807, 1819, 1837 and 1857. And while quantitative changes might have been in favour of labour, what of qualitative changes, and the psychological impact of the new, industrialized urban environment? The problem of what were the exact social effects of the technological and transportation revolution remains unsolved.

Trade unionism picked up in strength to some extent in the later 1850's, with the increase of railroad building, the gold discoveries in California and the general business revival. At least ten new national unions were set up including the Typographical Union (1850), the Hat Finishers' (1854), the National Union of Machinists and Blacksmiths (1859) and the National Moulders' Union (1859). Only three of these new, more practical and well-organized national unions emerged from the crisis of 1857; but the effects of this blow were much less prolonged. Meanwhile the courts had shifted their line of attack from the question of whether unions were 'conspiratorial' to the question of what were the legal means unions and labour generally could adopt to achieve their ambitions and fulfil their needs. In the case of *Commonwealth* v. *Hunt* (1842) the right of workers to form unions was finally admitted. Legal controversy over strikes and boycotts remained for many decades and constantly involved unions in costly litigation.

SUGGESTED FURTHER READING

CLARK, V. S. *History of Manufactures in the United States* (New ed., 3 vols., Washington, 1929).
COMMONS, J. R. et al. *History of Labour in the United States* (4 vols., New York, 1918).
HANSEN, M. L. *The Atlantic Migration, 1607–1860* (Cambridge, Mass., 1940).
TAYLOR, G. R. *The Transportation Revolution, 1815–1860* (Vol. IV in Rinehart & Co's *Economic History of the United States* New York, 1951).
WARE, N. J. *The Industrial Worker, 1840–1860* (Boston, 1924).

IV

INTERNAL IMPROVEMENTS

The significance of the Transportation Revolution and Internal Improvements – 'Trails' and rural roads – Turnpikes: the Cumberland Road (1806–38) – 'Plank' roads – The Erie Canal (1817–25) and the Canal Mania – River steamboats; the Steamboat Act (1852) – The coming of the railroads: state and city competition; the transcontinental plan – Railroad financing before 1860 – The triumph of rail transportation.

AMONG the many interacting elements involved in industrial change on the nineteenth-century scale, the 'transportation revolution' was not only the 'linking factor', articulating the whole process; in America at least the coming of the turnpike roads, canals, river steamboats and railways was the *essential condition* of the opening-up and subjugation of the entire continent. Not only did frontier settlements depend upon transportation lines for their economic life, but the very existence and location of settlements was chiefly determined by them. Especially after 1850 railway building often *preceded* settlement and railway companies organized immigration to the areas flanking their own lines—immigration not merely from the East but from the continent of Europe. The creation of demand and extension of markets due to transport developments was at least as significant a factor in American industrialization as technological innovation. Finally the *political* benefits of the transportation revolution were enormous; it is indeed doubtful whether the United States would have long remained united but for the economic integration facilitated by transport developments, to say nothing of the vital need for the communications themselves, without which the administration and government of such a vast area would have been impossible.

The transport history of the years up to 1860 can be made to fall into three convenient categories, though not into neat chronological periods. We must deal with turnpikes and road improvements, with canals and canalized rivers, and with railways and steamboats. The turnpike roads reached their greatest years of growth between about 1790 and 1814. Meanwhile, from about 1807 onwards, the river steamboat rose to a position of great importance in the national economy. Its heyday was the '50's. The construction of canals was, most significant between the years 1817–50 and that of railways from about 1830 onwards. These developments were never accepted by the nation with complete unanimity or approval. When they were undertaken at federal or state expense or encouraged by the governments such 'internal improvements' became the object of heated party and sectional politics. Generally speaking Western farmers, whose basic need was communication with Eastern markets and ports, strongly supported internal improvements. The North-east and coastal towns, desiring cheaper foodstuffs for their increasing urban and industrial populations, were prepared to favour these improvements and thus became aligned politically with the Westerners in this matter. Eastern manufacturers and Western farmers were to see eye to eye on the question of internal improvements if not on many other affairs. The significance of this we shall notice later on. Moreover, land speculation and transport developments were inseparable, not only because of the governmental policy of land-grants but also because land values inevitably rose with the coming of the turnpike, canal and railway.

Before the so-called 'turnpike era' Americans depended for transportation facilities upon waterways and crude tracks. Early settlements had to be strategically placed and were mainly confined to the seacoast and the banks of navigable rivers. Therefore penetration of the interior was at first very slow and when population did spread out the movement was restricted to navigable streams and the most-frequented overland routes. Unil the Revolution and indeed for some time after, the American economy looked Eastwards back across the Atlantic, and depended upon transoceanic contacts. Nevertheless despite the infrequency of long distance travel in the colonial period, there were several established 'trails'. Daniel Boone's route from Watauga, North Carolina, to Boonesborough, Kentucky (the 'Wilderness Road' trip of 1775) has already come to our notice in considering Westward expansion. Other 'traces' or 'trails' to the *South-west* were: one from the river Potomac and settlements in Virginia and South Carolina to Nashville and Memphis, Tennessee via the Cumberland Gap; and the famous Santa Fe Trail (Spanish) from St. Augustine, Florida, across the Mississippi westwards to Santa Fe, New Mexico. This eventually stretched out to California and was travelled by stage-coaches in the '50's. The *North-west* trails included three: one from the Hudson river to the upper Susquehanna, which then turned westwards along the boundary of New

York and Pennsylvania to Lake Erie (later occupied by the Erie Railroad); one from Philadelphia to Harrisburg, Pittsburgh, and down the Ohio to the Mississippi valley; and one from the river Potomac through western Virginia and Pennsylvania to the Monongahela river and so to Pittsburgh. To the *North*, one route via the Hudson river to Lakes George and Champlain in Canada was that used by the Revolutionaries who invaded Canada. Another trail went by the Hudson and Mohawk rivers in New York, then by portage to Wood Creek into Lake Oneida, and thus by means of the river Oswego to Lake Ontario.

These long, arduous and dangerous pioneering trails were the exception. By the time of the War of 1812 on the other hand, a network of rural roads or tracks, atrociously surfaced and barely passable in bad weather, covered the settled areas. The phrase 'turnpike era' is something of a misnomer because with all their drawbacks (e.g. lack of permanent bridges) these rural tracks were really more important the country over than were the turnpikes. The latter, as G. R. Taylor has pointed out,[1] merely connected large towns and led westwards across the mountains, an improvement on the 'trails' just mentioned. The countless country roads, on the other hand, had been linked up to a considerable extent and by about 1816 a more or less continuous 'highway' linked Maine to Georgia.

Like Britain, America passed through an era of road building financed by turnpike trusts collecting tolls from those who used the roads. The trusts were private stock companies encouraged to take such action by Westward migration, increasing national feeling, prosperity and growing foreign commerce resulting from European wars, and by the obvious weaknesses revealed during the War of 1812 when inadequate roads almost rendered all movements of troops and supplies impossible. The first American turnpike road was that from Philadelphia to Lancaster (a distance of about sixty-two miles), built in 1792-4 at a cost of $465,000. Well constructed on a firm stone foundation with a gravel surface and well located in a populous area, the Lancaster Turnpike was from the outset a financial success. Its rapid effect was to produce a spate of turnpike road building and during the following three decades hundreds of state charters permitted the planning and construction of thousands of miles of roads. In New York State 135 companies had by 1811 built some 1,500 miles of road; in Pennsylvania 86 chartered companies built 2,200 miles of road. Turnpike roads led logically to the construction of turnpike bridges, and out of this flurry of activity emerged at least one major achievement: the 'National Pike' or Cumberland Road which was first projected to join Cumberland, Maryland, with St. Louis. It took the passing of over thirty Congres-

[1] *The Transportation Revolution* (New York, 1951).

sional Acts and the federal expenditure of $6,821,200 between 1806 and 1838 to complete and maintain the road as far as Vandalia, Illinois, from which point it was not extended the remaining distance.[1] The acceptance of the idea of a *nationally* subsidized highway did not come except after vigorous debate and widespread political and legal disagreement between 'strict-constructionists' (who believed in interpreting the Constitution narrowly to exclude federal enterprise and intervention) and 'broad-constructionists' (who believed in a wide interpretation of the Constitution and a strong federal government). Behind the long-winded Constitutional exegesis which paralysed Congressional debates over this issue lay meaningful economic and political hopes and fears, which we shall examine in Chapter VI. Suffice it to note at this stage that the road, despite its very slow progress, constituted when building ceased in 1838 the principal highway to the West. Cutting down the travelling time from Baltimore to Wheeling from eight to three days and halving freightage costs, the Cumberland Road brought local prosperity along the length of its 834 miles of all-weather surface.

Turnpike road construction whether by federal, state or (as in the majority of cases) private means was most evident in the North and North-east. The turnpike 'craze' ended in New England about 1806 although much building continued into the 1820's. Pennsylvania and New York possessed the greatest mileage, the bulk of the construction in the latter state coming immediately after the War of 1812. The fever hit the Old North-west in the '20's and '30's, mainly in Ohio. Few roads were completed, however, except in that state, and even these were inferior. In the Upper South, Maryland was the most progressive, possessing about 300 miles of toll road by 1830. No important roads appeared in Virginia (despite the permissive Turnpike Act of 1817) until the '30's. The turnpike era in South Carolina ended fairly abruptly when state appropriations were terminated in 1829. During the years 1823-8 several short and two fairly long toll roads had been built there under direct state auspices at a cost of $120,000. Road building in the Deep South was either desultory or non-existent, though many plans were doubtless made. As late as 1835 Harriet Martineau's[2] strictures on Southern travel were extremely severe and those of Arthur Young on the roads of England of half a century before compare favourably.

The decline of turnpikes was not entirely due to canal and railway competition, for it had begun before their competition became effective. Few if any turnpikes were as economically successful as the Lancaster Pike and on the whole they failed, in handling such bulky

[1] Those interested in the complete story should try to obtain Philip D. Jordan: *The National Road* (Indianapolis, 1948).

[2] Op. cit., vol. II.

and perishable goods as dominated the economy, to provide a sufficiently cheap mode of transport for any considerable distance. They failed to prove a sound investment and indeed were often hard put to make ends meet at all. Similarly the short-lived boom in timber-surfaced roads came to an end with the crisis of 1857. Appearing first in New York State (via Russia and Canada) in 1844 these 'plank roads' spread quickly for short distance uses all over the settled areas. Although the original costs were low, the maintenance and replacement costs were, as with turnpike roads, very high. There was much evasion of payment in both cases—'shun-pikes' or roads around toll points being quite common.

The greatest triumph in transport development before about 1840 was undoubtedly the Erie Canal. Canals had existed in the eighteenth century, and as early as 1777 proposals were made to link the river Hudson with the Great Lakes by water. [In 1817 the legislature of New York State sanctioned by Act the construction of a canal from the Hudson to Lake Erie, financed by loans most of which were British. This scheme was completed in 1825 at a total cost of over seven million dollars and covering a distance of over 360 miles. The Erie Canal was a complete success, tolls exceeding interest charges before the project was fully completed. When tolls were finally abolished in 1882 some 120 million dollars had been collected. According to H. V. Poor[1] the Erie Canal drastically reduced travelling time from Buffalo to New York from twenty to six days, and slashed freight charges to one-twentieth of the original (100 dollars per ton to 5 dollars per ton). He wrote:

'The success of the Erie Canal had an electric effect upon the whole country, and similar works were everywhere projected. The States of Pennyslvania, Maryland, Ohio, Indiana and Illinois at once embarked upon elaborate systems designed to give every portion of their State the advantage of such works. . . .'

Farm land in New York State doubled in value and New York city, the population of which also doubled between 1820 and 1830, established its hegemony over Philadelphia as the leading American seaport. The new canal linked the Old North-west more closely to the North East than it had ever been linked by way of the Mississippi or St. Lawrence valley to the South or Canada. A decade after its completion the New York legislature ordered a vast enlargement of the whole project, finally achieved in 1862. Tonnage carried by the Erie continued increasing in spite of railway competition up to 1880, when its highest point was attained. This was a handsome return on a daring and courageous State investment which had met much

[1] *Manual of the Railroads of the U.S. for 1868–9* (New York, 1868).

political opposition and faced great geographical and engineering hazards.

So much for 'Clinton's Big Ditch' as it was called; the history of the 'canal mania' of the '20's and '30's which terminated after much overspeculation in the crisis of 1837, can hardly be termed the story of the Erie 'writ large'. Canal construction was heaviest in Pennsylvania, Massachusetts, Maryland, Virginia, Ohio, Indiana and Michigan. The first three states of this list feared respectively for the commerce and prestige of the cities of Philadelphia, Boston and Baltimore, and tried to build trunk-line canals to compete with the Erie. Pennsylvania constructed a canal system between Philadelphia and Pittsburgh (1826–34) at a cost of $10 million; Massachusetts proposed to divert some of the Western commerce from the Erie Canal and New York to Boston by way of a Boston canal to the river Hudson, but the scheme did not work out and Boston had to suffer; Maryland was slow in taking similar action but began instead the first railroad contact with the West—the Baltimore and Ohio—in 1828. Virginia and Maryland together took up an old plan to link the East coast with the river Ohio by way of a canal along the river Potomac. This, the 'Chesapeake and Ohio', was begun in 1828 and came to a halt at Cumberland in 1850 after countless setbacks and losses. The canal cost $11 million (the bulk of which was provided by the State of Maryland) and the venture was largely unsuccessful owing to the competition of the Baltimore and Ohio railway and to the failure of the canal to cross the mountains to the Ohio. In addition to these trunk-line canals, several short 'tidewater' canals were built all along the coast from South Carolina to New England. Chief among these were the waterways used to haul anthracite coal from the Pennsylvania mines to Baltimore, Philadelphia and New York. The interior canals of the Middle West formed a third group of great economic significance, linking the river Ohio with Lake Erie and the river Illinois with Lake Michigan. The largest of these, and incidentally the largest canal ever built in America, was the 'Wabash and Erie' (1832–43). Over 450 miles in length, it connected Evansville on the Ohio with Toledo on the shores of Lake Erie, going by way of Terre Haute, the river Wabash and Fort Wayne.

Only the tidewater canals were financed by private sources. The others were predominantly public schemes and most of them were unprofitable. The railways came close on their heels, they were subject to weather conditions and provided a slow and cumbersome method of transport. Nevertheless canal mileage in the U.S.A. increased from 100 or so miles in 1816 to 1,270 in 1830, 3,320 in 1840 and 3,700 in 1850. Why? The demand for better transportation was so strong, and the canals were infinitely superior to the mule-train and cart, although of small significance for passengers. They immediately stimulated production, diverted existing trade, opened up former wildernesses, forests and mines, and created markets. Before the Miami and Erie Canal was completed in Ohio in 1845 neither grain nor pork was exported from the north-western section of the state through which it passed. One year after the canal was opened the amounts exported through it totalled 2,000,000 bushels of grain and 125,000 barrels of pork.

It was, however, an over-expansion of internal improvements, especially of canals, which helped to bring about the financial crash of 1837.[1] Many states simply had to repudiate their debts and many more 'sold out' to private concerns, disavowing any further public investment. So the railroad era which was already more than embryonic was to be financed by private individuals and corporations.

The river steamboat and the railroad both underwent great expansion after the crisis of 1837. The '50's proved to be the 'golden age' of the river steamboat but it was in 1807 that Robert Fulton first took his 'backwoods sawmill mounted on a scow and set on fire'—the *Clermont*—up the river Hudson. Its first voyage, New York to Albany, was a distance of 150 miles covered in 32 hours. The side-paddle wheels on this 133-feet-long craft were driven by a British steam engine made by Boulton & Watt. Invented 'with a view to the navigation of the Mississippi from New Orleans *upward*', the *Clermont* combined several elements of earlier inventions attempted by such people as John Fitch (whose *Thornton* ran a regular packet service on the river Delaware for some time after 1790), John Stevens of New Jersey and James Rumsey of Maryland. By the end of the 1812–14 war steamboats were no longer uncommon on the Delaware and Hudson, and in 1811–12 the *New Orleans* had steamed from Pittsburgh to New Orleans in eleven days' running time (and faced Indian canoes, flood-waters and a minor earth tremor). In the spring of 1815 Brownsville, Pennsylvania, was reached by a steamboat travelling upstream from New Orleans, the journey taking one month. From that date progress was very rapid, especially when in 1824 Fulton's monopoly was set aside. The trip from New Orleans to Louisville took less than five days by fast steamer in the '50's, and in 1870 in a famous race, the *Robert E. Lee* beat the *Natchez* by steaming from New Orleans to St. Louis in three days, eighteen and a half hours. Steamers were mainly used on the Mississippi, Missouri and Ohio, the Mississippi achieving its position as America's greatest commercial artery by 1850. Almost 600 steamboats were in commission in that year in the United States, and many of them were more

[1] A fuller treatment of the crisis of 1837 is contained in Chapter VI, below, pp. 77–8.

than 300 feet in length and carried 300 to 400 passengers not including cabin-class travellers. Steam navigation of rivers in California and Oregon developed quickly in the '50's after the gold discoveries, some of the boats actually rounding Cape Horn in the process.[1]

State and federal aid to steamboat navigation was both small and indirect. Unlike the turnpike, canals and railways, steamboat companies received no direct money or land grants and none of their stock or bonds was purchased by governmental bodies, except in Georgia. Attempts were made on the other hand to improve river navigation, widen and deepen streams and remove 'snags' and obstructions. Such work was undertaken directly by state governments or *ad hoc* chartered companies and received some federal aid in addition. The first Congressional act regulating steamboats was passed in 1838, and was followed by a more wisely framed and effective measure in 1852: the Steamboat Act. At first the railways often stimulated a greater development of steamboat navigation: this was especially true where water navigation was essential to connect railway lines, for instance across Lakes Erie and Michigan and on Long Island Sound. Once *through* rail routes were completed, however, the steamboats were doomed. They shared the physical and economic disadvantages of the canals and were outpaced and eventually even outpriced by the railroads. The latter combined greater speed with more direct routes and an all-year-round time-table mainly unaffected by weather and temperature with regularity of service.

T. P. Kettell,[2] the famous Southern economic and political writer, said of the 1830's:

'The excitement in relation to canals and steamboats was yet at its zenith, when the air began to be filled with rumours of the new application of steam to land carriages and to railroads.... In 1825 descriptions came across the water of the great success of the Darlington railroad, which was opened to supply London with coal, and which had passenger cars moved by steam at the rate of seven miles per hour. The most animated controversy sprang up . . . (and) with the national energy of character, the idea had no sooner become disseminated than it was acted upon.'[3]

The railway boom in the United States came at roughly the same period as that in Britain (unlike the canal mania, which had already reached its peak by 1793 in Britain). Several native American experi-

[1] A definitive study of this subject has been made by L. C. Hunter: *Steamboats on the Western Rivers* (Cambridge, Mass. 1949).
[2] See Chapter VI, below, pp. 90–2.
[3] *Eighty Years' Progress* (Hartford, 1869).

ments had been attempted with varying degrees of success before the construction of the Stockton and Darlington line. The stimulus afforded by this English achievement and by the later Rainhill Trials of 1829 was immeasurable, however. The first locomotive to operate on a commercial track in America was in fact the *Stourbridge Lion*, a British engine. Like most of the other British locomotives imported in this early period it was much too heavy for American needs. The 'Baltimore and Ohio Railroad', planned as we have seen to protect the interests of Baltimore in the competitive struggle for Western communications, was the first important commercial railroad. It made use in 1830 of a much lighter American locomotive, Peter Cooper's *Tom Thumb*. Begun in 1828, the company had thirteen miles of track in operation by May 1830, but it did not finally dismiss experimentation with sails and horse traction until the *Tom Thumb* was accepted. Curiously enough from the point of view of popular generalizations about 'the agrarian South', it was in South Carolina that the second railroad in the United States was built. Moreover this line, the Charleston and Hamburg, was running a regular passenger service as early as 1831 and when completed in 1833 constituted the longest railroad in the world (136 miles). By connecting Charleston with the Savannah river it hoped to divert the rich cotton trade from the port of Savannah at that river's mouth. In 1830–1 the Massachusetts legislature chartered three railway companies to build outwards from Boston. These were completed in 1833 and by 1841 a through connection was made from Boston to the river Hudson. Rapidly the state of Pennyslvania gained on the pioneers Maryland and South Carolina with the Philadelphia and Columbia (1834), the Philadelphia and Trenton (1834), the Philadelphia, Wilmington and Baltimore (1838) and the Philadelphia and Reading (1839). By 1840 all the larger eastern seaboard states had a considerable mileage except Maine. No significant lines had been built beyond the Appalachians but the total U.S. mileage had leapt during the decade from 73 (1830) to 3,328 (1840). Canal mileage had increased from 1,277 to 3,326 during the same time; but during the 1840's grew to only 3,698 miles. Railway mileage by 1850 was 8,879, and by 1860, 30,636. New York had overtaken all the other states for railway mileage by 1850, Massachusetts being a very close second, Pennsylvania a more distant third, and Georgia and Ohio fourth and fifth. In 1860 the competitive order was: Ohio (nearly 3,000 miles), Illinois (2,800 miles), New York, Pennsylvania and Indiana (all well over 2,000 miles); followed by Virginia, Georgia, Massachusetts and Tennessee. The New York Central in 1850 established a through connection with the Great Lakes, in 1853 linked Chicago and in 1854 the Mississippi with New York. St. Louis and New York were linked in 1855 and the Mississippi was bridged the following year. By 1860 several lines stretched almost to the very edge of the Western frontier. In the South progress was comparatively slow despite the early start of South Carolina: population was less dense, inter-regional trade less active, labour and capital fairly immobile. In the 1850's Southern ports made attempts to retain the valuable trade from Kentucky, Missouri and Illinois, 8,000 miles of railroad being constructed to connect up the South-west. New Orleans was joined with Chicago; Savannah and Charleston with Atlanta, Nashville and thence to the Ohio; and Mobile almost linked up to the system by a line going north to contact the east–west route from the Virginian coast to Memphis on the Mississippi. The idea of a trans-continental railroad, suggested as early as the 1820's, became an outstanding political issue during the ante-bellum decade (1850–60). Congress split on sectional lines and the question of a northern or southern route for the railroad could not be settled until the South had seceded from the Union—although Jefferson Davis as President Pierce's Secretary of War had successfully advocated the 'Gadsden Purchase' in December 1853 of a piece of Mexican territory through which he hoped a southern trans-continental line would pass. Chicago, St. Louis and Memphis were keen rivals in the political struggle, each claiming a prior right to a transcontinental rail connection. But for the line built across Nicaragua in 1855, however, and Jefferson Davis's plans, nothing substantial was achieved before the Civil War.

Over 30,000 miles of railroad were built between 1830 and 1860. How was this immense expansion financed?[1] In the '30's private capital was mainly used and loans at high rates were much supported in England. With few exceptions railroads were built by private corporations under state charters. Private capital was however quite inadequate, and the state governments stepped into the breach either by supplying credit or in some cases by building railroads themselves. Also most of the state charters gave wide privileges to the railroad companies and placed few if any restrictions on securities and fares. The railroad 'mania' swept aside normal American doubts about 'monopolistic practices', some states actually granting monopoly rights to certain railroads (as in Massachusetts, New Jersey, Georgia, Louisiana, Kentucky, and South Carolina). The Camden and Amboy Railroad thus received exclusive rights to rail transportation between Philadelphia and New York. Freedom from property taxes and the right to establish railroad banks were privileges often included in state charters. In the '30's the number of railroad banks that were established, while helping to finance construction undoubtedly contributed to the disastrous growth of 'wildcat' banking.

[1] A standard work on railroad financing is: *Public Aids to Transportation*, 4 vols., (Washington Government Printing Office, 1938–40).

A huge amount of direct financial aid was given by state and local governments to private railroad companies—state debts attributable to railroads reaching the total of $43 million in 1838. Local and municipal aid probably exceeded even this state figure. So in the East, South and West towns, cities, counties and states lavished money on railroad loans and investments. By 1861 Virginia, for instance, had supplied $21 million, Missouri over $25 million; Texas had donated 5,000,000 acres of state lands to stimulate railroad construction.

Before 1850 *federal* aid to railroads did exist (for instance in the reduction of tariff duties payable on iron used in railroad building, operative between 1830 and 1843) but it was mainly after that date that it assumed great significance. In 1850 the policy of making federal land grants to roads and canals of more than merely local significance was extended to railroads. This extension may have been stimulated by the shortage of state credit caused by the speculative 'crash' of 1837; but it was forced through Congress by a temporary alliance of Southern and Western states who demanded grants for a railroad from northern Illinois to Mobile, Alabama. By the act the states of Illinois, Alabama and Mississippi were allowed alternative sections of land in a strip six miles wide on each side of the proposed line. The states were then to give the land to the railroad companies, who either sold it or sold bonds secured by a mortgage on it. Thus constitutional difficulties regarding the rôle of the Federal Government were side-stepped. The land came eventually to make up parts of the Illinois Central and the Mobile and Ohio railroads, and totalled 3,736,005 acres. Federal property and troops were to be transported by the railways without charge and Congress was to fix the rates for mail. In 1852, 1853, 1856 and 1857 Congress acted upon this precedent by granting land to ten states and, through them, to forty-five railroads. Although these grants amounted to 18,000,000 acres they were belittled by the subsequent Congressional gifts to the transcontinental lines in the second half of the century.[1]

The less fortunate aspects of railroad history: the speculation and corruption over the vast land grants, the political chicanery, the immense waste in bitter competitive struggles and 'rate wars', and the problem of preferential rates and hasty, shoddy building—these questions became much more noticeable and noticed in the post-Civil War years. Some of the more successful canals continued to expand their business, but it is broadly true that by 1860 the railroad had established its hegemony in the field of American transportation. An illustration of this was given in the *Preliminary Report on the Eighth Census, 1860* (op. cit.), which declared:

[1] See G. R. Taylor, op. cit., Chapter V.

'It is well ascertained that our railroads transport in the aggregate at least 850 tons of merchanise per annum to the mile of road in operation. Such a rate would give 26,000,000 tons as the total annual tonnage for the whole country. If we estimate the value of this tonnage at 150 dollars per ton, the aggregate value of the whole would be $3,900 million. Vast as this commerce is, more than three-quarters of it has been created since 1850.'

SUGGESTED FURTHER READING

HUNTER, L. C. *Steamboats on the Western Rivers* (Cambridge, Mass., 1949).
JORDAN, P. D. *The National Road* (Indianapolis, 1948).
RIEGEL, R. E. *America Moves West* (Revised Edition, New York, 1947).
TAYLOR, G. R. *The Transportation Revolution, 1815–1860* (Vol. IV in Rinehart & Co.'s *Economic History of the United States*. New York, 1951).

V

TRADE AND FINANCE

Early trade difficulties and the growth of merchant shipping 1789–1807 – Neutral trading: the Jay Treaty, the Continental System and Orders in Council and the Embargo Act (1807) – Origins and consequences of the War of 1812 – Rise and decline of the merchant marine, 1814–1860 – Early financial problems – Hamilton and Jefferson – Hamiltonian finance: tariffs, excises, the U.S. Treasury, the Funding Act (1790), coinage and the first U.S. Bank (1791) – Tariff controversy up to 1860 – Jackson, Biddle and the Second U.S. Bank.

DESPITE the hesitancy with which the phrase 'the Critical Period' was used in Chapter I to describe the years between Independence and the ratification of the Constitution, the outlook in this period was certainly gloomy for commercial and shipping interests, and especially so for the smaller firms. American trade was for a time excluded from Spain, Holland and France, and in the Mediterranean American shipping was constantly at the mercy of Tripolitan pirates. As for trade with England, Pitt's belief in the need to grant generous trade terms to the newly-United States once the war was decided, was mainly ignored. The Orders in Council of 1783 were restrictive, and English opinion was swayed by Lord John Sheffield's *Observations on the Commerce of the American States*.[1] Sheffield claimed that as Americans had demanded by force the right to be 'foreigners' they should therefore receive no privileges whatsoever under the English Navigation Acts. 'Nothing can be more weak than the idea of courting commerce', he said, and added:

'It will not be an easy matter to bring the American States to act as a nation; they are not to be feared as such by us. . . . It will be extreme folly to enter into any engagements by which we may not wish to be bound hereafter. . . . No treaty can be made with the American States that can be binding on the whole of them.'

[1] London, 1783

In any case Lord Sheffield believed, with some justification, that America would be obliged to trade with England. His opposition to the idea of an Anglo-American commercial treaty was echoed by the English government in 1784-5, when American overtures were rejected.

The result of this attitude was the exclusion of Americans from trade with the British West Indies until 1830. This was of the greatest disadvantage to the young nation. The British sugar islands had taken an important part in Colonial trade; the prohibition of American commerce meant the subsequent loss to the Yankees of the rich 'three-cornered' trade. Soon, however, this was to be replaced by Baltic trading, by the opening to Americans of some of the Caribbean ports of Spain, France, Holland and Denmark, and by the readiness with which American captains took to privateering. The most striking and significant innovation was the American attempt to trade with the Orient. The opening-up of the New England-N.W. China route began when in 1784 the *Empress of China* sailed from New York to Canton; in that same year the *United States* left Philadelphia for India. Thus was originated a 'new epoch' in international history: the small beginnings of Western commercial and cultural influence on China and Japan. Moreover in 1789 a revolution broke out in France which was soon to lead to large-scale European war. Up to 1807 at least the United States had a golden opportunity, as a leading neutral nation, to expand her commerce. This opportunity, with the help of Hamilton's sound financial policy, she took. No sooner had the conservative Federal Constitution been largely agreed upon than the new Congress enacted legislation to encourage a revival of merchant shipping and foreign trade. The first Tariff Act (4 July 1789) gave genuine aid to native shipping by allowing a 10 per cent reduction of duties on goods imported in ships built and owned by Americans. Tea directly imported from the Far East in American ships was to pay only 50 per cent of the normal duty. Tonnage duties on alien ships was 50 cents a ton; on alien-owned but American-built vessels, 30 cents; and on American-owned and -built vessels, 6 cents. By 1798 the Federal Government was using its small navy to make reprisals on Tripolitan pirates. During the long European wars the British Navy drove much French and Dutch competition from the seas, and the lucrative carrying-trade fell increasingly into American hands. Neutral trading was dangerous but highly profitable until about 1807; from that date until 1815, however, the hazards and difficulties increased. In 1807 the American maritime boom reached its climax; the tonnage of shipping engaged in foreign trade had increased from just under 350,000 tons (1790) to almost 850,000 tons; the value of total exports had multiplied fivefold from $20 million (1790) to over $108 million (including re-exports); and the value of total imports had multiplied sixfold from $23 million (1790) to $138½ million. The proportion of this trade carried in American ships increased from 23·6 per cent (1789) to 92 per cent (1807) and between 1798 and 1812 more than 200,000 tons of American shipping was sold to other nations.

One year after 1807 American imports reached only $57 million. They had been more than halved. Similarly, exports were drastically cut to one-fifth (from $108 million to $22 million). How did this disastrous change come about? To comprehend this we must know something of the so-called 'Continental System', that mutual blockade established by the belligerents in the Napoleonic Wars which raged in Europe from 1793.

Both France and Britain sought to employ methods of 'economic warfare' against each other. England aimed to enforce the 'Rule of 1756' which stated that trade not open to neutrals in time of peace should not be available in time of war. This enforcement was aimed at France and the United States, the latter having begun to take over once again the 'long haul' of West Indian sugar across the Atlantic. French merchant ships were unable to run the English blockade and therefore threw open the trade routes (from Nantes and Bordeaux to Martinique and Haiti) to the Americans. The Anglo-American friction over British boarding of American vessels at sea and the wide definition by the British of the term 'contraband' led to the posting of John Jay, an American Supreme Court Chief Justice, to the Court of St. James in May 1794 to treat with the British Government. The 'Jay Treaty' which was thus produced did not put an end to the searching of neutral vessels and the impressment of American seamen (often mistakenly deemed 'deserters') but it did recognize several basic rights of the United States as a neutral power and allowed American ships (of not more than 70 tons) to trade in the West Indies. Meanwhile France held that the United States was bound by the treaty of 1778 to aid her in her struggle against Britain and was furious at the American willingness to negotiate a treaty with Britain. Opinion in the United States fluctuated between pro-French and pro-British attitudes, but on this occasion very nearly came to war with France. A temporary agreement was reached in 1800. After the turn of the century, however, when the commercial clauses of the Jay Treaty lapsed, Britain reinvoked the 'Rule of 1756'. Between the renewal of the war in 1803 and the peak American commercial year of 1807, over 500 American vessels were seized by Britain and almost 400 by France. Napoleon's Berlin and Milan Decrees (1806 and 1807) and the retaliatory British Orders in Council which followed them established the 'Continental System' and cut out neutral trading altogether. The Napoleonic measures declared what was in effect a 'paper blockade' of British ports, forbidding all trade with them and with ships sailing to or from British territory, which were considered 'good prize' and liable to seizure by French men-of-war. The Orders in Council on the other hand stated that all ports belonging to France or her allies were subject to blockade and that no neutral could trade with them *without* first entering a British port. In 1807 therefore American shipping and commercial interests were in a dangerous international position. They were the only important neutral traders and carriers, and between 1807 and the outbreak of war with England in 1812 they lost 750 vessels. Despite the fairly lax enforcement of the system by the British and the theoretical and flimsy nature of Napoleon's 'paper blockade', considerable damage was caused to American shipping and the important 'triangular' trade was once more disrupted.

President Jefferson tried at first to resolve the problem by imposing economic pressure rather than appealing to force, and passed in 1807 an Embargo Act prohibiting the sailing of American ships to foreign ports. The cumulative effect of all these measures on American import and export figures we have already observed. After these heavy American losses and much internal political opposition, the Act was repealed in 1809. A Non-Intercourse Act was substituted in its place, forbidding trade only with Britain, France and their possessions. In 1810 this was also repealed, all commercial restrictions being annulled. In addition the offer was made that if either of the two chief belligerents, England or France, would waive their decrees in favour of the United States, then the Federal Government would renew the Non-Intercourse Act in return, to act against the other contestant. Napoleon repealed his decrees and the Non-Intercourse Act was revived against Britain in March 1811.

Anglo-American relations were becoming as strained as U.S.-French relations had been in the late 1790's, and on this occasion the disagreement was not patched up or successfully ignored. The War of 1812, as it is usually called, was however not solely the result of such incidents as the firing by *H.M.S. Leopard* on the American ship *Chesapeake* and the impressment by the English of four of her men in 1807. Such incidents were frequent, and often occurred—to the exasperation of American witnesses—very near the U.S. coast. Congress declared war on Britain on 18 June 1812. Castlereagh had already revoked the Orders in Council on 16 June, but two days earlier. President Madison's justification for recommending war to Congress was fourfold: the illegal impressment of American sailors by British men-of-war; the British violation of the three-mile limit; the 'flagrantly illegal' Orders in Council; and the British attempts to blockade American ports. But 'maritime rights' were only the ostensible reason for a war with England. Throughout the Western frontier territories the belief had for a long time been widely held that British intrigue lay behind each new defensive move made by the Indians. In the Indiana Territory around about 1809 a new Indian leader emerged: Tecumseh, the son of a Shawnee brave, who, with his brother 'the Prophet', tried both to unite and to reform his race. His desire was to put an end to constant annexation of Indian territories by white men, make his people virtually teetotal (and so free them from the white man's trickery) and reduce all contact between the two races to a minimum. Accordingly he hoped to form a great confederation of the Indian races east of the Mississippi. Where the Tippecanoe Creek meets the river Wabash, Tecumseh established a settlement in 1809. The clash between his braves and white settlers which came about in 1811 was mainly engineered by the whites themselves. Much of the responsibility lay with General Harrison, Governor of Indiana Territory (and President of the United States during the last month of his life in 1841). At all events, the Indian settlement was destroyed on 6 November 1811 when Harrison gathered a force of 1,100 men and fought a pitched battle with Tecumseh. The Indians used rifles of British manufacture and it was true that Canadian authorities had encouraged the new Indian confederation. When the Congressional decision was taken in June the following year, the inland and Western states—Vermont, Ohio, Kentucky and Tennessee—voted unanimously (except for one vote) for war with England. And, what is more surprising, perhaps, when we consider the emphasis laid on maritime rights in these years, the maritime areas of New England were unanimously *opposed* to war. In the first place conservative New England was mainly anti-French and pro-British and many of its inhabitants believed that the war was the product of Napoleonic machination. In the second place, war with Britain would strike mercantile New England a crippling blow, as had the Embargo Act of 1807. A repetition of such a disaster was to be avoided at all costs. The mercantile viewpoint, even though it led in 1814 to a serious threat of the secession of New England from the Union and the signing of a separate peace, can be more fairly understood in the light of actual events: foreign trade in 1814 was reduced to a quarter of even the badly reduced total of 1808. When the war ended imports amounted to only $13 million and exports to $6,900,000.

Maritime rights were the excuse and the battle of Tippecanoe the occasion for the outbreak of the 1812–14 war. But what united the West against Britain was not simply a suspicion that she had a hand in Indian wars. Solid economic motives came into play. The real initiative for the war came from a strongly represented group in Congress headed by Henry Clay and John Calhoun, the 'Warhawks' or Western expansionists who had their eyes on Canadian forest land. Territorial expansion and the hopes of developing a rich fur trade were pressing factors in Western politics. The South-west was particularly land-hungry and, unsatisfied even by the Louisiana Purchase, hoped for Florida from Spain and eventually for Mexico. The demand for war was thus the expression of 'frontier nationalism' and of the feeling that the two chief stumbling-blocks to territorial expansion on the American continent were the Indians and 'foreign'-held areas (such as Canada). Congressman John Randolph declared in 1812:

'Agrarian cupidity, not maritime rights, urges the war. Ever since the report of the Committee on Foreign Relations came into the House, we have heard but one word—like the whip-poor-will, but one eternal monotonous tone—Canada! Canada! Canada!'

To some degree the situation was exacerbated by the Western economic depression brought about through the trade restrictions caused by the international predicament.

The war was primarily fought on sea, although there was an American invasion of Canada and an English invasion of the United States, both of which failed. In 1813 York (Toronto) was destroyed by the Americans and in 1814 Washington by the British. The famous battle of New Orleans, which later helped to assure General Jackson the Presidency, was fought after peace had been declared. The treaty of Ghent (1814) made no mention of neutral rights but dealt instead with boundary disputes and fishing rights. We have observed already that the War of 1812 (or the 'Second War of Independence' as ardent nationalists styled it) stimulated manufacturing developments by throwing Americans on to their own resources. The shutting off of imports, the release of capital from shipping and commerce and the existence of abundant raw materials facilitated the growth of the cotton, iron, woollen and metal industries. In the South-west, Andrew Jackson had cleared the way of Indians and migration westwards to the rich 'Black Belt' areas was now possible.

A rapid expansion in American trade began at the end of the War of 1812. British goods formerly starved of markets by war and the Continental System, flooded into U.S. ports. Imports increased in the four years 1814–18 from $13 million to almost $122 million. Exports grew from under $7 million to well over $93 million. The demand of the expanding English cotton industry for American cotton seemed insatiable, while other exports included wheat and flour, naval stores, timber, fish and whale products and some manufactured articles. The panic year of 1819, however, made serious inroads on foreign trade, exports falling to $50 million and imports to $87 million. From 1819 recovery was slow and steady up to 1830. New York city, as we have seen, gained predominance in both domestic and foreign commerce when the Erie Canal was opened in 1825; similarly the port of New Orleans gained by the coming of the steamboat and the movement of population west of the Appalachians. From 1830 to the crash of 1837 foreign trade again underwent an expansion, as a result of international trade agreements, a reduced scale of tariffs, the need to market a considerable and increasing domestic surplus of agricultural goods, the improvements and innovations in sea transportation, and basically, as a result of the 'natural' increase in commerce due to population growth and increased productivity. Just before the crisis of 1837, exports reached the value of nearly $129 million and imports almost $190 million. Regular steamship services joined New York and Liverpool and American commerce was principally with the U.K. and northern Europe.

Recovery from the 1837 crisis was already well under way by 1840, when total exports were $132 million and total imports $107 million. But fluctuations continued until about 1846, after which expansion was rapid down to the outbreak of Civil War. The repeal of the English Corn Laws by Peel in 1846, together with the hurried measures of famine relief which he had already begun in Ireland, stimulated the export of American grain and foodstuffs. Further, the American tariffs (which had been raised in 1840) were decreased, and the gold discoveries in California, Colorado and Australia gave impetus to commerce. The slowness of overland routes to the gold areas of California greatly increased the demand for shipping. This together with other factors led to an abnormal production of American shipping, which was followed by a sharp regression. Among these other factors were: the development in the 1840's of American 'clipper ships' (the fastest sailing-ships afloat); the Anglo-Chinese wars of the 'forties and 'fifties, which threw part of the Chinese trade into American hands; and the European Revolutions of 1848 and the Crimean War, which also indirectly benefited American commerce. The days of the clipper ships were numbered, however, and the crisis of 1857 helped to precipitate the ultimate crash in a shipbuilding industry unprepared for the change-over to steel ship production. The old trade routes declined (Brazilian coffee began to capture the American market, at the expense of Oriental tea, for instance), capital found new outlets in industry, canals and railways, and America turned from her merchant marine to the subjugation and internal development of the continent. The decline of merchant shipping was accentuated by the Civil War. This dealt it a blow from which it had not recovered by the time of the First World War.

The financial history of the United States between Independence and Civil War must take into account two principal problems: the

National Bank issue and the tariff issue. To understand either we must go back to the state of affairs existing immediately after the Revolution. It will be remembered from Chapter I that the new government of 1783 was faced with challenging financial problems. It lacked the wherewithal of administration—revenue. It laboured under a heavy national debt, to which it was proposed to add the burden of state indebtedness. A currency famine of long-standing led debtors to agitate for some kind of relief legislation. State governments had frequently given way to demands for a 'cheap' money policy, and flooded the country with worthless paper currency. The problem of providing for private credit being a national issue, now also devolved upon the Federalist government set up in 1789 under the new Constitution. The revenue question leads us to a brief consideration of tariff policy; the currency and credit question leads us to the National Bank issue.

Both problems, however, merely illustrate different developments of a central theme on the final nature of American society, a theme reiterated throughout American history. Jefferson represented the leaning towards a 'broader, freer' democracy and upheld American agrarian ideals; Hamilton represented the leaning towards a closer Union, a stronger Federal government and stimulated and expanding national industry. The struggle between these two basic attitudes to American government, law and economic life forms that theme.

Alexander Hamilton (1757–1804) was born in the Leeward Islands. His father was a Scots merchant and his mother the daughter of a French Huguenot physician and planter. It was a complicated marriage and the parents were not prosperous. Alexander was saved from a career in a general store however (which he had already begun at the age of twelve) by the benevolence of several aunts and the intensity of his ambition for university training. He entered King's College (Columbia University) in 1773, and almost immediately entered the pamphleteering war against British control. He took a commission and command of an artillery company in the war in 1776 (at the age of nineteen) and fought alongside Washington, becoming his personal secretary and aide-de-camp in 1777, with the rank of lieutenant-colonel. Through a marriage in 1780 to Elizabeth Schuyler he entered one of the highest and most influential New York familes. Two years later he entered the Continental Congress and was admitted to the Bar after five months' intensive study, in 1783. From the start Hamilton favoured a strong Federal government and part of his early legal work involved a defence of Federal against State authority.[1] He was a delegate to the Annapolis Convention in

[1] *Rutgers v. Waddington* in which Hamilton maintained that the (federal) peace treaty between Britain and the U.S.A. overrode the laws of the State of New York.

1786, and indeed it was Hamilton who secured the unanimous adoption of the idea of a further Convention in Philadelphia to discuss the possibilities of stronger Union. In 1789 he became the first Secretary of the Treasury of the new Federalist government.

Thomas Jefferson (1743–1826) was born in Albemarle County, Virginia, on the edges of Western settlement at that time. His parents may have been of Welsh extraction. The father was a surveyor and landowner; the mother came from a family of social distinction. Thomas was educated in classics at a local school, entering William and Mary College in 1760. His main college interests were mathematical and scientific; but his other than academic connections during these years were equally important. He hobnobbed with the greatest Virginia families and was an accepted member of the high-class social clique. Admitted to the Bar in 1767, he became a successful lawyer until the time of the Revolution. Two years later he became a member of the Virginia House of Burgesses, where he remained until it ceased in 1775. From the outset aggressively anti-British, he helped to draw up the Virginia Resolves. His *Summary View of the Rights of British America* (1774) has been called the greatest literary contribution to the American Revolution next to the *Declaration of Independence* (for which he was in any case mainly responsible during his first year in Congress 1775–6). From 1779 to 1781 Jefferson was Governor of Virginia; in 1783 he became a member of Congress once more and did much committee work, helping to draft at least thirty-one State papers in six months. He advocated the adoption of the dollar as a unit of currency and the abolition of slavery in all the Western territories after 1800. His appointment as American ambassador to France occurred in 1785, when he succeeded Franklin. During his four years as ambassador (up to the outbreak of the French Revolution) Jefferson doubtless found much to his taste in France, especially the philosophy of the physiocrats. For Jefferson was one of the world's most famous 'perfectibilists': he believed in Natural Rights and Natural Law; in the unlimited capacity of Man for progress; in land as the source of all wealth; in the need for complete freedom of economic and intellectual commerce. Of a prosperous landowning background, Jefferson was politically an advanced liberal; of an unhappy and unstable background, Hamilton was politically a conservative. In 1789 Jefferson became the first Secretary of State under the new Constitution, and in this position came increasingly into conflict with Hamilton over foreign policy, economic policy (particularly the Bank of the United States) and over the 'true' interpretation of the Constitution. The hostility between these two men and the bodies of interest and opinion they represented had by 1792 become implacable and sadly divided the Washington administration. At the very end of 1793 Jefferson resigned from the cabinet, but in the election of 1796 became Vice-President of the United States (under Adams). Four years later another election, that of 1800, made him President of the United States, a position he held for two terms until 1809.

Jeffersonian democracy meant a centrifugal tendency in government and 'States' rights'; an agrarian republican ideal; a minimum of law and regulation; international free trade. Yet Jefferson passed the Embargo Act in 1807 because he believed in the first place that American prestige was all-important and in the second place that Europe could not do without American trade. Hamiltonianism, however, although conservative in politics was revolutionary in economics. It was the doctrine of the future America rather than of an ideal agrarian past. Hamilton would diversify economic life, encourage shipping, create and protect home industries by legislation and tariffs, and build up a centralized government, national in scope and powerful in character—fit to control an expanding industrial and mercantile nation. Behind the two men lay entrenched interests: planting-slaveholding groups behind the Virginian; mercantile-shipping-financial groups behind his opponent.

Hamilton's aims as Secretary of the Treasury for the young Republic were: to establish national credit by 'funding' the National Debt (i.e. converting it into long-term bonds and providing sufficient revenue both to cover its interest charges and ultimately to retire it); to make the Federal Government undertake responsibility for the debts of the several states under a similar funding scheme; to establish a Bank of the United States by governmental authority but under private control, as a medium uniting business and government in the task of developing national commerce. This would not only extend commercial credit but would facilitate government fiscal operations. Hamilton's sources of government revenue were to be import duties and internal taxes. Also he proposed the sale of public lands in large 'parcels' on credit.

Taking the chance offered by the new federal Constitution, Hamilton achieved the enactment of a Tariff Act (July 1789) which though primarily for revenue purposes gave slight 'protection' to certain interests.[1] Specific duties were placed on about thirty commodities and a low *ad valorem* duty on others. More important, however, Congress set up the primary administrative organization for collection and supervision of the federal customs. The tariff itself was by no means satisfactory to Hamilton, being neither high enough nor protective enough for his purposes. His famous *Report on Manufactures* (December 1791) suggested twenty-one increases in existing rates, four government subsidies to industry and five reductions in rates on raw materials. The Report was a clear statement

[1] See above, p. 57.

of the Protectionist view—the need to encourage domestic industries and safeguard them against foreign competition. A new Tariff Act of March 1792 increased the average rate to 13½ per cent, accepting eighteen of Hamilton's proposed increases and three of his reductions. Already sectional alignment was clarifying: a unanimous Pennsylvania vote and an overwhelming New England majority vote (all but two) favoured the Act. A consolidating Act was passed in March 1799.

Hamilton's second source of revenue was internal taxation, which incidentally served to 'bring home' the meaning of federal government inside the nation. Excise taxes were thus imposed in 1791, 1794 and 1797. The Whisky Insurrection of 1794, of which the excise tax on domestic distilled spirits was the immediate cause, gave the Hamiltonian Federalists a further opportunity to demonstrate the authority of the Federal Government. The rising was successfully put down by the militia.[1] In addition to spirits, snuff, wine, sugar and carriages were taxed. Auctions had to be licensed, as had documents after 1797. Income from these excises was quite small, however (only $180,000 in an average year of the mid-nineties), and in July 1798 Congress levied a $2 million direct tax, to be apportioned (according to Constitutional requirements) among the various states' according to population. The direct tax included land, buildings and slaves but was administered in such a complex way that only half the levy had been gathered in by 1801. Proceeds from the land sales were practically nil for the immediate future—by 1798 the Treasury had collected only $100,000 for the 1,300,000 acres sold.[2]

After the first measures had been taken to raise a revenue, a bill was drafted by Hamilton to establish the permanent U.S. Treasury to replace the temporary Board of Treasury. The body was to have a single head, nominated by the President and completely responsible to him. Hamilton's plans for making this office, the Secretary of the Treasury, a highly powerful and influential one, came to naught as Congress gradually asserted its control over the Department, relegating the Secretary to administrative duties. In 1796, for instance, Congress set up a standing Ways and Means Committee in the House of Representatives to supervise continuously the financial needs of the government and to initiate revenue measures. The Secretary of the Treasury could merely submit his estimates to the standing Committee, and the chief result was the control of fiscal arrangements by the legislature rather than (as in Britain) by the executive.

With a certain amount of revenue assured and fiscal institutions founded at least in their early crude forms, the urgent problem was

[1] See Chapter I, above, p. 6.

[2] These sales were regulated by the Acts of 1785 and 1796, discussed in Chapter II, above, pp. 16–17.

to establish government credit. Hamilton's *First Report on the Public Credit* (1790) assumed the national debt to stand at something over $54 million and state war debts at $25 million. Of the first figure some $27½ million represented all domestic debt, about which there was much controversy and discontent. The Funding Act of 1790 redeemed certificates of indebtedness at par, and most of the paper money at a valuation of 100 to 1. The assumption of state debts by the Federal Government was achieved only by a temporary alliance between Jeffersonian 'Republicans' and Hamiltonian 'Federalists' in which the latter agreed to the Southern demand that the federal capital be located on the Potomac. Much opposition to Hamilton's funding scheme and to the payment in full by the Federal Government of U.S. and state debts arose from the fact that such payment would give a huge windfall profit to wily speculators. Even during the debates over the Act several such speculators had sensed the direction things were turning and bought up certificates from the original holders at very low prices. Was it more important to prevent this manipulation than to build up the credit and prestige (national and international) of the United States Government? Hamilton thought not. He went on to establish a U.S. coinage system,[1] advising the free coinage of gold and silver at a ratio of fifteen to one, the decimal system and the dollar as a unit, of a value as equivalent as possible to the Spanish milled dollar. His ratio overvalued silver (the international market price of which began to fall soon after American coinage commenced), and in accordance with 'Gresham's Law' gold disappeared from circulation. As American silver dollars were accepted at face value in Spanish-American possessions, despite their lighter weight than Spanish milled dollars, they drained away to the West Indies. The conduct of economic life came to rest almost wholly on bank-notes, and Hamilton accepted paper payment of government dues although the Revenue Act of July 1789 specifically prohibited it.

Finally we come to the keystone of the Hamiltonian system: the Bank of the United States. Hamilton believed strongly in the need for a national bank modelled on the Bank of England. This could act as the fiscal agent of the government, provide stability for paper currency, and expand commercial credit. The Jeffersonians rationalized their deepfelt opposition to the idea in legal arguments about the need to construe the Constitution 'strictly'. Jefferson himself in his capacity as Secretary of State wrote to President Washington:

'The incorporation of a bank and the powers assumed by this bill (July 1791) have not, in my opinion, been delegated to the United States by the Constitution.'

[1] *Report on the Establishment of a Mint* (April 1791).

Hamilton's reply to this argument was the doctrine of 'implied powers'. He said:

'It is unquestionably incident to sovereign powers to erect corporations.'

Also, the Constitution, he claimed, had given Congress the authority to set up any medium to help the government to execute its constitutionally ordained functions. The Bank would enable the U.S. Government to collect taxes, regulate coinage, borrow money and spend funds. In addition it would encourage lower rates of interest by increasing the supply of money.[1] Thus although the Republicans insisted that banks increased usury and speculation, led to a drain of specie due to the competition of paper money, and diverted capital from agriculture, the Act to charter the Bank became law in February 1791. Only one Northerner voted against and three Southerners for the measure. The Act gave the Bank twenty years lease of life and a capital of $10 million, of which 20 per cent was to be subscribed by the Federal Government. Notes could be issued up to the amount of total capitalization, and were receivable in taxes if they were redeemable in specie. Interest on loans and discounts was not to exceed 6 per cent. During the first decade of its life the first Bank of the United States was quite successful, but opposition to its operations arose due to 'foreign interests' —almost 75 per cent of its stock was held in alien hands, though foreign owners had no voting power. In addition the numerous banks chartered by several of the states were keen rivals to the national institution, largely because the notes of non-specie paying banks were being driven out by the national bank's demands that paper be redeemed. So in 1811 the charter of the U.S. Bank was allowed to lapse.

All Hamilton's immediate schemes had been adopted but he was forced to resign in January 1795 and Congress began to develop machinery to prevent any future Secretary of the Treasury from wielding so much power. He had turned worthless paper into marketable securities, and provided for their redemption by taxes which were moderate and yet protectionist. Under his regime the U.S.A. acquired excellent financial credit and confidence, which was in part responsible for the revival of prosperity during the last years of the eighteenth century. But his more long-term hope—the consolidation of the Union—was still far from realization, for in the process he had obtained many enemies and found much opposition. America was not yet ready for the Hamiltonian Revolution although she finally took to it with an astonishing exuberance after the Civil War.

It now remains for us to outline the history of tariffs and of the National Bank question up to 1860, whilst striving at the same time

[1] *Report on a National Bank* (December 1790).

to keep political details down to a minimum. Without the artificial aid of a protective tariff the eventual growth of large manufacturing concerns in America was assured by the existence of abundant raw materials and an expanding home market which is even now, in the mid-twentieth century, far from saturation-point. Yet the American tariffs certainly helped to accelerate industrial growth, besides accentuating sectional differences and influencing the cost of living. Up to 1816 tariffs had been primarily meant for revenue purposes and were only incidentally protective, but the impetus given to the economy by the War of 1812, followed by the post-war depression due mainly to European competition, led to much agitation in favour of a strictly protective tariff. The tariff imposed during the war was due to expire in February 1816, but Congress extended its life until June pending a decision on tariff policy.

The decision taken was in favour of protection, and received the support of the 'Warhawks' who had helped to bring about the war. Under the new tariff the general rate of duty imposed was about 20 per cent, but cottons obtained special protection. The scheme had considerable support in the Southern states. Similarly the tariffs of 1818 and 1824 met with little strong opposition. To put it rather simply, farmers and manufacturers saw eye to eye because they were united in a common struggle against the depression of 1819–21. Both wanted markets for their goods; both fell back on the home market idea and supported protectionism. Henry Clay, the spokesman of the West, united the nationalists under his leadership in support of what he called the 'American System': protective tariffs to encourage native industries, which would in turn stimulate urbanization and so provide a bigger and expanding domestic market for agricultural produce; federal 'internal improvements' financed mainly by tariff revenues, to ensure the transportation without which farmers could not hope to market their goods. Clay finally managed to persuade Western farmers to accept the idea of a National Bank, and the alliance between North-east and North-west was then completed. Obviously the 'domestic market' appeal for protection was most successful with Western grain-farmers and North-eastern manufacturers, rather than with Southern cotton-planters who depended chiefly on foreign markets.

Perhaps the phrase 'North-eastern manufacturers' is vague and inaccurate, at least where the 1820's are concerned: New England remained basically commercial and most manufacturing was centred in the textile industry. It was textiles, however, which had gained protection by the tariffs of 1816 and 1818. Split between shipping, mercantile and industrial interests, New England held a divided vote until about 1830 when she was won over to the protectionist view. The South, once expansion to the rich cotton lands of the Gulf basin was ascertained, turned completely against protection and led by an ex-Warhawk, Calhoun, began to agitate against 'Northern' influences in the national economy. In 1824 an increase in tariffs brought the average level up to 33⅓ per cent. Four years later the 'Tariff of Abominations' (1828) imposed heavy duties on iron, wool, hemp and finished woollens, and an average rate of 41 per cent—the highest of any tariff up to 1860.[1]

The outcry in the South was immediate, although most Southerners expected Andrew Jackson, the newly elected President of the United States, to take action of some kind. He was after all a slaveholder and plantation-owner. The Jackson party, which claimed to champion the 'Common Man', derived its power from Western farmers and Eastern proletariat. It was democratic, *laissez-faire* and strongly opposed to monopoly of all kinds, but was at the same time an alliance of widely divergent and even opposed groups: it combined Western farmers who supported an 'easy' money policy; ex-Jeffersonian 'hard' money men who opposed the National Bank; Southern 'States rights' men who demanded low tariffs and opposed federal intervention; nationalists; urban workers and rising captains of industry alike. What unity Jacksonian Democracy possessed was derived chiefly from a common reaction to Hamiltonian economics, as continued by the Clay-Adams group of National Republicans.

It was not Andrew Jackson but Henry Clay and a representative from South Carolina, George McDuffie, who introduced amendments to the Tariff of Abominations. The plans of both Clay and McDuffie were rejected in 1830; but McDuffie's demand that the tariffs be lowered was not entirely ignored. In 1832 Congress reduced duties to an average of 33 per cent. Unfortunately this was quite inadequate to satisfy the Southerners, once roused; it left the hated principle of Protection intact and made a mockery of McDuffie's plans of an overall reduction to a maximum of 12½ per cent. In November 1832 the state of South Carolina issued a 'Nullification Ordinance' declaring null and void the federal Tariff Acts of 1828 and 1832 and threatening to secede from the American Union if the federal authorities tried to impose the laws by force. In December President Jackson issued a proclamation against nullification and was re-elected with an overwhelming majority of electoral votes. He maintained the inviolability of the Union and threatened if necessary to use the Army and Navy to enforce the tariff. The Force Act of 1833 which would enable him to use coercive measures was a dead letter, for thanks to the negotiations between Clay and Calhoun a compromise was achieved in time.

Frequently writers have praised Jackson for his 'firm stand' on this occasion and for his statesmanship and executive ability. Perhaps

[1] For an analysis of voting by sections on this Bill, see below, p. 85.

this judgment fails to take into account many factors. If Clay and Calhoun had not been *more* statesmanlike and had not striven for a compromise, what would have ensued? Viewed in this light, Jackson's 'firm stand' becomes a blundering threat of force which tended to make an eventual solution more difficult and obscured the hopes of compromise. Calhoun insisted on 'States' rights' but was ready to accommodate conflicting interests. Whatever be the final judgment of history upon this episode, the compromise tariff of 1833 was a victory for the South and the trend in tariff history from that date until 1860 was generally downwards. The 1833 measures laid down that all duties were to be cut to a maximum of 20 per cent by 1842. The Whigs increased tariffs slightly in 1842 but three years later the Walker tariff undid their work. Further reductions came in 1857.

In the same year as South Carolina's threat of secession and Jackson's 'firm stand' (1832) the President vetoed the re-chartering of the second Bank of the United States. We know already that the charter of Hamilton's first Bank had been allowed to lapse in 1811. Five years later the second Bank was founded (1816) on the same lines as the first, but larger and with strengthened powers. It was supported by the same agrarian party which had opposed the re-chartering of Hamilton's Bank. To understand this change we do not have far to look, for the years between had suffered the 1812–14 war with Britain. If this war was ineptly fought it was stupidly financed. The abolition of internal taxes by the Jeffersonians made the U.S. Government dependent on tariffs for most of its funds in a period when tariff revenues were falling off due to shrinking European trade. Thus the Treasury had to rely fairly continuously on loans. Congress sanctioned a loan of $11 million in March 1812, for instance, but by the summer Gallatin, the Secretary of the Treasury, was forced by desperate lack of funds to authorize an issue of $5 million worth of Treasury notes. Ultimately $37 million was issued and although these notes were not legal tender for private transactions they did in fact get into circulation as money and had an inflationary effect. A further $16 million loan was sanctioned in February 1813 by which time over $13 million worth of federal bonds and notes had also been sold by the Treasury. The war years witnessed a vast growth in the number of state banks from 88 (1811) to 208 (1815) and a consequent over-issue of their notes. Thus ineffective taxation, coupled with cumulative over-borrowing to meet the increased government expenditure of war-time and a flood of state bank-notes, led to inflation in which American prices rose to the highest point for the century. Not until very late in the proceedings did the Federal Government wake up to the need for tax increases both to provide revenue and to help to absorb the enormous volume of currency. It took in fact a suspension of specie payments in the summer of 1814 to persuade Congress to take action. A special session in September 1814 enacted increases in direct taxes, excises, postage rates and duties which added $4½ million to the revenue. This belated manœuvre was of little avail; post-war currency consisted mainly of a mass of bank-notes and a smaller number of Treasury notes, all of fluctuating value. Out of this chaos grew the support among national leaders generally (including 'agrarians') for some form of national banking institution. One bank bill was passed by Congress in January 1815, only to be vetoed by President Madison. Finally in April 1816 the Bank Act, allowing the new body a twenty-year charter and capital of $35 million (of which one-fifth was to be subscribed by the government), became law.

What had happened between the passing of that Act and 1832, to support President Jackson's refusal to re-charter the second Bank of the United States? At first the new Bank had met with great difficulties and had itself become the victim of the wave of post-war speculative inflation it had been set up to check. The Baltimore branch of the Bank collapsed in 1818 when the very limits of credit expansion had been reached. Meanwhile the state banks increased their hostility to the national body and several state governments followed the lead of Maryland (1817) in imposing taxes on the U.S. Bank's various branches. This struggle came to a head in 1819 when the Maryland branch of the U.S. Bank refused to pay a state stamp duty on its notes. The federal Supreme Court upheld the constitutionality of the Bank by a decision in its favour in the case *McCulloch* v. *Maryland*. In and after 1819 the Bank was reorganized by Langdon Cheves (a South Carolina lawyer) whose severe methods of credit restriction brought it financial soundness once more. Cheves resigned in 1823 and was replaced by an aggressive and positive leader, Nicholas Biddle, with whom Jackson was fated to have his famous struggle a decade or so later. Biddle reversed the policy of his predecessor as president of the U.S. Bank, and expanded its circulation, its loans and deposits and its ownership of stocks and real estate. He tried to make it a real central bank with control over the national money market. Thus the issue of Bank notes increased from $4½ million worth (1823) to $11 million (1828) and finally to $19 million worth (1831). Earnings also increased and by 1828 a surplus of $1½ million had accrued. From 1828 until its charter expired in 1836 the Bank managed to pay dividends at the rate of 7 per cent per annum. By upholding specie payments for its own notes and cajoling state banks to do likewise, the U.S. Bank encouraged the creation of a stable national currency; by basing its business in the West and South on capital raised in the Eastern states it succeeded in making credit and currency more easily available where it was formerly lacking; and finally it provided the Federal Government with speedy and economical loans whenever such financial injections were needed.

Despite these achievements the U.S. Bank gained only the hostility of the state banks and of debtor groups. Nothing it did could satisfy some sections of the community: when Cheves restricted credit between 1819 and 1823 and foreclosed securities on unpaid loans the Bank became the chief owner of real estate in several Western cities, and earned the title 'the Monster'. The Bank's deflationary measures were blamed for the crash of 1819—which in truth they could have at the most only accelerated. Debtor pioneering areas of the South and West bitterly resented Cheves' credit restrictions. Moreover the state banks had profited from the inflation and currency chaos and did not wish to return to specie payment until they were forced to do so by political pressure and by the U.S. Bank.[1] Yet on the other hand, when Biddle assumed control and *reversed* these policies, the Bank met the opposition of the 'hard' money men (especially after the election of Jackson to the Presidency in 1828) who distrusted all banks and all paper currency, blaming them for inflation and speculative booms and depressions. Biddle's expansion of business became as unpopular as Cheves' restrictions. State banks still resented the U.S. Bank as a controlling influence on their operations, and the growing class of entrepreneurs demanded *laissez-faire* and shouted down all 'monopolistic' tendencies. In fact the National Bank issue was by no means a clearly cut 'sectional' dispute between on the one side creditor commercial and industrial North-East favouring a centralized monetary system, control over local banks and checks on inflation, and on the other side debtor agrarian and planter West and South favouring a decentralized monetary system, freedom for local banks and credit expansion.

'Tsar Nicholas' Biddle was a forceful banker but scarcely an astute diplomatist. Not only did he treat the change in political climate since 1828 with scant regard and underestimate the strength of the opposition forces, but he applied for re-charter of the Bank in January 1832, four years before the old charter was due to lapse and in a presidential election year. Jackson was eventually re-elected with an electoral vote of 219 as against opposition votes which combined together did not reach 70. Two years earlier, ignoring the doubly expressed confidence of the House of Representatives in the Bank, President Jackson had suggested the idea of a bank as a branch of the Treasury, which could deposit but not proffer loans. In the following year he received the overt support of Senator Benton ('Old Bullion') who declared in the Senate that the Bank tended to enrich the rich and impoverish the poor, was unfavourable to small capitalists and injurious to the labouring classes and was controlled by private

[1] Specie payments were resumed on 20 February 1817.

individuals, many of them foreigners. His speech was a rallying-point for all anti-Bank opinions: 'hard' money protagonists, agrarians, urban proletariat and 'States' rights' men. 'Old Bullion' was perhaps rather more of an orator than he was an economist.

The fate of the Bank became mixed up with the trend of political events. The cabinet was divided over the question and Jackson seemed to wash his hands of it when in December 1831 he publicly declared it an open question to be decided by 'an enlightened people'. Those anti-Jackson forces which grouped themselves under the Whig banner and Henry Clay, however, made the Bank the main plank of their platform in the same month in a convention at Baltimore. It was Clay who encouraged Biddle to be immediate in his demand for a new charter. Congress enacted a bill to continue the Bank (with some limitations) on 3 July 1832. Taking the risk of losing sectional votes in Pennsylvania and elsewhere, Jackson vetoed the bill a week later. In the November elections his opponent Clay suffered an overwhelming defeat. The cause of the U.S. Bank was well and truly beaten.

During the remaining four years until its charter lapsed the Bank was torn by inner dissensions between its dictatorial leader and its administration. Biddle made desperate attempts to force on the country a realization of the need for a national bank: in August 1833 he opened a deflationary campaign and began to restrict credit as severely as possible. The crisis he succeeded in bringing about in 1834 had an opposite effect to that he desired, however, for it alienated the business groups who suffered from the financial stringency, and convinced waverers of the power of the Bank not for good but for evil. He ceased this irresponsible trial of strength in September 1834 and two years later 'Biddle's Bank' expired as a 'Bank of the United States'.[1] An attempt was made in 1841 by Henry Clay to create a third U.S. Bank, but it was vetoed by President John Tyler. Instead the system of using state banks as government depositories was continued. There is still no highly centralized banking system in the United States.

SUGGESTED FURTHER READING

DEWEY, D. R. *Financial History of the United States* (11th Ed., revised, New York, 1931).

[1] For opposed views on the struggle over the second Bank students should refer to A. M. Schlesinger, *The Age of Jackson* (op. cit.), for an anti-Bank argument, and B. Hammond's articles in the *Journal of Economic History* (vols. VI and VII, May 1946 and May 1947), for a pro-Bank argument.

JOHNSON, E. R. *et al. History of the Domestic and Foreign Commerce of the United States* (2 Vols., Washington, 1915).

TAUSSIG, F. W. *Tariff History of the United States* (8th Ed., New York, 1931).

TAYLOR, G. R. (Ed.) *Jackson versus Biddle: The Struggle over the Second Bank of the United States* ('Problems in American Civilization' Series, Amherst College, Boston, Mass., 1949).

VI

THE CRISIS: CIVIL WAR

The functioning of the American economy to 1860: the panics of 1819, 1837 and 1857 – 'Origins' of the Civil War: varying interpretations – The economic and social basis of sectionalism: abolitionism and the moulding of mental attitudes; the Westward movement and slavery-extension; public lands; tariffs; the U.S. Bank; internal improvements – Changes in sectional alignment after 1830 and the 'removal of the Alleghenies' – The South and the election of 1860; Southern economic grievances.

THE American Civil War (1861–5) represented the breakdown of a national democracy. We are about to examine the economic and social background to this tragic failure, but before doing so must take a glimpse, however brief, at how the economic machinery worked during the preceding half-century. This is not the place for a full consideration of the functioning of the American economy up to 1860. Yet a separate mention of the crises of 1819, 1837 and 1857 is clearly called for and may perhaps give some indication of the nature of cyclical problems before the Civil War.[1] The economic effects of the major wars have been considered as far as possible in earlier chapters; peacetime fluctuations were dependent upon factors native to America beyond the 'normal' cyclical breakdowns common to nineteenth-century capitalism. The United States was made more sensitive to fluctuations, for instance, by the westward development, which took place with great rapidity and was accompanied by boom conditions and speculative crazes in land. The reaction on the rest of the economy often precipitated or at least played an important part in bringing about general crises. Unstable financing, too, which characterized the whole of the period, frequently led to minor breakdowns which had a potentially cumulative effect. Transport developments, increased specialization and the extension of market areas made the various sectors of the country

[1] A detailed account is given in W. B. Smith and A. H. Cole, *Fluctuations in American Business, 1790–1860* (Cambridge, Mass., 1935).

increasingly interdependent, thus accentuating the above tendency. It was becoming as difficult to localize economic disturbance as it became to localize warfare in the twentieth century.

The principal crises which the American economy underwent up to World War I were those of 1819, 1837, 1857, 1873, 1893 and 1907. Of these the first three concern us here, all of which were stimulated among other factors by monetary over-investment. In 1819 the other factors included speculation in Western lands, over-rapid commercial expansion since the Peace of Ghent,[1] and industrial instability. The panic was the climax of post-war maladjustments. The sudden contraction of credit by the U.S. Bank under Cheves and by local banks cannot be deemed the prime cause of this first general crisis in United States history, but it is obviously true that such a stringent emergency measure would not have been necessary but for the wild over-expansion which preceded it. The dislocation of foreign commerce, on the other hand, was influenced by a purely external factor—the sharp decline after 1818 in the European demand for American foodstuffs, which had been considerable during the post-Napoleonic War period. Prices fell drastically, specie payments were suspended, industry and trade halted and unemployment made widespread. The West was badly hit and tried to remedy the situation by a new expansion of credit and currency. By 1823 the tide was once more turning, and Biddle took over at the U.S. Bank from Langdon Cheves, to inaugurate a policy of expansion there also.

The collapse of 1837 was precipitated by the issue of President Jackson's *Specie Circular* (July 1836) which directed government land agencies to accept nothing but specie in payment for public lands. This brought to an abrupt end a feverish land speculation carried on with inflated bank-note issues, which had begun about 1833. In the North-west speculation had been stimulated by rising grain and livestock prices; in the South-west by rising cotton prices. Urban land values had also risen, especially in growing cities such as New York and Chicago. The gradual inflation of land values generally was to a great extent the result of rapid transportation improvements, especially the building of canals.[2] Land sales had reached a peak in 1836 when Jackson's circular was issued. Speculation had been facilitated by the great increase in loanable funds afforded by the rising number of banks after 1832 and the enlarged bank-note circulation. The U.S. Bank, coming to an end, transferred its assets to Western banks. Moreover a further increase of loanable funds had been caused by an unusual inflow of foreign capital and specie, which went directly into business and speculative activities, such as canal-building.

Then came the change. The *Specie Circular* brought a drastic fall in land prices and eventually a restricted supply of specie itself—

[1] See the earlier section of Chapter V, above. [2] See Chapter IV, above.

for the Treasury would not redeposit coin with the banks. Also the supply of both foreign and domestic loanable funds was cut short: the former by the panic of 1836 in England (due partly to the previous drain of specie to the U.S.A. and partly to the collapse of the English railway 'mania' of that year); the latter by the payment of the Federal Government's surplus from the sale of public lands to the individual states in quarterly instalments in 1837. This allocation implied a transfer of government funds from Western to Eastern banks, and forced Western banks to contract their loans, thus restricting total domestic money supplies. Non-monetary factors exacerbated these difficulties: cotton began to fall in price and decrease in demand; crop failures in 1835, 1837 and 1838 necessitated wheat imports and caused much distress among farmers. By May 1837 every American bank had to suspend specie payments, which were not generally resumed until 1839. A wave of bankruptcies ensued, and deflation and readjustment was to continue for five years. The Western and Southern states and Pennsylvania suffered the worst of the long depression; New England the least. The final collapse of the U.S. Bank of Pennsylvania (all that was left of Biddle's Bank, chartered by the state of Pennsylvania since 1836) in 1841 led to a further succession of specie suspensions in the South and West. Prices reached a record low level in 1842-3, unemployment became severe and widespread and hundreds of banks failed.[1] Business conditions did not begin to recover until about 1845—eight years after the speculative 'bubble' had burst.

The third crisis of the pre-war period was that of 1857, a very acute disturbance mainly financial rather than industrial, and fairly short-lived. There had been a consistent recovery after 1845, due chiefly to increased agricultural exports (with the potato famine in Ireland in 1845, Peel's relief measures there and the repeal of the English Corn Laws in 1846) and the rise in foodstuffs and cotton prices. After the European revolutions of 1848 came almost a decade of prosperity and economic expansion for the United States. Prices rose particularly steeply after 1852 and agriculture, industry and commerce flourished, accompanied by a renewed expansion of bank credit and the number of banks. There was a fresh land boom in the West and South-west and a further increase in demand for American foodstuffs and shipping was occasioned by the bad European harvests of 1853 and the Crimean War (1853–6). The price of Southern cotton and Southern slaves mounted steadily and there was a 'mania'

[1] The loss of federal funds in the state banks had influenced Congress to set up the *Independent Treasury* in 1840 (repealed in 1841 by the Whigs; re-established in 1846 by the Democrats). This became the depository for federal funds and facilitated their easy distribution from one section of the country to another.

for railway investment in other areas,[1] supported by much foreign capital. England alone had about $400 million invested in American enterprises at this time. The increase in credit was of course also stimulated by the flood of gold from California, first discovered there in 1848. In 1850 California gold production ($36 million) exceeded the annual average world production of the preceding decade, and a year later reached $56 million.

The crash came when in August 1857 the Ohio Life Insurance and Trust Company, which had $5 million involved in railway construction loans, failed to meet its Eastern liabilities. New York banks immediately began to contract their loans and by October most of them had agreed to suspend specie payments. Banks all over the country followed New York's lead (except in New Orleans) and failures were numerous. Railway companies found themselves unable to obtain credit to meet interest obligations, while at the same time their traffic in many regions could not be expected to yield a fair return for long enough, until the areas they had 'opened up' had been settled and consolidated. As many as fourteen companies failed in one month.[2] Railway construction ceased almost completely, Western land speculation came to an abrupt halt, imports declined and unemployment was severe.

The Federal Government under President Buchanan did little or nothing (on principle), except to post troops to protect government buildings in New York city because of the deep labour unrest, unassuaged by municipal poor relief measures. While Buchanan knew that over-extension of credit had played a significant part in the crisis, he did not believe that the Federal Government could or should attempt to regulate state banks. Still less would he have envisaged a regulation of production. The cycle worked itself out: expansion and increased production had led to speculation; a sudden tightening of credit in 1854 had led to much doubt and loss of confidence; one large failure brought a chain-reaction; credit was curtailed, production halted, workers thrown out of employment and a period of liquidation and depression ensued; finally the credit contraction and a certain amount of financial reorganization led to a recovery, and the process was ready to recommence.[3] Recovery was in this particular case fairly rapid and by 1858 most banks were able to resume specie payments. Business achieved a 'healthier' condition until the

[1] See Chapter IV, above, pp. 53–4.

[2] The New York and Erie, the Illinois Central and the Michigan Central railroads all filed petitions of bankruptcy.

[3] It is interesting to note that some contemporary writers thought in 1857 that the invention of the telegraph had much to do with the panic, because it enabled bad news to travel so rapidly, making it impossible to ocalize iquid ation.

coming of the Civil War three years later. Whilst the Southern states did not feel the repercussions of the panic of 1857 as severely as the North-east and the West, their experience seemed to support the Southern sectional claim that by seceding from the Union the South could establish a more stable economy of its own.

Three years after the crisis of 1857, the state of South Carolina resolved to secede from the American Union (20 December 1860), the six further states of the Deep South following its example almost within a month. We cannot, unfortunately, trace in any detail the fascinating trend of political events which led up to this calamity. It is within our scope, however, to 'gather together' facts concerning the economic and social evolution of sectionalism, otherwise scattered under the subject headings of the preceding chapters. What follows will therefore be to some extent a recapitulation of events already mentioned elsewhere. It is emphatically not an attempt to explain the 'causes' of the American Civil War, for it is necessarily restricted to a consideration of economic factors. Moreover it involves, even within this relatively restricted field, an understandably great simplification of complex facts. Perhaps no part of American history has been more minutely studied than the ante-bellum period. In place of the old devil theory of war maintained in the decades immediately following Appomattox, and in place of the interpretation of the war as a 'moral conflict' over slavery, grand mechanisms of interpretation have been evolved in the present century. The Beards' pseudo-scientific economic interpretation of the '30's has been supplanted by the 'cultural conflict' analysis of 'cultural anthropologists' like Osterweis. The whole field of social psychology has been systematically raided for material to back up rather flimsy and sweeping historical methods. Unfortunately we cannot consider the psychological, constitutional and legal, political, cultural or ethical interpretations of the Civil War here, except to say that they exist.

The sectional conflict is being discussed in this chapter; but it may well be that the Civil War was one phenomenon and sectionalism another. An explanation of the latter need not give the answer to the questions: Why did the War come? Why did it come when it did, instead of at any other crucial point in the history of sectionalism? It may be necessary to make a distinction between the 'causes' of sectionalism and the 'causes' of the Civil War. It is apodeictic that the war was based on the sectional struggle, but the study of this struggle alone does not justify economic determinism in the interpretation of the war.[1]

[1] Modern writers like the late J. G. Randall and A. O. Craven strongly doubt the alleged 'inevitability' of the war. They tend to think that it was

Bearing all this in mind and taking a 'calculated risk', we might say firstly in our treatment of the economic background that although there were sections within sections, and although sectional allegiances were never clear and varied from issue to issue, it remains perhaps broadly true that the cleavage between North-east and South came to dominate the political and economic scene in the 'antebellum decade'. Venturing still further onto thin ice, perhaps we might add that the former became caught in the throes of an economic revolution which was to make it a 'dynamic', industrial, commercial and creditor section; but the latter remained largely a 'static' agrarian and debtor section tied to an economy of staple crops (despite several Southern attempts to diversify the economy). Northern economic expansion was accompanied by a high rate of population growth and urbanization—a growth which greatly exceeded that of the South. So it has been claimed that in the sectional struggle the South was 'fighting against the census returns'. She became a 'conscious minority' and the North a consciously expanding majority which could afford to moralize about Southern institutions, especially about slavery—around which all the anti-Southern ideas revolved—because the North had found it to be uneconomic many years earlier. When the economic interests of the sections clashed, as they did over federal internal improvements, the national bank, the idea of a protective tariff, and the development of the public lands, crises occurred. The South felt that she was rapidly becoming an economic colony of the North, and her traditional prestige and power in national affairs seemed to be declining.

For a treatment of slavery as an economic and social institution in the Southern states, the reader should refer to earlier pages.[1] The abolitionist movement which began in the North as the work of a small group of religious fanatics swelled to become a general vilification of Southern society and Southern people and an implicit claim that the North had the monopoly of human virtues. The reaction on Southerners was to make them build up imposing but impossible rationalizations of Southern society and in particular of slavery—based on religious, political, historical and pseudo-biological grounds. There is some truth, therefore, in the view that 'cultural nationalism' underlay many of the economic and political arguments used by Southern leaders. This alone would never have brought the

precipitated by the work of minority groups of religious and political fanatics placed at strategic points—'fire-eaters' in the South and 'black Republicans' in the North. One might call this the 'conspiratorial' view! For a good discussion see the *Report of the Historiography Committee of the Social Science Research Council* (New York, 1947) by H. K. Beale ('What Historians have said about the Origins of the Civil War.')

[1] See Chapter II, above, pp. 20–22.

nation to the brink of a great civil war, however. Before about 1830 there was already an abolitionist movement in the Northern states, mainly on a religious basis. The Quaker preacher Benjamin Lundy was perhaps the most famous reformer of the early period. By 1827 slavery was prohibited all over the Northern states and the movement seemed to be dying away. As Southern slavery and cotton-production recovered and rose to great importance in the Southern and in the national economy, the abolitionist movement in the North had a rapid revival in the 1830's. But the revived movement under such forceful and extreme leaders as William Lloyd Garrison, Wendell Phillips, Theodore Parker and Theodore Weld replaced Lundy's moral persuasion with outright denunciation. Garrison's paper the *Liberator* declared in its first number (1 January 1831).:

'I will be as harsh as truth, and as uncompromising as justice. On this subject I do not wish to think, or speak, or write, with moderation . . . I am in earnest—I will not equivocate—I will not excuse—I will not retreat a single inch—AND I WILL BE HEARD.'

It is certain that no modern scholar would deny that the cause of the abolitionists was a just one, and that slavery could have no part of any civilized community. But many abolitionists were ill-balanced fanatics who failed to see the forces of Evil anywhere but in 'the South' and were slow to come to the aid of industrial labour, for instance, in their own native states. Perhaps men like Garrison and Weld and women like Harriet Beecher Stowe (who wrote *Uncle Tom's Cabin* in 1852, based mainly on Weld's pamphlet, *Slavery as it is, the Testimony of a Thousand Witnesses*, 1839) did most to perpetuate the stereotypes and popular myths which filled the literature and debates of the ante-bellum years. To many Northerners their Southern cousins were mainly large planter-aristocrats,[1] uneducated yet overbearing and conceited braggarts, violent of passions, self-indulgent, impatient, jealous and avaricious, improvident, idle and cruel in the extreme. So they were portrayed by the Northern abolitionist historian Hildreth.[2] To many Southerners on the other hand their Northern cousins were wildly extreme Puritans, hypocrites and misanthropists, living in 'moral deformity and hideous gloom' and unfit for civil or religious freedom because of their 'fierce, fantastic intolerance'. So they were portrayed by the Southern paper *De Bow's Review* in 1860. The *Review* went on to say that for all their 'human' failings, the Southern planters were a gallant, high-spirited, chivalrous and generous race, direct descendants of Anglo-Saxon blood. Whereas the Bible was the source of all Southern law, in the North

[1] See Chapter II for a more balanced account.
[2] *Despotism in America*, 1840.

only the Almighty Dollar and metal were worshipped. The Southern social system (including slavery) was, if we are to believe *De Bow's Review*, 'founded on the revealed laws of God'.

Soon after the *Liberator* was founded, anti-slavery societies sprang up all over the North and West and a federation of groups was established in Boston in 1832: the New England Anti-slavery Society. A year later the American Anti-slavery Society, an even larger federation, was founded by Garrison and his colleagues in Philadelphia. By 1840 there were about 2,000 societies with a total membership of perhaps 175,000. During the '30's abolitionism had become no longer derided, feared and hated, but a well-organized movement with a definite propaganda. It began to attract more famous Northerners, men of standing and of liberal disposition, such as the poets Whittier and Lowell and the scholars W. E. Channing and F. Wayland. Oberlin College was founded by a student faction from the Lane Theological Seminary in Cincinnati, and became a Western centre of abolitionism. The 'stormy' period of abolitionism was well over by 1840, although as late as October 1835 Garrison had been dragged through the streets of Boston wearing a halter. The opposition came mainly from Unionists who opposed Garrison when he advocated *Northern* secession and called the Constitution:

'A covenant with death and an agreement with Hell.'

In the following decade, however, more and more conservatives were drawn into the movement as different methods were adopted. A. Y. Lloyd[1] divides abolitionists into three groups: radicals (like Garrison and Weld) who began the violent agitation which first stirred the South to answer; thinkers and scholars (like Channing and Wayland) who based their arguments on Natural Rights and an enlightened rationalism; and finally politicians, who reaped the benefits of their predecessors' work, beginning in the 1840's, by linking abolitionism with other sectional issues.

This combination was not difficult to achieve, because in the national political arena the slavery controversy took the form of Northern opposition to the *extension* of slavery to the Territories which were being acquired as America moved westwards. Thus slavery became inextricably mixed up with the sectional politics of federal land policy. As we have already observed in Chapter II, Congress had no authority to regulate slavery in any state of the Union but it had the power to do so in the Territorial phase of a state's evolution. Each time a new Territorial government was formed a Congressional crisis occurred, because the position secured for slavery in the new area was likely to determine its status when the Territory became a state. As the population and wealth of the South

[1] *The Slavery Controversy* (Chapel Hill, N.C., 1939).

relatively declined toward 1860 so did its strength in Congress. But a Territory which became a 'free' state added yet another two Senators and several Representatives to Congress to represent Northern interests. Southern politicians wished to prevent this and to expand the slave-holding area in a western and southern direction. The crises and compromises of 1819–20 and of 1850 were stages in the growth of this problem.[1]

Besides the abolitionist and slavery-extension questions in the years up to 1861 the economic interests of the sections clashed over four other groups of problems: the disposal of public lands, the tariff, the U.S. Bank and federal internal improvements. From the beginning it was a matter of opinion whether public lands should sell at high prices over a long period in order to conserve public resources and provide government revenue, or sell very cheaply to pioneers to hasten settlement and strengthen the democratic process. The latter policy was generally favoured however, and an Act of 1796 stated that single sections of 640 acres (one square mile) should sell at two dollars per acre. Between 1800 and 1820 the size of the smallest sections was cut down to 80 acres, instalment buying was introduced (and abolished again in 1820) and the price reduced to 1 dollar 25 cents per acre. By 1820 therefore $100 would buy an 80-acre farm. 'Pre-emption' rights were legalized in 1841. Each of these measures was highly controversial although throughout the cheap land policy predominated. Up to about 1830 sectional alignment over land policy[2] was that the North-eastern manufacturing and commercial states generally favoured high-priced public lands and feared a labour shortage due to the drainage eastwards of able-bodied families. On the other hand they did not want the Federal Government's revenue from high-priced lands to remove the need for tariff revenue, and therefore favoured the allocation of such profits to the individual states according to population. Western settlers of course demanded a cheap or free land policy, and the Southern coastal states at this time maintained a fairly neutral position. After about 1830 a change came in this alignment; as the slavery question grew, the South came to oppose a cheap land policy because it would encourage rapid settlement of the West by small pioneer (and therefore non-slave-holding) farmers, but the North-east was willing to support Western land policies in order to obtain Western co-operation on other matters, particularly tariffs. Sectional voting for the Pre-emption Bill of 1841 was thus: *North-east* (Connecticut, Delaware, Maine, Massachusetts, N. Hampshire, N. Jersey, N. York, Pennsylvania, Rhode Island, Vermont and Maryland), 72 for

[1] See Chapter II, above, pp. 29–30.
[2] See Potter and Manning: *Nationalism and Sectionalism in America* (New York, 1949).

and 44 against; *South* (Alabama, Georgia, North and South Carolina, Virginia, Louisiana, Mississippi, Tennessee), 18 for and 62 against; *West* (Illinois, Indiana, Kentucky, Missouri, Ohio), 27 for and 12 against. The Republican Congress passed the Homestead Act a year after the outbreak of Civil War, thus bringing to a logical conclusion its pro-Western policy: land was to be given freely to bonafide settlers.

The tariff as a sectional dispute was most notable in the 'middle' period, the 1820's and '30's, when it led to the second threat of secession from the Union. The idea had first been raised in New England during the War of 1812, and the 'Tariff of Abominations' of 1828 resulted in an adoption of the same threat by South Carolina. Despite the Nullification Ordinance (1832), however, a compromise tariff was hammered out in 1833.[1] The Southern feeling was that she paid tariffs to protect Northern industries and to support the prices of Northern goods which she had to buy herself. Though the tariff issue had largely passed by the time of the ante-bellum decade, it had given much publicity to the notions of 'Southern rights' and secession. Voting on the tariff of 1828 (22 April) showed a clear sectional trend, even though the anti-tariff group could expect some Northeastern support because of the wool tariff and the traditional concern of some coastal towns (e.g. Boston) for freedom of trade. The *North-east*[2] voted 73 for and 34 against the tariff (although Maine opposed it unanimously, and Massachusetts with a vote of 2 for and 11 against); the *West* voted for the tariff, 29 to 1; the *South* opposed the tariff, with a combined vote of 3 for and 59 against (the only 3 votes for the bill coming from Virginia).

The disputes about the U.S. Bank were not so clearly sectional, as a brief backward glance at the preceding chapter would show. It is very generally true that the North-east as a creditor area favoured a centralized monetary system, with control by a central bank over the issue of local banks in order to check inflation, and that the South and West, as debtor areas lacking capital and currency, opposed the central bank idea and control over local credit issues. But state banks in New York and the North-east generally as well as those in other sections were extremely jealous of both Hamilton's U.S. Bank (1791–1811) and the Second U.S. Bank (1816–36). Northern proletariat opposed the Bank as the supporter of paper-money policies; but people who supported paper money also opposed the Bank because it restricted local issues. Western hatred of the Second Bank became particularly strong in 1819 when it earned the name 'the Monster' by calling in Western loans, helping to cause the collapse of local

[1] See Chapter V, above, pp. 69–71.
[2] Sectional area names include the same states as for the Pre-emption Bill.

banks and taking over vast forfeited territories.[1] In 1832 however it was only President Jackson's veto which prevented the Second Bank from having its charter renewed. The vote of 3 July 1832 in the House of Representatives was 107 for and 85 against: the *North-east* favoured the renewal of the charter 68:35 (Maine and New Hampshire opposing almost unanimously, New York opposing by a good majority); the *West* co-operated with the North; the *Southern states* (with the exception of the three *South-western* states, Mississippi, Louisiana and Tennessee, which were evenly divided, 8:8) opposed the rechartering with a vote of 12 for and 35 against.

The internal improvements question was probably the most important of all the sectional issues except slavery and slavery-extension. Certainly it was the most dangerous to the South for it was ultimately to split the old alliance between South and West, and thus ensure the victory of the North in any conflict which might occur. Curiously enough it was Jefferson who inaugurated a policy of internal improvements at the expense of the Federal Government (i.e. out of *national* revenues), when in 1806 he recommended that Congress be allowed to support a national system of roads and canals. Such a scheme was detailed in the Report by Gallatin, the Secretary of the Treasury, in 1808. Even though he believed public expenditure to be usually unproductive, Gallatin had already in 1803 strongly supported the Louisiana Purchase. His Report of five years later suggested using the enormous surplus revenue at the rate of $2 million a year for ten years, to build turnpike roads and canals and to improve rivers. Such a long-term plan for public enterprise was not equalled in America until the twentieth century. Neither was it accepted however in 1808.

The construction of a national road, authorized by Congress in 1806, did not begin until 1811 and did not cease until 1838. This was the Cumberland Road, from Maryland to Illinois.[2] Other developments were slow, but Henry Clay hoped to combine the question of internal improvements with those of tariffs and the U.S. Bank, and to bring about the co-operation of North-east and West on this programme: the *American System*. His plans, and the progress of federally aided improvements, suffered a setback in 1816 when the Bonus Bill was vetoed by President Madison. This had meant to use the surplus of $1½ million paid by the U.S. Bank to the Federal Government, for the building of national roads and canals. Furthermore in 1831, a year before he prevented the rechartering of the U.S. Bank, President Jackson vetoed the Maysville Turnpike Bill, which had been passed by Congress to give financial aid to the building of a road from Mays-

[1] For a consideration of the U.S. Bank's peculiar position throughout its existence, see Chapter V, above, pp. 72–4.

[2] For details on internal improvements, see Chapter IV, passim.

ville to Lexington, both in Kentucky. The Jackson administration however was forced by changing economic circumstances to spend more federal money on internal improvements than ever before: the West was continuing to grow at an unprecedented rate and demanded such improvements, and federal surpluses were increasingly heavy. Between 1829 and 1836 over $25 million were spent on roads, canals, fortifications, rivers and harbours, lighthouses and public buildings. The policy of making federal land grants to railways as well as roads and canals was begun openly by the Act of 1850, forced through Congress by a temporary alliance of Southern and Western states. Before the outbreak of the Civil War, $18 million worth of land had been donated by Congress to railway companies.

This growth brought a change in sectional alignment by causing cleavage between West and South. The rapidly expanding population of the West, with no seaboard, found freight rates to be excessively high. What was already a high production was thus being cramped. The river link with the South was becoming inadequate for Western needs; some direct and cheap connection with the East and with Europe was obviously required. Under Henry Clay the whole of the Ohio valley was solidly united for internal improvements. Clay managed to reconcile farmers and manufacturers to the idea of a national economy but had little influence on planters and shipowners. Moreover the actual success of internal improvement schemes had the effect of linking North-east and West by main lines of communication such as the Erie Canal from New York, the double line of canal and railway from Philadelphia to the river Ohio, the Baltimore and Ohio railway from Maryland, and the Chesapeake and Ohio Canal from the same state (although this never finally reached Ohio). A new alignment between North-east and West was thus clinched, and what was in effect the 'removal of the Alleghenies' counteracted the political and economic consequences of the Mississippi. The Erie Canal, for instance, linked the Old North-west more closely to the North-east than it had ever been linked by way of the river Mississippi to the South, or by the St. Lawrence valley to Canada.

Up to about 1830 the most logical sectional alignment seemed to be an alliance of West and South: the seaboard South felt much more strongly about low tariffs than she did about land policy and was willing to give way on the latter to obtain Western support for the former; similarly the West was more interested in cheap lands than in tariff policy, and the South-west was in any case in favour of a low tariff. The North-east, with its demands for high tariffs and dear land, its general support of a national bank and its lack of deep interest in internal improvements until the late '20's, seemed unlikely to come to political terms with the West. Between about 1830 and 1860 however there was a distinct realignment of sections: the North-east whipped up enthusiasm for internal improvements and began to support (with rather less enthusiasm) a cheap land policy, thus retaining Western support for higher tariffs. So Northern voting for the Maysville Turnpike Bill of 1830 was 63 in favour, 35 against, although in 1817 its vote for the Bonus Bill had been almost evenly divided, 52:51. Western approval of the Maysville Bill was almost unanimous (27:1), but Southern opposition to internal improvements had grown considerably, alienating the West with a vote in 1830 of 12 for, 51 against the Bill. In 1817 Southern voting had been less marked in its rejection, 24:28. Similarly, on the public land question, the Southern view became after 1830 further and further removed from that of its former Western ally. Three factors helped to cause this: the development of Northern attacks on Southern institutions, the fierce defence by the South which this produced, and the expansion of cotton-production. Southerners refused to allow Western lands to be disposed of in such a way that slavery and slaveholders were precluded, either by economic or political pressures. So it was that an alliance of West and North-east defeated the South in the election of 1860, and in the war that followed shortly after. In the years immediately preceding the outbreak of war it seems clear that the processes of history had produced a unique situation; two events occurred in 1856 which illustrate this. Firstly, the most important prairie railroad was completed: the Illinois Central, managed by Yankee capitalists and partly financed by them and by Congressional grants, reached Cairo (where the Ohio joins the Mississippi) from Chicago. Secondly a new political party emerged, the Republicans, with a platform uniting West and North.

The presidential election of November 1860[1] brought in Abraham Lincoln of Illinois. During the ante-bellum decade the last bonds of Union had seemed to snap when the national political parties and national churches split and reformed on sectional lines. The Whigs disintegrated after 1852, the Democrats finally split in 1860 and the Republicans emerged as the anti-slavery-extension party on an openly avowed sectional basis. Lincoln became a minority President, and it seemed to the South that her drifting decline would now be hastened and completed unless action was taken. After the failure of the compromise manœuvres of 1860–1, war broke out on 12 April 1861 at Fort Sumter, Charleston, South Carolina.

Were the Southerners correct in their belief that Lincoln's election presented an immediate menace to Southern institutions? Not only was he a minority President but the very opposite of a fanatic. The 'abolitionist' minority of the North had little influence in the Republi-

[1] See the table concerned, facing.

STATISTICAL ANALYSIS OF THE ELECTION OF 1860

States	Total Popular Vote	Democrat Douglas %	Const. Unionist Bell %	Republican Lincoln %	S. Rights Democrat Breckenridge %
NORTHERN STATES					
Conn.	118,840	32·3	5·9	32·8	29·0
Ill.	339,693	47·5	1·0	50·7	0·8
Ind.	272,143	42·5	2·0	51·0	4·5
Iowa	128,331	47·5	1·0	50·7	0·8
Maine	979,918	23·3	2·1	64·1	6·5
Mass.	169,175	20·3	13·2	63·0	3·5
Mich.	154,747	42·1	0·2	57·2	0·5
Minn.	347,799	34·2	0·2	63·4	2·2
N.H.	65,883	39·2	0·6	60·0	3·2
N.J.	121,125	52·0	—	48·0	—
N.Y.	657,133	46·2	—	53·8	—
Ohio	442,441	42·3	2·7	52·4	2·6
Penn.	476,442	3·5	2·7	56·3	37·5
R.I.	19,951	38·7	—	61·3	—
Vt.	42,844	16·0	4·6	78·9	0·5
Wisc.	152,180	42·7	0·1	56·6	0·6
Cal.	118,840	32·4	5·7	33·0	28·8
Ore.	14,410	27·4	1·2	36·6	34·8
Total % of N. States		34·5	2·4	54·4	8·7
BORDER STATES					
Del.	16,038	6·4	24·1	23·8	45·7
Ky.	146,216	17·5	45·2	0·9	36·4
Md.	192,512	36·5	45·1	2·5	45·9
Mo.	165,518	35·5	35·3	10·3	18·9
Va.	167,223	9·8	44·5	11·6	44·1
Total % of Border States		14·7	38·1	9·7	37·5
SOUTHERN STATES					
Ala.	89,357	14·2	31·2	—	54·6
Ark.	54,053	9·7	37·2	—	53·1
Fla.	14,347	2·6	37·9	—	59·5
Ga.	106,365	10·9	40·3	—	48·8
La.	50,510	15·1	40·0	—	44·9
N.C.	96,230	2·8	45·7	—	50·5
S.C.	—	—	—	—	100·0
Miss.	69,120	4·8	36·2	—	59·0
Tenn.	145,324	7·8	47·7	—	44·5
Total % of S. States		7·5	35·1	—	57·3

can party, which they had scorned and disowned. Southern political power had a long tradition and was still quite firmly entrenched except in the Executive branch. Finally, many Northern vested interests were opposed to extreme action of any kind. Slavery itself was in any case limited geographically; the struggle over slavery-extension was one over 'an imaginary Negro in an impossible place' because Western physical conditions would not have permitted the development of plantation slavery on an economic basis—the terrain was quite unsuitable. It was precisely the secession of the Southern states and the outbreak of war which empowered Lincoln to do all those things which the South feared.

Nevertheless, although no immediate menace existed there was good reason to believe that a more distant threat was implied by a Republican victory. There was little guarantee, for instance, that the Northern Democrats would remain pro-slavery voters, or that the Republican party would not exclude the South from all share of the patronage. Politics had openly assumed a sectional character and the South had come to the end of a long period of political control over the Federal Government. If such considerations were not tangible enough, there was always the Southern complaint that she had become a mere 'economic colony' of the North. Among the numerous exponents of this view was Orr of South Carolina who pointed out in the *Charleston Courier* of April 1855 how the South depended on the North for all its manufactured goods and most of its bare necessities of life. He wrote:

'Where came your axes, hoes, scythes? Yes, even your plows, harrows, rakes, axe and auger handles? Your furniture, carpets, calicos, muslins? The cradle that rocks your infant to sweet slumbers, the top your boy spins, the doll your little girl caresses... all are imported (from the North).'

T. P. Kettell, however, author of *Southern Wealth and Northern Profits* (1860), marshalled an imposing array of dates and statistics to show that the South was the great wealth-producing region and the North an economic leech, dependent on Southern raw materials yet drawing the lion's share of the profits. Kettell argued that this economic inequality resulted from the concentration of manufacturing, banking, shipping and international trade in the North. New York was the centre for the marketing of export crops, not New Orleans or Charleston. The Southern planter was paid by English importers in bills of exchange, the market for which was in New York where ready money could be obtained for them. When the demand for bills was low, this negotiable paper would be depressed; if the demand were high on the other hand, some speculator rather than the Southern producer would reap the profit. Southern planters were con-

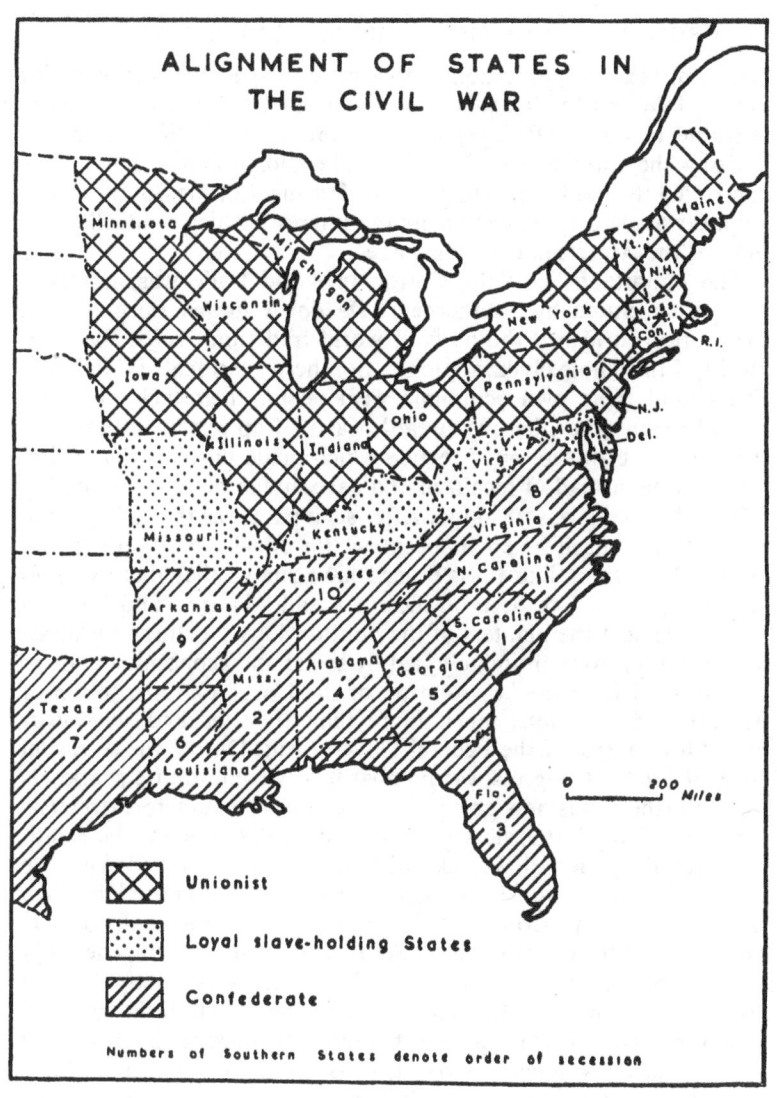

vinced of vicious speculation in this cotton paper, the factor of risk involved by Northern brokers in giving money for a future claim (payable in 60 or 90 days) being ignored. In addition to monopolizing the foreign export business the North almost completely controlled the banking system, to the detriment of the South. Heavy tribute was paid to Yankee shipping interests which controlled the bulk of the American carrying-trade.

The importance of King Cotton in world trade was, however, often exaggerated by Southerners: *De Bow's Review* once claimed that cotton furnished the basis of world trade and 'ruled the commerce of the whole civilized globe'. Southern 'nationalists' failed to understand their own economic weaknesses, their lack of liquid capital for instance, because wealth was tied up in slaves and land. It is true that an economic regime which made business depression nation-wide instead of localized and gave undue rewards to middlemen and brokers was unsound. After such panics as that of 1857 the South viewed itself as an innocent victim of wild Northern speculation. But writers like P. S. Foner[1] have shown that there was no alliance between Northern businessmen and labourers and Western farmers against the planters of the South. Many Northern businessmen, after all, were intimately tied by social and economic bonds to the South. They *feared* dissolution of the Union and disruption of normal trade relations much more than they disliked slavery or hoped for control of the Federal Government. During the secession crisis of 1860–1 Congress was bombarded by compromise proposals from Northern business groups.[2] The claim of Southern extremists therefore, that Northerners were systematically robbing the South and provoking her to war-like action, must be accepted with the same reservations with which one accepts the Northern claim of a vast 'Slave-Power Conspiracy'. Above all, the agrarian conservatism and lack of resilience of Southern institutions impeded any self-help such as moves to diversify the Southern economy. Several Southern Commercial Conventions were held, but little came of their proposals to establish direct trade with Europe, to encourage the growth of Southern ports such as New Orleans, to improve commercial education, to enact better banking laws and to improve methods of marketing cotton. Such reforms were never carried out intelligently by state or local governments. The remedy for Southern economic grievances, other than self-reform, lay solely with Time. For this the South refused to wait.

[1] *Business and Slavery* (New York, 1941).
[2] On this subject see also K. M. Stampp: *And the War Came* (Baton Rouge, Louisiana, 1950).

SUGGESTED FURTHER READING

CRAVEN, A. O. *The Coming of the Civil War* (New York, 1942).
EATON, C. *History of the Old South* (New York, 1949).
LLOYD, A. Y. *The Slavery Controversy* (Chapel Hill, N.C., 1939).
POTTER and MANNING *Nationalism and Sectionalism in America* (New York, 1949).
RANDALL, J. G. *Civil War and Reconstruction* (New York, 1937).
SMITH and COLE *Fluctuations in American Business, 1790–1860* (Cambridge, Mass., 1935).

PART TWO

Emergence of American Capitalism 1861–1917

VII

INDUSTRY AND COMBINATION

Civil War financing; the National Bank Act (1863) – The Southern economy – Northern industrial growth: chief factors – Iron and steel – Other minerals: sulphur, salt, aluminium, zinc, lead, copper, coal – The automobile industry and mass production – The Industrial Revolution in the South – Business consolidation: reasons and methods; pools, trusts and holding companies – Standard Oil.

FOUR years after the surrender at Appomattox courthouse the Special Commissioner of the Revenue, David A. Wells, estimated the money cost of the Civil War to the United States Government as well over $4,000 million—a sum fifty-two times greater than the national debt outstanding in 1861.[1] But this was not all: Wells calculated the cost of war pensions to be about $200 million, and added the losses and expenditures of the Confederate Government ($2,700 million) and of the several states, counties, cities and towns. He thus arrived at an estimate of the 'aggregate destruction of wealth, or diversion of industry which would have produced wealth' since 1861: $9,000 million. Wells points out that this sum is in excess of the entire increase of wealth, as returned by the census, for the whole country from 1850 to 1860.

A far-reaching effect of the extremely high cost of the war was to make the Federal Government much more important in the national economy than it had ever been before. A large federal debt has been produced by every major war involving America; the present debt after World War II is one hundred times as large as that left by the Civil War. Even so, the latter was enormous to contemporaries, and federal debt-management policy[2] was bound to affect every aspect

[1] *Report of the Special Commissioner of the Revenue, 1869*, IV-VI, (Washington, D.C., 1870). The sums were: $4,172,000,000 and $76,500,000.

[2] A subject that lies outside the scope of this book, despite its importance. For advanced students there is a specialized work: R. T. Patterson: *Federal Debt-Management Policies, 1865–1879* (Durham, N.C., 1954).

of economic life after 1865. During the emergency, the authority of the central government was extended over fiscal, banking and monetary affairs, and met with little resistance.

The United States Government financed the war by increased direct and indirect taxes, by bond issues and by currency inflation. As the national economy remained mainly agricultural (and the Southern economy almost wholly so), taxation was extremely difficult. In consequence there was an unhealthy dependence on paper-money issues and loans in both North and South. The United States Government raised only 22 per cent of its income from tax revenues; the Confederate Government only 5 per cent.

It would not be censorious to say that the financing of the war was bungled by both sides. Yet at the same time the difficulties faced were heavy: there was no fund of financial experience to draw from, national income was only $140 per head, the revenue system was inelastic, there was no income tax, excises had not been enforced for decades, and loans required Congressional authorization in every detail. The currency and banking system was chaotic and weak: there were 1,600 state banks and 7,000 kinds of bank-notes, more than half of which were worthless. The Federal Government itself, under the Independent Treasury (set up in 1840 after disastrous losses of federal funds in state banks),[1] used only 'hard' money. In the North, the government blundered along without any planned long-term policy until the spring of 1863. Two years earlier it had believed that the war would be short and decisive; the struggle had proved to be long, tedious and costly. Taxation was thus not definitely resorted to until it was almost too late. The Morrill Tariff Act (1861) of the old Congress restored duties to pre-1857 levels, before Salmon P. Chase took over the Treasury for Lincoln. The measure yielded little, because the outbreak of war seriously hit foreign trade. Chase thought taxes should be introduced only to cover sinking fund and interest needs of new loans. As far as loans themselves were concerned, he unwisely depended on short-term issues, and the Treasury was thus forced to raise funds continuously throughout the war, while at the same time meeting short-term obligations. Congress authorized a $250 million loan in July 1861, and an omnibus revenue bill in August that levied a $20 million direct tax on real property, a 3 per cent income tax on earnings over $800 a year, and new or higher duties on tea, sugar, coffee and other goods. Altogether during the war years loans amounted to about $2,600 million, taxation yielding only a quarter of that amount—$667 million.

Specie payments were suspended in December 1861 owing to an increase in hoarding (the result of bad military news and the govern-

[1] See the section on the crisis of 1837 in Chapter VI.

ment's hesitancy in tackling monetary problems) and to Chase's refusal to modify his 'hard' money notions; he insisted that payments to the Treasury should be in specie. The money market was upset and it was impossible to float new federal loans. Accordingly, after much debate and disagreement the Legal Tender Act was finally passed in February 1862 providing for the issue of $150 million in U.S. notes ('greenbacks'). Further Acts (July 1862 and March 1863) brought the total of paper money issued by the U.S. Government during the war up to $450 million. The greenback issues inaugurated an inflationary movement, and specie payments were not resumed until 1879.

In July 1862 a more vigorous tax policy was accepted after a long, three-month debate, and in February 1863 the National Bank Act was passed. Its aims were: to provide a safe, uniform, national currency replacing the notes of the 1,600 state banks; to create a market for federal bonds, the government being still in need of loans; and to drive the notes of state banks out of circulation. The last was achieved by a federal tax of up to 10 per cent on note-issue, enacted in March 1865, and the sale of government bonds was stimulated by Jay Cooke's campaign. In October 1862 Chase made Cooke—a highly successful speculator and banker—the general agent for the sale of 6 per cent bonds authorized under the Loan Act of February 1862. Cooke had already sold over 20 per cent of the 1861 notes, and with a group of 2,500 agents working under him, he carried out a national publicity campaign which sold $364 million by January 1864. He reaped a huge personal profit—probably a good deal more than the $220,000 he estimated publicly—and the success of his techniques earned him the title 'the financier of the Civil War'. In his railway schemes of nine or ten years later, Jay Cooke was not so fortunate.

The important banking reforms and institution of a national currency achieved by the 1863 Act did not become fully effective until the Civil War was over; but they were an essential factor in the growth of a national industrial economy with a continental domestic market.

Northern military strategy during the war was to encircle the South, blockade her ports, and defeat her armies inland. For her part, the South held an exaggerated belief in the need of the world for her cotton, which was expected to perform the triple function of bringing aid from Europe, financing the rebellion and forcing acquiescence from the North. But Europe needed North-western wheat as badly as Southern cotton, and European cotton-importers were already overstocked at the opening of the war and able to manage for some time. In addition there was a strong anti-slavery group of Northern sympathizers in England, and the Northern blockade in any case forestalled all Southern hopes regarding cotton.[1]

On the other hand there was a temporary quickening of economic processes in the South, stimulated by war and blockade. Manufactured goods had now to be made there, household industries revived and small munitions factories were set up by the Confederate Government and by entrepreneurs. On the plantation, the collapse of the cotton market and the need of supplying troops brought about a switch from cotton to foodstuffs—an uneasy change with slave labour. The marketing of foodstuffs became a mere gamble as the transport system rapidly deteriorated.

The same factors—war and blockade—that had proved beneficial to the South in the short-run, destroyed in the end much more than they had ever created. Ultimate economic losses under the Northern blockade and the devastation of her countryside by the ebb and flow of war reduced the South to a morbid condition. The post-war military regime imposed on her by the Northern victors (once Lincoln's restraining hand was removed) served to perpetuate this condition until 1877. 'Reconstruction' remains a euphemism, despite the attempts of recent 'revisionist' scholars to prove otherwise by suggesting that many 'quietly constructive' social and political developments took place during the period, and that corruption and chicanery were common to all groups.[2] Perhaps the chief economic problems inherited by the South from the Civil War were: the abolition of slavery, which cost $3,000 million and left the racial problem quite unsolved; the disruption of the plantation system; and the collapse of the financial system.

By contrast, while the South made painful, slow attempts to rise from the chaos and destruction caused by the war and exacerbated by Reconstruction, industrial development in the North was so remarkable as to constitute a second 'Industrial Revolution'. Among the factors involved in this gigantic growth were vast supplies of raw materials and the means of power: nearly half the iron resources of the world, two-thirds of its copper, one-third of its lead; plentiful anthracite and bituminous coal; and vast prairies and forests supplying timber and the needs of agriculture. Abundant capital at the command of captains of industry for investment and a great and

[1] For a detailed account of Confederate financing, see E. Q. Hawk: *Economic History of the South* (New York, 1934), Chapter XIV.

[2] We can go no further into the political history of these years; but there is a useful book for quick reference to several of the many points of view about 'Reconstruction': E. C. Rozwenc, (Ed.): *Reconstruction in the South* ('Problems in American Civilisation' Series, Amherst College, Boston, Mass., 1952).

growing labour force also help to explain the acceleration of economic progress after the Civil War. Both the flood of immigration and natural increase presented American industry with this labour supply. Over 28 million immigrants were added to the American population between 1860 and the opening of the 'depression decade' of the twentieth century. The increase was much greater in the North and West than in the South, and between 1870 and 1900 the total population of the United States rose from 38½ million to over 76 million. Looked at from the opposite end of the economic process, this vast growth in numbers formed the basis of the huge, insatiable domestic demand that is the key to American prosperity. Moreover, transportation facilities—the linking economic factor—did not fail to keep pace with developments in other fields. New processes and machines became available, including the typewriter (1874), the refrigeration freight wagon (1875), the telephone (1876), the 'gasoline carriage' (1879) and, above all, electric light and power (1882) and the first successful attempts at flight (1896 and 1901). In addition to available raw materials and power, abundant capital and labour and improved transportation, economic growth was aided by high protective tariffs and freedom of internal interstate commerce.[1] The *laissez-faire* policy of the Federal Government, while it necessarily involved much wastage of resources, overlapping and uneconomic construction, nevertheless assured that exploitation would be rapid.

By the turn of the century America had become the leading industrial nation of the world, and this leadership had changed from fine work to mass-production. There was a westward and southward shift, apparently towards raw material supplies: the coal, iron ore and petroleum of the Middle West, the cotton and timber of the South. Iron and steel replaced timber and cotton, however, as the basic American industries, although by 1914 meat-packing was the leading industry in value of product. Industrial growth continued very unevenly to the 1930's.

The outstanding innovation in the industrial history of the period 1861–1917 was probably the rise of the iron and steel industries. Pig-iron production in the United States increased from under one million to over 43 million tons during the years 1861–1917. This was due in part to the invention of new processes for converting iron into

---

[1] Moreover, the *laissez-faire* character of the Constitution was made more explicit by the addition of the Fourteenth Amendment (ratified 1868), which later proved so useful in the protection of business corporations from any kind of state interference that it has often been claimed that this was in fact the true intention of its framers. (For a vigorous article based on fresh research on this question, see J. F. S. Russell: *The Railroads in the 'Conspiracy Theory' of the Fourteenth Amendment*, in the *Mississippi Valley Historical Review*, Vol. XLI, No. 4, March 1955, pp. 601–22.)

steel, and in part to the discovery of new resources of ores.[1] Also federal tariffs which were almost prohibitive constituted in effect an 'indirect subsidy' to the American iron and steel industry. The wartime Act of 1864 had raised the average rate on dutiable commodities from 37 per cent to 47 per cent. Yet the Civil War was not in itself a sufficient stimulus to this industry, the loss of the normal market being so great as merely to be met by the war demand. By 1873 the production of pig iron had nevertheless risen to more than $2\frac{1}{2}$ million tons, and it was more efficiently produced. That year can perhaps be regarded as the turning-point in the change-over from charcoal to coal and coking in iron production—a move which had occurred in Britain in the late eighteenth century.[2] The Bessemer process (despite Kelly's independent work earlier in Kentucky) was first extensively applied in 1865 when Bessemer steel was made from the non-phosphoric and non-sulphurous ores of Lake Superior and New Jersey. The first American steel rails were rolled in Chicago in 1865. Other centres of steel production which arose included Cleveland, Toledo and Milwaukee; but it was Pittsburgh, at the centre of the Appalachian coal-fields and well placed for water and rail transport, that came to dominate the scene. In the '80's, however, Birmingham, Alabama, became a Southern rival, when the coal and iron deposits of the Southern Appalachians came to be exploited. By 1937 the American output of iron and steel overtopped the combined total productivity of Britain, Germany, France, Italy and Japan by some 2 million tons. The American industry surpassed Britain in both technique and quantity; it achieved important economies of large scale which kept its products at very competitive prices in world markets; it was quick to apply chemical science to iron and steel production and to introduce electric furnaces; and extensive vertical and horizontal integration took place until in 1901 the giant United States Steel Corporation or 'billion dollar monopoly' was established. This owned and mined 65 per cent of the Lake Superior ores, owned five large docks and an extensive fleet, ran its own trains on its own railway system, and produced 50 per cent of the total steel production of the U.S.A. The combine was capitalized at the sum of $1,400 million and by 1924 had made an agreggate net profit of well over $2,000 million. *Vertical integration* (the control by a single corporation of all the elements going into the making of a single product at all levels—raw materials, transport, manufacture, distribution, finance and advertising) gave an enormous amount of independence, and *horizontal integration* (the combination of all manufacturers of

[1] See *Historical Statistics of the United States, 1789–1945* (U.S. Bureau of Census, Washington D.C. 1949), p. 149 (Series G 93–101). There was a 20-fold growth in the first half of the century. (See above, Chapter III).
[2] See above, Chapter III, pp. 34–5.

one product) made it easy to control price and production levels. The U.S. Steel Corporation combined these various advantages.

It is true that the rise of an immense iron and steel industry was the basic condition of the emergence of America as a world industrial power in the later nineteenth century; but this was the chief aspect of a wider transition—the rapidly increasing dependence of the American economy on the mineral industries as a whole. The decades following the Civil War saw the deepening and extension of mines, the introduction into manufacturing of 'new' minerals and a greater use of well-known ones, and the replacing of wood by coal as the principal fuel. Between 1870 and World War I total American mineral production increased twenty-one-fold in real value, reaching an annual estimate in 1920 of nearly $7,000 million. Minerals of note besides iron and steel included of course coal; also copper and lead production expanded appreciably. Sulphur production multiplied fifty-fold in the second half of the century, although at that time the bulk of the raw material—pyrites—was imported from Spain. It had gained many significant industrial uses, as sulphuric acid. After 1900 came a truly spectacular rise: vast strata of native American sulphur were discovered in Louisiana and Texas, and technical innovations in sulphur-mining coincided with the rise of the oil industry and the opening of adjacent petroleum fields which could provide plentiful cheap fuel. Yearly output increased from 8,000 tons (1903) to over 1,000,000 tons (1917),[1] and America became an exporter of sulphur. Another mineral which came into great demand in the last quarter of the nineteenth century owing to the rise of the chemical industries was salt. Used in meat-preservation and for household purposes before the Civil War, native salt had been obtained chiefly from Syracuse in upper New York State and from the upper reaches of the Ohio valley. But more than half the American consumption was imported from England and elsewhere. There were no major technical innovations in the salt-mining industry, the main processes including drilling, forcing water down the bores, and pumping up the brine. After 1865 however fresh strata of rock salt were discovered in New York, Louisiana and Michigan and these were developed as greatly enlarged uses were found for salt in the expanding chemical industries. The tariff on salt, which had been repealed in 1807 despite its good yield, was renewed at a high rate; thus although foreign salt continued in use along the seaboard, domestic production grew much faster than imports.[2] The American demand for salt tripled between 1890 and the closing of World War I.

[1] See V. S. Clark, op. cit., Vol. II, pp. 820–1. The industry was stimulated by the heavy demand for explosives in World War I.

[2] Salt may have played a minor part in the rise of Chicago as a meat-packing centre: it was used as ballast on return journeys by ships taking

Among the lesser minerals aluminium, manufactured from bauxite ore imported from British and Dutch Guiana, is nowadays controlled by one of three close monopolies established near large sources of electric power, such as the Niagara Falls, the Tennessee valley and areas in Washington State. As a light, pliable metal, aluminium is essential in the aircraft industry and has also invaded the domestic utensil, automobile, wire and cable and electrical industries, to name but a few. The industry did not appear until the late 1880's, however, when three commercial methods of reducing aluminium were invented by Americans—Cowles, Castner and Hall—in 1885-6. Production leapt from about 80 pounds (1883) to $7\frac{1}{2}$ million pounds in a decade, whilst costs fell consistently until in 1891 aluminium replaced cast iron in the building of the dome of Philadelphia's city hall, reducing the weight of the tower by 400 tons. Two years later the price fell to 50 cents a pound (from $20 to $32 in the mid-'80's). The United States produced well over half the world's total of aluminium (c. 900,000 metric tons) in 1945. Zinc-mining has become of commercial importance in several states, especially Oklahoma, Kansas, Tennessee and Missouri. Production increased from 700 tons (1873) to over 63,000 tons (1893) in the last quarter of the nineteenth century; the United States is now the world's leading producer of this metal.[1] Associated geologically with zinc, and sometimes extracted from the same mines, is lead. Large deposits of low-grade lead ore have been worked in south-eastern Missouri since 1869 when prospecting first began there. In addition lead was also found in the Rocky Mountains associated with silver ores; in 1871 the completion of a railway link made it possible to exploit the deposits of Nevada and Utah which had been traced two years earlier. In the '80's the Leadville, Colorado region rose to prominence, and in the '90's Cœur d'Alene, Idaho. The official *Minerals Yearbook* for 1947 placed lead-producing states in the following order, according to quantity: Missouri, Idaho, California, Illinois. U.S. consumption of lead is about a million tons, in comparison with the 300,000 tons used by the U.K. In 1938 America produced almost 370,000 tons, world production being nearly 1,850,000 tons. Mexico came second (311,000 tons), South America and Australia third (307,000 tons each), and Africa fourth (not quite 70,000 tons). By 1945 the United States was still in the lead with a slightly increased figure of 389,000 tons, Mexico still second, Africa

Western grain down the Erie Canal from the Upper Lakes. See V. S. Clark, op. cit., Vol. II, pp. 123-4.

[1] World zinc production increased from 98,000 long tons (1865) to 1,400,000 long tons (1945), and in recent years the American percentage of this production has expanded. Thus percentages in 1937 included: U.S.A. 33 per cent, Belgium 14 per cent, Canada 9 per cent; in 1947 these had become: U.S.A. 49 per cent, Belgium 8 per cent, Canada 10 per cent

and Australia third, and South America fourth. Australian, South American and Mexican lead production had fallen in quantity, whilst that of the United States and Africa had increased. In 1889 American producers formed a trust, after years of severe competition, which was reported to manage 95 per cent of United States lead production. This was regularized in 1891 under the name National Lead Company.

The American copper industry during its most significant years of growth was closely linked with the electrical industry. With the invention of the telegraph came a demand for miles of copper wire. A transcontinental telegraph service was achieved by 1861; three years earlier Queen Victoria and President Buchanan had exchanged greetings via an Atlantic cable, and by 1866 a regular transmission of transatlantic messages was possible. Other inventions, electric motors and light bulbs and electrical apparatus of all types, increased in volume and variety from the early 1880's, assuring the prosperity of the copper industry. In the earlier half of the century this industry was widely scattered, operated by numerous small-scale mines mainly in the Atlantic coastal states, north and south. In the mid-40's the rich deposits of Lake Superior ores in northern Michigan were first tapped, and a copper 'fever' reached its speculative climax in 1846; in south-eastern Tennessee and adjoining parts of Georgia, a similar boom occurred in the '50's. By the beginning of the Civil War the U.S. was extracting about 8,000 tons of copper per year, of which 75 per cent came from the Michigan deposits. Western copper fields were opened up in the 70's and '80's and Michigan's hegemony was successfully challenged by Montana and Arizona. Montana's production surpassed that of Michigan in 1890 and by 1910 well over half the national output of copper came from the Western mines. Fifteen years later Arizona produced 43 per cent of the American total, Montana 30 per cent and Michigan only 8 per cent. Annual copper output increased at a quicker rate than iron and steel, to 900,000 tons during World War I. Britain lost her leading position as the world's producer to the U.S. in 1895. American copper production has tended to decline in recent years, from 635,000 short tons (1920) to 604,000 short tons (1946); but she remains the chief world producer, Chile being the second (398,000 short tons, 1946) and Rhodesia having risen to third place (205,000 short tons, 1946). The growth of large monopolistic business units has been very noticeable in the American copper industry. Profits were extraordinary before the First World War, the Calumet and Hecla Mining Company paying an annual average dividend to shareholders of 144·5 per cent. Four large firms dominated the mining of the ore (producing 51 per cent of total output in 1929) and four large firms dominated its smelting, two of the latter being two of the former also. One of these two—the Anaconda Copper Mining Company—also refined the copper and manufactured the products (through a subsidiary). Its assets totalled $750 million in 1929.

This rapid survey of the economic history of the American mineral industries has omitted two basic products: coal and oil. As the latter industry is to receive treatment further on in a wider context, we shall confine our attentions at this juncture to coal. In Chapter III it was noted that Abraham Darby's success in smelting iron with coal instead of charcoal (1709) passed almost unnoticed in the United States despite its revolutionary implications for his native England. This was because timber was abundant in America and entrepreneurs were mainly concerned with the need for labour-saving devices. The changeover to coal did not come about completely until the 1870's, and railways and steamboats burnt timber as their principal fuel. Urbanization was a central factor in the transition: local timber supplies proved insufficient for large concentrated populations and industries, and coal was not only cheaper but more compact and economical. The widespread domestic and industrial use of coal depended ultimately on freight transportation improvements.

Mention was made in Chapter III of the distinction between bituminous ('soft') and anthracite ('hard') coals. 'Eastern' deposits (in Pennsylvania and Virginia) are anthracite, and 'Western' deposits (in western Pennsylvania, eastern Ohio, West Virginia, Kentucky, Tennessee and Alabama) chiefly bituminous. There are also even vaster bituminous strata in Michigan, much of Illinois and south-western Indiana; in a north-south belt crossing Iowa, Missouri, Kansas and Oklahoma; and even further west, in the Rockies (as in Utah, Colorado, Wyoming and Montana).[1] Bituminous deposits far exceed anthracite deposits, and are also well suited for making the coke needed in the Cort process of the iron industry.[2] But Western demand remained inelastic at a low level, and consequently technical methods were found to overcome the disadvantages of anthracitic supplies in the East. By 1856, 121 furnaces in the Eastern iron industry smelted with anthracite, which became the leading industrial fuel in the ante-bellum decade. In this period the centres of mining for both hard and soft coal were to be found in Pennsylvania. Canals and later railroads were built to connect the hard-coal mines of the north-eastern part of the state to the coast, the mining and the transportation of coal becoming integrated. Despite the complaints of the Pennsylvania state commission of 1833, by 1870 most of the

[1] States listed according to estimated coal reserves (1947) come in the following order: Wyoming, N. Dakota, Montana, Colorado, Illinois, W. Virginia, Kentucky, Pennsylvania. The last three produce the most coal at present.

[1] See Chapter III, above, pp. 34–5.

anthracite district was owned by a small group of railway corporations. Anthracite consignments increased almost twenty-seven fold in the thirty years 1834–64, attaining an output of 10 million tons.

In the 1850's the bituminous mines of western Pennsylvania around Pittsburgh produced an annual average of 5 million tons. As a source of heat and power bituminous coal lay behind the industrial growth of Pittsburgh, and shipped (via improved navigable tributaries) down the river Ohio, it performed a similar function for Cincinnati (Ohio), Louisville (Kentucky) and, to a lesser extent, St. Louis (Missouri). This cheaply mined opencast soft coal cost under a dollar a ton, and by the '70's was steadily displacing anthracite for all industrial purposes. Hard coal was increasingly limited to domestic household uses, for which it is more suited because it emits less smoke in burning. The vertical and horizontal integration which characterized the anthracite industry was less noticeable in bituminous production, partly because soft-coal deposits were and are very widespread; organization was confused and conditions fluctuated. There were large corporations and small 'wagon mines'; irregular little mines working only in season ('snow-birds') and large 'captive' mines belonging to steel and railroad companies and supplying only company needs. In 1920 there were well under 200 producers in the anthracite business, but over 12,200 in the bituminous fields.

At the opening of this century some 90 per cent of American energy needs was met by coal; but by World War I production began to decline. Although contraction began first in anthracite output, the soft-coal industry was affected the worst by the severe depression of the 1920's. This depression was to a large degree the result of external factors, such as the competition of new power and fuels—petroleum, natural gas and hydro-electric power; but it is also true that mining capacity in the United States under private control was developed far in excess of any reasonably estimated demand, and heavy unemployment of both men and plant ensued. Extraction techniques were wasteful, adopted with a short-term view for quick profits. (Thus, the United States, with much easier geological and mining conditions to face than, say, Great Britain, has the highest accident rate in the world: three to four miners killed per thousand employed, each year. The coal-mining industry has had a very troubled labour history.)

By 1945 new fuels had so replaced coal that it met only 47 per cent of American energy requirements. Total production fell from under 600 million metric tons (1920) to under 360 million (1938). The 1938 figure represented 32·5 per cent of total world production;[1] this had risen once more by 1946 to 48·9 per cent or over 537 million metric

[1] Excluding the U.S.S.R.

tons. Of this amount, Pennsylvania and West Virginia produced about a third each.

The coal, iron and steel industries supported and were in turn stimulated by the massive automobile industry which grew up after 1900. This industry not only revolutionized American agriculture but began a 'renaissance' of road-building, heralding a new era in transport history. The European invention of the internal combustion engine was speedily assimilated in America by such men as Olds and Ford. Experiments with automatically propelled land vehicles had taken place in America since the early nineteenth century, but it was in 1893 that the first practicable car with a petrol engine was produced there. Work went ahead in the '90's on the commercial possibilities of the new vehicles, and the Census of 1900 gave them a mention. In that year about 3,700 were made in the U.S.A., most of which were steam-driven; 500 were 'electric carriages' and only 300 petrol motor-cars. Ten years later annual output was 187,000 motor-cars, valued at over $200 million. The manufacturing of 'automobiles' had already become a major industry. By 1921, 10 million motor-vehicles were registered in the U.S.A.; by 1928, well over 23 million (76 per cent of world registration). Passenger-car production fell from over $3\frac{1}{2}$ million a year in the late 1930's to almost nil by 1945, owing to the drastic change-over to war-time production. But it is characteristic of American industry that within the brief space of five years, 1945–50, production leapt from rock bottom to $6\frac{1}{2}$ million cars a year.

Besides its great significance in the history of transportation,[1] the automobile industry had an invaluable contribution to make to the development of modern American industry as a whole: the technique of mass-production. The initiative was taken when in 1908 Ford decided to make a single standard type of motor-car, the famous 'Model T'. He had formed the company in 1903, at which time R. E. Olds (whose firm was established in 1897) was already turning out 4,000 cars a year. Ford's aim was: to build sturdy, reliable cars at a cheap price so that they would last five years and then simply be replaced; and to provide interchangeable, standardized repair parts at such low prices that it was cheaper to buy new parts than repair old ones. During its first fifteen months the firm produced 1,700 cars and by 1907 was making over 8,000. It was the slump and contracted output of 1908 (6,400) which helped to determine Ford to make his Model T. The car was a great success and continued without basic modifications until 1927.

Two years after the Model T was introduced, a special plan was laid out by the firm near Detroit. This at first used the static assembly process, under which it took about fourteen man-hours to

[1] See Chapter X, below.

assemble a chassis. By 1914 the time for this work was cut down to under two man-hours by the adoption of the continuous-belt mass-production process. As this system eventually evolved, raw materials (such as coal and iron ore) entered one end of a Ford factory, to emerge at the other as a finished motor-car. Great economies of scale were achieved, and the basic price of the Model T fell from $950 in 1908 to $290 in 1924. Annual production in the latter year was well over 1½ million cars and 200,000 trucks. More than 15 million Model T's were turned out during the two decades of its production. To win labour support for the intensification and speeding-up involved in 'continuous-flow' production, Ford brought in an impressive labour policy in 1914, including the eight-hour day and basic wages for certain classes of worker of five dollars a day.[1] The mass-production technique spread from the car industry to many other important manufacturing concerns: iron and steel, paper, chemical products, petroleum, electrical and domestic utensils and processed foods.[2]

Meanwhile the forces of the Industrial Revolution had at last made themselves felt in the South. In the first place we must remember that many of the new developments already mentioned took place in southern states: sulphur production was confined to Louisiana and Texas, the latter state dominating the world market by 1925; Louisiana contained much of the rock salt discovered after 1865; aluminium came to be manufactured in the Tennessee Valley, depending as it does on large sources of electric power; Tennessee became a zinc-mining state in the later nineteenth century, and Alabama an iron and steel producer.

Such industries were, for the most part, new anywhere in the United States. Of the older, more established ones, the textile industry showed a marked tendency to drift to the South. An early advocate of Southern industrialization had been William Gregg (1800–67), who in 1848 opened a cotton factory at Graniteville, South Carolina. But his success did not lead to a general introduction of mills in the South before the Civil War; indeed the city of Charleston had forbidden the use of a steam engine within its precincts in 1836, and Gregg wrote:

'... This power is withheld lest the smoke of an engine should dis-

[1] For a fuller account see Allan Nevins, *Ford: The Times, The Man, The Company* (New York, 1954. With the collaboration of F. E. Hill). For the whole industry see the older book, R. C. Epstein, *The Automobile Industry* (Chicago and New York, 1928).

[2] The important 'agricultural industries' such as meat-packing and milling are dealt with below, under agriculture. A paper industry grew up behind high tariff walls, centred at Holyoke, Massachusetts, and the United States was exporting paper by 1870.

turb the delicate nerves of an agriculturalist: or the noise of a mechanic's hammer should break in upon the slumber of a real estate holder or importing merchant, while he is . . . building on paper, "the Queen City of the South".[1]

It was not until the 1880's that the southward migration of the textile industry began to take place. The Atlanta Cotton Exposition of 1881 led directly to the sale of mill equipment in the Southern states worth $2 million. The Raleigh Exhibition of 1884 and the New Orleans fair of 1895 had similar effects.

Nearly 80 cotton factories were built in the South in the 1880's and twice that number in the 1890's. Spindles increased eight-fold in quantity in these twenty years, to over $4\frac{1}{4}$ million. By 1926 Southern spindles constituted 57 per cent of the national total, numbering over $17\frac{1}{2}$ million and being housed in 814 cotton mills. New England had lost over 2,400,000 spindles between 1922 and 1926, while the South gained almost 1,700,000. Owing mainly to a 50 per cent lower labour bill, cotton manufacturing costs were 15 per cent lower than in New England. The Carolinas, Georgia and Alabama headed the list of Southern textile states.[2]

As with the textile industry, the centre of oil production began to move southwards after 1875, from Pennsylvania to West Virginia, Kentucky, Missouri and Tennessee; and after 1900, Texas, Oklahoma, Louisana and Arkansas made their entry into this branch of economic activity. The oil industry by its later history aptly illustrates a tendency common to American industry as a whole: the trend towards business consolidation. We are about to examine the causes and methods of consolidation in the later nineteenth century.

In 1860 America was largely a country of small-scale local industries, despite the spectacular growth before the Civil War in some branches of the economy. As late as 1880 agriculture was still the main source of material income. (Even Great Britain did not finally revoke her agrarian traditions until the '80's, according to R. C. K. Ensor.) In the twenty years 1880–1900 the balance was tipped and the U.S.A. became primarily a manufacturing nation. The factory system had been given impetus by the Revolution, the War of 1812 and the Civil War, as it has since been rapidly advanced by two World Wars. Development was, on the whole, gradual and confined almost entirely to the North-east until the Civil War. But by 1900 America

[1] For further information see B. Mitchell, *William Gregg, Factory Master of the Old South* (Chapel Hill, N.C., 1928).
[2] See V. S. Clark, op. cit., Chapter 34 for spindle figures of individual states in the revival period. Materials developed in the South since 1930 include artificial silks and rayons, especially in Virginia and Tennessee.

produced half as much as all Europe and about double the total industrial production of the United Kingdom. Even this seems small when compared with American productivity in the twentieth century. At the time of the outbreak of World War I she was very nearly economically self-sufficient; as for World War II, one year after Pearl Harbour she was producing more war materials than all the Axis Powers together. It seemed increasingly clear therefore that the economic fate of the United States was to become a determining factor in that of Europe and of the world.

Industrial and business units in America in the second half of the nineteenth century were characterized by increasing size. Capitalization per firm rose eight-fold between 1850 and 1880 for instance, and the rise of giant combines was seen, such as United States Steel, the International Harvester Company and Standard Oil. How and why did this consolidation take place?

Some explanation of the question *How*? will be given by examining the growth of the Standard Oil Company. At present we are chiefly concerned with the *Why*?

Firstly, a distinction should be made between 'normal' large-scale growth, and artificial 'combination'. The consolidation movement accelerated a tendency towards large-scale industry which was coming in any case. The evolution of the corporation was both cause and effect of this general trend.

While combination was especially important after 1897, large-scale growth was already discernible in the immediate post-Civil War years. The Union victory in 1865 proclaimed to the world that America was to be a nation, and inspired a new confidence at home and abroad. In this social and political environment, supported by high protective tariffs, American industrialists were eager to apply technical innovations, expand their horizons and develop new organizational methods. The technical innovations—cumulative in their effects—not merely facilitated but made imperative the adoption of large-scale operations. In particular, power resources were vastly expanded, water-power giving way universally to steam, the older and more inefficient steam-engines giving way to high-speed compound turbines, and both being supplemented by electric power towards the end of the century. Scientific and technical developments were justified by a great expansion of the marketing area, made possible by transportation and communication improvements: the railway, postal service, telegraph and telephone, and later the motor-car and radio. The evolution of new forms of industrial organization capable of handling large operations, and of raising the capital to initiate them, seemed in the logic of history. Both limited liability and flexibility of management were essential to these corporate structures. Their complex business operations were aided by such mechanical inventions as the typewriter,[1] cash register and adding machine, and by the study of scientific management.

The more specific origins of the consolidation movement proper have been a subject of voluminous writing including the four important tomes devoted to it by the Industrial Commission, working under the Federal Act of 1898.[2] The movement began in the '70's, reached a climax between 1897 and 1904, slowed down and then revived in the 1920's, taking in its stride the new industries (motor-car manufacturing, radio, films), the retail trades, banking and public utilities.

The Industrial Commission concluded that the chief motivating factor behind combination was the fear of excessive competition. Uncontrolled economic forces were already bringing about the emergence of large-scale firms and the elimination of weak and small concerns. Competition between the remaining contestants was often so fierce as to destroy the profits of each. The three-fold hope of the industrialist who chose to combine was thus: to increase profits by cutting competitive losses, to wield monopoly power to raise prices, and to lower costs of production through economies of large scale. The third of these hopes was rarely uppermost; the immediate aim was market and price control irrespective of reductions in costs.

Consolidation was thus a conscious attempt by American businessmen to increase their share of the national income. The last quarter of the nineteenth century was a period of high productivity and (despite the huge wastage of national resources) of large returns for society. Entrepreneurial earnings, however, did not undergo a comparable increase. Despite the tide of immigration and the opening of the West, demand for the new enlarged productivity was not infinite, and the competitive scramble for markets led to so-called 'overproduction', gluts and price falls. The wholesale price index, for instance, fell from 174 in 1866 to 68 in 1897. This deflationary tendency was exacerbated because business men, burdened with large fixed capital, did not halt production and await the absorption of the surplus. Too many expenses continued. Instead firms remained under production in the hope of meeting their fixed costs. This of course stimulated further price reductions (and is said partly to explain the steady deflation and 'hard times' after 1893). Business turned to

---

[1] The first patent for a writing machine was taken out in London in 1714, but the first practicable, marketable machine was produced in Ilion, New York, in 1874 by E. Remington & Sons, a firm of gun-makers.

[2] *Report of the Industrial Commission*, 19 Vols. (Government Printing Office, Washington, D.C., 1900–2). Vols. I, II, XIII and XVIII (Europe) concern consolidation. Vol. XIX is the *Final Report* which summarizes the findings. The Commission contained members of both houses of Congress and nine presidential nominees; it made extensive use of leading contemporary economic 'experts'.

monopoly for salvation from 'free competition'. Major technical improvements did occur in the steel, mining, textile and other industries when a larger scale of operation was achieved. These were not, however, the only results.

Industrialists combined to increase their profits; but sometimes survival itself was the question. The financiers and bankers who became promoters of combinations, on the other hand, never feared for their existence. Indeed as a group they perhaps gained more pure profit than any party to the transactions. Stockbrokers and investment bankers functioning as middlemen in selling corporate securities rose to an important position within the economy; their eager pursuit of financial gain was frequently an important element in the formation of individual combinations.[1]

Further contributing factors were federal tariffs, patent laws and land policy, and the division of powers within the federal legal structure. One witness called before the Industrial Commission claimed that the Dingley Tariff Act of 1897 (imposing an average level of 57 per cent—the highest of the century) was 'the mother of all trusts'. Heavy 'protection' certainly helped to encourage the formation of the American Sugar Refining Company, of which the witness was president. Federal land-grants also favoured the growth of monopolies in national resources, and federal patent laws (giving inventors the exclusive right for seventeen years to make, sell, lease or simply shelve any original innovation) encouraged the 'collecting' of patents by firms with monopolistic intent. Thus the United Shoe Machinery Company became 'overlord' to the shoe industry by collecting 6,000 patents covering all aspects of shoe manufacturing, and dictating the terms on which it was prepared to lease them. Firms owning leading patents could of course fix high prices for the industry as a whole.[2] Moreover, the laws of several states were by no means inimical to the setting up of monopolies, and the division of power in the federal legal structure made it well nigh impossible to prohibit combination generally. New Jersey, West Virginia and Delaware welcomed monopolies, the seven greatest industrial combines in the U.S. being incorporated in New Jersey between 1891 and 1902.[3]

[1] Eliot Jones in *The Trust Problem in the United States* (New York, 1924) estimated promoters' profits in forming the U.S. Steel Corporation to be about $62,500,000 (p. 288).

[2] The specialized study of this aspect is W. Hamilton, *Patents and Free Enterprise* (Temporary National Economic Committee, Monograph No. 31. Government Printing Office, Washington, D.C., 1941). Otherwise see H. U. Faulkner, *The Decline of Laissez Faire, 1897–1917* (Vol. VII of Rinehart & Co's. *Economic History of the United States*, New York, 1951), pp. 158–160.

[3] i.e. American Sugar Refining Co. (1891), Amalgamated Copper Co.

We must now consider the question of method, with the Standard Oil Company as model. Once more, certain distinctions must be made. In the iron and steel, coal-mining, oil and sugar refining, salt, tobacco, cotton yarn, whiskey-distilling and shoemaking industries among others, more or less informal arrangements for limiting production or for price-fixing gave way gradually to more permanent monopolistic forms—industrial pools, trusts and holding companies. How did these various forms differ?

It is difficult to define any one of them exactly, in fact writers so often confuse them from the outset, or begin analytically but end up ignoring their own distinctions. Any given combination or 'merger'[1] may be difficult to 'catalogue' at any given moment. Neither is a chronological view very helpful. It is true to say that pools were the prevalent form of combination from about 1873 to about 1887, trusts in the '80's and early '90's, and holding companies from 1897 to 1904. Yet all three forms were revived in the 1920's, and a writer claimed in 1915 that pools had not declined after 1887 but on the contrary still exceeded other forms of combination in number.[2]

Perhaps pools have been insistently returned to as a form of combination because they offer several advantages but do not seriously impair the autonomy of individual concerns. They are essentially loose organizations of independent firms, most commonly established to control prices and supply. More often than not, a central administrative committee assesses penalties for 'overprŏduction' or infringements of price agreements; sometimes sales areas are allotted to specific firms in relation to estimated productive capacity (as in the meat-packers' and wire-nail pools[3]); sometimes even central selling agencies are established. Early pools existed in the cordage, salt and anthracite industries, and later in gunpowder and whiskey production. The Michigan Salt Association was founded in 1868, the Steel-Rail pool in 1887 and the Associated Pipe Works in 1894. However, pools were not enforceable in the courts, being essentially 'gentlemen's agreements'. In their looseness lay also their ultimate weakness: they frequently broke up and reformed, only to dissolve once more. As

(1899), American Smelting and Refining Co. (1899), Standard Oil Co. (1899), Consolidated Tobacco Co. (1901), U.S. Steel Co. (1901) and International Mercantile Marine Co. (1902). See J. Moody, *The Truth About the Trusts* (New York, 1904), p. 453.

[1] This word is used with a general comprehensive meaning, as for instance in H. F. Williamson (Ed.), *Growth of The American Economy* (New York, 1944), pp. 618 ff.

[2] Faulkner, op. cit., p. 164.

[3] In 1902 this device reached an international scale, by the agreement between the American Tobacco Company and the Imperial Tobacco Company of Great Britain.

'conspiracies in restraint of trade' pools were contrary to the Common Law, and were also explicitly forbidden by the Sherman Anti-Trust Act of 1890.

Trusts were resorted to in the 1880's as a firmer and more durable type of combination, the first example being Standard Oil (1879), followed by the Cotton Oil Trust (1884), the Distillers' and Cattle Feed (or 'Whiskey') Trust (1887) and similar organizations in the sugar, lead, cordage and other industries. While the term 'trust' has a very vague and general connotation, in particular it implies a form of combination which goes further than the pool itself but remains true at least to the letter of the laws of various states which prohibited a corporation from owning the stock of another corporation. It implies the surrender of voting stock in competing concerns to a board of trustees, in return for trust certificates. The companies thus combined are managed as a whole by the trustees, and the holder of trust certificates takes a part of the general proceeds. Thus the individual investor is no longer concerned with the condition of a particular company and the board of trustees has its hands free to dismantle plant, discontinue lines, buy new companies and expand business in any direction. These advantages were gained by Standard Oil in 1879.

Eventually various legal decisions found trusts to be illegal and they came under fire from social reformers and writers such as Henry George, H. Demarest Lloyd and Ida M. Tarbell. The social and political reaction against trusts forms an important part of the Progressive Movement (1890–1917) dealt with in later pages.

Holding companies developed chiefly after the Sherman Anti-Trust Act (1890), the election of McKinley (1896) and the Dingley Tariff Act (1897). They were not a popular form of combination at first, but soon spread when it was realized that they enabled trusts to transform themselves fairly easily into legal bodies. A holding company was a concern which acquired control over other companies either by outright purchase or by acquiring the majority of their stocks. This was made possible by the state legislation of New Jersey (1889, 1893), New York (1892), Delaware (1899), Maine (1901) and elsewhere, although many states continued to prohibit the ownership of a corporation's stock by another corporation. Ultimate control is of course centralized in a holding company, but it is important to remember that administration is generally decentralized. A legally incorporated company acquires ownership of stock in other companies which remain ostensibly independent (therefore beyond the reach of anti-trust laws); but the directors of the holding company have voting control over the other concerns.[1]

The largest holding company in the period 1897–1904 was the

[1] A further form of combination is the 'interlocking directorate', in which one man is on the directing board of several concerns. This was not

United States Steel Corporation, chartered in 1901 in New Jersey. The Standard Oil Trust was attacked by the state of Ohio in 1890 and invalidated in 1892 on the same Common Law grounds that Louisiana had used to dissolve the American Cotton Oil Trust in 1887. Rockefeller kept his empire together on the basis of 'community of interest' until 1899 and then turned Standard Oil into a holding company.

Standard Oil was one of the earliest and most profitable of American monopolies and soon came to symbolize all the successes and evils inherent in this form of organization. John D. Rockefeller,[1] its founder, was born in 1839 and began work at the age of sixteen as a book-keeper in a commission merchant's office in Cleveland, Ohio. In 1859 with his savings and parental aid he supplied half the capital for a business in grain, hay and meats: Clark & Rockefeller. The firm made some $17,000 a year during the Civil War and in 1863 John D. took up oil-refining, buying out his partner two years later. The new business, Rockefeller & Andrews, had a capital stock of $200,000. The Englishman Andrews dealt chiefly with the manufacturing, and Rockefeller with the buying and selling. A critical moment was experienced in 1867, but disaster was averted by a timely injection of capital from a rich Ohio brewer, Harkness. In 1870 the title Standard Oil Company of Ohio was adopted, and the capital stock of a million dollars had multiplied five-fold by 1877.

Oil-refining was bitterly competitive. From the start Rockefeller grasped the need for stringent internal economies. Thus he undertook to maintain all incidental and related services rather than pay other producers. Standard Oil sought to possess its own tank cars, storage depots, plumbing and drayage service, and its own cooperage plants for the making of oil-barrels (the timber for which came from forest land owned by the company, the iron hoops being also of its own make). Small articles, such as barrel-bungs, were subject to strict economy and supervision. But economy alone was insufficient to make a great company: Rockefeller also speculated. For instance

llegal before 1914, although the Pujo Committee of 1913 disclosed extensive interlocking among the largest corporations, banks and insurance companies: 180 individuals (the directors of 18 major banking houses) held 746 directorates in 134 companies with a combined capitalization of $25,000 million. The Clayton Act (1914) limited interlocking but was fairly ineffective. The Transportation Act (1920) prohibited interlocking in its own field except by permission of the Inter-state Commerce Commission; but the latter granted over 2,500 applications between 1920 and 1928.

[1] The authoritative biography is A. Nevin's revised work, now called *Study in Power: John D. Rockefeller, Industrialist and Philanthropist* (2 vols., New York, 1953).

he purchased new fields in Ohio where the oil had an unsuitable sulphur base—but in a short time Standard Oil chemists had overcome the difficulty and a large profit ensued.

In his relations with the railroads Rockefeller typified the mental attitude of the monopolist of his day. In 1873 there were three major railroads competing in the Oil Regions for the lucrative traffic afforded by the industry. These railways served three cities, each of which was determined to dominate the refining stage of the industry: Cleveland, Pittsburgh and Philadelphia. In addition refineries existed in New York and Baltimore. The eventual success of Cleveland in establishing its hegemony was the result not only of natural advantages, but also of Rockefeller's relentless ingenuity. While Cleveland had the advantage of summer transport by water and good rail-canal connections to New York by the Erie and New York Central railroads and the Erie Canal, Pittsburgh was well placed near the source of the raw material and had the river Allegheny for transport, and Philadelphia was best located for the Eastern market and export trade. In the '60's and '70's open bargaining and discrimination in freight carriage rates by shippers and railroads was widespread, although a 'common carrier' had theoretically no right to show partiality. Rockefeller was neither the originator of 'rebates' nor the sole refiner who demanded them from carriers; but he was certainly the most successful and unscrupulous in negotiating for preferential treatment. After failing to secure sweeping rebates in the notorious South Improvement Company scheme in 1872 (judicially quashed by the Pennsylvania legislature after complaints from small companies), Rockefeller managed in the summer of the same year to cajole refiners to form a pool—the National Refiners' Association—with himself as president. This pool controlled during its existence some four-fifths of America's refining capacity. As it threatened to reduce still further the price of crude oil, the producers opposed the refiners' pool by halting pumping. Eventually an agreement was made on both sides to check output of both crude and refined oil—the 'treaty of Titusville' (23 December 1872)—but this broke down, and Rockefeller's refiners' pool was dissolved six months later (24 June 1873).[1]

Standard Oil merely continued to strengthen its position in the industry, by entering the pipe-line field, continuing rebate contracts with railways and building or acquiring large Eastern plants and terminals. Rockefeller bought out nearly all the Cleveland concerns and between 1874 and 1877 took over extensive refineries in Philadelphia, Pittsburgh and New York. By 1879, Standard Oil refined 90 per cent of American oil, and Rockefeller's real aim was to set up an interstate combination without getting into the public eye; so the Trust was formed. Ever since 1872 the new acquisitions of the com-

[1] See Nevins, op. cit., I, pp. 162–76.

pany outside Ohio had been placed in the hands of a 'trustee', usually H. M. Flagler, the company secretary. The acquisitions remained nominally independent, but the profits went to the Ohio company, despite the laws prohibiting ownership of corporation stock by another corporation. But this device was too vague and very doubtful in law. What was Flagler a trustee for? The situation was regularized when the Standard Oil Trust was established in 1879. Nine trustees received the stock of the forty component concerns, giving trust certificates to shareholders in return. The combination was now capitalized at about $70 million. In 1892 the trust agreement was invalidated as we have seen, and seven years later Standard Oil became a holding company. Having gone through most of the chief forms of combination, it dominated the oil industry for several decades. In 1911 the government charged that Standard Oil of New Jersey practised price-discrimination all over the United States, operated at least seventy companies under the guise that they were independent, and paid $326 million in eight years on an original investment of $70 million. It would undercut prices of competitors in some districts and recoup losses by imposing higher charges in others, where its monopoly was more complete; it employed espionage on competitors and bribed first-class men working for rivals; it bought up companies surreptitiously and thus obtained trade secrets; it tried to cut off supplies of crude oil to its rivals and force transport companies to deny the competing refiners access to markets. On the other hand Standard Oil management was more efficient and its leaders were undoubtedly men of vision and high administrative ability, even though these qualities alone are not sufficient to explain the rise of the giant oil monopoly.

The Supreme Court ordered the trust to be dissolved on 15 May 1911. The 'trust-busting' movement which had led up to this event is particularized in greater detail in another chapter.

SUGGESTED FURTHER READING

CLARK, V.S. *History of Manufactures in the United States* (New ed., 3 vols., Washington, 1929).

FAULKNER, H. U. *The Decline of Laissez-Faire, 1897–1917* (Vol. VII in Rinehart & Co.'s *Economic History of the United States*, New York, 1951).

JONES, E. *The Trust Problem in the United States* (New York, 1924).

MITCHELL and MITCHELL. *The Industrial Revolution in the South* (Baltimore, 1930).

NEVINS, A. *Study in Power: John D. Rockefeller, Industrialist and Philanthropist* (2 vols., New York, 1953).

—*Ford: The Times, The Man, The Company* (New York, 1954. With the collaboration of F. E. Hill).

VIII

THE WESTWARD MOVEMENT AND AGRICULTURE

The post-Civil War 'frontier': the 'miners' frontier' and the Great Plains; the buffalo, Indian wars and the Dawes Act (1887) – Land policy – The 'ranchers' frontier – The invasion by the farmer and 'closing' of the frontier (1890) – The Agricultural Revolution: mechanization, reclamation, specialization – The 'agricultural industries': implements, meat-packing, canning, milling – Government intervention – Agricultural education.

THE Civil War which raged between 1861 and 1865 was probably as distant and as unreal to many frontier folk as the Boxer Rebellion of 1900 in China was to most English people. The eternal struggle with Nature, the subjugation of new lands and their native Indian inhabitants, and the wresting of precious metals from the earth continued unabated.

When war broke out, there were already two 'frontiers': firstly, the traditional Westward-moving line, halted since the '50's on the edge of the Great Plains[1] (from central Minnesota to the southeastern corner of South Dakota, through eastern Nebraska and Kansas, excluding Oklahoma, but dividing Texas); secondly, the Far West 'mining frontier', hardly a line at all, but comprising a few thousand settlers between the Rockies and the Pacific coast, lured by gold to make a perilous overland journey across the Great Plains, a long sea trip around the Horn, or a sea and land voyage across the Isthmus of Panama. Between the two more or less settled areas lay the High Plains—the 'Great American Desert'—treeless and often waterless 'prairie', inhabited by herds of wild buffalo and nomadic Indian tribes. The story of the last frontier is chiefly that of how ranchers and then farmers filled in the great intervening space.

[1] The frontier line of 1860 is a boon to geographic determinists: it follows with remarkable closeness the 'edge' of the Plains, especially in Texas.

In the spring and summer of 1849 thousands of war veterans and adventurers had made their way to California, in search of gold. By 1850 the population of the area numbered about 100,000 and it was admitted as a state into the Union. The western slopes of the Sierras were scattered with more or less ephemeral mining camps, and during the next fifteen years various gold 'rushes' followed upon discoveries in Colorado, Nevada, Arizona and Idaho. Few miners were lucky, the majority remaining to exploit the wealth of less precious minerals or to supply goods and services to the mining communities and farms.[1] Enough migrants remained behind to form the Territory of Jefferson (1859), which had a population of some 35,000 according to the census of 1860, and was admitted as the State of Colorado in 1876. Meanwhile, silver was discovered—the richest deposits in the West—in the extreme western part of Utah Territory[2] in 1859. This 'Comstock' Lode attracted sufficient settlers to establish Nevada as a State of the Union within five years (1864), and for long remained the basis of Nevada's economy.

The advance of the Eastern frontier line was delayed by several factors, including the need for transportation, water, some economical type of fencing and a plough sturdy enough to cut the hard prairie sod. The Plains had long been regarded as desert (although suitable in fact for maize and wheat cultivation and for dairying). Until the '50's the pioneers had encountered mainly well-watered and wooded land and had conditioned themselves to meet the requirements of such an environment; but the Plains offered quite a different terrain, lacking timber for houses, fences, implements and fuel, and lacking water for crops, cattle and humans. In addition there were the Indians. So it was that until the '70's and '80's the Great Plains were merely 'the highway to the Far West', and were left, undisturbed except by passing migrants, to the Indian and the buffalo.

With the eastwards advance of the mining frontier and the extension of the network of transportation came a revival of the Indian Question, firstly in the mountain lands and eventually in the Plains themselves. In a series of bloody wars the Indian tribes were tragically depleted in numbers and herded into small 'reservations'. Two principal factors explain the defeat of the red men by the white men: firstly, the latter's superior strategy and improved weapons; secondly —and a much deeper explanation—the rapid extermination of the buffalo. The nomadic life of the Indians was closely intertwined with that of the buffalo, without which that life would not have been possible. The beast provided the native with hide for clothing, meat

[1] Agriculture is today the principal occupation of the Mountain states.

[2] Established by Congress in September 1850, this Territory included the whole of modern Utah and Nevada together with parts of Wyoming and Colorado. Utah State proper was admitted in 1896.

(eaten fresh or preserved in the form of 'pemmican') bowstrings, lariats and fuel.

There were two vast herds, one north and one south of the central overland route, and their destruction began in earnest after the Union Pacific railroad was connected with the Central Pacific at Promontory Point, Utah, in 1869. For two years after this, the white man continued to hunt buffalo for sport, but in 1871 a powerful economic incentive was added: a Pennsylvania tannery found a method of using buffalo hides for commercial leather. Hired teams of hunters were sent out, and by the mid-'80's the animal was practically extinct. Its numbers had been reduced from a roughly estimated total of about thirteen million to a mere specimen handful of thirty-four by 1903.[1]

The Indian wars themselves were sporadic, drawn-out affairs and they can most easily be understood if divided according to region. From this view there were two chief areas—mountains and plains—each having northern and southern sectors.

The subjugation of the natives of the northern mountain zone (Snake and Bannock tribes in Oregon and southern Idaho, and Ute Indians in Utah and Nevada) followed the pattern adopted in earlier years by the forty-niners, who murdered most of the 150,000 peaceful Digger tribe of California. The miners intermittently fought, bribed and cheated the primitive tribesmen between 1850 and 1855 and in 1861 the Ute eventually ceded most of their territories to the Federal Government, in return for a small 'reservation'. The Indians of the southern mountain area were not so easily subdued; the ferocity and tenacity of the Apache and Navajo warriors kept prospectors out until the '50's, when military invasion took place. Haphazard fighting in those years gave way to serious war between 1860 and 1864. Both tribes were defeated, the Navajo being dispatched to a reserve at Fort Sumner (1865) and the Apache to a number of small reserves in New Mexico and Arizona (1871–3).[2]

The Indians of the Plains were even more intractable: they were excellent horsemen and warriors and their bows were more effective than the muzzle-loading rifle. (In the '50's the Colt six-shooter helped to weight the scales in the white man's favour however.) The idea of retaining the whole of the Great American Desert as 'one big reservation' fell through with the gold discoveries and transportation improvements of the '50's and '60's; the demand grew to 'clear' Kansas and Nebraska which were organized as Territories in 1854.

[1] See R. A. Billington's standard work, *Westward Expansion: A History of the American Frontier* (New York, 1949), p. 668.

[2] During the war the famous Colonel Kit Carson trapped as many as 7,000 Indians at one time. Nearly 9,000 were captured and over 600 killed in, one year, 1863–4.

By 1860 this demand was fulfilled, but the movement did not end at that point. A gold discovery in Colorado brought the invasion of 100,000 miners from the East, urged on by the slogan 'Pike's Peak or Bust!', who proceeded to oust the Cheyenne and Arapaho from their territory—despite the entente of Fort Laramie (1851) in which the Federal Government had promised to preserve definite tribal boundaries. Refusing to accept a further imposed treaty (Fort Lyon, 1861), many Cheyenne and Arapaho took to the warpath in Colorado, Wyoming, and elsewhere. There was much savagery on both sides, especially in the winter of 1864–5,[1] but peace was secured in October 1865. The two tribes accepted new reservations and the Kiowa and Commanche surrendered all claims to central Texas, Kansas and eastern New Mexico. Uneasy peace reigned in the South-west until the Red River War of 1874–5, which signified complete defeat for the Indians.

The chief battles in the northern area of the Plains were fought in the Sioux wars of 1865–8 and 1876. A federal attempt to connect Montana to the East by the 'Powder River Road' was the immediate cause of the first; the advance of the North Pacific railroad, the Black Hills gold rush (1875) and corrupt administration of the Indian reservations, were the causes of the second. It was in the war of 1876 that Custer foolishly disobeyed orders and was forced to make his 'last stand' at the battle of the Little Big Horn (25 June). Despite this victory the tribes surrendered in October and Chief Sitting Bull fled to Canada, to add to the worries of the overworked 'Mounties'. This marked the end of major Indian wars although an epilogue, as it were, was the religious revival of the Teton Sioux of South Dakota and the 'battle' of Wounded Knee (1890), in which the Americans used the Hotchkiss rapid-fire gun with murderous effect.

In the East there was a considerable body of pro-Indian, humanitarian thought, led by reformers like Carl Schurz and Helen H. Jackson, whose *Century of Dishonour* (1881) played a similar rôle in the Indian question as did *Uncle Tom's Cabin* in the Negro question. The Congressional Committee on the Condition of the Indian Tribes (1865) decided it was cheaper to keep Indians in reservations at federal expense than to fight them, and from 1871 a policy was developed of breaking down tribal barriers and dealing with Indians as individuals rather than as separate nations. This culminated in the Dawes Severalty Act (8 February 1887), the first genuine attempt to civilize the Indian and educate him in the essentials of agriculture and social life. Land was to be divided among tribal members, those receiving grants to be admitted to full United

---

[1] In particular the 'Chivington Massacre' (29 November 1864) when 450 Indians, including women and children, were butchered in the early hours of the morning (Sand Creek, Colorado).

States citizenship. In 1901 the 'Five Civilized Nations' of Oklahoma, and in 1924 all remaining Indians, were also given citizenship.

Before the Eastern line of settlement could continue from where it had halted in the '50's, it had not only Indians and technical difficulties of the terrain to face. Federal land policy encouraged the land speculator rather than the 'homesteader', and between the late '60's and the late '80's ranchers used the great intervening plains and refused to give way to farmers.

Over 1,150 million acres of the public domain were 'alienated' between 1785 and 1914, 757 million acres being disposed of in the second half of the period. Of the total amount, 950 million acres were handed over to individuals, corporations and states, and 200 million acres kept in reserves.[1] The rapid rate of alienation after 1861 was governed by a series of Acts, including the Pre-emption Act of 1841 (repealed in 1891), Homestead Act (1862), Morrill Act (1862), Timber Culture Act (1873), Desert Land Act (1877), Timber and Stone Act (1878), Carey Act (1894) and Reclamation Act (1902). Huge federal grants were given to states and railroad corporations, and smaller areas given over to Indian reservations and forest reserves or national parks.

The central measure was of course the Homestead Act of 1862, which had legalized the donation of free land by the government to bonafide settlers and was the culmination of a traditional 'cheap land' policy. The act gave to any U.S. citizen (or intended citizen) 160 acres of free land if he had been settled on it for as long as five years and if it showed definite 'improvement'. Although it prohibited the raising of loans against 'homestead' land until possession was legally confirmed, the Act put no restrictions on transfer of ownership or maximum size of holdings. Its commuting clause was seriously abused, speculators obtaining vast tracts at only $1·25 an acre; the General Land Office was inefficient and the State Land Offices often corrupt. Much of this failure was inherent in the Act itself. Written by Easterners, it ignored the real geographical and economic conditions of the West. For instance, conditions of low precipitation west of 97° demanded either small-scale irrigation farming or large-scale 'dry' farming—more often the latter. A tract of only 160 acres was thus quite useless except east of the 97th meridian. West of this, 3,000 acres might have been a more economic size for a farming unit, but the Federal Government failed to take this into account until after World War I. The land given to individual states under the Morrill (agricultural colleges) Act of 1862 was eventually sold on the open market to the highest bidders and the homesteader could not possibly compete in such sales. Land-holding in fact became con-

[1] This left almost 291 million acres of public land in 1914, unreserved and not alienated.

centrated at an early date and before 1890 only 3½ per cent of the land west of the Mississippi went to actual homesteaders. The Homestead Act was thus only a theoretical triumph for the notion of small-scale land-holding. The holdings of speculators tended to cause a widespread dispersion of population, which necessitated the construction of railways across sparsely populated areas and raised the costs of local government. A constant feud raged between settlers and speculators, resident and absentee owners. On the other hand it must be admitted that 'speculation' was not necessarily or entirely inimical to resourceful colonization and development.

Finally, another enemy of the settler was the cattleman. The extermination of the bison and federal victories over the Indians in the late '60's and early '70's made the Great Plains available for the range cattle industry. It was discovered quite fortuitously that cattle could survive the bad winters of the Kansas, Nebraska and Wyoming region and fatten up on the pasturage afforded by the Plains. Almost simultaneously an opportunity of marketing the cattle from the same region was supplied by the transcontinental railroad. Texas ranchers thus began to send their yearling 'steers' each spring 'on the hoof' to the central and northern plains,[1] guided by cowboys along the long and arduous trails. Fattened on northern pastures the cattle were then shipped to the packers of the mid-western cities. This was *transhumance* on a scale probably unprecedented in history.

At first costs were negligible owing to lack of competition; ranching spread rapidly, the strain of stock was improved and Eastern capital introduced. By 1880 the industry was firmly established throughout the Plains, and cattle were being bred in the northern region. A 'longhorn' costing $7 or $8 in Texas would breed (if satisfactorily crossed) steers fetching up to $50 or $60 in the North. The cattle population of Kansas thus increased between 1860 and 1880 more than sixteen-fold (to over 1½ million). That of Nebraska multiplied thirty-fold (to over 1,100,000), and in Colorado, Wyoming and Montana numbers increased from negligible amounts to 790,000, 520,000 and 430,000 respectively.

The 'Cattle Kingdom' lasted no more than a couple of hectic decades. In the twentieth century it was to provide—posthumously—a boon for the film industry; but its real as opposed to its romanticized existence was conditioned by several hard economic factors. In its beginning was its end: the railroad that shipped its cattle to market eventually brought back in return settlers and farmers. Also good transportation and communications played no small part in the

[1] Cattle were first introduced into southern Texas by the Spaniards in the eighteenth century. The climate and vegetation were so ideal that a great cattle range already existed in the Nueces valley when Americans first invaded Texas.

immense speculative 'mania' of 1882–5. As the cattle boom developed uncontrollably, prices soared and capital poured into the industry from the East and from Europe. In 1881 the Prairie Cattle Company of Edinburgh declared a dividend of 28 per cent. Bidding in the East for cattle with which to stock Western ranges was bitterly competitive.[1] During the mania thousands of would-be 'ranchers' and millions of cattle swarmed over the Great Plains and neither men nor beasts could be supported. Veteran ranchers began enclosing their ranges to protect them from the new invaders, and countless stockbreeders' protective associations were organized.

The basic conditions for a slump existed by 1885: the Plains were heavily overstocked.[2] A series of historical accidents provided the 'immediate' cause of the collapse which came between 1885 and 1887: the bad winter of 1885–6, the withering hot summer of 1886 and the almost legendary winter of 1886–7 that killed off cattle in their thousands. The great 'livestock corporations' that had emerged could not stand the strain and went under in 1887.

Meanwhile from the South-west, over the Rockies via New Mexico, came sheep-farmers, and sheep in their hundreds of thousands. More important still from the opposite edge of the Plains the homesteader moved inexorably on, enclosing and farming, adapting himself at last to his new environment—with the help of barbed-wire fencing (first patented by J. F. Glidden of Illinois in 1874 and by the '80's made cheap owing to heavy competition in the wire industry), steel ploughs to cut the resisting prairie (in general use by the late '70's), and windmills to pump water (not in general use however until the '90's, because of the high cost of drilling operations). By 1890 the Great Plains were in the possession of the farmer and the 'rancher's frontier' was at an end.

In the same year the Superintendent of the Census stated that the 'unsettled area' had been 'so broken into by isolated bodies of settlement that there can hardly be said to be a frontier line'. Officially, the frontier was 'closed'. That is not to say that the Westward movement came to an abrupt end. It did not. There was perhaps little first-class *free* land left in 1890, but there was still much inferior land from which modern methods could extract a yield, and there was an abundance of *cheap* land. The 'closing' of the frontier therefore brought no 'sudden' or emphatic economic changes. The fact remains, however, that large-scale territorial expansion on the North American continent was now over. Many writers have pointed to

---

[1] The demand was so overwhelming that between 1882 and 1884 the numbers of eastern cattle transported westward as range stock *balanced* the numbers sent east to market (Billington, op. cit., p. 683).

[2] There were 9 million head of cattle in Wyoming alone in 1886—a figure beyond comparison with those given above for 1860 to 1880.

this when analysing the 'great aberration' of the 1890's that turned the American Republic into an 'imperialist' nation. More than any other single factor the existence of a boundless area of unoccupied land to the West helped to differentiate the economy of America from that of Europe. It allowed a free expansion of population and the absorption of masses of immigrants. It helped to shape the monetary, banking and transportation systems and dictated the direction and content of foreign trade.[1]

While the Great Plains were being claimed and reclaimed, nothing short of an 'Agricultural Revolution' was being enacted, or rather being consolidated (most of the technical developments necessary for the revolution had already appeared by 1860; only refinements and adaptations were now necessary). After 1860 innovations were applied for the first time on an extensive scale, and it was in part their adoption that enabled the farmer to assert his ascendancy in the West. The 'Agricultural Revolution', however, implied not only one but three factors: mechanization, reclamation and specialization. These alterations did not occur *in vacuo*; they took place in a social context, and brought ever-widening currents of social and political change in their wake. Not only were farms mechanized and scientific agricultural methods taken up, but there was a rapid growth of government interest in and aid to farming, a widespread movement for agricultural education, and a spate of agrarian discontent.

In 1910 there were over 6,300,000 farms, as against 2 million in 1860. This three-fold increase compared with a two-fold increase between 1785 and 1860. Average farm acreage in the second half of the century, on the other hand, fell from almost 200 (1860) to 138 1910). The total farmed acreage doubled, reaching nearly 880 million. Wheat production in 1910 was almost four times the 1860 figure, corn three and a half times, and cotton production three times.

On a wider view agriculture did not do so well: industrial growth was much greater, and consequently the proportion of the national wealth represented by agriculture fell considerably, from 56 per cent in 1850 to 21.8 per cent in 1912. Even though agriculture was made a subordinate part of an industrial economy, its growth was still if anything too rapid, depressing the price of foodstuffs, and (despite the increase in productivity) bringing diminishing returns for the farmer and distress to the farming class. There was an absolute increase in farm population over the period, but a steady fall in the proportion of the total population inhabiting farms.

Interest in conservation, irrigation and scientific method was stimulated by the official 'closing' of the frontier, and after about 1896

[1] See the last section of Chapter II, above.

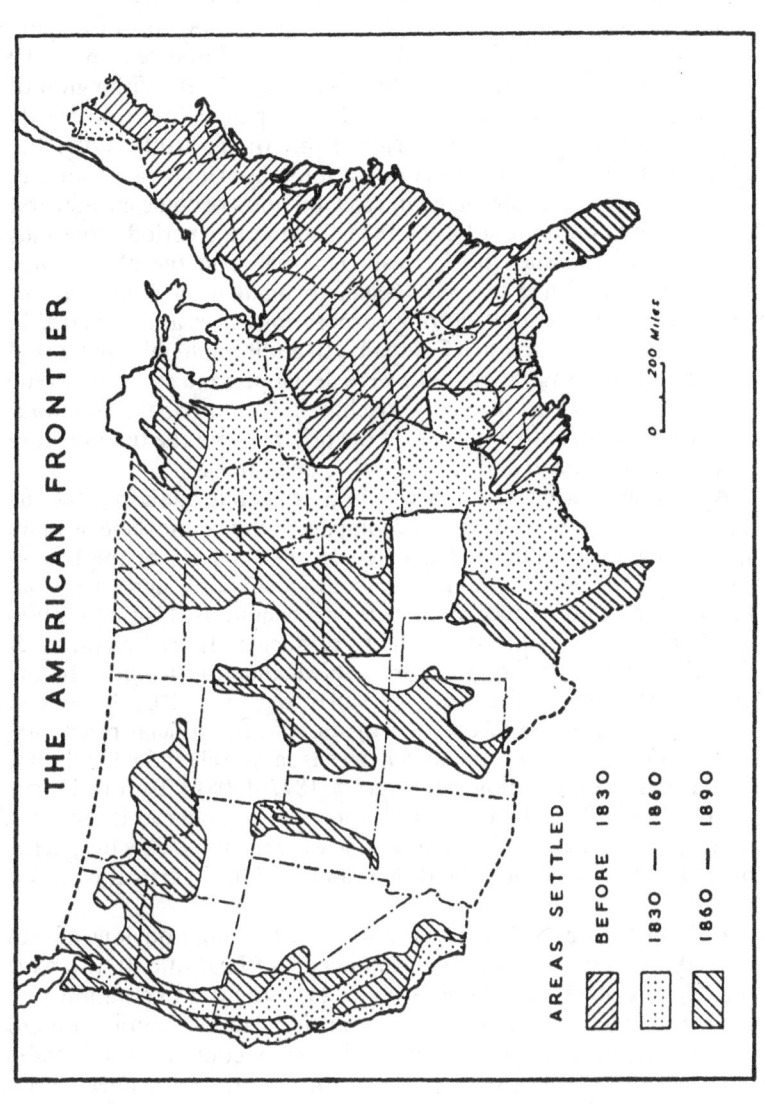

rising prices and land values, improved road transportation and more efficient machinery brought about better conditions for the farmer. By 1910 agriculture had attained some degree of stability.

Perhaps the most significant technical innovation was in reaping methods. A series of increasingly efficient inventions led up to the manufacture of the modern combine harvester. C. B. Withington of Wisconsin, by introducing his wire-binder patent in 1874, greatly improved upon an earlier harvester of the Marsh brothers of 1858. This was soon replaced, however, by John Appleby's twine-knotter which had been first considered in 1859, but did not come into general manufacture and use until after 1875. During this period thousands of patents were issued on harvesting devices and the McCormick firm (first established in 1847) began to build up a monopoly. In 1902 six harvester manufacturing corporations were amalgamated in the International Harvester Company. In addition, highly specialized ploughs and improved windmills were developed and as early as 1860 steam was applied to threshing machines. Total agricultural labour costs were soon cut to a quarter of the original, and the time spent in preparing the ground and sowing cut to one-fifteenth.

Agricultural mechanization was in a sense but one aspect of the industrial revolution. It was accompanied by a movement more specifically agricultural and devoted to the interests of the land—namely the increasing attention paid to reclamation and irrigation. Early irrigation on a successful scale was seen in the Mormon settlements of the arid state of Utah. Here ancient Indian methods of diverting mountain streams were copied and transformed. In the Gadsden Purchase area also, the valley region had by 1890 been entirely reclaimed by means of irrigation from artificial reservoirs. The history of this and similar schemes is inevitably linked with that of the first Conservation Movement (1877–1908).[1] By the Desert Land Act of 1877, the Federal Government announced its concern for irrigation schemes, although the measure proved ineffective, benefiting on the whole only herdsmen and fraudulent irrigation companies.

In 1894 the Carey Act checked some of the more obvious abuses by making water rights an inalienable part of land title. It also gave the 'Desert States' a million acres of land each, on condition that they 'reclaimed' them. The land was sold at nominal prices (about 50 cents an acre) to people who had already contracted to reclaim land and to purchase water rights from the state governments (at a cost of about $30 to $40 per acre of irrigated land, payable in instalments). Several states took advantage of the Act, but generally its effect was limited to the most fertile and easily irrigated areas. In any case, as it applied only to public lands the scope of the mea-

[1] See Chapter XII, below, pp. 202–4.

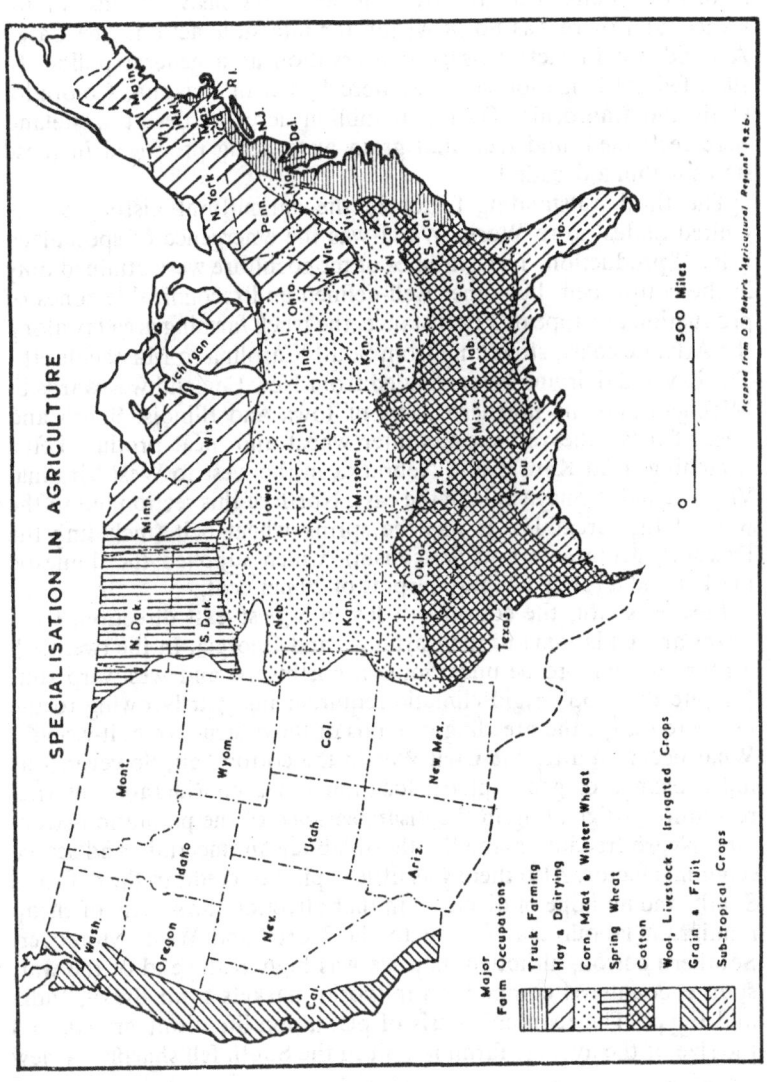

sure as a reclamation act has continually narrowed with the constant alienation of such lands under other enactments. Many problems remained to be solved after 1900: farmers were left quite unable to reconstruct dams after the frequent and very heavy floods for instance, and there was no provision for interstate action. The Carey Act did not in fact envisage conservation as a general policy. In 1902 federal irrigation schemes were begun in Arizona, Colorado, Utah and California. Over two million acres of desert wasteland were reclaimed, and fruit and grain were being produced in these states within a decade.[1]

The third outstanding factor in the agricultural history of the United States up to World War I was the emergence of specialized belts of production. The extremes of monoculture were attained only in the cotton belt, but other well-defined and recognizable zones of production did appear. For instance, the truck farming area lay along the Atlantic coast, stretching from South Carolina to Massachusetts. The hay and dairying belt extended from New England westwards to Michigan and the northern parts of Iowa and Illinois. South and west of it lay the vast corn, winter wheat and meat product belts, stretching from Kansas and Nebraska in the west to West Virginia, Virginia and Pennsylvania in the east. North of this section but to the west of the Great Lakes was the spring wheat belt (including the Dakotas, Minnesota and Wisconsin), which supplied the domestic market and a foreign export surplus of 20 per cent.

Further south, the cotton belt lay in a west–east direction, from Texas and Oklahoma to the Carolinas and Georgia. In the twentieth century it seems to be undergoing a northward and westward shift (despite the crop's rigid climatic requirements) partly owing to the desire to escape the breeding-grounds of the destructive boll-weevil.[2] What occurred after the Civil War in the cotton belt, however, was not a change of geographical location but a considerable internal revolution, originating in the disappearance of the plantation structure. Negro freedom made Southern labour an uncertain and scarce economic factor. Also there was little capital or credit in the defeated South, and no hope of diverting in that direction the stream of cheap immigrant labour that flowed to the North and West. Moreover, Southern cotton, although its price was high at the end of the war, soon encountered competition in world markets from Brazil, India and Egypt. The economic basis of plantation life disintegrated, and the size of the average farming unit in the South fell sharply. A new

[1] For further developments after 1900 see below, Chapter XIII, pp. 222–8.
[2] See Chapter II, above, p. 19. The boll-weevil migrated from Mexico to Texas in about 1892 and since then spread over the whole cotton belt. In so far as it led to the diversification of agriculture in the South, its effects have not been entirely bad.

character rose to prominence within the Southern economy—the country merchant—who helped recovery by accepting credit, but exerted over the small planter and farmer a rigid control. Crops were mortgaged by 'crop liens' even before the seeds were planted, and this system of financing certainly helped to cause 'overproduction' and agricultural depression in the South. Another device engendered by the decline of the plantation was 'sharecropping'. This was a system of tenancy for the Negro and the landless white who had no means of buying land and would not work for wages. The rent was paid in kind, by sharing the crop with the landowner. By 1880 sharecropping was a widespread Southern institution. While the crop lien and sharecropping systems involved many social disadvantages, cotton production nevertheless doubled between 1860 and 1899. During these years, Texas, Mississippi and Georgia became the leading three cotton states, the order having formerly been Mississippi, Alabama and Louisiana. Texas and Tennessee became centres of cottonseed milling, over 300 mills being built in the south.

A further specialized belt was formed by the Mountain States and semi-arid parts of the Plains (Montana, Idaho, Wyoming, Nevada, Utah, Colorado, Arizona and New Mexico). Its agricultural production was chiefly wool and livestock. The three Pacific coast states (Washington, Oregon and California) were a grain and fruit producing region. Obviously these belts were not exclusively devoted to the produce that characterized them. Even the cotton belt produced timber, corn, wheat and livestock, and no mention has been made of non-agrarian products such as minerals. An important citrus-fruit industry grew up and was to be found in several areas, including California, the Rio Grande part of Texas, New Mexico, Arizona and Florida.

The mechanization and expansion of agricultural production gave rise to several new industries which, because they depended heavily on farming, are sometimes called, perhaps ambiguously, *agricultural industries*. These included the manufacture of farm implements and machinery, meat-packing, the canning of fruits, vegetables and a variety of 'processed' foods, and milling. From its inception in 1847 until 1902 the McCormick firm dominated the agricultural implement industry. About 4,500 McCormick reapers were already in use in the grain areas by 1850, and when combine harvesters came upon the scene the firm was quick to snatch up inventions (e.g. Withington's wire binder of 1874) to improve its models. The 200 firms competing in this sphere were cut down to six, which amalgamated in 1902 to form the International Harvester Company, supplying over 80 per cent of American needs until World War I.

The combine harvester had untold effects on American grain production, which in turn necessitated large-scale improvements in the handling, transporting and storing of grain. Steam power, the introduction of grain 'elevators' (capable of holding up to 1 million bushels in storage and of loading ships at the rate of 10,000 bushels an hour), and co-operative bulk handling not only filled the gap but did so with great economy. The increase in cereal production was twice as rapid as the growth of population, and export totals leapt until the United States supplied at least half the total needs of the wheat-importing countries.

The meat-packing industry still contains firms whose history goes back beyond 1865, such as Swift, Armour, and Morris, but it was the Civil War that provided the chief stimulus. In 1850 Chicago was not an important meat-packing centre; by 1865 it led the nation. The reasons for this rapid transformation are to be found in canal and rail transportation developments, in the war, in the growth of the range cattle industry and in the change-over in the Chicago area from wheat to corn cultivation. Corn implies, in the United States, pigs because they are traditionally fed on it.[1] The change from wheat to corn thus brought a huge growth in the number of pigs raised in the belt after 1865. In Chicago and Cincinnati the packing industry chiefly dealt with pigs (because there was a much steadier demand for pork than for beef) until the introduction of refrigeration.

By 1870 most of the larger abattoirs had rooms chilled with natural ice, and experiments were being made to introduce chilled freight wagons. Ten years later, wagons cooled by a continuously circulating current of chilled air were quite common, and sales of fresh beef to Eastern markets were now possible. The numbers of cattle slaughtered in Chicago doubled twice between 1875 and 1890, and the city became the world's largest abattoir.[2] The packing industry began vertical integration by taking over transport and farming, and besides achieving great economies of scale, put to good use many fatty and other 'waste' products previously thrown away, making many important by-products such as lard, soap, tallow, glue and fertilizer. After 1890 new centres further west and south came into prominence, including Omaha (Nebraska), St. Joseph (Missouri) and Fort Worth and Dallas (Texas).

Up to 1900 the chief canning states were Maryland and California. The industry began in Europe but was developed most fully in the United States, and was given a clear and unmistakable impetus by the Civil War. When Gail Borden opened his first condensed-milk canning factory in New York in 1861 its entire output was acquired

[1] See F. A. Shannon, *The Farmer's Last Frontier* (Vol. V in Rinehart & Co.'s *Economic History of the United States*, New York, 1945), pp. 165–9, for a discussion of the 'corn–hog cycle'.

[2] Upton Sinclair's famous novel *The Jungle* is a grim picture of the social conditions associated with the rise of this industry.

by the Union Government to supply troops. The canning of fruits and vegetables was also stimulated by military contracts. Later factors in the industry's expansion included the use of calcium chloride (to give higher temperatures and extend the range of foods that could be canned), the mechanization of can-making (1885), increased bacteriological knowledge and control, urban growth, and specialization by area (e.g. Maine for sweet corn, Wisconsin for peas, Alaska for salmon).[1]

New York, Pennsylvania and Illinois were the three principal flour-milling states in 1870, but during the next two decades the mills of Minnesota (especially at Minneapolis) developed new milling processes, captured the domestic and broke into the foreign markets. By 1890 Minneapolis was turning out over seven million barrels of flour annually, almost 90 per cent of which was controlled by four large corporations. The milling interests encouraged and exploited railway growth and made the city the wheat-marketing centre for the whole North-west. After 1890 Minnesota in turn encountered the competition of new milling centres in Kansas (which in 1892 was the leading wheat-producing state), Texas, Oklahoma and New York (Buffalo). Buffalo is America's greatest milling centre nowadays, with the advantages of easy distribution to Eastern markets, cheap (lake-steamer) transportation of North-western and Canadian wheat, and cheap power. Minneapolis has declined and the chief milling companies moved to Buffalo which surpassed its rival in output in 1930. This change is symptomatic of the decline of the North-west as a wheat area, the declining quality of its wheat and the change-over to dairying on a considerable scale.[2]

Such changes did not proceed without the notice and interest of the Federal Government. Since 1865 in fact both federal and state authorities had attempted to align themselves with economic forces by initiating and encouraging developments in scientific farming. The federal Department of Agriculture began in 1862 and a special Bureau of Animal Husbandry (set up in 1884) initiated research in animal diseases. The Department eventually accrued a variety of powers, including control over the import and export of animals, the administration of the Pure Food and Drugs Act (1906), the Cotton Futures Acts (1914 and 1917) and the Federal-Aid Road Act (1916), and regulatory authority over forestry work (1905) and meat inspection. Georgia instituted the first state Department of Agriculture

[1] For quick factual reference to this and other industries (e.g. dairy products, beverages, baking) use the *Encyclopaedia of the Social Sciences* (New York, 1930–5).

[2] This is mentioned briefly in H. F. Williamson, op. cit., pp. 437–43. The chief work however is V. G. Pickett and R. S. Vaile, *The Decline of Northwestern Flour Milling* (Minneapolis, 1933).

in 1874 and other states followed suit (e.g. Tennessee, 1875). A division of labour developed: agricultural colleges supervised experimental and extension work, and the state Departments regulated standards of production by investigating adulteration and the issue of false substitutes, and by enforcing quarantine and other methods of checking pests and diseases.

Regulations alone however could do little. To effect a change of any depth and significance it was necessary first to bring about a change of 'heart' in the men concerned. Agricultural education was an attempt to do this.

The Ohio Enabling Act of 1802, governing the admission of Ohio to the Union, was the first federal measure to contain a clause providing that one 'section' out of each 'township' should be granted to the state, the proceeds from which were to be used for education. In 1803 the special Act governing the Mississippi Territory contained a similar clause. But the first state college specifically intended to teach agricultural sciences was begun by Michigan in 1857. In 1862 the Morrill Act made the land-grant college system more general: it gave each state a land grant of 30,000 acres for each Representative and Senator it had in Congress, provided that it established at least one college within five years. No minimum sales value of the land was imposed, and there was much speculation. Most states sold it for about one and a quarter dollars an acre. (Ezra Cornell, however, managed by skilful speculation to obtain an endowment of about five and a half million dollars for Cornell University (Ithaca, N.Y.) out of the sale of New York State's western land allotment.) On the whole the new colleges lacked financial backing and came up against the shortage of trained agricultural instructors and the rooted opposition of the older academic institutions. The second Morrill Act (1890) gave federal cash grants to the new colleges, thus enabling them to overcome economic difficulties and achieve academic standing. In addition it liberated funds for the creation of separate Negro colleges in Mississippi, Alabama, Florida, the Carolinas, Virginia and Delaware. Morrill's work was extended by the Smith-Lever (1914) and Smith-Hughes (1917) Acts, and colleges were supplemented by agricultural research stations, of which the first to receive public support was set up in Connecticut in 1875. The Hatch Act of 1887 provided for research stations in all states possessing a land-grant college and gave an annual grant of $15,000 to each state for the purpose. This grant was doubled by the Adams Act (1906) and was further enlarged in the 1920's and '30's.

At the turn of the century American farmers were gradually emerging from a long status of economic inferiority, and rejecting provincialism and obsolete agricultural methods. The older settled areas, encouraged by state and federal authorities, began to abandon monoculture and its concomitant evil—soil erosion—and turned increasingly to crop rotation, careful tillage, the use of manure, artificial fertilizers, and machinery, and the adoption of irrigation. The exhaustion of 'free land' which was signified in 1890 by the 'closing of the frontier' marked the beginning of the end for frontier farming. Some years of relative prosperity and calm for the farmer were to follow. There could be little doubt however that the chief purpose of American agriculture was now usually deemed to be to facilitate domestic industrial growth by producing large farm surpluses. These agricultural exports almost covered the total cost of American imports, and also constituted a large share of American exports. But the great collapse which was to come in the twentieth century was merely obscured from general view by the curve of rising prices.

SUGGESTED FURTHER READING

BENEDICT, M. R. *Farm Policies of the United States, 1790–1950* (New York, 1953).

BILLINGTON, R. A. *Westward Expansion: A History of the American Frontier* (New York, 1949).

SHANNON, F. A. *The Farmer's Last Frontier: Agriculture, 1860–1897* (Vol. V in Rinehart and Co.'s *Economic History of the United States*, New York, 1945).

WEBB, W. P. *The Great Plains: A Study in Institutions and Environment* (Boston, 1931).

IX

AGRARIAN UNREST AND LABOUR

The Granger Movement, 1867–86: Co-operative schemes, Granger laws and the Wabash decision (1886) – The Currency Movement and Farmers' Alliances – Populism, 1890–6 – The return of prosperity – The post-war Labour Movement – Trade Unionism: the National Labour Union; the Knights of Labour; the American Federation of Labour. Unrest in the '80's and '90's: the Pullman Strike (1894) and its implications – Labour in 1917; the I.W.W. and after – Character of the Labour Movement in America.

STATE and federal interest in agriculture was partly the result of the agrarian unrest that was a principal element in American political and social history after 1865. The debtor West became caught in post-war economic insecurity and the effects of the crisis of 1873, and the struggling farmer found it difficult even to meet the interest on his loans. To survive in a society that favoured industry and business and respected organization in general, the American farmers had to organize themselves. This was not easy: they were vast in numbers, extremely diverse in interests and background, and widely dispersed. The sectional controversy and the Civil War had done much to destroy any unity they might have previously displayed. But, out of sheer desperation, a series of farmers' movements emerged, each motivated by particular empiric grievances rather than an over-all plan. They advocated a variety of reforms: railway and anti-trust legislation, currency inflation, government aid for research and education, government loan facilities, and land reform. They worked through 'third parties' and by pressure on the two major parties.

The Patrons of Husbandry was the first important farmers' grouping that emerged. It was a secret 'fraternal' order, begun in 1867 by Oliver H. Kelley, an agent of the new Department of Agriculture. Its ritual, titles and constitution were based on farm life, and its aims were mainly educative and social. In 1868 local lodges were established called 'granges', from which the members received their more frequent name, Grangers. Kelley's hope was to improve social and cultural conditions in rural communities and induce farming men and women to adopt scientific ideas.

At first the order grew but slowly. Then in the early '70's, the creeping paralysis of economic depression made itself felt: eight and a half thousand local lodges were established in the crisis year alone (1873), and by 1875 the National Grange could claim as many as 20,000 branches. This accelerated growth was accompanied by a distinct change in outlook. Farmers of the North-west had seized upon the Grange as a means of attacking a particular problem of great concern to them at that time: railway abuses. The Patrons of Husbandry had become a vehicle in the war against transportation monopoly.

Nevertheless this was not their sole concern. They tried to encourage the use of co-operative enterprises (dairies, warehouses, grain elevators) for instance, and spread a deep hostility to 'middlemen', retailers and the artificially maintained prices of manufactured goods. States Granges operated insurance companies, banks (as in California), agricultural implement factories, packing plants and co-operative retail shops. These ambitious co-operative schemes failed disastrously in both spheres, distribution and production. The 'Rochdale Pioneers' plan did not take root so well in the Midwest as in England, and the Granger industrial concerns came up against the powerful hostility of the railway companies and private manufacturers.[1]

Despite its failure in this respect, the Grange did give farmers valuable experience and education in co-operative effort and stimulated the spread of farmers' political parties, especially in the years 1873–6. These gained control of several state legislatures and managed to force through Granger laws (restricting the activities of transport and elevator corporations) in Illinois, Wisconsin, Iowa and Minnesota. The new state constitution adopted by Illinois in 1870 proclaimed:

'The General Assembly shall pass laws to correct abuses and to prevent unjust discrimination and extortion in the rates of freight and passenger traffics on the different railroads in this state, and enforce such laws by adequate penalties.'

Accordingly in 1871 the state fixed maximum passenger rates, required freight charges based solely on distance and set up a regulatory board of railway and warehouse commissioners. When the Illinois Supreme Court invalidated the law, the Grangers simply voted a recalcitrant judge out of office, passing a more efficient law

[1] See S. J. Buck, *The Granger Movement* (Cambridge, Mass., 1913).

in 1873.[1] The next year an elaborate code was passed by the Iowa legislature, dispensing with the commission idea and fixing instead by direct statute the rates for all railroads within the state. California, Missouri, Nebraska and several Southern states put condemnations of railroad abuses into their revised constitutions in the '70's. The U.S. Supreme Court upheld the Granger laws against the railroads in four cases in October 1876, the most famous of which were *Munn* v. *Illinois* and *Peik* v. *The Chicago and Northwestern Railroad*. On the whole, though, the laws were difficult to enforce and the powerful railroad companies employed very skilful lawyers. In any case the depression of the '70's temporarily slowed down railway building and caused some anxiety lest construction should stop in the West altogether. Rate wars, moreover, resulted in a permanent lowering of freight rates, and this weakened the position of the Grangers. Ten years after it had sanctioned the laws, the U.S. Supreme Court reversed its view in the case of the *Wabash, St. Louis and Pacific Railroad Company* v. *Illinois* (1886). Its decision destroyed 90 per cent of the state railroad rate laws by definitely and explicitly limiting the authority of individual states to intra-state commerce. Only Congress could regulate interstate commerce, by legislation that was national in scope. The Interstate Commerce Act (1887), that was the logical outcome, is dealt with in Chapter X.

The decay of the Granger movement was to some extent the measure of the resurgence of the currency issue. Western farmers were anxious about the currency. They found interest rates high and loans difficult to obtain; they were controlled by Eastern financiers; they had to accept Eastern prices for their crops, and submit to extortionate railway rates. What happened in the sphere of monetary policy was therefore of central importance to them, and in the '80's they became involved in the Greenback, Free Silver and Populist movements.

At first farmers were slow to accept the inflationist notions adopted by the Greenback and Free Silver men.[2] The pro-Greenback party called the National Labour Union, for instance, appearing in 1866, had been chiefly an industrial wage-earners' movement. Its failure in the Presidential election of 1872 (when its candidate O'Connor polled under 30,000 votes) caused the initiative to pass to agrarian interests, and by 1876 a new group had formed, mostly with farm support. This was the Independent National Party established at Indianapolis with Peter Cooper as its leader, and representative members from Illinois, Indiana, Michigan, Iowa, Kansas and Missouri. In the election of 1876 Cooper gained a negligible 82,000 votes (but an increase over

[1] On the 4th of July in the same year the *Farmers' Declaration of Independence* was announced.

[2] For a fuller treatment of these movements see Chapter XI, below, pp. 186–9.

his predecessor). Finally, the Greenback Labour Party was founded at Toledo in 1878, with strong agrarian support from all the Middle West, and it gained one million votes and fourteen Congressmen in the congressional elections of that year. An avowed agrarian, J. B. Weaver, was the party's Presidential candidate in 1880 and he polled 307,306 votes, almost all of which came from the upper Mississippi valley—the former stronghold of the Grangers.

The Greenback party, lacking support from the urban proletariat, could not withstand the termination of the depression, the rise in prices and improved crops, and the effects of the Specie Resumption Act (1875) which provided for the resumption of cash payments on 1 January 1879, and made paper money circulate like gold. The party declined rapidly in the early 1880's and its most prominent leaders later joined the Populists.

The currency question was now changing to one of *free silver*, and former Greenbackers adopted the idea of the free and unlimited coinage of silver (at a ratio of 16 to 1) to replace their discredited 'Greenbacks'. Silver-mining interests and debtor Western farmers combined to urged the re-monetization of silver, the former because they believed this would increase the value of silver (which had fallen owing to vast silver discoveries like the Comstock Lode in Nevada) and the latter because they believed that free coinage of silver would mean a cheaper dollar.[1]

At the same time the vacuum caused by the collapse of the Granges was being filled by the Farmers' Alliances which were modelled upon them—the National Farmers' Alliance in the Northwest and the Farmers' Alliance and Industrial Union in the South. The southern group, which fused various spontaneous unplanned growths (e.g. the Agricultural Wheel of Arkansas, the Texas State Alliance and the Farmers' Union of Louisiana) was established in 1888 to prevent the 'encroachment of concentrated capital and the tyranny of monopoly'. The northern group, less closely knit, was first formed in 1880 by Milton George, a Chicago editor of a farmers' paper, the *Western Rural*. Within a decade it was fully organized in ten North-western states, the bulk of its power coming from the wheat areas of Minnesota, the Dakotas, Kansas and Nebraska.

A Convention at St. Louis in 1889 failed to unite the two wings of the movement, the rift being the result mainly of conflicting economic needs, such as the competition between North-western lard and butter and its Southern substitute, cotton seed oil.[2] But resolutions were drafted that included demands for 'free silver', nationalization of the railways and telegraph companies, land reforms, government subsidies to agriculture and a hint of tariff reform. In the election

[1] See *ibid*.
[2] J. D. Hicks, *The Populist Revolt* (Minneapolis, 1931), pp. 114–25.

struggle of 1890 the Farmers' Alliances merged into the now more prominent third party—the People's Party, or Populists.

In the decade after 1887, agricultural depression returned to the Middle West in an intensified form. Drought on the Great Plains cut Kansas corn production from 158 million bushels (1885) to 55 million (1890). The Farmers' Alliances were reluctant to enter the political arena, and nothing was to be gained it seemed from either of the two major parties. The result was the appearance of the People's Party more or less informally in 1890 in Kansas, Nebraska and South Dakota. The Populists of the North-west allied themselves at first with the Democrats, and despite the Knights of Labour element in the party, it was on the whole an agrarian movement demanding currency inflation and attacking silver demonetization as the 'crime of 1873'. Several federal Senators and Representatives and one or two State Governors were elected in 1890 on platforms that favoured the Populists, and in Kansas the party secured a working majority in the state legislature. This victory urged on the zealots and a national political party was formally announced at the Cincinatti Convention of May 1891.

Although Populism ended in a whimper, it certainly began with a bang. The St. Louis Convention (February 1892) declared:

'We meet in the midst of a nation brought to the verge of moral, political and material ruin. Corruption dominates. . . . The people are demoralized. . . . The newspapers are subsidized or muzzled; public opinion silenced; business prostrated, our homes covered with mortgages, labour impoverished and the land concentrating in the hands of capitalists. . . . From the same prolific womb of governmental injustice we breed two great classes—paupers and millionaires.'

About 1,400 delegates in Cincinatti had already pledged themselves to a programme in which many of the aims of industrial labour (such as the eight-hour day, universal manhood suffrage and the direct election of the Senate) stood side by side with agrarian demands. The *National Economist* was begun as the official organ of the party, and during the summer of 1892 Western and Southern sections, temporarily united by the enthusiastic spirit of the day, wholeheartedly cheered the 'Omaha Platform'. This conceived three great reforms: in finance (free silver), in transportation (nationalization), and in public land policy (opposing excessive grants to private corporations).[1]

[1] Additional demands were: a graduated income tax, postal savings banks, the Australian ballot, the Initiative and Referendum, and the 'Sub-Treasury' Scheme produced earlier by the Southern Alliance (government loans to farmers based on crops deposited in federal warehouses and elevators).

The ex-Greenback nominee and Civil War veteran James B. Weaver was chosen to head the Populist ticket in 1892, and won over one million votes in the country and twenty-two in the electoral college. The People's Party swept Nevada, Idaho, Colorado, Kansas, much of Nebraska and parts of Wyoming; carried off ten seats in the federal House of Representatives and five in the Senate; put about 1,500 county officials and state legislators in office, and triumphantly predicted an irrevocable victory of the 'people' over the 'plutocrats' for 1896.

The fateful, scurrilous presidential campaign of 1896 did not fulfil this prophecy. The Populists supported the Western and Southern Democrats under fiery William Jennings Bryan, and McKinley won the presidency for the Republicans on a platform that defended gold, protective tariffs and a 'firm hand' in foreign affairs. Sixteen years of Republican rule ensued (McKinley, T. Roosevelt, Taft) and after-events revealed 1896 to mark the climax of the currency struggle. Poor European and Indian harvests led to a rise in the price of American agricultural staples, large-scale production expanded pushing up foreign trade figures, and the strain on gold was relieved by a threefold increase in world gold output. The amount of money in circulation increased and the Currency Act of 1900 established the gold standard.

Like the Greenback movement, Populism was wiped away by the rising tide of prosperity. Many of the demands of its followers (post office banks, direct election of Senators, railway legislation, inflation, and above all, higher farm prices) were eventually achieved—in good time. Like the Greenbackers too, the Populists conceived no plan for economic and social reorganization, and but for railway nationalization, they fought mainly for ephemeral—even local—reforms to meet particular needs. This was not at all like the empiricism of, say, the Fabians in England, an empiricism within a general plan of social regeneration (in the case of the Fabians, democratic socialism). They had, in brief, little to offer that could hold a party together over any considerable length of time, little to offer that could outlast historical change or an upward slope of the trade cycle.[1] This is not to imply by any means that America had heard the last of agrarian unrest; the calm was but a long interlude.

The Granger movement, Populism and Free Silver clouded over and obscured the Labour movement. Labour organization in the decades after the Civil War was in any case uncertain and confused: its leaders alternately embraced and rejected politics, accepted and discarded various theories for social regeneration varying from the

[1] This is a personal conclusion. It is thus even less 'established' than the 'established' conclusions of text-book tabulations.

Single Tax to Anarchism, and attempted to form a united confederation—but left out unskilled, casual and Negro labour.

Nevertheless the economic revolution and the Civil War helped to break down parochial barriers and stimulate organization on a national scale. The number of workers in unions increased from about 170,000 in 1869 to about 300,000 in 1871, and by 1872 thirty-two national trade unions were established, including bricklayers, shoemakers, typesetters, ironmoulders, miners and locomotive engineers. At the same time, however, there was a vast increase in population and an even higher rate of increase in the proportion engaged in industrial labour. The number employed in factories, mines and railroad transportation multiplied five-fold between 1860 and 1900, reaching about 5 million. Trade union enlistments at no point in this period exceeded a fifth of the total labour force. It seems that most of the time the bulk of the workers were convinced by rising wage-rates that a negative policy was the best policy, and, with notable exceptions, acted in conformity with the brittle employers' philosophy expressed in Carnegie's short-sighted but famous essay, *Triumphant Democracy* (New York, 1888).

But, of course, capitalist development was uneven, and during cyclical business crises employers continued to resort to such traditional techniques as intermittent unemployment and wage-cuts. During the late nineteenth century America was made painfully aware by a series of events of what might happen during a clash of the two opposed forces, Capital and Labour. The railroad strike of 1877, the mining strike of 1886, the steel strike of 1892, and the famous Chicago strike of 1894, were overt examples of 'class warfare'.

Firstly, however, we must examine the growth of trade unionism. Immediately after the Civil War, in 1866, William H. Sylvis of the Ironmoulders' Union tried to federate American labour and reform organizations in the National Labour Union. A Congress of seventy-seven delegates met at Baltimore and endorsed a platform the central plank of which was the eight-hour day. Ira Steward, a Boston machinist and leading light in the Machinists' and Blacksmiths' Union, was the chief working-class theorist of the eight-hour day. His supporters claimed:

> 'Whether you work by the piece or work by the day,
> Decreasing the hours increases the pay.'

Steward aimed at the ultimate abolition of profits through their absorption into wages, and he wanted to bring this about gradually, by legislation. In the same year that Sylvis established his National Labour Union, Steward organized the Grand Eight-Hour-League of Massachusetts, which was copied by several other states. Two years later President Andrew Johnson signed a bill proclaiming the eight-hour day for federal employees on public works, thus setting a similar example to that set by President Van Buren in 1840.[1] Eight-hour legislation was enacted by several states in the '60's (New York, Illinois, Wisconsin, Missouri and Connecticut in 1867 and California in 1869), but was normally weakened by the lack of provision for inspection.

The other aims of the National Labour Union included producers' co-operatives and the admittance of Negroes, newly emancipated, to trade unions. The majority of its members favoured arbitration and conciliation rather than strike action and were mildly 'reformist' in outlook. They involved themselves not only with the 'co-ops' that became discredited in the late '60's and early '70's, but with such 'third party' movements as the currency agitation. The prestige of the N.L.U. with industrial labour declined rapidly, no trade union sending a delegate to the congress of 1871. As we have seen, it suffered disastrous political defeat (as the National Labour and Reform Party with a Greenback platform) in the presidential election of 1872.

Adopting Professor Perlman's phrase,[2] two 'nuclei' survived the crisis of 1873 and depression of the '70's that dislocated most of the organized labour movement. These were the Noble Order of the Knights of Labour and several unions grouped around the International Cigar Makers' Union which eventually became the American Federation of Labour.[3] The Knights of Labour organization was founded in Philadelphia in 1869 by Uriah S. Stephens, a tailor and ex-candidate for the ministry. It began as a secret, ritualistic group with a three-fold aim: to educate public opinion on the need to give Labour a just share of the wealth it created, to advance legislation 'to lighten the exhaustiveness of toil', and finally to give each other mutual aid in times of distress. The Order grew quickly and by 1873 had eighty local assemblies. A centralizing move was made in that year, the seat of control being called 'Assembly No. 1'. During the '70's the Knights gained many new members owing to the defection of trade union organizations. The number of national unions was reduced from over thirty to six by 1878, and total membership from about 500,000 to 50,000.

---

[1] See Chapter III, p. 42. The 1868 Act did not apply to work contracted out to private employers. [2] Op cit., p. 68.

[3] Three further movements, all of which failed to survive in the '70's, were: the Knights of St. Crispin (a shoemakers' organization established in 1867), the Industrial Brotherhood (a loose federation of about thirty national trade unions), and the Sovereigns of Industry (a consumers' co-operative organization established in Massachusetts in 1874 and finally dissolved in 1880).

Another cause of the expansion of the Knights of Labour was the miserable failure of the railway strike of 1877 followed by wage-cuts and retaliatory 'blacklisting' of prominent unionists by employers in Baltimore, Pittsburgh, Chicago, Toledo and St. Louis. A kind of general strike ensued, accompanied by wild disorders.[1] In Pittsburgh a pitched battle developed, the militia killed seventeen demonstrators, and five million dollars' worth of damage was done to railway property. Employers everywhere took heavy reprisals—and the secrecy of the Knights attracted new followers.

During the 1880's the Order grew to five and a half times its former size, and returning economic prosperity in 1879, together with the election of a new 'Grand Master Workman' (T. V. Powderly), brought about the abolition of secrecy. The 'hard times' after 1884 led to further increases in membership and forced the leaders to accept, albeit reluctantly, the notion of 'industrial warfare'—the use of strike and boycott. Under the leadership of Powderly the Knights of Labour became a national force and took an important part in many national strikes. A strike against wage reductions was called in February 1885 on three railways of the Gould system—the Wabash, the Missouri Pacific and the Missouri, Kansas and Pacific. It was successful in preventing the reductions and forced from the unscrupulous Jay Gould a promise that he would not use the black-list, and would in future submit disputes to arbitration. These sensational results swelled membership to 700,000 and the Knights even managed to squeeze from Congress a law prohibiting the importation of cheap contract labour.

In the following year, though, they overplayed their hand. A strike was called in March 1886 on the Gould railroad in the Southwest that brought business to a halt and alienated public opinion. In May the Knights were forced to the point of unconditional surrender. 1886 was a year of great upheaval generally: the nation was swept by 'sympathetic' strikes and lock-outs, and waves of destruction. The rank and file of the Knights of Labour gave their support to the May Day strikes organized by the Federation of Organized Trades and Labour Unions of the United States and Canada[2] in favour of the general adoption of the eight-hour day, and three days later the Haymarket Riot (Chicago) came as the calamitous climax.

[1] In the anthracite region of eastern Pennsylvania the defeat of a miners' union in 1869 led to the growth of a secret organization—the Molly Maguires—which used terrorism and assassination. Its leaders were caught and executed in 1876. It is now known that part of the violence was instigated by the employers themselves, as an excuse to dissolve the organization.

[2] A body set up in 1881 modelled on the British T.U.C., which later became the more famous American Federation of Labour.

A mass meeting was called to protest against the killing of strikers of the McCormick Corporation by the police. Anarchist speakers (members of the so-called 'Black International') addressed the crowd, and tempers became frayed as the police advanced to disperse the meeting. A bomb was thrown. One policeman was killed, seven civilians fatally injured and fifty or more wounded. After a trial which caused an outcry in labour and socialist circles in Europe as well as America (e.g. in William Morris's paper, *Commonweal*), eight men were convicted of murder and four actually executed.[1]

The Knights of Labour, along with other labour groups, were wrongly blamed for the Haymarket affair, and 1886 proved to be the turning-point in their history. The Order had included too many conflicting demands and pressure groups. It had supported, during its existence, the eight-hour day, 'free soil', feminism, officially recognized arbitration machinery, co-operation, abolition of child and convict labour, a graduated income tax, post office savings banks, nationalization of railroads and telegraph services, full legal protection for trade unions, factory and mines acts, public health codes, abolition of the contract system for public works, and the setting up of a Bureau of Labour Statistics. These diverse social reforms were too attractive to its leaders, who gave little time to trade union affiliation and organization. No reserve fund was maintained and strikes were called with little or no preparation. Moreover, the failure of the great South-western strike of 1886 and of all the 200 co-operative enterprises begun by the Knights (none were left by 1888) had a bad effect on internal morale and external prestige. Nothing succeeds like success. At the opening of 1886 the Knights of Labour had seemed strong, unified, and well directed; at the end of the year the same organization seemed overcentralized, torn by internal dissensions and jealousies, and lacking in sound leadership.

In 1893 when the last blow was struck—the replacing of Powderly by a farmer-editor—membership had dropped to 10 per cent (70,000). But a new organization had already established its hegemony over the American labour movement. This, the American Federation of Labour,[2] was firmly fixed on a craft basis. An idealistic hope of uniting labour of all skills, creeds and colours was certainly not the 'unspoken major premiss' of A.F.L. philosophy. Far from it. Leaders trained in European (and especially British) methods, like Gompers, Strasser and McGuire, were motivated by a hardbitten, 'job conscious' attitude quite unlike the Owenite enthusiasm

[1] Of the remaining four, one young man committed suicide in prison in a particularly ghastly, bungling way, and the rest were pardoned by Governor Altgeld in 1893.

[2] See Lewis L. Lorwin, *The American Federation of Labour* (Washington, 1933).

of the 'Knights' of Labour. Their principal goals were to secure decent wages and fair hours, build up closely knit unions of skilled artisans and legalize collective bargaining. Very similar in aims to the conservative 'Junta' that ruled the T.U.C. in Britain until the socialist revival of the '80's, the A.F.L. made no attempt to become a comprehensive Labour Movement and eschewed politics or the notion of independent labour representation.[1]

The A.F.L. was first organized in Pittsburgh in 1881 and then reorganized five years later. Gompers, who became its President from 1882 until his death in 1924 (except for one year), had already experimented successfully with the International Cigar Makers' Union, concentrating on building a national union of artisans with a well-organized central authority and paid secretariat, a union fund, regular union dues, and a mutual 'benefit' system covering illness and death. By 1879 the Cigar Makers' had become a 'model' union on these lines. Membership of the A.F.L. was restricted to trades and labour unions, representation in the federation being based on membership numbers. A 3 cents subscription per head was to provide a permanent revenue. Membership increased from 50,000 (1884) to 190,000 (1890) and gained heavily from the decline of the Knights of Labour. At the outbreak of World War I, the A.F.L. had fully two million members, and most of the national trade unions were affiliated to it. It had fought stiff opposition in the '90's and suffered defeat in two steel strikes.[2] It was weakened by the crisis of 1893 and ensuing depression. But it had led a successful revival of the eight-hours movement and in at least one member-union, the Stove Moulders', permanent arbitration machinery was set up, officially recognized by the employers (1891). The greatest period of growth up to World War I was after 1895, and especially in the five years 1900–5, when membership trebled.

Meanwhile about 24,000 strikes had occurred between 1880 and 1900, half of them ending in the defeat of the workers and a third of them being successful. A spectacular outbreak was the famous Homestead strike (30 June to 20 November 1892), organized by a powerful union, the Amalgamated Association of Iron and Steel

[1] See, among others, S. Gompers, *Seventy Years of Life and Labour* (2 vols., New York, 1925), and Louis Reed, *The Labour Philosophy of Samuel Gompers* (New York, 1930).

[2] Employers' associations were formed—such as the Stove Founders' National Defence Association (1886), the National Association of Manufacturers (1895) and the National Metal Trades Association (1899)— to assist members to fight strikes and unions. For instance, they enlisted strike-breakers and armed private 'detectives', hired lawyers to fight court cases and lobbied Congress to pass bills favourable to their interests.

Workers, at a branch of the Carnegie Steel Company. The trouble was over a wage disagreement, and the employers fought back bitterly hiring 300 Pinkerton detectives who fought a pitched battle with strikers. About ten people were killed and the Governor of Pennsylvania ordered the National Guard to stand by. An attempt on the life of an unpopular member of the steel company's staff (H. C. Frick) by an anarchist turned public opinion against the Homestead men, and the strike ultimately failed. Only a fifth of the 5,000 strikers were re-employed by the firm and those taken back had to renounce their union membership. Other steel firms in the Pittsburgh region also refused to have dealings with the Amalgamated Association of Iron and Steel Workers; this once-proud union was shattered, and its leaders blacklisted.

Even more important was the Pullman strike in Chicago in 1894, organized by the American Railway Union (an early example of a 'vertical' or industrial union) under the radical socialist, Eugene V. Debs. This strike presents a useful microcosm of industrial labour relations in late nineteenth-century America. Firstly, it illustrates three chief forms of intervention in disputes at that time: the use of state militia and federal troops (increasingly common after 1877); the use of the judiciary (although the courts made no lasting contribution to industrial peace, favouring Capital as they did); and the use of public mediating and conciliating agencies. Secondly the strike presents typical examples of the conduct and opinion of both Capital and Labour. Thirdly, and like many of its kind, it involved the participation of groups not parties to the original quarrel, and focused intense local and national feeling on several sensational 'incidents'. Finally, it was of long-term significance because it marked the beginning of a legal and legislative struggle extending over many years.

The prelude to the trouble at Pullman's Palace Car Company was the crisis of 1893. Prices fell, failures were numerous, unemployment was widespread and strikes almost continuous. In May 1894, a year after the depression began, a serious strike occurred at Pullman—the town which housed Pullman workers in dwellings built and owned by the company. Wages had been cut, although salaries remained untouched and profits totalled four million dollars. Even so, the strike might have worn itself out if both employers and workers had not had affiliations with larger and stronger groups, the actions of which turned a local dispute into a national crisis.

Several weeks before trouble broke out about 4,000 Pullman men had joined the new American Railway Union. The union held a Convention in June, and because they could make no headway in negotiations with their employers, the Pullman workers appealed to the Convention for help. Response was readily made: a complete boycott of all Pullman coaches. As these coaches were included in almost all American trains, a nation-wide railway strike was threatened unless they were detached. When the threat of boycott proved to be inadequate the A.R.U. called a full-scale strike, and at one point in the proceedings (in July) it seemed possible that all organized labour in America would join in the strike sympathetically. Gompers, in his capacity as President of the American Federation of Labour, put a stop to this at a conference in Chicago, and limited A.F.L. action to a strongly worded statement supporting the strikers. It is probable that he thought the battle was already lost.

But the scope of the strike continued to widen as the federal and state governments became active participants. The central government was implicated because Olney, the Attorney-General, had to safeguard the passage of regular trains carrying U.S. mails, and take legal action against any person obstructing them. On the advice of several district attorneys and local federal judges, President Cleveland ordered troops to the troubled zones. Almost immediately a constitutional dispute arose between the state governor and Cleveland regarding the rôle of federal and state action in industrial disputes.

A further complication was added by the intervention of the judicial arm. The aim was to prosecute Debs and his associates in one of two ways: firstly by claiming they had violated federal criminal laws (e.g. obstruction of the mails and 'conspiracy in restraint of trade'), and secondly by inculpating them through civil law, by use of the 'injunction'. The main criminal charge of 'conspiracy' fell through, but the civil charge was much more successful. An 'injunction' is an order issued by a court of equity commanding someone to do, or restraining him from doing, an act which would violate the personal or property rights of someone else.[1] The violation of an injunction constitutes contempt of court and is thus punishable by fine or imprisonment. On 2 July the government secured a 'blanket' injunction from a federal court forbidding 'all persons whomsoever'

---

[1] There are several kinds of injunction: *mandatory* (commanding the performance of a specific act), *preventive* (a restraining order), *interlocutory* (to prevent a danger immediately threatened, whilst the court decides the pros and cons), and *permanent* (the final decree of the court). Labour injunctions were first used in England in 1868 but the decision was criticized and the precedent not followed, though the Trade Disputes Act of 1927 did empower the Attorney-General to use the injunction against the application of trade union funds for 'illegal' strikes. In the U.S.A., however, the labour injunction took firm root. It was used successfully by federal courts against engineers on strike against the Chicago, Burlington and Quincy Railroad in 1888, and against railway strikers in the early '90's, and was justified by reference to the Interstate Commerce Act (1887) and, ironically, the Sherman Anti-Trust Act (1890). (See *Encyclopaedia of the Social Sciences*, op. cit., Vol. 8, for quick reference. Otherwise, use Frankfurter and Greene, *The Labour Injunction* (New York, 1930).)

from interfering in any way, even indirectly, with the operation of the railways. Debs and three colleagues were then arrested (for the second time) on the charge of contempt of court and the case was eventually carried to the Supreme Court of the United States which, by its decision, promptly placed the use of the injunction in labour disputes upon a strong legal basis (27 May 1895). Debs served a six months prison sentence.

The meaning of all this was not lost on industrialists, and during the following two decades the injunction was used as one of the most formidable weapons in their armoury in the struggle with labour. Woodrow Wilson promised to restrict its sphere of action in his 'New Freedom' programme, and the Clayton Anti-Trust Act (1914) exempted non-profit-making labour and agricultural organizations from the 'restraint of trade' clauses. The Act had little practical effect, however, and no genuine relief came for labour until the Norris-La Guardia Act (1932) put a halt to the misuse of federal judicial power by prohibiting the issue of injunctions in cases of official, publicized strikes financed by orderly trade unions, and in cases of 'peaceable assembly'. All cases of contempt springing from violation of injunctions were to be assured of trial by jury.

The significance of the Pullman strike of 1894 lies also in the fact that it heralds the beginning of the emergence of the Federal Government in its function of mediator in industrial disputes. President Cleveland established an investigating commission, and some of its recommendations were embodied in the Erdman Act (1898), a measure which set up machinery for arbitration between certain classes of railwaymen and their companies and strengthened the mediating powers of the central government. In 1913 the Newlands Act extended these provisions, and there has been ever since a growth of government responsibility in conciliation and arbitration.

Three further groups in the world of organized labour up to 1917 were: the United Mineworkers of America, a powerful 'industrial' union entirely outside the A.F.L.; the four great Railway Brotherhoods, also outside the A.F.L. and consisting of the Locomotive Engineers (organized at Detroit in 1863 and first called the Brotherhood of the Footboard), the Order of Railway Conductors (founded 1868), the Locomotive Firemen and Enginemen (founded 1873) and the Railroad Trainmen (founded 1883); and thirdly, the Industrial Workers of the World, otherwise known as the I.W.W. or 'Wobblies'.

The I.W.W. was formed in 1905 from various dissident radical and socialist splinter groups such as the Western Federation of Miners and the Socialist Trade and Labour Alliance. It was headed by William D. Haywood, who in 1907 was acquitted on a sensational murder charge arising out of a violent labour dispute, and who had assimilated the principles of French syndicalism. He was supported, though splits were soon to appear, by the Marxian socialist Daniel DeLeon (leader of the Socialist Labour Party) and by Eugene V. Debs, already famous for his generalship in the Pullman strike of 1894. The aim of the Wobblies was, according to their manifesto:

'One great industrial union embracing all industries, providing for craft autonomy locally, industrial autonomy internationally, and wage-class unity generally.'

In fierce reaction to the craft conservatism of the A.F.L., they appealed to the unskilled, as did the 'New Unionists' in England after the triumphant Dock Strike of 1889. Textile workers, migratory harvest hands, Western lumberjacks and exploited immigrants all found a place among the Wobblies. Ignoring the vigorous attacks launched upon them by Gompers (who feared for his respectability) and the A.F.L., they advocated a revolutionary programme aimed at the complete abolition of the 'wage system'. Nothing short of a general strike could solve the social problem, for their motto was 'an injury to one is an injury to all'—in direct contradiction to the *sauve qui peut* policy that had emerged among the craft unions. Perhaps the chief activities of the I.W.W. were the Lawrence strike of 1912 and the unsuccessful Paterson textile strikes of 1912–13. It achieved little else, mainly because of its heterogeneous membership and complicated internal dissensions. The Western Federation of Miners seceded in 1907, only two years after the founding of the movement, and in 1911 joined the A.F.L. The 'rump' split into two sections in 1908 with headquarters in Chicago and Detroit, one favouring revolutionary political action and its rival 'direct' industrial action. Government persecution, further dissensions, lack of financial support and the 'anti-Red' hysteria of 1917–20 drove the group out of existence. At no time had its membership exceeded sixty or seventy thousand.[1]

During World War I, which America entered in 1917, employment figures were high and the government and industry eagerly sought the co-operation of the trade unions. In the space of five years (1915–20) the A.F.L. increased its numbers from two million to over four million, and there was a flowering of labour relations councils and the like, in an effort to step up productivity. From about 1920 to the New Deal, however, a very different state of affairs existed. Only the strongest unions survived the depression and the all-out attacks from employers, A.F.L. membership fell to well under three million by 1925, and many unionists turned once more to the radicalism they had rejected earlier. Such bodies as the League for Progressive Political Action (dominated by the railway unions) sprang up, and the

[1] See P. F. Brissenden, *The I.W.W., a Study in American Syndicalism* (New York, 1919).

A.F.L. executive endorsed Robert La Follette, the Progressive party candidate, as its presidential nominee for the 1924 election. This was unsuccessful, but in the 1930's radicalism was to infect the A.F.L. still further and lead to an important splinter movement—the C.I.O.

Glancing back from 1917 over the history of organized labour in the U.S.A. we may well ask what comparisons can be drawn between American and British experience. We may ask, for instance, why no independent labour party has developed in the U.S.A., and why the idea of socialism, democratic or otherwise, has apparently failed to take root.[1] There are several reasons for this; but these reasons are not immutable or scientific laws—American society, like any other and more than some, is undergoing constant change. Immigration, the Westward movement and sectionalism, the federal political structure and the written constitution, have all been powerful factors operating on the history of Labour in America.

It can no longer be held that immigration caused widespread or prolonged displacement of native labour, because for one thing the number of jobs increased 300 per cent during the same years that total population increased 200 per cent (1870–1930). It is doubtful whether immigrants created fewer jobs through their function as consumers than they filled as workers, even in the early period. Speaking before a House of Representatives Committee on Immigration and Naturalization on 20 March 1946, a member of the C.I.O. said:

'Naturally a labour organization representing six million American workers would not be inclined to support measures which would threaten the job security of its own members. However, the C.I.O. realizes from past experience that immigration is automatically checked in periods of unemployment while it rises in periods of prosperity.... The best and most enlightened thought on this subject opposes arbitrary, prejudiced, and superficial legislation to curtail immigration into the United States.'[2]

Another argument about immigration has been that it delayed 'unionization' and thus held up the labour movement, because immigrants were hard to entice into unions. It must be remembered, however, that the bulk of the immigrants were unskilled labourers, and American unions remained organized on a skilled, craft basis until very late in labour history. On the other hand it remains true that employers discovered that unrestricted immigration was a useful

[1] A useful recent article on this subject is Henry Pelling, 'The American Labour Movement: A British View', in *Political Studies*, Vol. II, No. 3, October 1954, pp. 227–41.

[2] Quoted in W. S. Bernard (Ed.), *American Immigration Policy* (New York, 1950), p. 96.

weapon to use against recalcitrant unions. One thing is certain: the ethnic problems of immigration made their impact on trade unions no less than elsewhere. While there is much in the claim frequently asserted that America has less 'class consciousness' than Europe, there can be no doubt that *group* loyalties, ethnic and religious, have been fierce and deep-seated there. These loyalties have remained strong despite the spread of almost universally accepted criteria of taste and value in education, domestic life, dress and entertainments through such modern mass media as radio, films, television and high-pressure advertising. A high degree of vertical mobility in American society, while encouraging the persistence of individualist, *laissez-faire* notions among all classes, has not appreciably undermined group loyalties. The slowing down of immigration since 1918, however, obviously checked the growth of such ties, and helped to reduce conflicts within the American trade unions between ethnic groups.[1] Meanwhile 'dual' unionism developed despite the strong opposition of the A.F.L. The Amalgamated Clothing Workers for instance, led by Sidney Hillman and composed of East European Jewish immigrants, established its hegemony over the native United Garment Workers, from which it had originally seceded in 1914. (The A.C.W. was connected with the A.F.L. from 1924 to 1936, and became a founder-member of the C.I.O.)[2]

Whatever remarks are made about the now discarded 'safety-valve' theory (discussed in Chapter II), the Westward movement helped to retard American labour organization. Why stay behind in wretched unstable conditions and take the trouble to organize into legally ill-favoured groups in Eastern towns? 'Out West' lay an abundance of free farming land (or earth heavy with precious minerals), and freedom from restrictions of all kinds or the need to submit to an employer. In addition, 'individualism' suffused the documentary constitution, colouring every aspect of political and social life. The courts were always ready to invoke the written abstractions of the Fathers of the eighteenth century in order to safeguard in the nineteenth and twentieth, a one-sided 'freedom of contract' and 'property rights', and to suppress any hint of labour groupings which might conceivably be considered 'in restraint of trade'. 'The Constitution' hung around the neck of labour leaders throughout this period.

[1] Pelling, op. cit., p. 229.

[2] The Negro problem has, of course, not been affected by the slowing down of immigration. On the contrary it has increased in magnitude as Negro unionism has become more possible. The C.I.O. unions rarely practise discrimination, but it is still strong in the railroad brotherhoods where Negroes are denied promotion above certain grades. (Pelling, op. cit., pp. 229–30.)

The outcome of all this was that the American labour movement lagged at least half a century behind the British. Mr. Pelling has been able to compare the Knights of Labour of the 1870's and '80's with the attempts at general union made fifty years earlier in Britain, and the A.F.L. (founded under that name in 1886) with the 'New Model' unions, the first example of which in Britain was the Amalgamated Society of Engineers, established in January 1851. American trade unions have not been strong enough to enter politics on an independent basis or have despaired of the difficulties facing such action arising out of the federal structure of the political system and the complexity, expense and slowness of any major reforms of a socialistic nature. Their despair seems justified in the light of the case of *Lochner* v. *New York* (1905) when the legality of a mild New York statute restricting night work in bakeries was denied by the Supreme Court of the United States, on the grounds that the state was exceeding the limits of its right to protect public health.[1]

SUGGESTED FURTHER READING

BUCK, S. J. *The Granger Movement* (Cambridge, Mass., 1913).
COMMONS, J. R. et al. *History of Labour in the United States* (4 vols., New York, 1918–35).
FRANKFURTER, F. and GREENE, N. *The Labour Injunction* (New York, 1930).
HICKS, J. D. *The Populist Revolt*, (Minneapolis, 1931).
WARE, N. J. *The Labour Movement in the United States, 1860–1895* (New York, 1929).

[1] What the future holds in store for the American labour movement is perhaps largely a matter of conjecture. The reader can broaden the background of the above account by reference to D. W. Brogan's revised work, now called *An Introduction to American Politics* (London, 1954). Two opposed 'theories' of the movement are given by S. Perlman, *Labour in the New Deal* (New York, 1945) and *A Theory of the Labour Movement* (New York, 1926) on the one hand, and by Harold Laski, *The American Democracy* (English Ed., London, 1949) and *Trade Unions in the New Society* (London, 1950) on the other.

X

IMMIGRATION AND TRANSPORTATION

Immigration since 1861: change in origin after 1890; immigration theory; federal policy – The restrictive acts of 1882–1917 – The quota system (1921) – Railroad expansion to 1917 – Transcontinental lines – Financial scandals: the Credit Mobilier; Jay Gould – 'Empire builders': Hill and Harriman – Federal regulation, 1887–1910 – The Esch-Cummins Act (1920) – General decline of inland waterways; the Great Lakes and the St. Lawrence Project – The motor-car.

NEARLY half of the one and a half million people who migrated to the United States in the 1840's were Irish, the remainder coming chiefly from North and West Europe.[1] The latter region was also the predominant source of the thirteen million who migrated between 1850 and 1890. But after 1890 came a marked decline in immigration from such nations as Germany and the United Kingdom, followed by a fall in that from Scandinavia a decade or so later. Total immigration also slackened in the 90's, falling to three and a half million as compared with the five and a quarter million of the '80's. The 1900's, however, saw a huge increase, rising to eight and three quarter million for the decade as a whole. During the first thirty years of the twentieth century total American immigration numbered eighteen million.[2]

The nations which were the chief source of the 'new' immigration after 1890, were those of southern Europe: Italy sent over four and a half million; Austria, Hungary and the 'succession states' over four million; Poland and Russia almost four million. Overpopulation and persecution of minority groups such as Czechs, Jews and Poles in southern and eastern Europe and sometimes the desire to escape oppressive military service, help partly to explain the exodus to the

[1] See Chapter III, above, pp. 37–8.
[2] After 1930 came an emphatic drop to a comparatively meagre half million for the decade, followed by a rise to one and a half million in the 1940's.

New World. Also the advertising of American railway and steamship companies, who sent agents to Europe to organize migration and who subsidized fares, played no small part. Immigrants were often sent by special train from the port of entry to a prearranged spot on railroad lands. The American West and American industry cried out for cheap labour, and found it forthcoming.

It is generally true, however, that the bulk of the Russians, Italians, Austrians, Poles, Czechs, Magyars and others who made up the 'new' immigrants tended to settle in close groups in the growing cities of the United States and became first of all unskilled labourers in mines, in factories and on the railways. For instance, foreign-born workers constituted almost 80 per cent of the labour force of the Pennsylvania bituminous mines in 1909, over 90 per cent of these being from southern and eastern Europe. The pre-1890 immigrants on the other hand had a decided preference for farming and rural life and formed the majority of the population of states such as Minnesota, Illinois, Iowa, Nebraska and the Dakotas. The Irish, of course, provided the notable exception to this general rule.

Two further nations providing sources for immigration to the United States, more particularly after 1900, were her neighbours Mexico and Canada. About three-quarters of a million Mexicans, mainly illiterate and poor and employed as casual labourers in cotton and rice fields and in the oil industry, were to be found in Texas, Arizona, New Mexico and California in 1930. Over one and a half million Canadians emigrated to the U.S.A. after 1910, especially to the textile and lumbering regions.

The effects of immigration on labour history have been considered in the previous chapter. These effects are by no means certain and remain a subject of controversy among economic historians. But many other central questions also remain unsettled. What *caused* this migration from Europe to America, this largest movement of peoples in world history? Was it attracted by economic booms in the New World, or expelled by Malthusian dilemmas in the Old? In a recent work[1] Professor Brinley Thomas considers four principal waves of migration across the Atlantic, between the 1840's and World War I. From studying a mass of statistical data, he suggests several important correlations. On the whole he emphasizes the 'push' rather than the 'pull'; he believes that depressive factors in Europe, rather than attractive conditions in America, lay behind immigration. Each wave of migration from the Old World stimulated investment in the New—in transportation, in building and in mass-production machinery that could be used by heterogeneous, polyglot, unskilled

[1] *Migration and Economic Growth: A study of Great Britain and the Atlantic Economy* (Cambridge, 1954).

labour. Professor Thomas argues that these American booms were associated with periods of declining investment in Europe, the two conditions being to some extent compensatory and occurring in twenty-year stretches. The main factor in Europe conditioning migration was periodic pressure of population: there is a distinct relationship between the birth-rate and emigration figures.

Unfortunately we cannot consider in any further detail the origins of American immigrants or the present state of migration theory. Instead we must look briefly at the immigration policy of the Federal Government.

The first successful attempt to pass legislation restricting the immigration of aliens was aimed clearly at Oriental migrants—more particularly the Chinese coolies on the Pacific coast, who had been imported under contract as cheap labour to build the Central Pacific railroad.[1] The enlightened views on immigration held by a twentieth-century C.I.O. official (quoted in the last chapter) could hardly have gained much support among native American workers in the 1870's; there can be little doubt that much of the opposition to unrestricted immigration of aliens came from labour. This is not difficult to understand, however, in the light of actions by American employers. Oriental contract labour, with its low living standards, frugality and menial outlook, seemed to be a direct threat to native workers. In 1877, railroad employers imported Magyars and other East Europeans to break strikes; Slovaks and Poles helped to break a large coopers' strike in an oil plant in New Jersey; Slav labour was deliberately introduced to break strikes in Pennsylvanian coal-fields. Of course there was racial antipathy too, bursting the surface on tragic occasions, such as the race riots of 1871 in Los Angeles.

In 1877 a political party was founded by an Irish drayman, Dennis Kearney, called the Workingman's Trade and Labour Union, the aim of which was to exclude Chinese labour. Eventually some employers sided with the movement after several enterprising Chinese had themselves become employers, underselling their American competitors because they paid even less for their labour. The movement swelled, and in 1879 Congress was brought to the point of enacting a Chinese Exclusion Act. This was vetoed by President Hayes as contrary to the Burlingame Treaty of 1868, but the Chinese Government appeared indifferent as to the fate of its coolie citizens in America, and agreed to a new treaty in 1880. The Chinese Exclusion Act of 1882 prohibited for ten years the entry of Chinese labourers. It was renewed several times and finally made permanent in 1902.

[1] The Burlingame Treaty (1868) with China guaranteed unrestricted Chinese migration, and by 1870 there were 56,000 Chinese in the U.S.A., mainly in the Pacific coast states.

Three years after the signing of the second Chinese Exclusion bill, another federal restrictive measure was aimed at 'contract labour' and the flood of migrants from south and east Europe brought in by this device. The 1885 Act, strengthened in 1888, prohibited the import of contract labour and was passed under pressure from the Knights of Labour. In 1891 Congress went a step further by prohibiting advertising by employers and other direct methods of stimulating alien immigration. The Acts of 1882, 1891, 1893, 1903 and 1907 listed certain categories of 'undesirable' aliens who were to be excluded, including paupers, criminals, the insane, prostitutes, polygamists and those with 'contagious or loathsome diseases'. In 1897 Congress passed the first literacy test act, but it was vetoed by Cleveland who though it unfair; in 1917, however, a similar measure was passed over President Wilson's veto.

The literacy restriction, which it was hoped would restore the balance of immigration to the more advanced (and racially acceptable) nations of north and west Europe, did not seem to its admirers to fulfil their aims. With the coming of peace in 1918 they feared a fresh wave of migrants from a war-torn Europe. A new and more effective device was found in the 'quota' system, first introduced by the Emergency Quota Act, 1921. It provided a system of quotas for each country of origin, under which no nationality was to increase its number of foreign-born by more than 3 per cent of its total number in the United States in 1910. The quota base was altered in 1924 and again in 1927, when the system was extended to apply to all countries, including those in the Western Hemisphere previously not restricted, except Canada, Mexico and the independent Latin American states. 'Selective immigration' had received its full sanction.[1]

From immigration to transportation is a convenient and easy step, for they were interdependent and interacting factors in American economic growth. The railroads in particular opened up an inland continental empire, and developed an elaborate organization to people it by becoming large-scale 'colonizing' agents. Not only this, but their insatiable demand for huge capital funds brought an influx of European capital comparable in magnitude to the influx of European peoples. The need to pool the funds of many separate investors, both American and European, meant the adoption of the 'corporation' as the characteristic unit of American business. Indeed, railway history after the Civil War gives a striking illustration of the emergence of mammoth, interdependent industrial con-

[1] In 1907 Theodore Roosevelt made an agreement with Japan regulating the immigration of Japanese nationals, and in 1924 an Act finally prohibited their influx.

cerns, which by their growth, their financial organization and the problems they posed to the government, make the latter half of the nineteenth century distinctively the age of the railroad.

From 1861 to 1917 railroad building proceeded on an even larger scale than before the Civil War, and was helped by even larger land grants.[1] Over 30,000 miles of railroad were laid down in the years 1830–60; but construction in the second half of the century averaged 4,000 miles a year. The Civil War destroyed much rolling-stock and mileage in the South, but at the same time stimulated developments in the North and West, and the beginning of the first transcontinental line. In the years of greatest expansion railroad building was directly connected with the cyclical variations in economic growth. Temporary but severe setbacks occurred in 1873 and 1893 (in the latter year about 30,000 miles of line being thrown into bankruptcy). Nevertheless, mileage increased almost five-fold between 1870 and 1914, reaching a peak of 252,000 miles. This represented a total investment of some $15,000 million. By 1920 American railroads employed well over two million workers, and mileage exceeded that of the whole of Europe, constituting one third of the world's total.

The epoch of enthusiastic building came to a sudden halt with the First World War, though wartime retrenchment was not the principal reason. Between the two World Wars more miles of line were abandoned than constructed. Railroad expansion had been more rapid than population growth and the wild scramble for franchises, land grants and government aid, as well as the exaggerated optimism of railroad builders and speculators, led to unwise construction. Not only competing but wholly unnecessary lines were laid, in sparsely populated, barren areas which could scarcely support life at a subsistence level, let alone a railway service. Building surpassed saturation-point and the railroads put themselves into a precarious financial situation precisely when the success of the internal combustion engine brought the competition of motor-vehicle traffic in the passenger and 'short-haul' freight business. By the 1930's many American railroads were in a condition of chronic near-insolvency and World War II with its petrol rationing proved to be a blessing.[2]

Even more than most railway schemes the transcontinental lines depended upon government subsidies, and during the ante-bellum decade they became an outstanding political issue. Once war was declared, the North immediately understood that a Pacific railroad

[1] See Chapter IV for railway growth before 1861, and the origins of the land-grant system.
[2] For a competent technical account of the American transportation industries in recent times, full of statistical data, see H. Barger, *The Transportation Industries, 1889–1946* (New York, 1951).

was an essential measure to maintain contact with the riches of California and ensure the support of that state against the South. Accordingly on 1 July 1862 Congress chartered the first transcontinental railway: the Union Pacific Railroad Company was to build a line westwards from Nebraska, and the Central Pacific Railroad Company was to build eastwards from Sacramento, California, to connect with the Union Pacific. Both roads were to be subsidized by receiving ten alternate 'sections' of public land on each side of the track for each mile of line constructed and loans of from $16,000 to $48,000 per mile. Only American iron was to be used to build and equip the lines. Two years later, Congress doubled the land grant and extended further credit to the companies, because the investing public were slow to subscribe for stock. The lines of the two rival companies met—after bitter competition and almost open warfare between them—at Promontory Point, Utah, on 10 May 1869, and were joined by a gold spike driven in with a silver sledgehammer, amid great pomp and circumstance. The 1,086 miles of the Union Pacific and 689 miles of the Central Pacific linked up a railway system that brought the Atlantic and Pacific coasts within a week of each other.

Meanwhile Congress had chartered other companies, including the Northern Pacific (1864) to connect Puget Sound (Seattle) with Lake Superior, and the Atlantic and Pacific (1866) to build westwards from Springfield, Missouri. The latter was a financial failure and merged with the Atchison, Topeka and Sante Fe which extended across the deserts of New Mexico and Arizona and made contact with the Southern Pacific Railroad Company of California (and thus with the ports of southern California) in 1881. Another land-grant railroad, the Texas and Pacific (chartered in 1871 to construct westwards from Marshall, Texas, to San Diego, California), also met the Southern Pacific, at El Paso.

The transcontinental railroads represented an immense achievement in engineering in the face of heavy odds; but their building also had its seamy side. They were built by construction companies, controlled by the leading stockholders of the lines concerned, who thus played a dual rôle enabling them to acquire enormous illicit profits. For example, the Union Pacific was constructed by a Pennsylvania corporation called the Crédit Mobilier established in 1867, having gained its contract through Oakes Ames, who, besides being a member of Congress, had interests in both concerns. The construction company agreed to build 637 miles of railroad for $47 million, and its shares shot up in value to 400 per cent in February 1868. Ames thought it judicious to place the stock 'where it would do most good'; so he offered to several Congressmen shares in the Crédit Mobilier at par, in some cases himself advancing money to enable them to buy stock.¹ Charges of bribery were raised against members of Congress in the campaign of 1872 and a congressional committee of inquiry revealed that the Crédit Mobilier company had received $73 million for work costing under $50 million. It recommended the expulsion from the House of Ames (for bribery) and a government director of the Union Pacific, James Brooks (for venality). Though they were not expelled, the Crédit Mobilier gave its name to one of the most infamous financial scandals in congressional history and sapped public confidence in political and business morals.²

In the same year Jay Gould was forced out of the Erie, having made in any case a small fortune there since 1867. Gould led a fantastic career and was in and out of all kinds of shady and disreputable financial deals in the '70's and '80's—such as the scheme he concocted with Jim Fisk to corner the gold market, that ended in the 'Black Friday' panic of 24 September 1869. In 1873 he assumed temporary control of the Union Pacific, making some speculative gains on the side; but later, in opposition, he tried by judicious purchase of the Denver Pacific and Kansas Pacific Companies to encircle the Union Pacific. The last was forced to buy the other two from Gould at a high price, because he had built them up into potential rivals by taking over other lines with important connections. These other lines, including among them the Texas and Pacific and Missouri Pacific, gave him a substantial network in the South-west. Gould then bought the Wabash, thus gaining an eastern extension, began competitive construction in all directions, and entered an 'alliance' with the Southern Pacific directed against the Atchison, Topeka and Santa Fe. He fought ruinous rate wars, paid out unearned dividends and used numerous devices to get rid of his holdings while making a profit for himself and retaining control. He came into serious financial difficulties after 1884 and his dominions greatly shrank, though he made sure that others bore the loss.

A less disreputable 'empire-builder' and altogether a man of greater stature was James J. Hill, who rescued the Northern Pacific in 1893. This company had already laid 500 miles of track when the failure of Jay Cooke (who financed it) helped to precipitate the crash of 1873.³ With the help of German capital Henry Villard then took over and resumed construction, finishing the road in 1883. Ten years later, however, the Northern Pacific was again in difficulties and Hill seized his opportunity. In association with two Canadians, Lord Strathcona and Lord Mount Stephen, he proceeded to build up the

¹ James A. Garfield was among the politicians involved, and found this revelation an embarrasment in his presidential campaign of 1880.

² Similarly the Crocker Company that built the Central Pacific charged an average of $100,000 per mile—at least twice the actual cost.

³ For a brief account of this crash see Chapter XII, below, pp. 190–1.

Great Northern system, which by 1890 owned 2,775 miles of railroad in Minnesota, North Dakota and Montana, reaching the Pacific coast three years later. The prosperity of the North-west was bound up in this system: Hill founded communities, churches and schools, encouraged agriculture, bred cattle, opened banks and built ships to deal directly with the markets of the Far East.

The last of the empire-builders was E. H. Harriman, who rose to power by his successful working of the Illinois Central. After the crash of 1893 he emerged with a plan to 'rehabilitate' the great Union Pacific, which had failed disastrously to operate its 8,000 miles of line. Harriman linked together the Union Pacific, the Illinois Central and the Southern Pacific, besides buying the Baltimore and Ohio and other lines, and attempting unsuccessfully to extend into the Northwest. He died in 1909 and before long the Union Pacific resumed its normal size, the control of the Harriman companies having been compulsorily divided, under the anti-trust laws.

The whole economic life of the nation hinged on the railroads and their coming was hailed with unmingled joy, encouraged by legislatures, capitalists and common men alike. Yet, in the '70's and '80's this enthusiasm waned, changing in some cases to open animosity. The nation had lavished public and private wealth on the railroads; in return it was either reminded of its debt to 'the Christian men to whom God in His infinite wisdom has given the control of the property interests of the country' (by President Baer of the Reading Railroad), or merely 'damned' out of hand (by W. H. Vanderbilt). Grievances against the railroad companies included extortionately high rates, discriminatory charging, inefficient service, crooked financing and irresponsible speculation, the corruption of political life, utter disregard of public rights and monopoly. The 'third-party' movements of the second half of the century were all united in their condemnation of the railroads and their demand for legislation to check abuses. This was especially true, of course, of the farmers' movements such as the Grangers. The Granger Laws (mentioned more fully in Chapter IX) aimed particularly at preserving competition by forbidding the consolidation of lines; at putting an end to such abuses as the granting of free passes to public officials; at establishing schedules of maximum rates, and at prohibiting higher rates of charges for short hauls than for long hauls. When a series of legal decisions deprived the state legislatures of jurisdiction over interstate commerce the demand for railroad reform shifted its attention from the states to the Federal Government in Washington, and the wishes of the Grangers were substantially embodied in the Interstate Commerce Act of 1887. This marked a new phase in the relationship between the Federal Government and the national economy—although what little power possessed by the Commission set up under the Act, was quickly removed by Supreme Court decisions, and it became little more than a body to collect statistics, overburdened with a mass of detailed administrative work such as the examination of innumerable tariff schedules. Two famous Supreme Court cases in 1897 reduced the Interstate Commerce Commission, in the words of Justice Harlan, 'to a useless body for all practical purposes'. The *Maximum Freight Case* said the Commission had no authority to fix rates; the *Alabama Midland Case* nullified the long-and-short-haul clause of the Act on a verbal technicality.[1]

The railroad companies displayed a continued disregard for public opinion and law and the old abuses—rebates, discriminations, spreading monopoly and rising freight rates—remained unabated by the opening of the new century. The Roosevelt administration determined to strengthen the I.C.C., and passed the Elkins Act (1903) to clarify rebate regulations, and the Expedition Act (1903) which gave preference in the courts to cases 'of general public importance' brought by the Federal Government under the Interstate Commerce Act of 1887, the Sherman Anti-Trust Act of 1890 and similar measures. The Elkins Act was successful in checking rebates because it had the support of the railway companies, but when President Theodore Roosevelt suggested that the I.C.C. should be empowered to fix rates, the railroad opened up a vigorous campaign in the press and by sham public meetings, conventions, 'doctored' news and garbled facts tried to marshal 'public opinion' against the idea.

However, the Hepburn Act (1906) did manage to strengthen the I.C.C., enlarging it from five to seven members and extending its jurisdiction over other 'common carriers' such as express and sleeping-car companies and pipe lines. The Commission was empowered to fix 'just and reasonable' maximum rates and enforce standardized accounting. Violation of the Act was punishable by a fine of $5,000 a day, and it was swept through both House and Senate with overwhelming majorities.

Effective federal regulation of interstate railroad traffic was at last established, and in 1910 President W. H. Taft signed the Mann-Elkins Act widening the scope of the I.C.C. still further to include jurisdiction over telegraph, telephone and cable companies. More important, the Act cleared up the verbal technicality that had enabled the Supreme Court to render the long-and-short-haul clause useless, it empowered the Commission to suspend the operation of

[1] The main specialized work is I. L. Sharfman, *The Interstate Commerce Commission* (5 vols., New York, 1931–7). But the I.C.C.'s own Bureau of Statistics produced a useful factual volume, *Interstate Commerce Commission Activities, 1887–1937* (Government Printing Office, Washington, 1937).

any new rates for up to ten months until their justification had been established, and it set up a special Commerce Court (abandoned in 1913) to try railroad cases. Meanwhile the Supreme Court began to adopt a more helpful attitude towards the work of the I.C.C. In 1913 a Physical Valuation Act gave the Commission authority to carry out a valuation of railroad property in order to find a more scientific basis for fixing rates.

After America's entry into World War I, the railroads were taken over by the Federal Government. The Transportation (Esch-Cummins) Act (1920) returned them to private ownership, President Wilson having rejected both the demand by W. G. McAdoo (who was 'Director General of Railroads' during the war) that the wartime control administration be maintained for a further five years, and the demand by the A.F.L. for railroad nationalization. But in addition the 1920 Act completely revised federal railroad policy. The I.C.C. was increased in membership to eleven, and its hands were strengthened; it now had *general* control and could limit new construction, supervise financing and regulate rates and services But government aims regarding combination were startlingly reversed: carriers could pool both traffic and earnings, and were even encouraged to do so. The Commission was, in fact, asked to draw up a plan for railroad consolidation which would give the nation a limited number of competitive networks. A further innovation was the 'recapture clause' by which all companies earning a net operating income in excess of 6 per cent of the value of their property had to give half the excess amount to the I.C.C. to form a special loan fund for less prosperous railroads. Finally machinery was set up for mediation in labour disputes, including the unsuccessful Railroad Labour Board (replaced in 1926 by a Federal Board of Mediation).

The consolidation plan did not become effective, mainly owing to the opposition of the chief Eastern trunk lines, and the recapture clause soon came up against the inevitable adverse Supreme Court decision (May 1929), but nevertheless under the Act American railroads were comparatively prosperous and comparatively stable from 1920 to 1929.

Simultaneous with the growth of transcontinental railroads and a national rail network came the decline of the inland waterways.[1] The river-system runs mainly in a north–south direction, but freight movement since the 'removal of the Alleghenies' has been predominantly east-west. The greater speeds of railroads, their ability to carry bulky products over vast distances, and their relative freedom from restrictions on movement caused by climatic hazards, weighed heavily against canals and river transport. Railroad companies in America, as in England, were not averse to adopting unfair means to gain

[1] See Chapter IV, above, pp. 48–51.

control over canal and steamship lines either to operate or to discontinue them. Thus Mississippi river traffic declined steeply after 1880, and more than half the canals built before 1909 have since been abandoned. The work on the Panama Canal (opened in 1914) and the report of the Inland Waterways Commission (1908) brought a minor canal revival and attempts to deepen the Erie, Oswego and Champlain waterways. But of much greater significance was the agitation for the St. Lawrence Seaway and Power Project in the 1920's and '30's. Traffic on the Great Lakes had shown no appreciable decline; in fact it increased in the 1920's and has continued to do so. The total foreign trade of the Great Lakes ports amounted in bulk to 16 million short tons (of 2,000 lb.) in 1924, 5 million of which represented imports into the United States. In a peak year, 1928, this total rose to almost 24 million short tons, a figure not attained again until World War II. Then came a sharp recession with a more than 50 per cent fall to a bottom level of 10 million short tons a year in 1932 and 1933. Trade picked up in 1934 and began a steady rise in volume, broken only by a short setback in 1939, and by 1944 it amounted to a record total of almost 32 million short tons—double the 1924 figure.[1]

The main traffic nowadays is in ore, coal, grain, petroleum and limestone. The St. Lawrence Project, finally approved by the U.S. Congress in 1954 after years of delay in which the patience of the Canadians and of successive Presidents—Hoover, F. D. Roosevelt, Truman and Eisenhower—was sorely tried, is of vast economic importance. The existing system provides a continuous waterway stretching 2,300 miles into the heart of the continent, from the Atlantic to Port Arthur, in which the major bottleneck is the section from Prescott (Ogdensburg on the U.S. side) to Montreal. Below Montreal is a 35-foot channel, navigable by ocean-going vessels; above, the depth (1955) is only 14 feet. Even under existing conditions however, the tonnage of traffic on the Great Lakes waterway system *as a whole* exceeds that of the Panama and Suez canals combined. The plan now under operation is the more limited one of deepening the canal depth on the International Rapids section (Prescott to Cornwall) to 27 feet. This will only allow about 10 per cent of U.S. sea-going vessels to use the system, but a deeper construction, say to 35 feet, would involve too large an investment (about $1,500 million). The scheme should be completed by 1959, and will have far-reaching effects. Canada's economy is based on the world sale of a few major products which need long-distance haulage *within* the country; cheap transport is therefore essential. On the American side, there has been strong sectional opposition from the Eastern coastal

[1] *Historical Statistics of the United States*, op. cit., p. 214 (Series K. 132–45).

IMMIGRATION AND TRANSPORTATION

ports and Buffalo on Lake Erie has foreseen its decline, for a great deal of transhipment takes place there. The Eastern railroads to the Atlantic will certainly suffer initially, because they already bear high operating costs. But one important factor has greatly weakened all opposition: the winning over to the scheme of the big U.S. midwestern steel firms. The longterm prosperity of Ohio, Indiana, Illinois and Michigan seemed threatened by the predicted future shortage of ore and the need to *import* huge quantities before very long. Cheaper transport is also essential for the rapidly expanding industries of Canada in southern Ontario and in Quebec, which, like those in the U.S., are wanting ore from the newly opened Labrador mines.

What Canada also needs—especially for such industries as nickel, aluminium and copper smelting—is cheap power, and the St. Lawrence Project is of course also a hydro-electric power project. The area is capable of producing more energy in relation to constructed capacity than any other in the world, because the flow is so dependable and is backed by such huge natural storage reservoirs. New York State and New England are also short of power; but the Canadian need is greater, for that nation has had to fall back on costly steam-generated electrical plant at Toronto and Windsor and import coal for the purpose.

The economic effects of the St. Lawrence Project will be worldwide, but are still in the future (though not too distant).[1] What was by far the most important development in transport history in the late nineteenth and early twentieth centuries (from which we have deliberately strayed) was the introduction of the internal combustion engine and the automobile, which was in general use several years before America entered the First World War.[2] The social effects of the motor-car have surpassed those of trolleys and even of railways. The economic consequences of road transport impovements were to check for ever the development of street railways and 'electric cars', and to present the railroads with serious competition in the short-haul goods and in passenger traffic. The internal combustion engine brought a renaissance of road-building which far surpassed anything dreamed of in the old 'revolutionary' turnpike days. A system of well-surfaced roads spread over the nation within a couple of decades, aided by federal and state subsidies. Local electric railways were rapidly replaced by more efficient bus companies with greater coverage and adaptability. By the end of 1949 America had

[1] The above section on the St. Lawrence Project is based largely on an unpublished paper very kindly made available to the author by Mr. Robert Estall.

[2] The automobile industry has been dealt with above in Chapter VII; shipping is mentioned in Chapter XI.

about 36 million registered passenger cars and 8 million buses and trucks; in that year almost eight times as much inter-city travel was done by Americans in motor-cars (400 thousand million miles) as was done in trains in the peak railroad year of 1920.

SUGGESTED FURTHER READING

FAULKNER, H. U. *The Decline of Laissez-Faire, 1897–1917* (Vol. VII in Rinehart & Co'.s *Economic History of the United States*, New York, 1951).

HANDLIN, O. *The Uprooted* (Boston, 1951). (An unusual psychological study of migrants.)

RIEGEL, R. E. *America Moves West* (Rev. ed., New York, 1947).

STEPHENSON, G. M. *A History of American Immigration, 1820–1924* (Boston, 1926).

THOMAS, B. *Migration and Economic Growth* (Cambridge, 1954). (For advanced readers.)

XI

TRADE AND FINANCE

The merchant marine since 1861; federal legislation, 1891–1936 – Tariffs, 1861–1930: the triumph of protection – Changes in the amount, composition and direction of commerce – Economic imperialism and foreign investment: Latin America and the Far East – Finance since 1865: the National Banking system and the Independent Treasury, 1863–1913; the Federal Reserve system (1913) – Currency movements; Greenbacks and Free Silver; the Campaign of 1896; the Currency Act (1900).

CRUSHED by the Civil War, American merchant shipping revived as a direct result of World War I.[1] In both cases government action was a principal factor. The policy of restricting the registration of the national mercantile marine to American-built vessels (conditioned by an obsolete Act of 1789) had hindered the expansion of the American shipping business even before the Civil War; but in the post-war years, particularly when metal steam-driven ships began to replace wooden sailing-ships,[2] American capital had a clear tendency to be invested either in foreign ships or in coastal trade, from which aliens were excluded by an Act of 1817. English shipyards could turn out much cheaper vessels, and in any case there were other more attractive fields of investment for native capital within the United States, especially in manufacturing industries protected by federal tariffs. The heavy wartime taxes on shipping were not removed by Congress until 1868 and no effort was made to help shippers as their foreign competitors were helped. For instance, the last contract to carry mail lapsed in 1875 and was not renewed, no further step being taken until the Ocean Mail Act (1891)

[1] See Chapter V for developments before 1861.

[2] This replacement was not completed until the 1890's when the world's steam tonnage first surpassed sailing tonnage. Refrigerator ships were introduced about 1880, when steel began to replace iron in hull-construction also, and twin-screws came into use.

offered to pay mail subventions to American-built and owned ships.

The outcome of all this was that by 1913 American ships carried only 9 per cent of the value of U.S. foreign trade, as compared with about 75 per cent in 1860. British ships carried more than half, and German about 14 per cent; America was heavily dependent therefore on alien ocean transport.

With the outbreak of war in Europe in 1914 Congress repealed the 1789 statute and allowed foreign-built ships the right of American registration. In 1915 the Seamen's Act tried to ensure better working conditions, and in the following year the Federal Government agreed to provide marine insurance against war risks. A large shipbuilding programme was launched under the Shipping Act (1916), and on 16 April 1917, ten days after declaring war on the German Empire, Congress created an Emergency Fleet Corporation with a capital stock of $50 million. The government took over all private shipping, seized German vessels and commandeered or bought neutral ones, besides breaking all records at building new ships—though at a very high cost to the nation.

After the war, the Jones Merchant Marine Act (1920) sold to private enterprise much of the accumulated tonnage in government hands, on very liberal terms. In addition it provided for government-owned services (on certain trade routes), chartered out to private operators. In the '20's the percentage of foreign trade carried in native vessels varied between 30 per cent and 40 per cent. The White-Jones Act (1928) gave more favourable mail subventions and offered cheap loans for shipbuilders; but the first provision led to a public financial scandal and no one took advantage of the second. Therefore in 1936 the Merchant Marine Act established a comprehensive scheme of subsidies for both building and operation, and set up the U.S. Maritime Commission to administer the plan. At this time the American merchant marine represented under 15 per cent of the world's total; but by 1946, after a second global war, it represented over 60 per cent.

Much of the merchant shipping legislation we have briefly considered represents the demands of a resurgence of economic nationalism. Although important opposition minority groups have existed in the South and West it is broadly true that a neo-mercantilist spirit has dominated American trade policy since the Civil War, when a system of high protection was inaugurated. This is perfectly clear from a glimpse at tariff trends since the mid-century.

The account of tariff history given in Chapter V ends with the Act of 1857. Four years later the Morrill Tariff Act was imposed to meet the needs of war, but yielded little owing to the disruption of American foreign trade.[1] Tariff rates were increased again in 1864

[1] See Chapter VII for a consideration of Civil War financing.

and when peace came the average level was over 47 per cent. The report of the Wells Commission, announced in 1866, was ignored chiefly because of successful industrial expansion and the diversion of public attention to the need to remove direct taxes. From then on the control by industrialists of the Federal Government, the strenuous lobbying by protectionists, and the rationalization that the American workers must be saved from the unfair competition of the 'pauper labour' of Europe and elsewhere, ensured the success of a high-tariff policy. In 1867 after pressure from the Woollen Manufacturers' Association, Congress increased duties on woollens; in 1869 the copper interests gained an increase of duties, although their profits were already huge. Meanwhile an increasing Treasury surplus and the growing agitation of Western farmers was operating in the opposite direction, and in 1872 a reduction of 10 per cent was made on the protected industries—iron, wool and steel among them. This liberalizing movement was vitiated however by the crisis of 1873 and in 1875 high tariffs were again restored.

The annual surplus in 1882 was over $145 million and President Arthur's suggestion of a tariff commission was accepted by Congress. Curiously enough the commission, though composed chiefly of business men and presided over by the secretary of the Woollen Manufacturers' Association, recommended a substantial tariff reduction of from 20 per cent to 25 per cent in the interests of consumers and of 'general industrial prosperity'. The 1883 Act which ensued, however, has been justifiably called one of the silliest in the history of the American tariff. It was pushed through within hours of the end of a session by a Congress desperate to do something to stave off the possibility of more radical measures being taken in the new session—measures more in line with the commission's views.[1] Nominal reductions were made in some duties, and others were substantially raised.

Grover Cleveland was elected to the presidency in 1884. His party, the Democrats, had supported lower duties since the time of President James K. Polk (1845–9), but even so, by the '80's had a protectionist wing. Cleveland managed to startle both his party and the country by devoting the whole of his annual message of December 1887 to the question of tariff revision. The Democrats rallied and passed, by a strict party vote, the Mills Bill which hoped to reduce duties on pig iron, cotton goods and other articles and place raw materials on the free list. The Republican-dominated Senate refused to concur however, and Cleveland fought the electoral campaign of 1888 on the issue, gaining a popular majority but losing the presidency to Benjamin Harrison who captured the electoral college.

[1] See H. J. Ford, *The Cleveland Era* ('Chronicles of America' Series, New Haven, 1919), pp. 33–8.

The victorious Republicans immediately decided to try to stifle adverse criticism from one quarter by extending 'the protective system' to agriculture. The McKinley Tariff (1890) raised the average level to 49·5 per cent. Duties on wheat, corn, dairy products, meat, barley, hemp and flax were increased, and on woollen and cotton goods and linens. Powers were given to the President to impose duties on sugar, molasses, coffee, tea and hides (all of which were on the free list) if he should decide that duties imposed by foreign exporters of these goods were unreasonable. At the instigation of Secretary of State Blaine, who feared for America's foreign trade relations, a reciprocity clause was inserted in the Act.

Prices were immediately stimulated by the Act, and as Congressional elections were held in the following month (November), the Democrats were returned with an overwhelming majority. This tied President Harrison's hands, and prepared the way for a Democratic victory in the presidential election of 1892. McKinley had asserted in his hour of triumph that his Tariff Act was 'protective in every paragraph and American in every line and word'. In answer the Democrats claimed to denounce the Act as 'the culminating atrocity of class legislation'. Cleveland was returned to the White House with an outstanding popular vote and a considerable majority in the electoral college, giving the Democrats full control of both executive and legislature for the first time since the Civil War. The hour of free trade was at hand.

The Wilson-Gorman Act (1894) that resulted was a complete fiasco. In retrospect the long struggle of the Democrats and their final return to power in 1892 seems little more than an involved preface to a great *unwritten* work. What happened was that the reformist Wilson Bill passed the House but came up against strong opposition in the Senate from the protectionist wing of the Democratic party, led by Senator Gorman. The bill was radically altered in favour of protection and despite Cleveland's public strictures it became law without his signature. Two years later the Republicans regained power and rapidly introduced the Dingley Tariff (1897) which imposed an average level of 57 per cent—the highest of the century—and remained the unaltered law of the land for twelve years.

Economic change in the opening years of the new century, rising prices and America's industrial expansion and emergence as a great power, placed the high tariff protagonists increasingly on the defensive. Also the Dingley Tariff was severely criticized as 'the mother of all trusts',[1] and the growing expenses of federal government made it inadequate from the revenue viewpoint. Some attempt at revision was made in the Payne-Aldrich Tariff (1909), but the Senate hacked about the original bill, adding 847 changes in rates, chiefly upwards.

[1] See Chapter VII, above, p. 113.

The result was a slight extension of the free list to include hides, wood-pulp and petroleum, the institution of a Tariff Board, and a tax of 1 per cent on net corporate incomes of over $5,000.[1] Whatever economic and social effects the measure might have had, it certainly precipitated a split in the Republicans that led ultimately to the emergence of the Progressive party and the victory of the Democrats under Woodrow Wilson in 1912. As part of his policy under the 'New Freedom' (dealt with more fully in the next chapter), Wilson aimed at tariff revision. The Underwood-Simmons Act (1913), while it left the system still highly protectionist, made the first serious assault on it since the Civil War. Over 100 articles were added to the free list and rates were lowered on nearly 1,000, including necessities—food, clothing, and raw materials. The average rate was reduced to 29 per cent.

The First World War, like the previous wars of 1812–14 and 1861–5, brought an aftermath of protectionism. The Republicans replaced their opponents in 1921 and under Harding immediately enacted the Fordney Emergency Tariff, reimposing high duties on wheat, corn, wool, meat and sugar. This they regarded as a temporary stimulant, a stopgap to give them time to set about the complete reconstruction of the protective system. In this reconstruction farmers and the new industries that had sprung up during the war ('war babies') would be the chief beneficiaries. The Fordney-McCumber Tariff (1922) established the highest rates in American history, its only compromising feature being a special provision for flexibility, allowing the President to raise or lower duties by 50 per cent to equalize production cost differences in the U.S.A. and competing nations. This plan was ludicrous because neither Harding nor Coolidge had the slightest intention of lowering tariffs. Between them they made 37 changes: 32 upwards (butter, cheese, pig-iron, chemicals) and 5 downwards (live bobwhite quail, paintbrush handles, mill feed, cresylic acid and phenol).

[1] The Tariff Board made some investigation into comparative production costs but was suspected by Congress as an encroachment by the President. A Democratic Congress dissolved the Board in 1912 by refusing to appropriate its funds.

The *corporate income tax* was called an 'excise', because the Supreme Court had previously invalidated a Congressional attempt to impose an income tax under the Wilson-Gorman Act. President Taft meanwhile suggested a constitutional amendment empowering Congress to tax incomes. The amendment passed both chambers, many conservatives failing to oppose the bill because they thought it would never be ratified. In February 1913 it became law. (An up-to-date, well-written and highly competent book is Randolph E. Paul's *Taxation in the United States* (Boston, 1954). It is a hefty volume, three-quarters of which is concerned with events since the World Slump. Less advanced or less omnivorous readers will find the first five chapters most useful.)

Many other changes were still 'under consideration' as late as 1930 when the Act was superseded by the Hawley-Smoot Tariff. This brought even greater increases: the average rate on agricultural products was raised from 19·9 per cent to 33·6 per cent, that on metals from 33·7 per cent to 35 per cent, and that on wool and woollens from 49·5 per cent to 59·8 per cent. The economic effects of the Acts of 1922 and 1930 were disastrous. At home they stimulated monopoly and abroad they made it wellnigh impossible for European nations to repay their indebtedness to America in the form of goods, and brought reprisals such as the increased duties imposed on American products in France in 1927 and in Great Britain, Canada and elsewhere later. The Hawley-Smoot Tariff was clearly one of the decisive factors in the breakdown of the European economy in the 1930's.

During the late nineteenth and early twentieth century it is possible to trace definite changes in American commerce, changes in its amount, its composition and its direction. Changes in the *amount* of commerce reflect to a great extent American internal growth: the per capita value of imports and exports in the 1790's was $22; in the 1820's, however, when internal resources were considerably more developed, this figure fell to $10; by the 1870's it had increased again to $25, and after a regression reached $43 in 1914.[1] Between 1860 and 1920 American total exports increased in value by over twenty-one-fold, from about $400 million to about $8,600 million, whilst imports multiplied sixteen-fold, from $360 million to $5,780 million. In 1850 imports exceeded exports by $20 million; in 1920 exports exceeded imports by $2,800 million. The United States had become a creditor nation.

These vast alterations in value and bulk were accompanied by changes in *composition* by which the U.S.A. ceased to serve chiefly as a source of raw materials for Europe, but became instead an exporter of manufactured goods herself. Taking a yearly average for the 1850's, the commodity composition of American imports was: semi- and wholly-manufactured goods 63·3 per cent, manufactured and raw foodstuffs 27·1 per cent, raw materials 9·6 per cent. The composition of exports was: manufactured goods 16·3 per cent, foodstuffs 22 per cent, raw materials 61·7 per cent. Taking a similar average for the years 1901–5, import composition was: manufactured goods 41·3 per cent, foodstuffs 25·3 per cent, raw materials 33·4 per cent. Export composition was: manufactured goods 35·4 per cent, foodstuffs 34·3 per cent, raw materials 30·3 per cent. The average for 1911–15 reflects on the whole a continued change in the same direction. Import

[1] America remained much less dependent on foreign trade than many European nations however: the per capita figure for the U.K. in 1914 stood at the equivalent of about $108 and that of Germany at about $73.

composition was: manufactured goods 39·8 per cent, foodstuffs 25·3 per cent (this figure had fallen in the years between to 22·8 per cent), raw materials 34·9 per cent. Export composition was: manufactured goods 46·1 per cent, foodstuffs 23·1 per cent, raw materials 30·8 per cent.[1]

Statistics reveal a marked relative decline in the export of raw materials, accompanied by a rise in that of manufactured products. As for foodstuffs, the most significant factor was of course American grain. The figures given above offer little information on this score because they omit the chief period of grain exports, the 1870's and 1880's. We must therefore take a closer look at the five-year averages of composition percentages. In the '50's, as we know already, raw and manufactured foodstuffs took up 22 per cent of total American exports. Omitting the abnormalities of the Civil War, we find that the period 1866–70 saw little change in this situation (22·8 per cent). In the first half of the 1870's, however, foodstuffs took up 35·1 per cent of exports, and in the second half, 48·3 per cent—almost half. The year 1880 marked the climax of this rapid increase. In the late '80's the figure fell to 40 per cent, and although there was a recovery in the '90's the average for 1901–5 was only 34·3 per cent. This average percentage of total exports consisting of foodstuffs continued falling and by the years 1911–15 had reached 23·1 per cent. After World War I the decrease did not halt. The lowest proportion was that for 1936–1940: 9·3 per cent. After World War II it was again in the region of 20 per cent (22·9 per cent in 1946).

A noticeable change has been the increase in the export of manufactured foodstuffs as opposed to raw foodstuffs, especially during World War II when American canned, processed and dried foods gained even wider fame. During that war manufactured foodstuff exports represented 11·6 per cent of total exports, but raw foodstuffs represented merely 1·6 per cent.

Import statistics reveal much the same process in reverse. In the years 1915–20 raw material imports reached their highest proportion of total imports (40·1 per cent), whilst the influx of semi- and wholly-manufactured goods reached their lowest (31·5 per cent, of which well under half were finished products). Among the more important raw materials imported in recent years have been rubber, wood pulp, hides, skins and furs, wool, silk, copper, tin, petroleum, jute and vegetable oils. Imported foodstuffs have included coffee, tea, cocoa,

[1] Based on figures available in *Historical Statistics of the United States, 1789–1945* (U.S. Bureau of Census, Washington, 1949), p. 246, (Series M 56-67). The composition of foreign trade in 1946 was: *imports*: manufactured goods 37 per cent, foodstuffs 27·5 per cent, raw materials 35·5 per cent; *exports*: manufactured goods 62·2 per cent, foodstuffs 22·9 per cent, raw materials 14·9 per cent.

tropical fruits and nuts, and cane sugar. One imported manufacture of particular significance is newsprint, mainly from Canada and revealing serious exhaustion of American natural resources.

As an exporter of raw materials and foodstuffs the U.S.A. had sent most of her exports to Europe. With the change in quantity and in composition came a change in *direction*. Although Europe remains the principal market for American products, her position has declined in relation to other parts of the globe, especially Asia and Canada. In the '70's and '80's the proportion of total U.S. exports going to Europe reached its peak. In 1860 it had been 74·8 per cent, from which it rose to an average of 83·1 per cent for the years 1876–80. From 1880 until World War II it then declined steadily, reaching only 41·4 per cent in the years 1936–40. Of course, there was an increase during the war (to 56·9 per cent) and in 1946 the proportion of American exports bound for European markets stood at 42·1 per cent. In the same period, exports to Asia increased steadily from 2·4 per cent (1860) to 17·3 per cent (1931–5). During World War II this figure was cut down to 7·9 per cent, but in 1946 it stood at 13·8 per cent. U.S. exports to the rest of North America (both the northern non-U.S. and the southern non-U.S. parts) also increased more or less steadily from 15·7 per cent of total exports (1860) to 25·8 per cent (1926–30). In 1946 they stood at 26·1 per cent. Exports to South America have risen from 4·7 per cent (1860) to 11·8 per cent (1946), though the figures reveal considerable fluctuations. Those to Africa have increased slowly from 0·4 per cent of total exports in the years 1871–5, to 5 per cent in 1946.

Imports into the United States from Europe have shown a protracted decline, as a proportion of total American imports, since 1860. In that year they represented 61·3 per cent of the total, but by the years 1936–40 they were on average 25·3 per cent. For obvious reasons, they fell to 8·1 per cent in the period 1941–45, and in 1946 stood at 16·2 per cent. Imports from Asia increased from 8·3 per cent (1860) to 31·6 per cent (1936–40), but fell during the war, representing 18 per cent in 1946. The rest of North America has supplied an increasing amount of U.S. imports, its contribution rising from 19·2 per cent (1860) to 30·2 per cent (1915–20) and then declining to 23·1 per cent (1926–30). During the Second World War it rose once more (to 44·2 per cent), and in 1946 constituted 33·6 per cent of the total. South American imports rose from 9·9 per cent (1860) to 14·9 per cent (1891–5) and then fluctuated at a lower proportion before attaining 17·6 per cent in the years 1915–20. This, like that of the early '90's, was a momentary increase and by 1936–40 South American imports were 13·6 per cent of the total. During the war they increased and stood at 22·3 per cent in 1946. United States imports from Africa, like her exports to that continent, have remained small but nevertheless shown a steady increase, from 0.6 per cent in the years 1871–5 to 6·2 per cent in 1946.

The growing importance of American foreign trade, the extension of the internal transportation network, the 'closing' of the frontier and expansion of large-scale production under consolidated business organizations led to an urgent need to find markets, raw material sources and new fields of investment for surplus capital. The revival in the 1890's of the expansionist spirit of the '40's and '50's was thus no accident. Captain A. T. Mahan, the naval historian and publicist of the revival, made this very clear when he announced in the *Atlantic Monthly* in 1890:[1]

'Whether they will or no, Americans must now begin to look outward. The growing production of the country demands it. An increasing volume of public sentiment demands it.'

Although this imperialist tendency was a 'Great Aberration' for the American Republic, she was not alone in the world in her desire to acquire colonial territory. A new spirit was abroad, exemplified as much by Disraeli's shrewd and swift purchase of the Suez Canal shares as by the multilateral 'Grab for Africa'. Between 1870 and 1900 Great Britain attained an extra five million square miles of territory, France three and a half million and Germany one million. In these states as in America the economic basis of the 'New Imperialism' was to be seen in the acceleration of industrial progress in the preceding century. The problem of more production was for the present answered; for markets, raw materials and investment opportunities the Great Powers would go far—and the U.S.A. would follow their example. The New Imperialism, under whatever euphemism it masqueraded ('the white man's burden' or 'Manifest Destiny') was basically a question of economic exploitation of underdeveloped areas by economically advanced nations.

In the U.S.A. a further factor in the economic imperialism of the late nineteenth century was the country's gradual transformation from debtor to creditor status in the world at large. Until 1914, Great Britain, France and Germany were the only significant net creditors on international capital account.[2] Although America's direct foreign investments totalled in 1914 $2,600 million (mainly in Mexico and Canada), she remained a debtor nation. World War I brought a financial revolution, however, and was practically financed in its latest stages by American private and governmental loans. The

[1] In an article called 'The United States Looking Outward' (Vol. 66, pp. 816–24).

[2] For a useful discussion of this and related matters, see W. Ashworth, *A Short History of the International Economy, 1850–1950* (London, 1952).

United States ceased to be an international debtor. By 1922 she was a net creditor even excluding the huge sums owed to her by other nations in the form of war debts, and by 1929 her total direct foreign investments amounted to over $7,200 million. As a startling result of World War I the financial capital of the world shifted from London to New York.

The political policy of territorial expansion outside American continental boundaries was thus closely associated with the desire to protect growing foreign investments. This is not the place to consider in any detail the history of American foreign and imperial policy, yet this close connection with economic affairs necessitates some mention of the chief trends. The 'Great Aberration' chiefly concerned Latin America and the Far East.

In Latin America the Monroe Doctrine (1823) revealed an early United States interest, probably arising out of Southern desires to extend the area under slavery and the plantation system as well as out of distrust of European monarchies. In Cuba, however, American trade and investments had by the 1890's introduced a new and more compelling factor. Jefferson and John Quincy Adams, among others, had realized earlier the strategic importance of the island, close to American shores and commanding the entrance to the Mexican Gulf, and in 1848 Polk had even tried to buy it. In 1868 a ten years' war broke out in Cuba against Spanish rule, and when peace was restored the Spaniards reimposed their despotic control. Then in 1894 the Wilson-Gorman Tariff, reversing the earlier policy of the McKinley Act placing raw sugar on the free list, cut off the American market for Cuban sugar, which consequently was reduced to one-quarter of its former price. American investments in sugar and mining industries in Cuba at that time amounted to $50 million, while U.S.-Cuban trade had in 1893 exceeded twice that sum. In 1895 the Cubans revolted, this time aided by mass unemployment, and began to destroy sugar plantations. When the worst effects of the financial crash of 1893 were over, Americans, stimulated by garbled reports of Spanish 'atrocities' printed in various sections of the press and by the mysterious destruction of the U.S. battleship *Maine* in Havana harbour (15 February 1898), turned readily to the Cuban question. On 19 April 1898 Congress resolved that Cuba was independent and instructed the President to go to war with Spain to give credence to the statement. The Teller Resolution added that the government and control of the island would be given to its people. This was not so, for Cuba was ruled by the United States army from 1898 to 1902. Before it was finally handed over, yellow fever was stamped out by an American medical commission and the Platt Amendment (1901) was inserted into the Cuban constitution, stipulating that Cuba would never sign away its independence to any foreign power, never contract any public debt it could not pay, would grant the U.S.A. the right of intervention to preserve Cuban independence and protect 'life, property and individual liberty', and allow U.S. coaling and naval stations to be established on the island. This amendment was abrogated in 1934 but American interests in Cuba remained extremely active—direct investment there totalling over $660 million in 1936.

The Spanish-American War (ended by the Peace of Paris after 113 days of fighting) left the United States not only with the protectorate of Cuba, but with Puerto Rico as a colony. After eighteen months or so of military government, the Foraker Act of 1900 set up a civil administration in Puerto Rico, which was given the status of an 'unorganized Territory', whose people were not U.S. citizens. Free trade was established between the two countries in 1902. The Jones Act (1917) later gave full U.S. citizenship to Puerto Ricans, together with a Bill of Rights, an elected upper (as well as a lower) chamber, and a governor appointed by the President. Since 1900 the sugar, tobacco and fruit industries of the island have increased, and educational, sanitary and transportation facilities have been vastly improved. On the other hand the economy of Puerto Rico is by no means stable or satisfactory: its two chief crops are entirely dependent upon the American market, nearly all the businesses are owned by absentee American firms and most of the fertile land is controlled by American corporations. In the 1930's a class of landless proletarians emerged as farms were consolidated into larger sugar and tobacco plantations, absentee owners controlled about 60 per cent of total wealth, and 60 per cent of the populace were thrown into unemployment with the collapse of the U.S. market. Many natives emigrated to the United States.

A third legacy of the Peace of Paris was the renewed agitation for an Isthmian canal, thought necessary for military as well as commercial reasons. America was prevented from acquiring exclusive control of any such canal by the Clayton-Bulwer Treaty (1850) with Great Britain; but in 1901 the Hay-Pauncefote Treaty allowed her to build a canal if it were kept open to all nations on equal terms. Two years later Colombia refused to accept the Hay-Herran Treaty regarding payment for land to be ceded for canal construction, and shortly afterwards a revolt broke out in that country (3 November 1903) which was encouraged by the arrival of the U.S. gunboat *Nashville*. On 6 November America recognized the independence of Panama and rapidly signed a treaty with the new republic, gaining a canal zone ten miles wide in perpetuity, in return for $10 million cash and an annuity of a quarter of a million. The Panama Canal was completed in 1914.

The desire to protect American investments and political unrest in the areas concerned similarly helped to support the extension of U.S. protectorates over Nicaragua, Haiti and Santo Domingo. The Bryan-Chamorro Treaty (1916) gave the United States an option on a canal route through Nicaragua and a 99-year renewable lease on two small islands (Great Corn and Little Corn), in return for a payment of $3 million by the U.S. Government, to be used partly to settle outstanding claims by American banks. American marines had been landed in 1912 (at the request of the Nicaraguan Government) and remained in the country until 1925. Three years later they were brought back to supervise presidential elections, and not finally withdrawn until 1933. Similarly Haiti was occupied in 1915 when she was in a state of acute financial distress and internal anarchy, American forces being withdrawn in 1934. Santo Domingo had a national debt of over $32 million (two-thirds of it due to foreigners) in 1904 when Theodore Roosevelt first declared that the Monroe Doctrine could be extended to include 'the exercise of an international police power' by the United States in the New World. A U.S.-Dominican treaty was quickly drawn up by which the United States was to take over control of the collection of customs duties and ensure that 55 per cent of revenue was put aside as a creditors' fund. The Senate shelved the treaty, but Roosevelt established unofficial supervision over Dominican finances, which revealed a marked improvement. In 1907 the U.S. Senate ratified a new but similar treaty. American troops were sent to Santo Domingo to supervise elections in 1914 and remained in virtual control of the country from 1916 to 1924.

Other steps in United States-Latin American policy included the purchase of the Danish West Indies (the Virgin Islands) for $25 million in 1917, and the manœuvres of American financial interests in Mexico. U.S. investment in Mexican mines, oil, transportation and ranching was encouraged by the dictator Porfirio Diaz and took place at an average rate of $40 million a year between 1897 and 1914, total investments increasing more than four-fold to well over $850 million.[1] This was three times the investment in Mexico of Great Britain, who was the next important rival. The Mexican situation was complicated, however, by international rivalries, commercial competition against a background of tremendous profits, domestic economic instability and (from 1911 when Franciso Madero first led a revolution against the autocratic Diaz regime) almost continuous civil conflict. Madero's rising was financed in part by American oil men angered by Diaz's policy of playing off the British and American oil interests against each other. Madero was assassinated by the conservatives, who achieved a counter-revolution, perhaps with British help.

[1] See, among others, C. Lewis, *America's Stake in International Investments* (Washington, 1938), and S. Nearing and J. Freeman, *Dollar Diplomacy: a Study in American Imperialism* (New York, 1925).

The conservative government, however, was driven out by President Wilson and a new one, led by Carranza, found American support in 1914. In 1917 after further internal disorders a new Mexican constitution was drawn up nationalizing Church property, establishing secular education and declaring the inalienable right of the Mexican people to own their land, water and subsoil resources. All alien ownership of land and water rights within specified coastal and frontier zones was prohibited—but not retroactively. In 1938 the Mexican Government nationalized foreign oil concessions with promise of full compensation. The acceptance by the Americans of this expropriation owed much to the better diplomatic climate existing between the two nations. The principle of 'expropriation' of foreign property would appear again in the international history of the post-Second World War years.

Elsewhere in the New World, American economic imperialism was limited to investment, Canada being the second most important field in 1897 (to Mexico as the first) and the most important in 1914. American investment in Canada increased at a steady rate after the opening of the new century, principally because of the desire to acquire raw materials, to exploit the Canadian market and to obviate Canadian tariffs (especially after the increase of 1906) by making goods for sale in Canada in that country itself. Thus American capital has helped to develop the automobile, machinery, metallurgical, electrical, rubber, chemical, lumber, pulp and paper industries of the Dominion. By 1914 Americans had invested over $860 million in Canada, and by 1935 over $3,650 million. In Peru, Chile, Venezuela and Colombia, American capital was invested heavily in the mining of precious metals and copper and in oil production. In South, as opposed to Central, America the U.S.A. held investments totalling $635 million in 1914, over $3,000 million in 1929, and over $2,570 million in 1935.[1]

The second main area of interest for American expansion was the Pacific and the Far East. An early attraction for American commerce,[2] this part of the globe received renewed publicity with Perry's voyage to Japan (1854) and American trips to Samoa[3] and elsewhere.

Hawaii (the Sandwich Islands) was first discovered in 1778 by Captain Cook. In the 1820's several Boston missionaries emigrated to the islands and with gradual intermarriage gained political power.

[1] These figures include both direct and 'portfolio' investments but exclude U.S. Government loans. By comparison, American investment in Europe was almost $692 million in 1914, over $4,600 million in 1929 and $3,026 million in 1935. (See C. Lewis, op. cit., p. 606.)
[2] See Chapter V, above, p. 57.
[3] The U.S.A. acquired Tutuila (with Pago-Pago harbour) from the Samoan Islands in 1899.

Two groups of Yankees established close commercial contact with Hawaii—firstly the traders who sold its sandalwood to China, and later the whalers who used it as a supply base. From the 1840's sugar was grown in increasing quantities in the islands. U.S.-Hawaiian amity was assured by America's determined exclusion of England and France. In 1875 a reciprocity treaty placed Hawaiian sugar on the U.S. free list, exports to America thus increasing fifteen-fold by 1890. Hawaiian prosperity chiefly favoured the American beneficiaries, however, who had invested heavily in the islands. A constitution advantageous to property owners was forced upon the king in 1887, thus giving even greater power to the American planters, who held the best land and worked it with imported cheap labour from China and Japan.

Then in 1890 the McKinley tariff (placing raw sugar on the free list and giving a bounty to native American producers) caused great anxiety in the Hawaiian sugar industry: sugar was almost halved in price and property values slumped. When in the following year the new ruler, Queen Liliuokalani, demanded a democratic constitution embodying native rights, foreign capitalists panicked, demanded U.S. aid, and successfully brought about the abolition of the monarchy (16 January 1893). A treaty of annexation was drawn up, but President Cleveland's liberal qualms prevented further action in that direction. Hawaii became an independent republic until 1898, when she was annexed under the administration of President McKinley—the same McKinley whose tariff had been the chief cause of Hawaiian distress eight years earlier.[1]

The Philippine Islands and Guam[2] were ceded to the United States by Spain at the Peace of Paris, after an American payment of $20 million cash. Even before the treaty was ratified a Filipino revolution broke out (February 1899) and despite the commercial potentialities of the islands for sugar, hemp, coconut oil, tobacco, minerals, timber and rubber, their disadvantages were very great. Not only were there over forty different tribes speaking about ninety different dialects, but a large proportion of the population were illiterate, and transportation and sanitary conditions were extremely bad. A purely civil administration was established with some native participation and considerable material progress was made, even before the costly rebellion was put down in 1902. Once peace was regained a 25 per cent tariff reduction was allowed to Philippine products. Seven years

[1] After 1900 canning was introduced and Hawaii came to produce 80 per cent of the world's output of canned pineapples.

[2] Guam is an island with a very badly balanced economy, its chief importance being as an air passenger transit station (Pan-American Airways) and naval base. The naval commander acts as governor, and has a Congress which is purely advisory.

later free trade was conceded between the two countries except in sugar and tobacco, and in 1913 complete free trade was finally secured. The Jones Act (1916) gave a measure of home rule and promised American withdrawal on the institution of 'stable government'. There seemed little doubt that the Philippine adventure had cost and was costing the Federal Government much more than it gained in return, and in 1934 the Tydings-McDuffie Act—supported by American isolationists, agricultural interests in fear of competition and the A.F.L.—arranged for Philippine independence after a ten-year probationary period. This would have meant, of course, regular American tariffs, the imposition of an immigration quota, and the withdrawal of automatic U.S. military defence of the islands. But the Japanese put a stop to this by their invasion in World War II, which completely altered the situation: Philippine autonomy was finally confirmed on 4 July 1946, and the Philippine Trade Act of the same year promised U.S.-Filipino free trade for at least eight years.

The story of American investment in China, which centred around railroad construction, should be sought in further detail elsewhere,[1] if necessary. Here it can only be said that the high hopes of an 'illimitable market' in China and of 'fabulous trade' in the Pacific which would ensue from America's control of the Philippines, came to little. Greater stability and economic growth in Japan offered more chances for American enterprise and investment, but China proved disappointing. More American capital was tied up in missionary work there than in railroads, and total investments came to only $59 million in 1914.

American policy with regard to China was to check her territorial disintegration and maintain her economic integrity against the encroachments of Japan and Russia and the Western Powers—Great Britain, France and Germany. The conclusion of the Sino-Japanese War in 1895 left Japan with Formosa and vague rights over Korea. In addition the other Powers demanded long-term leases of certain ports from China. Encouraged by Great Britain, the American Secretary of State John Hay made an effort to keep the doors of China open to commerce. He sent notes to all the nations concerned on 6 September 1899, asking that no Power should interfere with any port within its 'sphere of influence', that no tariffs should be imposed other than those of the Chinese Government, collected by Chinese officials, and that there should be no differentiation between nations in harbour and railway rates. The Boxer Rebellion of 1900, in which the U.S.A. helped the other Powers to suppress anti-alien riots, gave Hay another opportunity to affirm the 'Open Door' policy of equal trading facilities for all nations. On 3 July 1900 he

[1] See, for instance, Lewis, op. cit.; Nearing and Freeman, op. cit.; and C. F. Remer, *Foreign Investments in China* (New York, 1933).

issued another circular message opposing further annexation of Chinese territory as a result of the rebellion and declaring that the United States intended 'to safeguard for the world the principle of equal and impartial trade with all parts of the Chinese Empire'. This policy was generally upheld despite such intrusions as the Russo-Japanese War (1904-5) and World War I, until the Japanese invasion of Manchuria in 1931. Taft's efforts at 'dollar diplomacy'— the substitution of dollars for bullets by encouraging railway magnates like E. H. Harriman to invest in Chinese railways—came to nought. Similarly his proposal through Secretary P.C. Knox that all Manchurian railways be neutralized (November 1909) was hastily rejected by Japan and Russia. In 1910 a British, French, German and American four-power banking consortium was set up to share equally in all Chinese loans, but American membership was withdrawn by Woodrow Wilson. Ultimately it proved impossible to substitute dollars for bullets in Far Eastern diplomacy; the door would have to be propped open with bayonets it seemed, despite the strong reluctance of the United States and the other Powers to take sufficient military steps to halt Japanese aggression.

The history of America's *external* trading and financial relations has now been outlined and illustrated. What of her *internal* financial history?

This has two principal themes in the years since the Civil War:[1] firstly the effects of the National Bank Act of 1863, the rôle of the Independent Treasury in monetary policy and the organization of the Federal Reserve System in 1913; secondly, the Greenback and Free Silver Movements, the Campaign of 1896 and the Currency Act of 1900. In other words we have to deal with banking structure and with currency reform.

The National Bank Act of 1863[2] was, as we have seen earlier, an attempt to market Civil War bonds and provide an adequate currency. It established a national banking system by creating a new department in the Treasury—that of the Comptroller of the Currency—which could give twenty-year National Bank charters to groups of not less than five stockholders with a certain amount of capital. The stockholders had to deposit bonds equal in amount to one-third of their capital with the Comptroller, and received in return National Bank notes equal to 90 per cent of the current market value (but not exceeding 90 per cent of par value) of the deposited bonds. The total issue of all National Bank notes was restricted to $300 million. To safeguard depositors, National Banks had to main-

[1] The financing of the Civil War itself has been dealt with in the opening pages of Chapter VII, in order to lend continuity to the text.
[2] Considerably amended in 1864.

tain certain reserves: those in central 'reserve cities' had to keep a reserve of 25 per cent of their deposits, made up of 'lawful money' and held in their own vaults. Banks in other cities also had to maintain a 25 per cent reserve, but half of it in their case could be kept on deposit in the banks of central reserve cities. Country banks must keep a 15 per cent reserve of which three-fifths could be kept on deposit in city National Banks of either category. The federal tax of up to 10 per cent on the note-issue of non-National Banks (imposed in March 1865) made it unprofitable for state banks to issue notes and began to drive them out of circulation. By October 1866 there were 1,644 National Banks, with a note circulation of over $280 million.

The most significant outcome of Civil War financing was this institution of a National Banking system. But the later history of the system was by no means smooth. Unlike the earlier U.S. Banks, it established a large number of relatively small banks scattered throughout the nation rather than a single central controlling bank. The Act faithfully reflected the centrifugal, individualistic tendency of the time, and the strong suspicion of consolidated authority in banking. Perhaps this was its chief weakness. Local control implied less experienced control; decentralization implied less unity of policy and hampered the formulation and execution of decisive action in times of financial crisis. Also, the state banks continued to exist, complicating the situation.[1] Moreover, although the currency secured by the Act was sound, it was inelastic. This was the second major flaw in the system. The amount of federal bonds held by banks —without which they could not obtain charters and National Bank notes—bore little or no relation to the demand for money. Looked at another way, this meant that instead of fluctuating with business demand, the number of National Bank notes in circulation tended to vary with the price of the federal bonds that were needed to obtain them—because this considerably affected the profit gained by issuing them at all. So when bonds were cheap in the 1870's note-issue was easy and profitable; but when bonds rose in price as many were redeemed in the 1880's, note-issue was difficult and unprofitable. The anomalous situation therefore came about that during the prosperity of the '80's when more currency was needed, less National Bank notes were available.

It will be clear that the notes were as unresponsive to short-term requirements (harvests, Christmas expenses and other seasonal demands) as they were to long-term requirements—a weakness disastrously well illustrated in times of financial panics. Other circulating media were also inelastic, and but for the growth of deposit

[1] These included state commercial banks, state savings banks and state trust companies.

banking and the expansion of the cheque system,[1] the need would have been very stringent indeed. As it was, the Comptroller estimated that under 10 per cent of the total volume of business was transacted in currency in the late '80's.

The failure of the National Banking system to provide an adequate money supply, especially during the crises of 1873, 1884, 1893, 1903 and 1907, led almost directly to the passing of the Federal Reserve Act of 1913. Several attempts were made in the interim to strengthen National Banking, but were on the whole ineffective. The Resumption Act (1875), for instance, removed altogether the 'ceiling' figure of total notes to be issued ($300 million), and in 1882 steps were taken to improve the competitive position of the National Banks by allowing those with a capital of under $150,000 to deposit only one-quarter (instead of one-third) of it in bonds with the Comptroller. In 1900 the Currency (or Gold Standard) Act, in so far as it affected the banking system alone, permitted National Bank notes to be issued up to the full par value of the bonds (instead of 90 per cent), reduced the minimum capital needs for banks in towns of under 3,000 population, reduced the tax on all bonds yielding under 2 per cent, if deposited to obtain National Bank notes (from 1 per cent to $\frac{1}{2}$ per cent per annum), and refunded the existing national debt in thirty-year 2 per cent bonds.

National Bank note circulation, which had reached over $340 million in 1874 and then fluctuated around that figure for a decade, began to decline after 1884 while other forms of money increased. In 1891 circulation was down to $168 million, but later on increased loans to cover such expenses as the Spanish-American War brought it up again, and by 1913 it was not far below $716 million.

Neither increased circulation nor reforms managed to avert a large-scale overhaul of the banking system in 1913. The Federal Government had already made a foray into the banking field (after a long armistice of almost half a century) when it created postal savings banks by an Act of 1910.[2] But although it met some opposition from government critics as a 'socialistic' measure, this Act was not their chief object of abuse. Those who distrusted and feared the growth of federal authority were greatly displeased even with con-

---

[1] Readers may recall that the use of cheques also expanded in England during the nineteenth century. Although the background to the two cases is very different, in some respects they are similar. In England the trouble arose out of Peel's Bank Charter Act (1844), the provisions of which were also inelastic. In both cases this expansion of 'credit currency' remained insufficient to meet the needs of crisis periods. See Sir John Clapham's *An Economic History of Modern Britain*, Vol. I: *The Early Railway Age* (Second Edition, Cambridge, 1930 (1926)), pp. 522-5.

[2] See D. R. Dewey, op. cit., p. 487.

ditions during the truce. Under the National Banking system the central government possessed no fiscal agent and with the lack of central bank control over credit, the Independent Treasury[1] (the government's chief depository) was forced to assume responsibility for various central banking functions. When in 1871–2 it took steps to meet a public demand for currency by issuing $6,137,000 in paper, opposition to the move was severe on the grounds that Congress alone should decide monetary policy and its authority should not be delegated to an uncontrolled Treasury official.[2] From 1890 to 1912 the Treasury acted as a genuine central bank, being considered as a lender of last resort.[3] Serious doubts soon arose as to its true place in the monetary system.

The Federal Reserve System set up by the Act of December 1913 did not adopt a central bank—despite the recommendations of the National Monetary Commission[4] in favour of such a move. Instead the nation was divided into twelve Federal Reserve districts, each with one Federal Reserve bank to act as a clearing house and bankers' bank for the member banks of the system. All National Banks were compelled and all other banks encouraged to participate by subscribing to the capital fund of their Federal Reserve district banks. They were to buy district bank stock amounting to 6 per cent of their capital and surplus, a cumulative dividend of 6 per cent to be paid on each share. District banks were empowered to issue Federal Reserve notes secured by 100 per cent commercial paper and a reserve of 40 per cent in gold or gold certificates. Their earnings in excess of 6 per cent were to be shared equally between their own surplus funds and the Federal Government. A Federal Reserve Board with headquarters in the capital was to supervise the whole structure, its seven members to include five presidential nominees, the Secretary of the Treasury and the Comptroller of the Currency.

The American Bankers' Association damned the Federal Reserve Act out of hand as 'socialism'; the Comptroller of the Currency declared future financial panics to be 'mathematically impossible'. In fact, the Act did greatly improve the National Bank-Independent

---

[1] Finally established in 1846. See Chapter VI, above, p. 78 n. 1.

[2] Later Congress did sanction a permanent currency increase to $400 million but President Grant promptly vetoed the Bill on anti-inflationary grounds. His message of 22 April 1874 is given in a standard work of reference, J. D. Richardson (ed.), *Messages and Papers of the Presidents, 1789–1897* (10 vols., Washington, 1907), Vol. VII, pp. 268–71.

[3] See E. R. Taus, *Central Banking Functions of the U.S. Treasury, 1789–1941* (New York, 1943). Thanks to a lucid style, this book is less formidable than it sounds. Chapters IV and V concern the National Banking period.

[4] Established by the Aldrich-Vreeland Act (1908).

Treasury system: it provided a more elastic currency, a centralized control of the discount rate and gold stock, a credit store for banks in emergencies, and a fiscal agent to connect the banking system with the Treasury. On the other hand the rivalry between National Banks and state banks was perpetuated, and the new system grew but slowly. By 1917 only thirty-seven state banks had volunteered to join it. As late as the 1950's it was still disabled by this dichotomy in the banking structure and inability to assert control over all commercial banks. For instance, in 1950 the Federal Reserve Board's request for a broadening of its authority to include control of consumer credit and the power to increase reserve requirements by 10 per cent for commercial as well as member banks caused a furor in Congress and in the banking world.[1] The request was studiously disregarded, and when the outbreak of the Korean War in June 1950 was accompanied by a panic growth of consumer sales and extension of credit the Federal Reserve Board looked on in impotent anxiety.

Currency reform supplies the second theme of financial history in this period. The 'Greenbacks' which were the subject of so much discussion were first introduced, it will be remembered, during the Civil War as legal tender paper money issued on government credit without metallic backing (Legal Tender Act, 1862). Before the war was over the Union Government had issued $450 million in Greenbacks and inaugurated an inflationary movement that sent their value down to about 43 cents each (1864). In the post-war years a deflationary policy was pursued, business and banking groups being successful in having some paper withdrawn. This explains the interest of farmers in currency affairs,[2] for those who had borrowed on a 40 or 50 cent paper dollar found themselves obliged to pay both interest demands and principal on an 80 or 90 cent dollar, and this while prices were in full decline. In 1874 came President Grant's veto (already mentioned) of a Congressional attempt to issue more Greenbacks, and in 1875 the Specie Resumption Act aimed at a further contraction of paper money (to reduce Greenbacks from $382 million to $300 million) and at resumption of cash payments on 1 January 1879. Provoked by this policy and by the after-effects of the 1873 crisis, the inflationist reformers—'Greenbackers'—fought a hard struggle in the elections of 1876, having considerable local triumphs but little national significance. Peter Cooper of New York, the presidential candidate of the ephemeral Independent National Party (Greenback), polled only 82,000 votes, and the victor was a Republican, the dull and mediocre

[1] In contrast, on the opposite side of the Atlantic a logical process had been completed four years earlier when the Labour government nationalized the Bank of England.

[2] See Chapter IX, above, pp. 138–41.

Rutherford B. Hayes. Two years later a new inflationist party emerged in Toledo, the Greenback Labour Party, with strong agrarian support. In the Congressional elections of 1878 it gained one million votes and secured fourteen Congressmen. This did not impede the successful completion of the resumption policy, as planned, at the opening of 1879. America returned to a metallic standard after seventeen years of irredeemable paper currency.

The Greenbackers fought the presidential campaign of 1880 with J.B. Weaver as their nominee, but their popular vote on this occasion fell disastrously to a mere 307,306—a defeat which heralded their decline. They lost the support of Labour to the Knights and their specific monetary arguments were vitiated by the ending of the depression, increasingly profitable crops and rising prices. Paper money, under the Act of 1875, circulated like gold and the old inflationist motif disappeared to be replaced with a new one: *Free Silver*.

The aim of the Free Silver men was to inflate the currency by re-establishing the free and unlimited coinage of silver at an inflated ration of sixteen to one. Free, unlimited silver coinage was first approved by the Act of 1792. From the Act of 1834 until 1873 its ratio had been sixteen to one, which overvalued gold. As a result silver was driven from circulation, and in 1873 the Federal Government, recognizing a *de facto* situation, discontinued the free coinage of silver. There was no protest at this time. But in 1871 Germany had adopted the gold standard, to be followed later by Holland and the Scandinavian countries. Also in 1874 the Latin Monetary Union (France, Italy, Belgium, Switzerland and Greece) limited silver coinage. Much silver bullion came on to the market as a result, precisely when American silver-mines were increasing output, especially in Nevada. As the price of silver rapidly dropped agitators in the silver-mining states and in the debtor West and South began denouncing demonetization as the 'Crime of '73'. In 1878 the inflationists were powerful enough in Congress to pass the Bland-Allison Act over the veto of President Hayes. This empowered the Secretary of the Treasury to buy between two and four million dollars' worth of silver bullion per month and to coin it into dollars at a ratio of sixteen to one. But although under the Act nearly 380 million silver dollars were coined between 1878 and 1890, the price of silver continued to fall. In 1888 the Republicans were successful and their candidate Benjamin Harrison became President. The faction from the silver states supported the McKinley Tariff and were accordingly rewarded with the Sherman Silver Purchase Act (1890). This authorized purchase by the Treasury of 4·5 million ounces of silver a month (about total national output), to be paid for in a new issue of paper money, the 'Treasury Notes of 1890', redeemable in either gold or silver and to be accepted as fully legal tender. Although the monthly purchase of silver was doubled, the Free Silver men remained unsatisfied; nothing short of 'free and unlimited coinage' would quiet them. The 'Omaha Platform' of the Populists in 1892[1] was headed by this measure, and in the election of that year their candidate the ex-Greenbacker J. B. Weaver polled over one million popular votes and twenty-two electoral college votes.

The circumstance that helped to bring the monetary struggle to a climax was the crisis of 1893 and the ensuing depression in which, by 1896, prices reached their lowest point for half a century. Also President Cleveland (who had been elected in 1892) was a 'gold Democrat' and, convinced that currency uncertainty was a principal factor in the collapse, he called a special session of Congress which repealed the Sherman Silver Purchase Act on 30 October 1893. The famous presidential campaign of 1896, that roused more excitement and attention than any since Lincoln's election of 1860, finally put an end to the long bimetallist controversy. The Western and Southern Democrats managed to displace Cleveland and supported instead a man much more in their favour, the orator William Jennings Bryan.[2] The Bryan Free Silver Democrats were joined by the Populists. On the opposite side the Republicans led by McKinley defended gold, protective tariffs, and a 'firm' foreign policy (meaning intervention in Cuba, control of Hawaii and purchase of the Danish West Indies). The emotional, slanderous struggle ended in a clear majority for McKinley who captured 271 electoral college and 7,035,638 popular votes, as against 176 electoral and 6,467,946 popular votes for Bryan. The latter's brilliant 'Cross of Gold' speech had been the keynote of the campaign. In it Bryan had made clear the underlying forces engaged:

'You come to us and tell us that the great cities are in favour of the gold standard; we reply that the great cities rest upon our broad and fertile prairies. Burn down your cities and leave our farms, and your cities will spring up again as if by magic; but destroy our farms and the grass will grow in the streets of every city in the country. . . . You shall not press down upon the brow of labour this crown of thorns, you shall not crucify mankind upon a cross of gold.'

The vote was cast on clear economic and sectional lines. Bryan won the Western states of Colorado, Idaho, Kansas, Nebraska, Montana, Nevada, South Dakota, Wyoming, Utah and Washington, the eleven states of the Solid South, and a 'border' state, Missouri.

[1] See Chapter IX, above, p. 140.
[2] Who was, according to an opponent, like the river Platte from which he came: five feet deep and a mile wide at the mouth. Bryan's eloquence earned him the title the 'Boy Orator of the Platte'.

After 1896 several factors mentioned earlier came into play: poor harvests in 1896 and 1897 in India and Europe which raised the price of American agricultural staples; increasing industrial production in the United States; a trebling of the world's gold production by 1900 owing to technological innovations and the development of new mines in South Africa and the Klondike; and an over-all increase in the amount of money in circulation. The demand for inflation disappeared in a period of relative prosperity for farmers, and at last the price trend began to tilt upwards. By the Currency Act of 1900 the government was able to establish a monometallic gold standard: all forms of currency must in future be maintained at parity with the gold dollar (25·8 grains, nine-tenths fine). A reserve fund of $150 million in gold coin and bullion was to be set aside to redeem Greenbacks and the 'Treasury Notes of 1890'. The last were removed from circulation and replaced with silver dollars. The Free Silver controversy was over.

SUGGESTED FURTHER READING

DEWEY, D. R. *Financial History of the United States* (11th edition, revised, New York, 1931).

JOHNSON, E. R. *et. al.* *History of the Domestic and Foreign Commerce of the United States* (2 vols., Washington, 1915).

TAUSSIG, F. W. *Tariff History of the United States* (8th edition, New York, 1931).

WILLIAMS, B. H. *Economic Foreign Policy of the United States* (New York, 1929).

XII

SOCIAL CRITICISM AND REFORM

The functioning of the American economy to 1917: the major crises; national income and living standards – Progressivism and the literature of protest; trust-busting; the Sherman Act (1890) and aftermath; the 'New Freedom' – Conservation – A note on 'laissez-faire'.

THE American economy experienced six principal crises up to World War I: three of these (1819, 1837, 1857) have already been mentioned in the concluding chapter of Part One. In this, the concluding chapter of Part Two, it is necessary to consider, very briefly, those of 1873, 1893 and 1907.

The events preceding the Panic of 1873 were not dissimilar to those preceding the earlier crises of the century: over-investment (this time in railroads—facilitated once more, as in the case of canals, by foreign capital) and unstable financing. Between 1865 and 1873 a railway mania succeeded not only in doubling the total national mileage but in stimulating a general boom and over-expansion in the iron and steel industries and agriculture. There was a total increase in national income which encouraged extravagance—the marginal propensity to import was high. Between 1860 and the crisis year imports increased 82 per cent (from $354 million in value to $642 million), but exports increased only 57 per cent ($334 million to $522 million). In addition to the capital outflow thus caused there was a drain of specie to pay annual interest rates on foreign capital (amounting to about $130 million); these losses were a danger signal but were blithely ignored.

Since 1871 money had been scarce and interest rates fluctuating and high. The crash came in September when the failure of a major firm—Jay Cooke & Co.—followed that of several minor firms engaged in railroad financing. Cooke—'the financier of the Civil War' —had over-involved his company in heavy investment in Northern Pacific Railroad securities. His bankruptcy precipitated a swift panic in which brokers and banks failed, the New York Stock Exchange was forced to close its doors for ten days, and cash payments were suspended by most banks. The disruption of the national economy brought little action from the national government; the Grant administration rose to its full height—and liberated $13 million in currency by repurchasing federal bonds.

By October New York was receiving injections of money from Europe and from the rest of the nation and the acute financial period was over. Cash payments were resumed, and the crisis deepened into a depression. For about five years the country suffered severe unemployment, wage cuts, strikes, bread lines, the closing-down of many manufacturing concerns (especially in the iron and steel and coal industries) and steeply falling agricultural and industrial prices.[1] Nevertheless a favourable balance of trade was achieved by a reduction of imports and expansion of exports encouraged by falling home prices and national income, demand elasticity for (luxury) imports being high. From late 1878 to 1883 there was a recovery, in which perhaps the central factors were foreign crop failures in 1879 and 1880, increasingly heavy American exports and an influx of gold. Railroad building and manufacturing revived and prices began rising. An acute setback was the financial crisis of 1884, again the result of wild railroad financing. The ensuing depression lasted a year, but there was no suspension of cash payments. About a million workers were thrown out of employment. Besides the railroads the main industry affected was iron and steel. However, the same two industries featured in the boom which soon developed out of the rapid recovery. There was also in the late '80's a speculative boom in Western lands and a renewed inflow of foreign capital.

In 1890 the economy paused slightly in its stride; in 1893 it staggered. Monetary factors were of particular significance in this second major crisis. Anxiety about American policy over the gold standard (owing to the bimetallist controversy and the Sherman Silver Purchase Act) led to withdrawal of considerable amounts of foreign capital, which together with the bankruptcy of several railroad companies (such as the Philadelphia and Reading) overtaxed the banking system. Western and Southern banks withdrew funds from New York, where cash payments were halted in July. A general contraction of the money market ensued. Almost 600 banks failed in 1893, the interior bearing the brunt of the strain. Commercial failures were three times the 1873 number, 15,242 houses going down. Railroad construction ceased, 74 companies collapsed and by 1895 no dividends were being paid on 60 per cent of railroad stocks. Factories and mines curtailed production and an estimated three million workers were unemployed (1894). The European demand for wheat fell off

[1] Distress was so universal and severe that two Congressional committees were appointed to investigate the 'causes' of the depression; they found, and failed to resolve, nearly 200.

and poor American harvests caused distress among the farming community. The depression that followed the panic lasted nearly four years, prices reaching their bottom level in 1896—the year of the great Bryan-McKinley presidential campaign. The 'hard times' explain much of the bitterness in that election and the severity of the Pullman strike of 1894.[1] Inflationists and Westerners claimed that the depression could be ended by increasing the currency through the free coinage of silver; conservatives blamed the crisis itself on silver. The former thought silver policy had not yet gone far enough; the latter thought it had gone too far. The conservatives forgot that most failures occurred in the West, where they could hardly be ascribed to a lack of confidence in the currency arising out of silver policy; the inflationists did not seem to realize that the great bulk of the nation's business was transacted not in currency but through cheques and demand deposits. President Cleveland, however, had the Sherman Silver Purchase Act repealed in October 1893[2] in order to protect gold and stop the drain on the Treasury. Although the drain in fact continued and the Federal Government had to buy gold (by selling bonds) twice in 1894, once in 1895 and again in 1896, conditions did improve during 1896, when the Treasury's financial position became more favourable and the gold drain ceased. A business revival began in the following year.

The Panic of 1907 is attributed nowadays chiefly—sometimes exclusively—to a banking failure. Contemporary opinion, however, was conflicting: the currency was once more blamed (the Aldrich-Vreeland Act of 1908 being the outcome); Roosevelt's 'trust-busting' policy was claimed by businessmen to be the central factor; rumours and blind fear in the financial world came in for severe castigation from newspaper cartoonists. The so-called 'rich man's Panic' of 1907 had been preceded by a smaller scare in 1903, felt most by the iron and steel industry and brought about mainly by the rapid overexpansion of holding companies and other 'mergers'.[3] In 1907 not only were heavy foreign and domestic capital funds concentrated in New York, but under the National Banking system many provincial houses had redeposited their reserves with New York banks, which practice had two dangerous results: firstly, both depositing and depository banks counted the same funds as reserves; secondly, the concentration at New York made reserves immobile and caused a tightening of the New York money market and a rise in interest

---

[1] See Chapter IX. In the same year 'General' Jacob Coxey, a Populist from Ohio led an 'army' of unemployed from the Mid-West to Washington to petition for federal relief action. He was arrested for walking on the grass and nothing was done by the administration to help the unemployed. See D. L. McMurry: *Coxey's Army* (Boston, 1929).

[2] See Chapter XI, above, p. 188.   [3] See Chapter VII, above, pp. 114–6.

rates twice a year, as farmers' deposits were withdrawn to meet the seasonal needs of sowing and harvesting. Thus in August and September 1907, when bank loans had reached a peak and reserves were almost down to the legal minimum (stimulated by speculation in holding and trust company securities, as in 1903), interest rates began to creep up and the Treasury had to make widespread deposits of federal funds (amounting to $28 million) in various banks to ensure that harvesting would take place. In October the Mercantile National Bank came into difficulties which when investigated revealed a case of wilfully irresponsible speculation. This led to a general disclosure of weakness among other institutions, and a run on the Mercantile National Bank spread elsewhere. On 22 October the giant Knickerbocker Trust Company, the largest in New York and one which held the deposits of 17,000 people valued at about $50 million, closed its doors. A full-scale banking crisis ensued, with a sharp drop in business activity and severe unemployment. While the members of the New York Clearing House decided to suspend cash payments, the Federal Government took steps to relieve the stringency. The Treasury deposited $36 million of federal funds in New York National Banks and set up a credit pool to extend loans to solvent companies in need. (J. Pierpont Morgan assumed control, and the U.S. Steel Corporation was allowed to assimilate the Tennessee Coal and Iron Company by permission of President Roosevelt.) The depression was brief and by 1909 business activity had revived, together with prices which continued rising until the spring of 1910. In 1911 came a recession in both prices and business activity, followed by renewed expansion until 1913. The year 1914 witnessed another crisis for which the outbreak of European hostilities was mainly responsible.

It seems abundantly clear from however brief a consideration of the crises of 1873, 1893 and 1907 and the minor ones in between, that the American economy functioned very imperfectly during the years dividing the Civil War from World War I. Stability and a uniform rate of economic growth are not the only criteria however. Changes in the composition and distribution of national income, in the working conditions and length of working time needed to produce it, in national health and efficiency and in the diversity and range of consumer choice should also be taken into account. So far scholars have failed to produce a methodical, universally acceptable basis on which to judge and assess 'living standards' differing in time and space. The subject remains, fascinating in its potentialities and challenging in its difficulties, but unsolved. A good deal of work short of this ideal has been done,[1] but it seems doubtful whether such a revolu-

[1] See for instance Chapter 45 of Professor C. W. Wright's *Economic History of the United States* (2nd ed., revised, New York, 1949) and the

tionary intellectual tool will ever be produced, for it would need to measure qualitative as well as quantitative factors.[1]

The *per capita* real income—the goods and services represented by the dollar income of each individual in the United States—has risen steeply since 1783. R. F. Martin has shown (in terms of constant 1926 dollars deflated by an index of the general price level) that between 1799 and 1937 there was a three-fold rise in *per capita* real income, from $214 to $602.[2] Even taking into account that part of this increase is represented by the economic change-over to an industrial economy and consequent transfer to the market of services formerly discharged in the home, the expansion is an undeniable measure of considerable material progress.

Between 1861 and 1918 *per capita* real income roughly doubled, reaching $599. But there were severe fluctuations in the curve, one such being the steep fall during and immediately after the Civil War when it reached a low level of $233 (1869). Despite the crises of 1873, 1884 and 1893 there was a steady increase in real income from the '70's to the '90's; in 1899 it stood at $456 and in 1909 at $530. In the early years of the twentieth century the steady nature of the curve vanished, although oscillations occurred within a continuing upward trend.[3]

'Real income *per capita*' gives us a useful economic yardstick; but what about the actual distribution of national wealth? Data on this subject were not readily obtainable until the income tax was re-established in 1913, although we do know that by 1889 at least six private fortunes exceeded $100 million and over sixty exceeded $20 million. By 1892 over 4,000 single individuals were worth a million dollars each, and in the following year it was estimated that 9 per cent of the families in the United States owned about 71 per cent of total wealth. After 1900 at least two fortunes actually exceeded $500

work of his former student E. W. Martin, *The Standard of Living in 1860* (Chicago, 1942). R. F. Martin, *National Income in the United States, 1799–1938* (National Industrial Conference, New York, 1939) and P. H. Douglas, *Real Wages in the United States, 1890–1926* (Cambridge, Mass., 1930) are both useful statistical works, central to this theme. Graduate workers and advanced readers should also be aware of the highly technical volumes published by the *National Bureau of Economic Research*, including S. Kuznets, *National Income, A Summary of Findings* (New York, 1946). An excellent comparative study of the living standards of the leading countries is Colin Clark's *The Conditions of Economic Progress* (2nd ed., rewritten, London, 1951).

[1] See Chapter III, above, pp. 42–3.
[2] R. F. Martin, op. cit., pp. 2–4.
[3] 1918 was a peak year after which real income *per capita* fell until 1921, rose irregularly to a slightly higher new peak in 1927 and fell steeply by about 25 per cent until 1933. In 1938 it stood roughly at the 1911 level.

million. In the twentieth century increasing taxation, gift funds and economic dislocation helped to disperse to some extent the older established fortunes.

The 1914 returns showed that 8,000 people had incomes exceeding $50,000 each. The number had increased to 43,000 people in 1928 but fell during the slump to below the 1914 estimate. By 1944 it was again up to 37,000. Moreover a Federal Government investigation in 1947 revealed that 8 per cent of all families and 'unattached' individuals received 30 per cent of national income, whilst 31 per cent (with incomes under $2,000) received only 9 per cent of national income. It thus remained true in 1947 that a large sector of the population had no proportionate share in national wealth.

In addition to the long-term increase in real income, material progress took the form of shortened working hours (reduced rather slowly from about 70 hours a week in the 1860's to 54–60 hours in 1909 for 76 per cent of the working force, and to over 60 hours for 9 per cent), improved working conditions and extended longevity (expectation of life at birth increasing from about 38·7 years in 1855 to 58·1 years in 1929 for males, and from 40·9 years to 61·4 years for females). Leisure time was increased and the number of goods and services available to consumers of all categories vastly augmented with the coming of electricity, domestic refrigeration, the motor-car, radio, films, canning and preservation of all types of foods from all types of climatic zones, the extension of popular education, innovations in plumbing, building and lighting—a 'mixed bag' of changes not all of them without disadvantages and drawbacks, but all of them diversifying consumer choice and most of them (in the United States) becoming available to most of the community. The result was that despite the recurrent breakdowns of the national economy and despite the uneven distribution of national income and sharp regional contrasts within the country, the 'standard of living' of the United States came to be generally accepted as the highest in the world—so much so that Professor David M. Potter has attempted an analysis of the American character in the light of economic abundance, and has thus recognized mass publicity—the constant 'education' of consumer demand—as the characteristic institution of American life.[1]

Nowhere is the old cliche 'Poverty in the midst of Plenty' more easily applicable than in the later years of the nineteenth century in the United States. Recurrent economic crises, maldistribution and unintelligent exploitation and wastage of natural resources gave rise to a rich literature of protest and to governmental intervention in

[1] *People of Plenty* (Chicago, 1955). See also J. K. Galbraith, *American Capitalism: The Concept of Countervailing Power* (Cambridge, Mass., 1952), p. 102.

economic life—to social criticism and social reform. From another viewpoint this was a decline of *laissez-faire* in both thought and policy. The trend of events from the 'Progressive Movement' of the 1890's via Wilson's 'New Freedom' to F. D. Roosevelt's 'New Deal' of the 1930's, should from this point of view be considered as a whole. As we shall see, the New Deal was very far indeed from 'socialism', but it was also very far from the 'jungle economics' of the '70's and '80's.

The years of 'Progressivism' (*c.* 1890–1917) form the second of the three major 'reform' periods of American history, the first being the 1830's and '40's and the third the 1930's. Each period had its prophets of complete social regeneration and reconstruction which it ignored, and each period was characterized by a central issue—central, but temporary. Thus the 1830's and '40's had abolitionism, the 1930's federal intervention to halt the depression, and the 1890's trust-busting. This seems to give a curiously *ad hoc* character to the three movements.[1]

The radical tradition in American thought and literature (if not in policy) is older than many non-Americans realize. For instance, although abolitionism overshadowed all other notions and movements in the 1830's and '40's, there were a number of socialist and labour intellectuals such as Thomas Skidmore, Frances Wright, William Leggett and George Simpson, not all of whom were immigrants. The Free-Soil Movement, too, had G. H. Evans and Horace Greeley, and the latter together with his colleague Albert Brisbane did his utmost to introduce European radical ideas, especially those of Fourier and Marx, into the United States. The Communitarians have already been mentioned in connection with the Labour movement before the Civil War, in Chapter III above. After Appomattox came a revival of various theories: feminism, international peace, temperance, Negro rights, conservation, Labour demands of all kinds, land reform, currency and taxation schemes, civil service reform, the 'cleansing' of corrupt city governments, social settlements and charity societies, and several shades of socialism from Marxian to Christian. By the 1890's, however—the decade of 'Progressivism' proper—the dominant theme was the hatred and distrust of 'corporate wealth' and monopoly.

Land and taxation reform were united in a single, highly effective appeal by Henry George's scheme for the taxation of land values (*Progress and Poverty*, 1879), which had repercussions in countries as far apart as Denmark and New Zealand, the British Isles and China. Currency reform was advocated by 'Coin' Harvey and William Jennings Bryan; civil service reform by E. L. Godkin, David A. Wells, Dorman Eaton and others; better city administration by

[1] See Chapter IX, above, p. 141.

Tom Johnson (a disciple of George), 'Golden Rule' Jones (Mayor of Toledo, Ohio) and a host of writers including Lincoln Steffens (*Shame of the Cities*, 1905) and W. T. Stead (*If Christ came to Chicago*, 1894); social settlements by Jane Addams, founder of Hull House in Chicago (1889); Utopian Socialism, or 'Nationalism' as it was called, by the novelist Edward Bellamy (*Looking Backward*, 1887); anarchism by Benjamin R. Tucker (*Instead of a Book*, 1893); 'interpreted' Marxism by many disciples including Adolph Douai of the Socialist Labour Party; Fabian and Christian socialism by Laurence Gronlund (*Co-operative Commonwealth*, 1884), the Rev. W. D. P. Bliss (editor of the famous *Encyclopaedia of Social Reform*, 1897), H. Demarest Lloyd, Professor Richard T. Ely and many other clergymen and academics. Henry Demarest Lloyd was also one of the chief 'Muckrakers' who stirred up discontent against the monopolies and gave the trust-busting movement much of its ammunition. In 1880 Lloyd wrote an article on Standard Oil in the *Atlantic Monthly* emphasizing its various underhand practices, and in 1894 produced a complete book on the subject: *Wealth Against Commonwealth*. This sensational attack was followed ten years later by Ida M. Tarbell's equally merciless *History of the Standard Oil Company* (1904). Muckraking works serialized in such magazines as the *American*, *McClure's*, *Collier's*, *Everybody's* and *La Follette's Weekly* gained an extensive public and made short work of monopolies in all fields from finance and insurance to meat-packing, transportation and copper manufacturing.[1] In addition the novelists filed their 'minority report': Upton Sinclair attacked the meat-packing industry in *The Jungle* (1906), Frank Norris wheat speculation in *The Octopus* (1901) and *The Pit* (published posthumously in 1903) and Winston Churchill political corruption in *Coniston* (1906). Novelists with a more specifically 'humanitarian' approach denounced working and housing conditions, John Spargo's *The Bitter Cry of the Children* (1906) and Jacob Riis's *Children of the Poor* (1892) and *Children of the Tenements* (1903) being particularly effective in this respect. Helen Hunt Jackson's *Century of Dishonour* (1881) has already been mentioned for the rôle it played in the Indian question; a similar part was taken in the Negro question by Booker T. Washington's *Up from Slavery* (1901).

In politics the Progressive Party itself was a faction of the Republicans led by Roosevelt; but *Progressivism* had a much wider connotation—its chief exponents being the Democrat William Jennings Bryan, the Republican Robert M. La Follette,[2] the Republican

[1] See C. C. Regier, *The Era of the Muckrakers* (Chapel Hill, N.C., 1932).
[2] 1855–1925. Governor of Wisconsin, 1901–1905; federal Senator, 1906–1925. He gained almost five million votes in the presidential election of 1924 on an 'Independent, Progressive and Socialist' ticket.

Theodore Roosevelt and the Democrat Woodrow Wilson. Some of its aspirations found expression in Roosevelt's 'Square Deal' and Wilson's 'New Freedom'.

The positive achievements of the 'Square Deal'[1] were few and far between. The clamour made by Theodore Roosevelt about 'trust-busting' was little more than a smoke-screen, not to cover tactical manœuvres, however, but to give the illusion of manœuvres which were not in fact taking place. Roosevelt assumed office as President in 1901 after the assassination of McKinley. The Sherman Anti-trust Act had already been passed under Harrison's administration eleven years earlier (July 1890); the second important anti-trust measure, the Clayton Act, was not passed until 1914—six years after Roosevelt left the White House for the wilds of Africa. More federal actions were taken against monopolies under the avowed conservative Taft than under his predecessor Roosevelt. Yet such was the success of the latter's publicity campaign that his name is for ever linked with 'trust-busting'.

The Sherman Act declared that joint action of any sort 'in restraint of trade' was illegal; that attempts to monopolize interstate or international commerce were criminal offences; that the Attorney-General, public authorities and private individuals could proceed against 'injurious combinations', and that violation of the Act carried a fine of $5,000 or a year in jail, or both. The Act did no more than confirm the desire of Congress to maintain 'free competition', and it was seriously weakened by the impossibility of defining, in a dynamic economy, such phrases as 'restraint of trade' and 'monopoly'. Clearly these lacked precise legal meaning and in practice their interpretation was left to the courts. True to form, the United States Supreme Court kept the interpretation within very severe limits, violating the spirit of the Act to uphold its letter. The first case under the Act to come before the Court was a Federal Government suit against the American Sugar Refining Company for acquiring the stock of E. C. Knight & Co. and three other independent concerns, in order to control over 95 per cent of the production of refined sugar in the country (*United States* v. *E. C. Knight & Co.*, 1895). The government suit was rejected on the grounds that the Sherman Act applied only to monopoly of interstate and international 'commerce', not to monopoly of 'manufacturing'. Moreover, by gratuitously adding that there were no limits in the Act on the rights of corporations to acquire and control property, the Court seemed to validate holding companies[2]—a form of consolidation that became extremely popular henceforth. During the years of greatest monopoly growth, 1897–

[1] For a brief review of the 'Square Deal' see G. Soule, *Economic Forces in American History* (New York, 1952) Chapter 17.

[2] For a definition of which see Chapter VII, above, p. 115.

1904, the Sherman Act was at its weakest, for the Court decision of 1895 remained in force until the *Northern Securities Co.* case of 1904 established that the Act would definitely apply to holding companies and the like (monopolies brought about by property transfer).

Roosevelt at least whipped up public opinion against 'trustification', if he managed to do little else. It was a major issue in his electoral platform of 1904 and during the campaign he committed himself to a vigorous prosecution of the Sherman Act. Being successfully elected he began moderate action two years later, initiating a series of government legal cases against monopolies that continued into the administrations of Taft and Wilson. Thirty-seven such cases were introduced under Roosevelt, forty-three under Taft (1909–12) and fifty-three under Wilson's pre-war administration (1912–16). As a result several of the most outstanding mergers were dissolved, including the American Tobacco Company and Standard Oil,[1] both in 1911. With these two memorable decisions came the introduction by the judges concerned of a new interpretative gloss—a distinction between 'reasonable' and 'unreasonable' trusts. It was held that the Sherman Act applied only to 'unreasonable' contracts in restraint of trade. This gave the Courts even wider powers and after the First World War they became increasingly hesitant to dissolve established combinations. In the *United Shoe Machinery Co.* case (1918) and the *U.S. Steel Corporation* case (1920) it was decided that a merger controlling the greater part of any given industry was not illegal if it were not engaged in either underhand agreements with or unfair competitive practices against its rivals. The mere size of a concern was not considered in itself an evil to be controlled, so long as lip-service was paid to the fetish of 'free competition'. By the mid-twentieth century the government and the courts alike had completely reversed many former views about giant mergers, and American economists were constantly emphasizing the rôle of such mergers in 'stabilizing' the economy (because of the long-term nature of their planning)—always provided of course that business directors could be persuaded to imbibe a little elementary economics.

Before this change of view came about, however, an attempt was made to strengthen the Sherman Act for its original purpose—not for use against trade unions but to restrain monopoly growth. This attempt took the form of two Acts passed in 1914, the Clayton Antitrust Act and the Federal Trade Commission Act. As these formed the

[1] E. V. Rostow in *A National Policy for the Oil Industry* (New Haven, 1948) reveals that although one company no longer dominates the industry monopolistic influences are still very strong. He thinks the existing legislation could be made to work—provided governments so desired—if oil companies were prevented from operating in more than one of the four chief sectors: production, refining, transportation and distribution.

heart of Wilson's 'New Freedom' they should be considered within the context of that reform programme.

Professor Woodrow Wilson, who had already gained considerable public attention as a scholar and educational leader of integrity (during his presidency of Princeton University) and as an opponent of corruption and maladministration (during his Governorship of New Jersey since 1910), won the presidential election of 1912 for the Democratic party. He gained 41·82 per cent of the popular vote and 435 out of 531 electoral votes. The Republicans were split between Taft and Roosevelt, the latter securing 27·45 per cent of the popular vote and 88 electoral votes as leader of the Progressives. Wilson's inaugural speech presented a programme of constructive economic reform the main considerations of which were the regulation of business, tariff changes, and currency and banking reforms. The Clayton Act was intended to supplement the Sherman Act by explicitly prohibiting certain trade practices favouring monopolistic growth that were not specifically included by the existing legal interpretation of that Act. Thus certain kinds of price discrimination and exclusive-dealing agreements and the acquisition by one company of its competitor's stock were forbidden. The Federal Trade Commission Act set up a Commission to enforce these provisions, composed of five members and empowered to investigate and make subsequent recommendations, in co-operation with the President, the Attorney-General and Congress. Its regulatory powers were restricted to the field of action laid down by the Sherman and Clayton Acts, however, and it thus did not represent a genuine extension of anti-trust regulations. The Clayton Act itself was not of much importance in the trust-busting movement; it was badly drafted, limited in scope and subsequently nullified by strict judicial interpretation. Samuel Gompers saluted the Act as the Magna Carta of Labour because it sought to limit the use of the injunction in labour disputes and exempted non-profit-making labour and agricultural organizations from the 'restraint of trade' clauses. His rejoicing was rather premature, however, and no genuine relief for Labour in this sphere came until the passage of the Norris-La Guardia Act of 1932.[1] As for mergers, they were as powerful as ever at the accession of F. D. Roosevelt in 1933; the trust-busting movement, although it may have had a salutary effect on business ethics and perhaps had even prevented the emergence of complete monopoly, had certainly failed to prevent the growth of oligopoly and the transformation of the national economy that this implied.

'New Freedom' policy regarding tariffs was to attempt to lower them. The Underwood Act of 1913 was successfully passed by Congress with the help of political 'patronage'—the Democrats having

[1] See Chapter IX, above, p. 149.

been out of office for sixteen years. It introduced the lowest rates since the 1857 Act, reducing the average level from 40 per cent to 29 per cent. This did not satisfy free traders but it did represent the first serious breach in protection since the Civil War. The Act lasted no longer than Wilson's presidency, and the return of the Republicans in 1921 brought an upward revision.[1] The income tax introduced along with the tariff reductions (to cover the estimated loss in revenue of about $70 million) proved more durable. Its use was made possible by a special constitutional amendment—the sixteenth—adopted by Congress in 1909 and ratified by the necessary number of states in 1913. The rates of the tax were low and affected a relatively small sector of the community, evasions were widespread and the number of exemptions high; the measure was merely a beginning.

One of the major achievements of Wilson's pre-war administration was in the field of banking and currency reform—the Federal Reserve Act of 1913. Its details and its place in the context of financial history are discussed in Chapter XI above. The report of the National Monetary Commission set up under the Aldrich-Vreeland Act of 1908 listed at least seventeen serious defects in the American banking system, and the report of the Pujo Committee (1911) revealed the existence of an immense money monopoly—a complex of interlocking directorates.[2] The Federal Reserve Act created a new national banking structure that linked the Treasury with the system, and provided a credit reserve for banking emergencies, centralized control of the discount rate and gold stock and a more elastic currency. Also it allowed National Banks to extend their scope by making real estate loans to farmers. The opportunity was soon taken, over $45 million having been loaned out by the summer of 1916. Even so, farm credit was still too restricted and in July 1916 the Federal Farm Loan Act tried to improve the situation for agriculturists. It established a Federal Farm Loan Board to supervise twelve districts in each of which there was a Federal Land Bank. The Land Banks were to extend credit on first mortgages, no loan to exceed 50 per cent of the value of the mortgaged land or 20 per cent of the value of permanent improvements. Interest was not to exceed 6 per cent. By 1927 over 19 per cent of total farm mortgage debts had been assumed by the Land Banks. While the Act at last brought down the burden of excessive interest rates which American farmers had to bear, it probably encouraged further incurring of debt.[3]

The reform legislation of Wilson's administration was not limited

[1] See Chapter XI, above, p. 171.   [2] See Chapter VII, above, p. 115 n.1.
[3] In addition the Federal Warehouse Act (1916) licensed warehouses which met certain requirements and empowered them to issue receipts against farm products which could be used as collateral for bank loans. See M. R. Benedict, op. cit., pp. 154–5.

to anti-trust, tariff and banking measures, although these formed the basis of the 'New Freedom'. La Follette's Seamen's Act (1915), introducing regulations for better working conditions and safety precautions, crowned years of struggle by the Seamen's Union; the Adamson Act (1916) established the eight-hour day on interstate railroads; the Keating-Owen Child Labour Act (1916) tried to restrict the employment of children under sixteen in mines and quarries and children under fourteen in factories, but was declared 'unconstitutional' by the Supreme Court in 1918; the Smith-Lever Act (1914) and Smith-Hughes Act (1917) provided federal aid for farm demonstration work and agricultural education; the Rural Post Roads Act (1916) extended federal aid to individual states to build primary and secondary interstate and connecting roads, and the Alaska Railway Act (1914) envisaged Alaskan railways built and owned by the Federal Government.

In the United States as in Great Britain World War I cut across the programme of social and economic reforms. Thus the Federal Reserve system had no sooner been set up than it had to be converted to finance national defence; the Underwood tariff was of little significance in a world of nations bent upon war-time production; the anti-trust laws became meaningless and irrelevant in a national economy similarly orientated.

Before considering the effects of the First World War on the American economy, however, there is one sphere of reform in many ways characteristic of the Progressive era which deserves individual consideration, namely the *conservation movement*. The history of conservation in the United States can be usefully divided into two; the first movement from about 1877 to about 1908, and the second—part of the New Deal—from 1933 onwards. Many of the economic and social problems that have been mentioned up to now in this book concern ultimately the allocation of benefits among those Americans who extracted, produced, processed and distributed products created from the physical resources of the nation. The unlimited fecundity of those resources was more or less taken for granted until very late in American history. Federal land policy—in its insistence that land be easily obtainable, widely owned and rapidly exploited—provides a good illustration of the official attitude towards natural resources. The enthusiasm for swift utilization was highly acceptable to contemporary *laissez-faire* economic thought, but it failed to take account of the enhanced destructive powers of advanced technology and the speed at which, in the modern age, forests could be cleared, crops harvested and minerals extracted. The natural resources of a continent could be wrested from the earth within several decades. A dangerously naïve assumption of *laissez-faire* was that any form of exploitation of natural resources could only add to national wealth.

This, of course, was not true. Soil-depleting types of agriculture, for instance, were well known long before the Civil War.

It was not until the late nineteenth century that the Federal Government woke up to the need to conserve soil and other natural resources to assure future supplies. In the late 1870's and '80's the four chief demands of those who advocated conservation were reafforestation, the encouragement of better farming practices to prevent soil erosion, the preservation of oil resources and the protection of wild animals (especially the buffalo). The first federal conservation measure was the Forest Reserve Act (1891) which authorized the President to set aside timbered areas within the public domain as forest reserves so that such areas could not pass into private ownership and be indiscriminately exploited. At one time the United States had possessed 800 million acres of forest land; by the opening of the twentieth century this was reduced to 200 million acres—one-quarter, of which four-fifths was in private hands and not likely to last very much longer. Before the 1891 Act the Land Office had for some time been pressing for forest reservations, as had the American Association for the Advancement of Science and the American Forestry Association, and had come across heavy opposition from Westerners. Under the Act three successive Presidents, Harrison, Cleveland and McKinley, set aside nearly 47 million acres. This failed to keep up with the rate of exploitation, however,[1] and Theodore Roosevelt (whose conservation policy was his most outstanding achievement in domestic affairs) speeded up the movement, setting aside a further 125 million acres. He also placed the national forests under a forestry bureau of the Department of Agriculture and put his personal friend Gifford Pinchot in charge. Pinchot was the first officially appointed professional forester in United States history, and a man of considerable ability and energy. Congressional opposition to Roosevelt's vigorous policy came to a head in 1907 when a bill was forced through which in effect repealed the 1891 Act. Roosevelt, however, managed to slip through an order establishing twenty-one forest reserves in the six timber states of the North-west before he agreed to sign the repealing Act.[2] The amount of good timber land in the public domain and not yet reserved was by then quite small in any case. Additions to reserves since 1907 have been made by purchase, under the terms of the Weeks Act of 1911.

Meanwhile federal encouragement had been given to reclamation and irrigation by the Desert Land Act (1877), the Carey Act (1894) and the Newlands Act (1902), all of which we have already mentioned

[1] The cost of producing an average Sunday edition of a leading American newspaper in the 1920's was about fifty acres of forest land.

[2] See R. M. Robbins, *Our Landed Heritage, The Public Domain, 1776–1936* (Princeton, 1942), Chapters 19 and 20.

above in Chapter VIII. In 1907 Roosevelt appointed an Inland Waterways Commission to investigate and publicize the related questions of water power, water transport, rivers, forests and soil conditions. The scheme for a national conservation conference grew out of this Commission's recommendations and was strongly supported by Gifford Pinchot. In March 1908 Roosevelt arranged a three-day meeting at the White House of state governors, Supreme Court justices, Cabinet members, Congressmen, business men, educationists and scientific experts, to discuss conservation problems. The result of this conference was the establishment of a National Conservation Commission of forty-nine members under Pinchot (which brought out a comprehensive three-volume report), the setting up of state conservation commissions in forty-one states, and the organization of an educational and propaganda body, the National Conservation Association, under President Eliot of Harvard University. Roosevelt added to the forest lands already withdrawn from entry about 80 million acres of coal lands, $1\frac{1}{2}$ million acres of land near water-power sites and about 5 million acres of phosphate lands. On the other hand he failed to persuade a hostile Congress to pass an act authorizing the permanent reservation by the Federal Government of all lands with coal, oil and natural gas deposits, and this policy did not become law until 1920. But for the Weeks Act of 1911 no important conservation measures were adopted between 1909 and 1933. The conservation crusade of 1908-9 ended in an anticlimax, and until the accession of F. D. Roosevelt the work of T. Roosevelt was allowed to lapse, further inroads being made into the nation's supplies of timber, coal, oil, natural gas, iron and other minerals. As a result of technological progress more energy was obtained from less fuel, low-grade ores were brought into use and new materials—such as plastics—introduced. Also the increasing scarcity and rising prices of some materials (timber for instance) did force industrialists to adopt less extravagant, wasteful and inefficient methods. But none of this was due to governmental action or performed for the sake of conservation as a general policy. It took a world slump to bring about the political, social and economic conditions necessary for the emergence of the second and most important Conservation Movement.

It has been said earlier in this chapter, and indeed it is generally accepted, that the later years of the nineteenth and the early years of the twentieth century witnessed a 'decline of *laissez-faire*' in the United States.[1] *Laissez-faire* itself is a concept not without ambiguity; the notion of its 'decline' is indeed tenuous and vague. The

[1] See for instance A. R. Burns, *The Decline of Competition* (New York, 1936), and H. U. Faulkner, *The Decline of Laissez-faire* (New York, 1951).

question of what *laissez-faire* means is perhaps better left to metaphysicians. If it means 'perfect competition' in any strict sense, then it has never described a state of economic affairs known to Man. If it means *more or less* 'perfect' competition then it is true to say that it 'declined' in this period—because of the emergence of 'trustified' capitalism. But there is another sense in which even an economy characterized by oligopoly can be called *laissez-faire*. That is, in the sense whereby *laissez-faire* implies a specific relationship between the government and economic life, in which the former pursues a deliberately negative policy in order to leave economic 'forces' untrammelled and 'free' to regulate themselves 'automatically' and according to 'natural' economic 'laws'. This string of doubtful categories is of little help to the economic historian who needs perhaps above all to achieve some consistency of interpretation; for from this point of view government intervention in economic affairs is unwarrantable 'interference' if businessmen think it limits their field of action, and acceptable 'protection' if they think it likely to increase their chances of profit. *Laissez-faire* thus does not imply opposition to State intervention in economic life, but opposition to certain types of intervention.[1] Government laws imposing heavy protective tariffs (as in 1890 and 1897), or donating huge stretches of public land to railroad promoters (as in 1850), although they meant that the State was playing a positive rôle in economic development, were not found to be particularly incompatible with *laissez-faire*. Grants to other sections of the community were not so acceptable, however; it was not until 1935 that the Federal Government found itself able to aid the aged and the infirm, and dependent children.

Taking 'intervention' to mean roughly what an average businessman of the period would have called 'interference', there is no doubt that federal intervention did increase in the later nineteenth century. Its growth was tortuous and gradual, becoming more noticeable in times of stress and more rapid when supported by public opinion. A beginning was made in moderating the worse excesses of 'individualism' piece-meal, supported at varying times by anti-monopolists, Christian socialists, conservationists, tax reformers, monetary reformers, anti-tariff men, bank critics, agrarian crusaders, labour leaders and economists. Perhaps the first major federal incursion before World War I (stimulated by the Granger Laws) was in the matter of railroad regulation: the Interstate Commerce Act (1887), the Elkins Act and Expedition Act (1903), the Hepburn Act (1906), the Mann-Elkins Act (1910), and regarding railway labour, the Erdman Act (1898), Newlands Act (1913) and Adamson Eight Hour Act (1916). The second major field for federal intervention was, of

[1] One could justifiably argue that this was a period not of *laissez-faire*, but of *neo-mercantilism*—which says very little for either phrase.

course, trust-busting: the Sherman Act (1890) and the Clayton and Federal Trade Commission Acts (1914). The third field was money and banking: the Currency Act (1900), the Aldrich-Vreeland Act (1908), the Postal Savings Act (1910) and the Federal Reserve Act (1913). Other areas included: education—the second Morrill Act (1890), the Smith-Lever Act (1914) and Smith-Hughes Act (1917); agriculture and conservation—the Desert Land Act (1877), the Forest Reserve Act (1891), the Carey Act (1894), the Newlands Reclamation Act (1902) and the Weeks Act (1911); and several humanitarian reforms—the Dawes Act (1887), the La Follette Seamen's Act (1915), the Child Labour Act (1916) and others.

These acts (all of which have been alluded to in their subject contexts in previous chapters) do not constitute a 'decline' of *laissez-faire*. The word 'decline' is too strong and misleading; *laissez-faire* was not overthrown by economic and political changes, it was *transformed*. This transformation, however, was not allowed to continue in a smooth or gradually evolutionary way; its path was blocked by the exigencies of a World War followed by a period of unprecedented economic prosperity associated with a dearth of social reform. As we shall see in Part III, the *mass* of reform legislation under the New Deal can largely be accounted for by this period of enforced quiescence after 1914, that held so many long-needed reforms in abeyance for twenty years.

SUGGESTED FURTHER READING

DORFMAN, J. *The Economic Mind in American Civilisation* (3 vols., Vol. III, 1865–1918. New York, 1949).

DOUGLAS, P. H. *Real Wages in the United States, 1890–1926* (Cambridge, Mass., 1930).

FAULKNER, H. U. *The Decline of Laissez-faire, 1897–1917* (Vol. VII in Rinehart & Co.'s *Economic History of the United States*, New York, 1951).

MARTIN, R. F. *National Income in the United States, 1799–1938* (New York, 1939).

SOULE, G. *Economic Forces in American History* (New York, 1952). (Especially chapters 14, 16, 17, and 18.)

PART THREE

America and the World Economy since 1917

XIII

WAR AND PROSPERITY

World War I: economic mobilization – The Council of National Defence; the War Industries Board; fuel, transportation, food and manpower – Financing the war – Gains and losses – Prosperity of the Twenties: 'balance of payments' and war debts problems; characteristics of the period; the construction, automobile and electrical industries – Consumers' goods and publicity – Agriculture before the Slump.

ON 2 April 1917 President Woodrow Wilson read his war message to Congress; four days later the legislature passed a joint resolution declaring war on the German Empire. Although the United States was involved in World War I for only nineteen months, the American economy was seriously affected by the conflict from the moment of its outbreak in Europe in 1914. Heavy demands by belligerent nations for American supplies and equipment sent up U.S. export figures for such products as munitions, iron and steel, copper and brass goods, raw materials (including grain and foodstuffs), motor vehicles, and animals for transport. Once these orders began to come through, the depression of 1914 was quickly dispelled. In 1916 the United States exported war munitions totalling $1,000 million in value—total exports being almost $5,500 million. Exports exceeded imports in the same year by well over $3,000 million. In 1917 total exports reached well over $6,200 million, exceeding total imports by over $3,280 million. The result of war demand was thus to expand the volume of American foreign commerce and create an extremely favourable trade balance.

All was not well however, for the Allies were running short of cash. Gold poured into the U.S.A. from Europe during 1915 and 1916; the British Government and its American fiscal agent, J. P. Morgan and Co., could not maintain sterling exchange, and the rate fell. The result, after much Congressional debate and disagreement, was the extension of U.S. loans to the Allied governments, which by 1917 amounted to almost $2,000 million. This financial help made a huge breach in the policy of strict neutrality laid down by Wilson in 1914. As it became increasingly clear that it was impossible to uphold neutral trading rights in such a war, American opinion moved gradually in favour of the Western Allies. An alteration of feeling was undoubtedly stimulated to some degree by economic interest: the war boom of 1916 was based on trade with the Allies financed by credit extended to them, the British blockade having prevented Germany from effective participation in such trade. A German victory would simply wipe out Allied debts to U.S. creditors.

American industrial and commercial organization had not been in any way re-adapted to meet the needs of this new European demand, and one of the first aims of the Wilson government after declaring war was to impose some plan on the chaotic struggle of private enterprise to fulfil its obligations. Before America entered the war though, certain changes had already been made. Firstly, the European demand for war materials had caused a partial industrial turn-over to wartime production; secondly, the Federal Government had taken steps to improve national defence by establishing an officer reserve corps and providing for an army of 175,000 men (National Defence Act, June 1916) and by setting up (under the terms of the Army Appropriation Act, August 1916) a Council of National Defence, consisting of the Secretaries of War, Navy, Agriculture, Commerce, Interior and Labour, its main function being to co-ordinate economic resources for national security and welfare and to create the conditions necessary for rapid economic mobilization at any moment. An additional advisory body of seven unpaid experts was chosen by the President to provide the Council with information. The 'experts' included the President of the Baltimore and Ohio Railroad; a successful Wall Street man, Bernard Baruch; a prominent surgeon; the President of Sears, Roebuck and Co.; and Samuel Gompers. The Council proved to be the parent body of most of the innumerable control agencies established after official American hostilities opened.

National crisis always emphasizes the necessity of collective action. Twentieth-century war, being the supreme crisis, produces a universal need for government regulation of private economic and political activities. In practice, however, no single or decisive line of action was taken by the American Government during World War I; the question remained undecided whether key industries should be taken over wholesale or whether private producers should be persuaded or cajoled to adopt their activities to the needs of the nation.

A series of empirical compromises ensued, and a mass of controlling and advising agencies were set up, transforming the mighty economy into a *more or less* regulated war machine—just as in the 1930's a similar mass of agencies managed somehow to fabricate a *more or less* national effort to beat the depression. As the New Deal agencies were saved not so much by their own efforts as by the coming of World War II, the agencies of the First World War were the more successful of the two. These latter bodies are perhaps most easily dealt with in a short space under several heads: industry (the War Industries Board); fuel (the Fuel Administration); transportation (the Shipping Board and Railroad Administration); food (the Food Administration); man-power (the War Labour Board); and finance (the War Finance Corporation).

Of all the agencies the most important—and the nearest approach to a central co-ordinating body—was the War Industries Board. It was set up by the Council of National Defence (8 July 1917) after the dismal failure of the short-lived 'General Munitions Board' to co-ordinate military estimates. Because it lacked any executive authority, the W.I.B. made little headway at first, and plans were advanced to replace it with a 'Munitions Department' similar to Lloyd George's Ministry of Munitions in the U.K. Wilson did not accept the idea however. Instead he reorganized the W.I.B., made it independent of the Council of National Defence, gave it executive commission to co-ordinate the national industrial, agricultural, and financial effort, and placed the energetic Bernard Baruch in charge (4 March 1918). In a short time Baruch became a kind of economic Supreme Commander, and the Board itself an economic General Staff. 'War Service Committees' were set up for each industry—somewhat similar to the 'Code Authorities' under the New Deal—to act as liaison bodies between the W.I.B. and producers. The Board's four principal means of control were: by issuing 'priority' orders (following the British example) to ensure the production and distribution of essential commodities, by enforcing conservation and standardization in industry, by price-fixing, and by commandeering. Baruch never in fact used the last method, although it was always useful as a threat to recalcitrant producers who refused to keep prices down to reasonable limits. As it was, the W.I.B. proved to be successful in its industrial expansion policy, but failed in its price-fixing policy to prevent inflation or the amassing of large, easy profits by many industrialists.

The Fuel Administration (set up under the Food and Fuel Control Act of August 1917) had as its foremost problem the unusual and severe shortage of bituminous coal, caused partly by its universal wartime demand, by traffic congestion, by an increase in normal domestic consumption during the harsh winter of 1917–18, and by labour shortage in the mines arising out of poor working conditions and the call of military service. By rationing luxury users, breweries, less important industries and the like, and by mediating in labour disputes and exempting miners from the draft, the Fuel Administration succeeded in increasing over-all coal production and productivity per man-hour underground. Average production per miner underground in 1914 was 833 tons a year; by 1918, it had reached 1,151 tons. There was always a coal shortage however, until the war came to an end.

The Shipping Board was established in September 1916 and its subsidiary, the Emergency Fleet Corporation, in April 1917. These two bodies came in for heavy criticism for procrastination and delay,[1] but they did enable the government to take over all private shipping, and to seize enemy and commandeer or purchase neutral vessels.[2] Internal transportation was controlled by the Federal Government through the Railroad Administration, which took over all rail and inland water transport facilities from 1 January 1918. Several schemes, including the 'Railroads' War Board' voluntarily established by the companies themselves, had already failed. The Railroad Administration was on the whole, and for the purpose it served, a success. W. G. McAdoo (the Secretary of the Treasury) was put in charge, and an Act of March 1918 guaranteed to each company a fixed return based on the average earnings of the three years 1914–17—years of high profits. Although a heavy deficit arose during the two years of government operation (mainly owing to a much slower rise in freight rates than in costs and wages), large additions were made to plant and a degree of 'rationalization' took place that would not have been otherwise possible. Facilities were interchanged, wasteful cross-hauls were excluded, needlessly competitive lines withdrawn from service, equipment standardized and accounting co-ordinated.[3]

The Food Administration was created in August 1917 only after bitter debate in Congress in which representatives of the farmers and the immense food-processing and distribution industries took a major part. These groups were thriving as a result of the huge expanded demand and the doubling of American food exports and agricultural prices. The Food Administration (under Herbert Hoover) did not establish retail rationing or price control; it tried instead to eliminate speculation in the wholesale markets, regulate wholesale prices and hasten the flow of distribution. The Food and Fuel Control Act of 1917 made it illegal to hoard, waste, or charge excessive prices for essential foodstuffs, but the Administration relied mainly on propaganda and persuasion rather than compulsion. 'Hooverizing'—being economical in the use of food in the home—became a patriotic by-word. For wheat and sugar, however, it was

[1] See G. Soule, *Prosperity Decade, 1917–1929* (Vol. VIII of Rinehart and Co.'s *Economic History of the United States*, New York, 1947), pp. 29–32.

[2] See Chapter XI, above, p. 168.

[3] For earlier and later developments in railroad history, see Chapter X above, pp. 157–63.

deemed necessary to create two special bodies: the United States Grain Corporation, organized with a capital of $150 million, abolished competitive purchase by buying grain from the producers (at a minimum guaranteed price) and allocating it to all mills according to the average 'grind' of each for the three pre-war years; the Sugar Equalization Board similarly bought raw sugar from the producers—in the United States, Cuba and Hawaii—paying varying prices according to local conditions, but selling it all at one price to American refiners, whose profit margin was regulated.

So much for industry, fuel, transportation and food; but what of man-power in wartime, on both the military and domestic fronts? On the military front the main federal measure was the Selective Service Act (18 May 1917) which demanded that all men aged between 21 and 30 should register. About ten million men were rapidly registered, of which nearly three million were taken immediately. Deferments were allowed generously in such employments as essential war industries and agriculture; unemployed able-bodied men were given a choice, under the 'work or fight' order of May 1918, between national service or essential labour. Altogether about 16 per cent of the American male labour-force was diverted into the armed services. On the domestic front this, together with the termination of immigration, exacerbated an already difficult labour problem. After a year of confusion and labour wastage characterized by a high turn-over, the government at last recognized the need for national standardization of wages and working conditions as far as possible. The National War Labour Board was established on 8 April 1918, consisting of five labour and five employer representatives, and two joint chairmen—ex-President W. H. Taft and a prominent liberal, Frank P. Walsh. The Board worked. Its arbitration decisions on disputes were widely accepted. In addition a War Labour Policies Board dealt in more detail with questions of labour mobilization, and a Housing Corporation had begun building workers' homes when the war ended.

Labour was eagerly sought during the war; there was an outgrowth of labour relations councils and productivity boards, and trade unions flourished, the A.F.L. increasing its membership from two million to over four million between 1915 and 1920.[1] This state of affairs soon altered in the '20's, but not all the advances made by Labour in the war were lost in the peace. The eight-hour day, for instance, became more or less general once the pressure of wartime production was eased, and the notion of a half-day on Saturday began to spread very gradually. As far as real income is concerned advances were very uneven, and the skilled and salaried groups or those workers in non-war occupations found that their spasmodic

[1] See Chapter IX, above, pp. 150–1.

wage increases were inadequate to meet the rising living costs, especially during the inflation of the immediate post-war years. Professional people and those on fixed incomes found it increasingly difficult to make ends meet during the war.

Meanwhile the Federal Government had its own financial problems. After 1917 it largely took over the financial task of waging the war, at a total cost to the nation (April 1917 to July 1919), excluding normal estimated peace-time expenditures, of about $32,700 million —according to Professor E. R. A. Seligman.[1] This figure should be compared with that for other wars: the Civil War (though it lasted, from the American viewpoint, twice as long) cost the government but an eighth or a ninth of the World War I total; the Second World War on the other hand cost eleven or twelve times as much (well over $360,000 million).

About 31 per cent of the total cost of the First World War was raised by taxation, the rest by loans. The Secretary of the Treasury, McAdoo, believed that taxation was the best means of war financing from the economic viewpoint because it cut down consumer purchasing-power, reduced competition and kept prices down. At first he hoped to derive at least 50 per cent of wartime needs from taxes, but deep antipathy to the idea existed in the country and prevented this. Taxation was a slow and lengthy process that did not provide immediate revenue. From the start the Treasury had to fall back on borrowing. Currency inflation (the issue of paper money), as adopted in the Civil War, was not envisaged at all in World War I.

In an attempt to aid businessmen and farmers, Congress established the War Finance Corporation on 5 April 1918. It was given a capital stock of $500 million, all subscribed by the government, and was empowered to make advances of credit to banks, trust companies, building and loan associations, and indeed to any concern or individual engaged in essential war-work. Farmers were assisted through the Federal Farm Land Banks set up by the Act of 1916 (discussed above as part of the New Freedom). The War Finance Corporation was assisted by a Capital Issues Committee, the function of which was to prevent diversion of credit into unwanted channels.

Government borrowing took two principal forms: firstly, the sale of short-term notes or certificates to banks at frequent intervals (e.g. the $268 million of 3 per cent certificates sold through the Federal Reserve System in April 1917, and the $600 million sold in three lots in May and June of the same year); secondly, the sale of long-term 'Liberty Bonds' in biannual, organized popular 'drives', not unlike the Jay Cooke campaigns of the Civil War. The four

[1] $9,400 million of this was loans to the Allies under the four Liberty Loan Acts (April 1917–July 1918) and spent on American goods in the United States.

Liberty Loans yielded $2,000 million, $3,800 million, $4,200 million, and $7,000 million respectively, and the additional 'Victory Loan' (March 1919) yielded a further $4,500 million—a startling revelation of the wealth reserves at America's disposal.

This type of borrowing resulted in credit inflation, which revealed itself in rising prices. The Bureau of Labour index number of wholesale prices (July 1914=100) shows a marked rise beginning in the winter of 1915. From 106 in December 1915 it climbed to 187 in July 1917. Government price controls then began to operate and considerably decelerated the rate of increase, so that by November 1918 (the war's end) the index stood at 206.[1] Even with the control policy, wholesale prices were thus more than twice as high at the end of hostilities as in 1914. This inflation must be taken into account when any comparison of pre-war and post-war conditions or any evaluation of gains and losses in various branches of the economy or of the American population is being attempted.

There can be no doubt that business corporations—and especially their leaders—gained most from World War I. Business acquisitions revealed themselves partly in the payment of increased dividends to investors but also (perhaps chiefly) in the building up of huge 'undistributed' surpluses. Many devices were adopted to evade taxation, and the 'official' figures given by firms themselves are not always a sound guide. These surpluses did enable companies to continue paying out dividends to investors during the later depression, when other sections of the community were not so fortunate. The most significant industrial gain was the large expansion of physical plant and equipment brought about by the war. Together with the stimulus given to the movement for standardization and interchangeability of parts (first publicized by the successes of Henry Ford[2]), this physical expansion led to a total increase in America's productive capacity. On the other hand, growth was uneven, and while the automobile industry quadrupled, the rubber industry trebled, the canned milk industry more than doubled and the iron and steel, meat-packing, and petroleum industries heavily increased their respective outputs, there was a severe contraction of house construction and (once the war was over) an equally drastic reduction in the artificially boosted war industries—especially shipbuilding and aircraft production.

Agriculture also had considerable gains during the war. Total output did not increase in any startling way, but it was *maintained* whilst prices for farm goods rose rapidly. For instance, the prices of raw agricultural products were 106 per cent higher in 1918 than in 1913. Even marginal farms prospered in a period when the real income

---

[1] It had risen 81 points in 19 months (December 1915–July 1917), and 19 points in 16 months (July 1917–November 1918).

[2] See Chapter VII, above, pp. 108–9.

of farmers increased 29 per cent (1915–18). Farm *labourers* were not so lucky, their real income rising by only 2 per cent in the same years.[1] In agriculture as in industry expansion was very uneven. The cutting-off of the British market dealt a solid blow to Southern cotton, for instance. Moreover, the farmers' gain in real income was often invested in further land acquisition rather than used to raise current farm living standards, and these investments were tragically swallowed up in the depression years.

The American economy underwent external as well as internal changes as a result of World War I. It was transformed from debtor to creditor status in the world at large (see Chapter XI); its financial capital (New York) became the world's; it acquired a large export surplus, distributed on an international credit basis, which created a bitter problem in the immediate post-war years.

This question of war debts will not be new to most readers: it is indeed an oft-told tale, fully considered from various national and international viewpoints elsewhere, in readily available sources.[2] It is easier to grasp if it is understood as a three-fold question, involving Allied debts to the United States, inter-Allied debts, and German reparations. The American Government consistently refused to recognize the connection between the debts the Allies owed it and German reparations (which it did not itself exact). Indeed there was no legal relationship; but there was a *de facto* economic relationship.

At the war's end European private and governmental debts to the United States amounted to about $12,600 million. The war had entirely disrupted existing fiscal and commercial patterns and turned former creditor nations into debtors almost overnight. European nations wholly unused to debtor status lost income formerly derived from U.S. assets and all hope of increasing their net U.S. holdings. On the other hand they now had heavy liabilities and the American Government pressed not only for current interest dues but also for 'amortization'—the repayment of the principal in regular instalments. There was a large gap in the 'balance of payments'. How was it to be filled?

---

[1] See J. M. Clark, *The Costs of the World War to the American People* (New Haven, 1931), p. 153.

[2] See W. Ashworth, op. cit., for an outline of the international position; C. Lewis, op. cit., for a statistical analysis of the debtor-creditor situation of the U.S.A.; J. M. Keynes, *Economic Consequences of the Peace* (London, 1919) for this economist's early views; Paul Einzig, *World Finance Since 1914* (London, 1935) for a restrospective view by a leading monetary expert; and U.S. Department of Commerce, Economic Series No. 23, *The United States in the World Economy* (Washington, D.C., 1943) for an official American source.

Europe had insufficient dollars even for current needs from the United States. The gap could be filled in at least three ways: by a drastic, perhaps tragic, cut in European importation of American products; by a heavy American importation of European goods; or by international gold movements. The first might have resulted in starvation in Europe and severe dislocation in American industry and agriculture; the second was not at all probable because of the crippling U.S. protective tariffs (which reached the highest level in American history with the Fordney-McCumber Act of 1922);[1] the third would certainly drain Europe's already diminished gold supply, disable her economy. and perhaps force her off the gold standard completely. To make matters worse, U.S. immigration quotas (see Chapter X above), introduced in 1921, prevented the movement of a fresh wave of migrants from a stricken Europe. The United Kingdom, in a vain attempt to save the situation, agitated for the complete cancellation of all war debts—despite the fact that it had itself lent twice as much to the Allies as it had borrowed from the U.S.A. But the American Government refused to accept the idea. 'They hired the money, didn't they?' complained Coolidge.

In the 1920's the position was relieved to some extent by refunding agreements, such as that between the U.S. and the U.K. drawn up in 1923, which lowered interest payments from 5 per cent to 3 per cent (for the first ten years) and to $3\frac{1}{2}$ per cent (for the remainder of the instalment period—lengthened from 25 to 62 years). The dollar shortage had already made itself felt, however, on American agriculture. The regime of high prices and high demand was at an end. Europe's purchasing-power was abruptly reduced and from early 1920 onwards American farm produce began to flood the world market, bringing down prices to 50 per cent of their former level within two years. Unlike businessmen, farmers could not or would not curtail production. Organized in small units, they each attempted to increase output still further in a vain hope of making a living. This only served to exacerbate their position and during the prosperity of the '20's American farmers fared very badly. In a sense they were sacrificed and Europe saved, for European consumption of American foodstuffs was maintained.[2]

Low prices for American agricultural products did no more to

[1] Also Europe could not pay as much in *services* as formerly, because the United States now had a large (perhaps even too large) merchant fleet, and its trade no longer depended on alien ocean transport. See Chapter XI, above, p. 168.

[2] Maintained that is, within the pattern of general decline in American foodstuffs exports in relation to total exports (see Chapter XI above). As other world agricultural zones were developed the U.S. became less important for the European food supply.

solve the fundamental problem—the dollar shortage and Europe's dependence on the economic stability of the United States—than did the various refunding agreements. Together with a third factor, their total effect was to hide the underlying weakness from general view. This third factor was the growth of American investments in Europe. It was perhaps the most significant and decisive of all three stop-gaps, for when it ceased (from the summer of 1928 onwards) international economic life came to a virtual standstill. Americans had begun heavy investment on the European continent partly as a result of the acceptance of the Dawes Plan in 1924. This plan, which was on the whole successful, was advanced to meet the immense difficulties in the reparations problem. Briefly, Germany could not pay heavy reparations to the European victors and at the same time cope with her vast domestic problem of inflation. The Dawes Plan gave a gold loan to Germany as a basis for a new currency, and was sensible enough to recognize her complete inability to pay reparations except in so far as she had an economic surplus to pay with. There is no doubt that this attempt to combat the reparation issue helped to stimulate American foreign investments. By 1928 these had risen to an annual $1,691 million. In the late twenties they were always at least three times the value of foreign investments within the United States, and America's net creditor position greatly improved, rising from $3,700 million (1919) to $15,200 million (1930).

Grossly simplified, the payments 'flow' after 1924 was on the following circular model: Germany paid reparations to France and the U.K. out of the inflow of (chiefly) American capital; France was thus enabled to meet her obligations in Great Britain; in turn Great Britain, out of its French and German receipts, could pay its debt charges to the United States. This system broke down, with serious results for Europe, once American investments terminated.

Despite the depressing complexities of post-war international finance (which are only hinted at above) and despite the poor condition of American agriculture, ebullience and expansion rather than gloom and contraction characterize the '20's, not less in the economic than in other spheres.[1] The sharp but short-lived recession of 1920–1 set the stage for the '20's. Some sections of the economy never recovered from its effects and remained black spots throughout the period; others swiftly regained lost ground and figured prominently in the upward surge of economic growth that was an extension of wartime prosperity. Thus agriculture and certain industries such as shipbuilding, textiles, leather, railroad equipment, and coal-mining did not recapture their position. Also Labour, which had suffered

[1] For instance, George Soule, op. cit., names the years 1917–29, 'Prosperity Decade' and explains the purpose of his book to be to lay bare the economic background of a period of 'froth and turmoil'.

critical unemployment in 1921 (almost five million), continued to bear much of the strain during the rest of the period; unemployment fluctuated at a high level, particularly in those areas of the economy which failed to respond to the general boom conditions.

But what of the prosperity itself? On which industries was it based? There has been much controversial writing on the '20's, but it seems certain that no one will in the future cast doubt on the rôle played by the new industries—firstly the automobile and secondly the electrical industries. Even more important in economic growth was the older group of construction industries. Although the crisis of 1929 came about after a speculative mania which was to a large extent 'artificial' because it was based on quick sales and resales of stock exchange securities, irrespective of their yield potentialities, one must not, as some secondary works seem to, confuse this mania with the 'real' underlying industrial expansion which had preceded it, and accord to the stock market panic the bulk of the responsibility for the Slump. On matters of this kind a good guide is provided by the works of the late Professor J. A. Schumpeter, who gives perhaps the most sound interpretation of economic expansion and recession yet produced—particularly for the student of economic history.[1] He emphasizes the rôle of 'innovation' (the introduction of a new production function) as the initiating factor in cyclical growth. On the Schumpeterian analysis we must look back to the boom of the '20's in the automobile, electrical and construction industries, and study them in their structural context of capitalist society, before we can understand the 'causes' of the crash of 1929 and ensuing depression.

Of course the situation in 1929 was complicated by international factors and a study of purely domestic affairs would not take us very far. Readers will already have noticed how this book becomes, in Parts Two and Three, increasingly concerned with international events, and conditions in other nations. Try how he may to cut away the thick factual undergrowth and make clear and intelligible the main themes of American economic history, try how he may to isolate the *national* economic experience of the United States, no writer could exclude extra-national factors. The emergence of an international economy after the Civil War, and especially after the decade 1870–80, makes nonsense of any purely national account of economic history. On the other hand, in the 1920's economic changes in the United States were much more likely to produce world-wide effects than changes in any other nation. Professor W. A. Lewis has pointed out that the ratio of United States imports to national income in 1929 was only 5 per cent, and that of exports only 6 per cent. Changes in American foreign trade have been dealt with in some

[1] A useful introduction to Schumpeter's work is R. V. Clemence and F. S. Doody, *The Schumpeterian System* (Cambridge, Mass., 1950).

detail in Chapter XI above—but this book is written from a European viewpoint, and foreign trade would probably receive less attention were it not. If we confine our attentions *mainly* to United States internal affairs in this brief treatment of the '20's (which follows and continues into the next chapter), the method is fully justifiable.

The National Bureau of Economic Research index of physical output for all U.S. manufacturing industries (1899=100) rose from 257 (1917) to 364 (1929), with a setback to 194 in 1921 and another to 266 in 1924.[1] Along with manufacturing, the construction industries underwent a similar expansion: the value of total output destined for domestic use of construction materials rose from $3,700 to $5,000 million (1919–29).[2] This building boom, shared by Europe in the same period, came in the United States not of course as a result of wartime destruction; but a major factor in the American housing shortage was the severe contraction of house construction during the war. Rents rose from a consumers' index (1935–9=100) of 93·2 in 1917 to a peak of 152·2 in 1925.[3] The construction boom had reached its climax in the years 1926–8, financed by a growth of the market for real-estate mortgage bonds and a flowering of building and loan associations. There was a huge extension of cities and within them a multiplication of apartment blocks and giant skyscraper offices. The characteristic skyline of modern urban America took shape whilst the outstanding urban mortgage debt was trebled.

The manufacturing industries in the prosperous '20's saw not only the emergence of large new branches but also the gradual transformation of several older industries as they were made much more efficient. Increased efficiency was the keynote of the '20's, and efforts were multiplied to 'put science into industry'. The index of output per man-hour (1939=100) rose from 45·3 at the war's end to 78·1 at the time of the crash.[4] Combined with this large increase in productivity came the stimulus of reduced federal taxes, low interest rates, high protective tariffs (for fortunate industries) and extended concentration of control—a revival of business consolidation. Profits rose, slowly at first and then more quickly after 1928.

It was shown in Chapter VII that by 1914 the manufacturing of what came to be called 'automobiles' was already a major industry. But it was during the war and post-war years that automobile production saw its greatest expansion. Annual production of passenger cars in 1910 was 181,000, in 1914 was 548,000, and in 1917 was 1,746,000. This figure fluctuated a little during the time that the U.S. was directly engaged in fighting; but the motor industry added to its production in 1917 over 128,000 trucks (as compared with an annual

[1] *Historical Statistics of the United States*, op. cit., p. 179 (Series J13–14).
[2] Ibid., p. 171 (Series H 49–50). [3] Ibid., p. 236 (Series L 40–7).
[4] Ibid., pp. 71–2 (Series D 213–17).

output of 25,000 in 1914 and 6,000 in 1910). In 1920 the United States produced nearly 1,906,000 passenger cars and 322,000 trucks. A peak production figure of almost 4,590,000 cars and 771,000 trucks was attained in 1929, when total vehicle registration exceeded 26,500,000.[1]

In that year, 1929, when so many industries reached their summit, the production of the automobile industry amounted in value to 12·7 per cent of total national manufacturing output; its employees constituted 7·1 per cent of the total labour force of the manufacturing industries; the wages it paid were 8·7 per cent of total manufacturing wages. The industry consumed 15 per cent of the nation's steel production, and revealed an insatiable appetite for petrol, rubber, glass, lead and nickel.[2] But its significance is not measured in these statistics alone, as earlier chapters have shown.

The motor industry directly stimulated the construction industries in at least two ways: by encouraging 'suburbanization' and by bringing about a renaissance of road building. Road construction was in itself an important minor factor in the expansion as a whole. Under the Rural Post Roads Act (1916) passed under Woodrow Wilson, the Federal Government had extended aid to individual states to build primary and secondary, interstate and connecting roads. As a result the total of federal and state funds spent on highway building between the passage of the Act and 1929 amounted to over $1,759 million.[3]

Much more important in the prosperity period were the electrical and radio industries. Not only was industry as a whole gradually adopting electric power but there was a vast and increasing public demand for electrical consumers' goods—household gadgets and aids such as electric irons, vacuum cleaners, refrigerators, and washing machines. The demand for and importance of the radio in both communications and entertainment undoubtedly gave it the status of a separate industry in its own right. The value of its output increased 25-fold between 1919 and 1929, from $15,124,000 to $388,476,000. As for electric power, its total production (including both electric utilities and industrial establishments) multiplied three-fold, from about 43,429 million kilowatt-hours (1917) to 116,747 million (1929).[4]

The expansion of the electrical industry was closely associated with another phenomenon common to both America and Europe—the abnormal demand for durable consumers' goods and articles pre-

[1] Ibid., p. 223 (Series K 225–35).
[2] Figures quoted in Soule, op. cit., pp. 164–5.
[3] Estimated from *Historical Statistics of the United States*, op. cit., p. 221 (Series K 189–91b).
[4] Ibid., p. 181 (Series J 49–96) and p. 156 (Series G 171–82).

viously regarded as luxuries. For example, the annual output of household refrigerators rose from about 5,000 in 1921 to 890,000 in 1929 and continued rising—unlike most products—even after 1929, to attain a peak annual figure of 2,824,000 in 1937.[1] Such purchases were made possible by a vast extension of consumer credit, i.e. of 'H.P.' sales, and by large advertising expenditures (about $1,782 million in 1929). The difficulty from the economic point of view about the demand for durable consumers' goods was that such demand tended to inject an element of uncertainty and instability into the economy, because it was based heavily on credit financing and because it was much less constant than that for the perishable staple commodities essential to everyday life. Advertisers tried (and still try) to get round this obstacle by stimulating the speedy casting-off and replacement of consumer goods of all kinds, by discouraging the notion that there is any particular value in mere durability, and by forever introducing real or feigned 'latest improvements'. That they have been to a large extent successful in the United States is evident from the way in which they are at present (1955) convincing American consumers that it is not the thing to be a 'one-car-family'.[2] But although in 1929 consumers bought 23 per cent more than they did in 1923, the period ended, nevertheless, in so-called 'overproduction'.

Before we can consider the events of 1929 to elucidate this point, we must first of all look more closely into the conditions of American agriculture before the Slump.

Irrespective of cyclical fluctuations in prosperity, the three decades to 1930 brought several radical changes in the American farming scene. Although there was a decline in farm population the nation still produced a food surplus. The very first United States census of 1790 had classified 94 per cent of the total population as rural. Since then there has been a sustained fall in this percentage. In the 1870's and '80's the national proportion engaged in agriculture fell below that engaged in other industries, and by 1910 the total farm population was about 32 million, as compared with a non-farm population of 60 million. The farmers had been reduced to a minority, albeit a

[1] Ibid., p. 186 (Series J 152–64).
[2] Their success on Americans is also shown in friendly arguments between English and American enthusiasts about the relative merits of the cars of their respective countries: the customary English arguments about the alleged durability of British engines rarely impress American manufacturers, not only because the evidence is scanty, but also because until very recently, at whatever level of quality, the British car market was so obviously underdeveloped. In the early 1950's an English audience once gasped (during an American trade union propaganda film about the horrors of unemployment and the need for unions) at seeing unemployed workers queue up for union food rations—and carry them to their waiting Fords.

WAR AND PROSPERITY

vociferous one. During the 1920's the net loss of people to American farms owing to migration was one and a half million, and by 1930 total farm population was about 30 million, while total non-farm was 92 million. Thus farm population had declined since 1910 at the same time that non-farm population had multiplied by one-third.[1] Under 21 per cent of those 'gainfully employed' in 1930 worked on farms. (During the depression years the shift to the towns was reversed, as thousands of the unemployed tried to find rural work or returned to their home farms; but this did not affect the general trend.)

There were at least four reasons why a food surplus could still be produced despite these tendencies. Firstly, the reclamation and irrigation measures begun in the early part of the century helped to increase production. The Newlands Reclamation Act (1902) extended the scope of the Carey Act of 1894 and provided direct federal aid in reclamation work. More important, it tried to devise a policy specifically suited to Western local needs. A revolving fund was established derived from public land sales, to be used in the building of great power and storage dams and irrigation canals. Settlers received their irrigated, improved lands free, as usual, but had to repay within ten years (without interest) the cost of federal construction activities. Federal irrigation schemes were begun in Arizona, Colorado, Utah, and California and by 1915 government investment in these plans totalled $80 million.[2]

Secondly, the spread of 'dry farming' technique had made large areas of semi-arid land usable, especially in the central High Plains. This method suited cereals, some forage crops and some orchard crops; but 'dry farming' was often unwisely over-extended, resulting in the blowing away of many acres of top-soil in the Plains. Thirdly, the Homestead Act of 1862 was modified to rid it of those defects which arose from its Eastern authorship,[3] and a series of Acts allowed homesteading on easier terms and in larger tracts in the arid regions. These included the Kirkaid Act (1904), the Forest Homestead Act (1906), the Enlarged Homestead Act (1909: allowing half-section homesteads on non-timber or mineral-bearing lands), the Three-Year Homestead Act (1912) and the Stock-Raising Homestead Act (1916). The last allowed land suitable for grazing but not for irrigation to be taken in whole-section grants (mineral and water rights being reserved). Unfortunately these measures encouraged large-scale homesteading by inexperienced people (e.g. war veterans under the 1916 Act), who were entirely unused to conditions in the semi-arid zones. Between 1900 and 1920, 112 million acres were acquired through the Acts, chiefly in the West. Eventually the Taylor Grazing

[1] Based on ibid., p. 29 (Series B 165–70).
[2] See Chapter VIII, above, pp. 128–30.   [3] See Chapter VIII, above, pp. 123–4.

Act (1934) removed 142 million acres of Western grazing land from entry, leaving it for lease only, under strict regulations preserving its natural grass coverage.[1]

The fourth and most important reason why agricultural production was maintained was that the mechanical advances of the previous century were continued. The central innovation in this respect after 1900 was the tractor. In the 1880's and '90's steam tractors were used to draw combine harvesters (that cut, threshed and sacked grain in one continuous operation). After 1910, and especially after 1920, these were replaced by petrol-driven caterpillar tractors. The new type of combine thus drawn enabled two men to harvest about four or five hundred acres in fifteen days—i.e. about thirty acres a day. Combines were used on the Great Plains, displacing seasonal labour. By 1927 there were over 11,200 of them in use, and the effect was to cut the price of wheat to a half and sometimes a quarter of its normal level. Farms of 300 acres or under were rendered uneconomic for wheat production. Meanwhile over 17,000 tractors were manufactured in the United States in 1914 and 32,000 in 1916. This total doubled within a year (to 67,000 in 1917) and then more than doubled again within the following year (to 161,000 in 1918). By 1929 there were well over 820,000 petrol-driven models in use, and the average cost of a tractor had fallen to $1,000. In mixed farming regions, however, the horse still prevailed, although mechanization (e.g. of potato planting and picking) was not entirely absent.

Unfortunately the maintenance of production did not in itself necessarily imply the prosperity of agriculture, though for some time after 1921 farmers themselves believed that the post-war distress would be short-lived, and continued to buy beyond their immediate needs, on the instalment plan. In the recession of 1920–1 agricultural prices fell to their pre-war level but other prices did not, and the farmers' purchasing-power remained greatly reduced throughout the '20's. This situation gave rise to the long struggle for so-called 'parity prices'—for the guaranteeing by federal action of farm prices on a par with a standard based (usually) on the years 1909–14. But prices did not attain pre-war parity before the Slump; the highest point they reached, in June 1928, was 93 per cent of parity. In addition farmers had to bear heavy losses when their countless mortgages, taken up in the prosperity years, were rapidly foreclosed and farm savings disappeared. Many farmer-owners were forced into tenancy or driven off the land, and great numbers of farm bankruptcy cases were concluded, their number rising annually from 997 in 1920 to a peak of 7,872 in 1925 (not falling below 1,000 a year until 1944). In numerous cases the banks had to go into farming themselves, being unable to sell the land they acquired.

[1] See M. R. Benedict, op. cit., pp. 319–21.

Some of the causes of this distress we have considered elsewhere. It is true that too much land was opened up, much of it in risky areas, and that this together with federal aid and encouragement, and continued mechanical progress, led to 'overproduction'. That is to say, a large margin of American farm produce (especially cereals and meats) was 'surplus', owing to maldistribution and increasing industrial unemployment at home and the loss of markets abroad. World wheat production increased by one-third in the '20's, but consumption did not expand proportionately. American growers met the competition of newer world zones. U.S. beef exports fell while Argentine exports rose, and although the American lead in pork exports was held, its share of world cotton output fell to just over half in 1930. Another factor in the loss of foreign markets was of course the creditor-debtor situation already analysed above, and prohibitive U.S. tariffs.

American farmers found it very difficult to adapt themselves to the new conditions. Though some turned to the production of luxury goods, not everyone (as Professor Shannon dryly explains) could operate blueberry or skunk farms. Demands for reform of all kinds soon arose, varying from tariff reductions to the greater use of agricultural co-operatives[1] and the wider utilization of farm waste materials in industry. Corporation and chain farming developed in an attempt to achieve economies of large scale. A California orchard corporation worked over 60,000 acres; a British group bought 45,000 acres of Mississippi cotton land; a Texas corporation established the largest rice plantation in the world. By 1925 there were over 8,000 of these combines, owning areas of up to 75,000 acres (at least in the wheat belt). Chain farms (such as the 600 farms under supervised tenants operated by the Aetna Life Insurance Company) were mainly the result of mortgage foreclosure.

Since Populism had been wiped away by the rising tide of agricultural prosperity in the late '90's and early 1900's, farmers had not been entirely without organization. Of the various farmers' unions that had been absorbed into the Alliances of the '80's and thence into Populism, the only one of any consequence that emerged intact was the Grange. It grew steadily but unspectacularly after 1900, and by 1915 had about 540,000 members. On the other hand, groups very similar to the early unions were revived on a fresh basis, including the Farmers' Union (established in Texas in 1902), the Farmers' Relief Association (organized in 1900 and merged with the Farmers' Union in 1906) and the American Society of Equity (founded in Illinois in 1902). There were several more or less unsuccessful attempts at national federation. During World War I a loosely

[1] Several large co-operatives became prominent in the 1920's in the wheat, livestock, cotton and fruit production areas, and in dairying.

federated 'Farmers' National War Council' had existed in the capital, and after the armistice its name was changed to 'Farmers' National Council' and it continued to meet. Its post-war platform included nationalization of railroads, mercantile marine, grain elevators and natural resources; reform of the meat-packing industry; a Single Tax on land values that would have brought joy to the heart of Henry George; an improved marketing system, and cheap farm credit. A more effectively organized rival body with very similar aims was the National Board of Farm Organizations, begun in 1917 principally under the auspices of the Farmers' Union. Like the National Council, it spent most of its time in lobbying, but it exceeded the Council in influence. Four other groups representing farm interests in Washington were the Farm Bureau Federation, the Farm Bloc, the Nonpartisan League and the Farmer-Labour Party.

The Farm Bureau Federation was a wholly unintended offshoot of the county organizations for local educational and demonstration programmes under the Smith-Lever Agricultural Extension Act (1914). By 1918 these local bodies had formed themselves into several state federations to consider mutual problems on policy matters far transcending education. The New York state Farm Bureau Federation called a convention at Ithaca in February 1919 to form a National Federation, and a constitution was drawn up at Chicago nine months later. The movement was finally and officially launched in March 1920, and by July of the following year its network covered forty-two states of the Union.[1] Though it had a first-class national organization, its aims were middle-class and 'reformist' and it had no particular appeal for the underprivileged or poorer class of farmers and farm labourers. After the war, for instance, it strongly supported the return of the railroads to private ownership, and in the '20's the more radical agrarian organizations such as the Farmers' Union attacked the Bureau for its friendliness to big business.

The Farm Bloc was an alliance between members of Congress representing farm states, organized in 1921 by Gray Silver, the Washington agent of the Bureau. In many ways it became more radical than the Bureau would have intended. Prominent members were Senators La Follette (Wisconsin), Kenyon (Iowa), Capper (Kansas) and Smith (South Carolina). The Bloc came to hold the balance of power in Congress and had considerable legislative success. For instance it forced through a group of measures in July and August 1921, including two amendments to the Farm Loan Act, one to increase the capital of federal Land Banks and extend their credit facilities, the other to raise the interest on farm loan bonds to the

[1] Those wishing to specialize on agricultural problems should see O. M. Kile, *The Farm Bureau Through Three Decades* (Baltimore, 1948) for further details.

investor without raising them to the borrower; an Act subjecting packers and stockyards to regulations against monopoly and 'unfair practices' (the Packers and Stockyards Act); an Act revised later in 1922 and renamed the Grain Futures Act, to control speculation in grain markets; and, finally, an Emergency Credits Act to finance the export of agricultural surpluses through the revived War Finance Corporation. These minor Congressional triumphs were of course totally inadequate to slow down the rate of agricultural recession.

A more direct attack was the McNary-Haugen scheme, presented to Congress as a Bill five times (once each year, 1924–8 inclusive), defeated twice in the House, shelved once, and passed twice in both House and Senate, only to be vetoed by President Coolidge. It went beyond the aims of the original members of the Farm Bloc by demanding a government export corporation for farm surpluses (not unlike the wartime Grain Corporation and Sugar Equalization Board in some respects) that would control marketing and virtually control prices.[1] A year after the veto of the fifth McNary-Haugen Bill, the new administration under President Hoover passed the Agricultural Marketing Act (15 June 1929). This set up a Federal Farm Board financed by a revolving fund of $500 million, to extend credit to agricultural co-operatives and encourage 'effective merchandising'. The Board was permitted to form 'stabilization corporations' to control surpluses and uphold prices. It was too late for this plan to come to anything, however, and the structure it established was engulfed by the New Deal.

The Farmers' Nonpartisan Political League was founded in North Dakota in 1915 and spread into fifteen Western states. In 1916 it gained control of the state government of North Dakota and began to execute a radical agricultural relief programme: state-owned elevators and warehouses, a state bank, exemption from taxation of farm improvements, a hail insurance fund, an industrial commission to organize state-owned and state-financed industries, and a Home Building Association to encourage home ownership by state loans to builders.[2] By 1922 however the League had passed its zenith in North Dakota, and in that year it lost the gubernatorial campaign. Its decline was caused by administrative inexperience, scandals connected with the state bank, rumours of the League's pacifism during the war and the opposition of Eastern financial interests.

The Farmer-Labour Party grew up partly out of the disfavoured

[1] See M. R. Benedict, op. cit., Chapter 10, passim.

[2] As Professor Benedict has pointed out, the 'socialism' of the League did not extend to farming; the notion was to socialize other businesses but run the state in the interests of farmers. (Op. cit., p. 188.) For a fuller treatment see T. Saloutos and J. D. Hicks, *Agricultural Discontent in the Middle West* (Madison, Wisconsin, 1951).

Nonpartisan League, but its main purpose was to unite farmers with industrial workers in a concerted agitation and programme of reform—an exceedingly difficult if not hopelessly impossible chimera. The problem that taxed the imagination of Lenin and brought the moral collapse of his successor Stalin, proved too onerous also for Parley P. Christensen, the Farmer-Labour Party's luckless nominee for the Presidency of the United States in 1920. He gained no electoral and 265,000 popular votes. The victor, Warren G. Harding, gained 404 electoral and over 16 million popular votes. Nor did Christensen prevent the separate nomination and campaigning of the able Eugene V. Debs (Socialist), or of W. W. Cox (Socialist-Labour) and R. C. Macauley (Single Tax). Two years later the party did elect one Minnesota candidate to the U.S. Senate. In the 1924 presidential campaign a loose alliance of Farmer-Labour men, A.F.L. members and Socialists supported La Follette on a Progressive ticket, and he won 13 electoral and almost 5 million popular votes; but even in that election there was a separate Socialist-Labour candidate and a Workers candidate. The Farmer-Labour Party fought independently in the two struggles that followed, winning only 6,000 popular votes in 1928 and 7,000 (under Jacob Coxey) in 1932. Not only was this 7,000 merely one-thirty-eighth of the 1920 figure, but the total electorate had increased from about 27 million to about 40 million. The agrarian radicals were, to put it mildly, in a distinct minority.

SUGGESTED FURTHER READING

BENEDICT, M. R. *Farm Policies of the United States, 1790–1950* (New York, 1953).

CLARK, J. M. *The Costs of the World War to the American People* (New Haven, 1931).

SOULE, G. *Prosperity Decade: From War to Depression, 1917–1929* (Vol. VIII of Rinehart & Co.'s *Economic History of the United States*, New York, 1947).

U.S. DEPARTMENT OF COMMERCE. *The United States in the World Economy* (*Economic Series*, No. 23, Washington, D.C., 1943).

XIV

SLUMP AND NEW DEAL

*The recession of 1927 – Long-term depressive factors –
Speculation – The Crash (October 1929) – Trends in the
1930's – Falling indices, 1929–33 – The New Deal:
Hoover and the R.F.C.; industry; credit; pump-priming;
labour and social security; agriculture and conservation –
Conclusions – The recession of 1937–8.*

IN 1927, two years before the great financial crash, a minor recession occurred in the United States associated with reduced rates of expansion (rather than absolute declines) in wages and salaries, consumption, factory output and investment. Also the (Bureau of Labour Statistics) wholesale price index fell 3·5 per cent in 1926 and 4·6 per cent in 1927. But dividends, interest and rent continued to expand at the same or at an increased rate.[1]

A positive fall was experienced by wages and salaries in the construction and mining industries and in commerce, and they gained very little in manufacturing. Thus there was a decline in the rate of increase of consumer spending and a striking drop in the sales of durable goods: the car market was saturated at the existing demand level and conditions (there was a fall in the total of the manufacturing labour force, besides the retarded growth in total earnings of those in employment), and in 1927 passenger-car production fell 23 per cent below the 1926 figure (from about 3,784,000 to about 2,937,000); also the housing boom was now over, many building workers being thrown onto the labour market. Factory output of non-durables continued at a slightly *increased* rate, the index (1935–9=100) rising thus: 1925—76, 1926—79, 1927—83. Output of durables in 1927 decreased, however, as we have seen, the index being: 1925—107, 1926—114, 1927—107. The index of total manufactures registered a fall of one point in 1927 (95 to 94), which seems more significant when

[1] See Soule, op. cit., pp. 318–23, for an extremely useful table of economic changes, 1923–9, adapted from National Bureau of Economic Research data.

viewed against the five-point increase of the previous year.[1] Finally, a small but distinct reduction of about $770 million in total private investment was accompanied by a deflationary Federal Government financial policy.

The 1927 setback did not develop into a major affair. Recovery was swift, and even the number of unemployed (which had risen from 464,000 in 1926 to 1,857,000 in 1928) fell in 1929 to 429,000—about 35,000 below its pre-recession figure.[2] Thus on 4 December 1928 in his annual message to Congress, President Coolidge was able to make that famous statement, so full of dramatic irony (for the historian as playgoer):

'No Congress of the United States ever assembled, on surveying the state of the Union, has met with a more pleasing prospect than that which appears at the present time....'

Ten months later the worst financial crash in history on the New York Stock Exchange had destroyed security values and brought untold personal tragedy to thousands. This crash was followed by a ten-years depression, of varying degrees of severity, that was brought to an end only by renewed global war.

The origins of the Great Depression lay beyond those of the Wall Street panic that had helped to precipitate it and symbolized it so dramatically. A glance back at the previous chapter would show that its origins lay beyond the unheeded 'rumblings' of 1927. They should be sought in the structural weaknesses that were merely concealed by the prosperity of the so-called 'New Era'. There was consistent agricultural distress, trouble in the coal, textile, shipbuilding, railroad, leather and other industries, and persistent unemployment. Some authorities claim that there was never under one and a half million unemployed throughout the '20's. (Certainly in bad years it was very severe—almost five million in 1921, three million in 1922 and over two million in 1924, according to the conservative National Industrial Conference Board estimates alone.) Dazzling successes on the roundabouts diverted attention from the sadly neglected and decaying swings. One could be too easily dazzled even by the prosperous 'roundabouts': the automobile, the building and to some extent the electrical and radio industries produced durable goods the demand for which could easily be withheld in times of stringency. In addition their sales were financed largely on credit.[3] Meanwhile, technological

[1] *Historical Statistics of the United States*, op. cit., p. 223 (Series K 225–235) and p. 180 (Series J 30–48).

[2] Ibid., p. 65 (Series D 62–76). These are National Industrial Conference Board figures.

[3] Outstanding consumer credit in 1929 was estimated at about $7,000 million.

innovation did not slacken, and employment did not increase proportionately with the increase of population. Despite the rise in real wages throughout the '20's as a whole, an increasingly larger percentage of the national income went in profits and undistributed surpluses, which helps to explain why the rate of increase of consumption was slower than that of production.[1]

Even in the years of prosperity, therefore, there were several incipient hidden factors, any one of which if it had become acute could have precipitated a crisis. In 1927, as the reader will have noticed, some of these factors emerged more clearly, but were swept aside in a final spurt of economic growth. There was a tendency to underconsumption and increasing maldistribution of income; a tendency to credit inflation, stimulated by sales organizations, mass advertising, loan associations, instalment purchase and the easy-credit policy of the Federal Reserve Board; a distinct possibility that investment opportunities would soon become wholly sequestrated (at least for a while); and fourthly, increasingly heavy and complex stock exchange speculation. It was of course the last of this selection of factors that did in fact come to a head.

The disastrous panic on the New York Stock Exchange in October 1929 initiated a *deflationary spiral* which was exacerbated—by a deflationary national wages policy after 1930; by a pressing weight of debt that, being repaid in a time of slump, also had a deflationary effect; by falling prices of primary products (agricultural goods and raw materials) which discouraged private investment throughout the 1930's; and by many bank failures (owing to farm bankruptcies and the drop in real-estate values) that also discouraged investment, stimulated currency-hoarding and consumed money.[2]

These failures were one of the principal trends in United States banking history during the '20's. Other features included a growth of banking consolidations, of chain and branch banks; an increase in instalment sales and bank deposits; an official easy-credit policy; and the extension of foreign loans to Europe and elsewhere. In 1925 there were nearly 28,000 commercial banks in the United States, of which about 9,500 were Federal Reserve member-banks. Between 1921 and 1929 (*before* the crash) 5,684 banks failed, owing to poor management, excessive loans, depreciation of assets and (above all) falling agricultural prices in the West. The surviving banks invested

[1] See, for instance, J. M. Clark, *Strategic Factors in Business Cycles* (New York, 1934), p. 106. In addition, consumption habits were changing: oil and natural gas were replacing coal, silks and rayons replacing cotton, tractors replacing horses and mules (and thus cutting down demand for oats and hay).

[2] A good brief analysis on the above lines is given in W. A. Lewis, *Economic Survey, 1919–1939* (London, 1949), pp. 51–7.

their increasing deposits in loans on real estate and for the purchase of stocks and bonds.

The Liberty and Victory bond campaigns of World War I inadvertently played an educative rôle in American life, familiarizing the public with the techniques of investment and stock exchange operations. After the war more and more people bought stocks and bonds, though sales did not cover such a broad section of the general public as is often claimed. Credit was easy and securities sold without difficulty. As the '20's developed speculation became more intense, huge volumes of securities were 'floated', and the process became much more complicated and subtle. In the orthodox way, business corporations make new issues and re-fund old ones in order to acquire fresh capital for business expansion. But in the Prosperity Decade big business could easily finance itself. This left bank resources free to make large collateral loans, helping to finance speculation for its own sake.[1] Those who made a profit in selling securities stimulated an unusually wide demand for them, through nation-wide advertising schemes. New securities were 'manufactured'—not because business needed extra investment capital, but simply because such securities could be sold at a good 'rake-off'. Not only were new companies invented but banks and investments promoters persuaded business corporations to re-fund old issues and float new ones for no particular excuse. In other words, the whole system was topsy-turvy: securities were not offered for sale in order to finance business expansion; on the contrary, business surpluses went into pure speculation. This was how the curious state of affairs described in the previous chapter came about—a speculative mania that was 'artificial' because it was based on hasty sales and resales of stock exchange securities, irrespective of their yield potentialities and with little or no reference to the business activities they were supposed to represent.

Investment 'trusts' grew up to take advantage of the fantastic market conditions. For instance, one investment banking house, Dillon, Read & Co., established such a trust in 1924—the United States and Foreign Securities Corporation—that eventually made thirty to forty million dollars on an original investment of five million. On the basis of these rich takings the bank then set up a new trust, the International Securities Corporation. Some of these trusts had ramifications so intricate and delicate both financially and legally, that their very promoters knew little of how they operated.[2] Many of them were irresponsible, and all helped ultimately to create an excess of supply of securities above the effective demand of public investors.

[1] In the three years 1925, '26, and '27, security loans of member banks of the Federal Reserve System increased 40 per cent, investments 20 per cent, and commercial loans only 12 per cent. See Soule, op. cit., p. 279.

[2] Ibid., pp. 298–304.

Before this came about stock prices continued to rise phenomenally. The price index for all common stock (1926=100) rose three-fold between 1920 and 1929, from 64·2 to 190·3. This index is too comprehensive to give a very accurate picture however. The common stock price index of coal companies for instance, actually *declined* by one-third in the same period, from 136·6 to 91. (By 1932 it had reached the gloomy depth of 11·8). The largest rate of increase was nearly six-fold, in retail trade common stock that rose from 31·7 to 178·5. The index of utility companies climbed from 54·5 to 234·6, that of industrial firms from 66·1 to 189·4, and that of railroads from 64 to 147·3.

New capital issues and re-funding issues of securities increased nearly 300 per cent in total value between 1920 and 1929, rising from about $4,000 million to almost $11,600 million. Nearly five times as many shares were traded through the New York Stock Exchange in 1929 (1,125 million) as in 1920 (227 million).[1] The 1929 figure represented about 58 per cent of the national total. A few streets away in the same city the New York Curb Exchange handled a further 25 per cent of the national total. Thus 83 per cent of the volume of stock sales in 1929 were concentrated in the two major exchanges in the same district of New York City.

The market value of all shares officially listed on the New York Stock Exchange alone, rose in the four years January 1925 to January 1929 from over $27,000 million to nearly $67,500 million, and the actual number of shares listed increased from 433 million to 757 million. Within the year 1929 itself this expansion accelerated and by 1 October the market value was over $87,000 million and the numerical total almost 1,050 million.[2]

What about the owners of all these shares? Not allowing for double-counting (most investors owning stock in more than one firm) there were about 20 million American corporation stockholders in 1929. One author has estimated the real figure of total investors to be about 9 million, and states that 80 per cent of total shares were owned by people with incomes of over $5,000.[3] (This scotches the long-held belief that a considerable amount of speculation was by small investors—the 'common man').

It was a pronounced minority of the American people, therefore, that engaged in the year of frenzied speculation immediately preceding the Crash of October 1929. A scandal on the London Stock Exchange in September caused a steep fall in prices there and a recall

[1] For these statistics and those in the preceding paragraph, see *Historical Statistics of the United States*, op. cit., p. 281 (Series N 212–220 and N 221–223), and p. 282 (Series N 228–32).

[2] Soule, op. cit., pp. 293–5. [3] Loc. cit.

of British funds from the United States. The larger speculators and men with inside knowledge foresaw trouble of some kind and began unobtrusively and gradually to liquidate their holdings. For all that, stock market prices continued to advance until 15 October. On that ominous day, when a prominent economist, Professor Irving Fisher, triumphantly announced that stock prices stood on 'a permanently high plateau', they fell 5 or 6 points. So universally pervasive was the optimism of the '20's—affecting consumers, businessmen, financial experts and academic economists alike—that in the first few days Professor Fisher, like many of his colleagues, believed firmly that the decline would not last and blamed it on the mistaken panic of small investors (the 'lunatic fringe', as he termed them).[1]

On Black Thursday (24 October) the New York Stock Exchange was flooded by selling orders, prices dropped precipitously, and almost 13 million shares changed hands. The leading bankers, themselves heavily involved, met together at the offices of J. P. Morgan and announced to an anxious world their agreement to support the market. Skyscraper offices hummed with activity throughout the night as hundreds of clerks laboured at piles of paper work.

Because business did not depend on bank credit, there were few business failures in the early stages; indeed some firms saw their cash balances expand as they called in loans. But on the 29th a new wave of selling orders engulfed the Exchange and a new fall in stock prices caused damage even to the strongest concerns: the American Telephone and Telegraph Co. (with 458,000 shareholders), General Electric and United States Steel. Fully 16 million shares were traded. A second bankers' conference at Morgan's brought no further response to support the market. J. D. Rockefeller tried to do something to check the price fall by declaring that he and his son were buying up common stock. Bankers then rallied and formed a $250 million buying pool. But it was to no avail, for although the fall was decelerated, prices continued to decline during the winter. By 1930 the price index of all common stock had fallen about 21 per cent below its 1929 peak of 190·3, to 149·8. In 1932 it reached its nadir—48·6. Between 1929 and 1932 retail trade stock fell to one-quarter (45·2), industrial stock to under one-quarter (46·5) and railroad stock to between a fifth and a sixth (26·4) of their 1929 prices. The index of utility companies did not reach its lowest point—slightly over one-quarter (68·9)—until 1934.

The economic history of the 1930's[2] can be divided into three predominant trends: a long decline (from September 1929 to the spring

[1] In England, J. M. Keynes thought that the slump would usefully liquidate unsound speculation.

[2] See, for an English analysis, L. Robbins, *The Great Depression* (London, 1934). A readable general American economic history of the period is B. Mitchell, *Depression Decade, from New Era through New Deal*

of 1933—Roosevelt's inauguration), during which business activity was halved; an equally long, irregular upward climb (until the autumn of 1937), in which the peak of 1929 was almost reconquered; and finally, a sudden steep fall (in 1937-8) followed by a general resurgence of economic activity arising out of the stimulus of international war and an increase in deficit spending.

By the autumn of 1932 one of the few indices that was rising was that of unemployment, which totalled according to National Industrial Conference Board figures 11,385,000 and according to other estimates about 15,000,000. The total of bank failures also leapt dramatically from 659 in 1929 to 1,352 in 1930, 2,294 in 1931, 1,456 in 1932 and 4,004 in 1933 (when United States banking collapsed completely). Gross national product was reduced by almost 50 per cent, 1929-33, falling from $103,800 million to $55,800 million. Of minor importance internally but indicative of the trend of events was the decline in foreign trade: the value of total imports fell from $4,399 million (1929) to $1,323 million (1932), and that of total exports from $5,241 million to $1,611 million. Both imports and exports were thus cut to about 31 per cent. The Bureau of Labour Statistics index of wholesale prices (1926=100) fell by one-third from 95·3 (1929) to 64·8 (1932). That of wholesale farm prices fell even more steeply than the general index, from 104·9 (1929) to 48·2 (1932).[1]

The long, gradual, uneven, uphill climb after 1933 was of course directly associated with the New Deal policies. These we must now consider.

For those who choose to study the New Deal at first hand there is an overwhelming mass of material of all kinds to sift through. Perhaps the best way to tackle the subject within the confined space available here and for the purposes of this book is by considering under several broad categories the main problems the Roosevelt administration faced in 1933, and then connecting them with the major New Deal measures.[2] Firstly however, what steps if any were taken by the Hoover government between 1929 and 1933 to meet the depression?

(Vol. IX of Rinehart & Co.'s *Economic History of the United States*, New York, 1947). For background use Dixon Wecter's *Age of the Great Depression* (New York, 1948).

[1] *Historical Statistics of the United States*, op. cit., p. 65 (Series D 62-76), p. 273 (Series N 135-40), p. 12 (Series A 101-16), p. 216 (Series K 158-67), and p. 233 (Series L 15-25).

[2] The best political introduction for the British reader is D. W. Brogan's *Roosevelt and the New Deal* (London, 1952) which has a useful bibliography. Also good—but unfortunately very brief—from an economist's viewpoint, is Chapter VIII of W. A. Lewis, op. cit.

There were three basic attitudes one could hold about the American national crisis in and after 1929. One could staunchly uphold a purely negative policy on the part of the Federal Government, on the theoretical grounds that the sooner and the more complete the deflation, the swifter the recovery. Alternatively, one could demand that, as far as possible and within mild limits, the deflation should be 'cushioned' by federal action. Or one could go all-out for positive and comprehensive federal intervention in economic affairs. The New Deal was the embodiment of the last of these three attitudes, the Hoover programme that of the second. None but a few fanatics seriously believed in the first.

The most important step taken by President Herbert C. Hoover was to establish the Reconstruction Finance Corporation (R.F.C.) in January 1932, with a capital of $500 million and authority to borrow three times as much if necessary. The R.F.C. was to extend credit on security to commerce, industry, agriculture, financial houses, railroads, and later to state and local authorities engaged in public benefit schemes. It loaned $3,000 million in the first eighteen months of its existence and brought assistance at an opportune moment to many concerns facing disaster. Undoubtedly the effect of its help was to retard the deflationary spiral to some extent. But two criticisms still stand against the scheme (whatever attempts are made by later writers to rehabilitate President Hoover as an earnest reformer). Firstly, it gave aid to the very bankers and businessmen whose short-sightedness had precipitated the Crash, instead of directly in the form of relief to the thousands of common people who bore the brunt of the tragic consequences. Dividend and interest payments were maintained throughout the Great Depression, and indeed in 1931 reached a peak figure of about $8,000 million—this in a period in which national income as a whole was more than halved. The poorer majority of the American people payed disproportionately for the blunders of the entrenched minority. Secondly, and more important still, the R.F.C. can be criticized because it was the *pièce de résistance* of the Hoover programme, not just one minor measure but the central reform. Apart from its institution all that was done was to form conferences with business leaders begging them to maintain wages and employment, and to urge the rest of the nation to nail the flag to the mast. Meanwhile the mechanisms of private charity broke down under the strains they could no longer bear, and internationally the situation was made infinitely worse by the Hawley-Smoot Tariff Act of 1930, that outdid the Fordney-McCumber Act in the levels it imposed.

Precisely when the nation was sickening of reiterated warnings to 'tighten its belt' and presidential prohibitions of congressional attempts to appropriate adequate relief resources, there came an election. F. D. Roosevelt obtained an overwhelming national mandate for his proposed New Deal. He won in 1932 almost 23 million popular votes and 472 out of 531 electoral votes.

When Roosevelt took over in 1933 the depression was at its very depths. The problems he met were as interacting and as interdependent as the New Deal measures he adopted to combat them. At the same time it is not straining 'the facts' too much to discern six *groups* of problems in 1933: there had been an overexpansion of capital plant and of production, particularly acute in agriculture; Labour suffered unduly from cyclical and technological unemployment and received an inadequate share of the national income; monopolistic practices, especially in the case of conscious interference with free movement of prices, seemed to many New Dealers to be a grave evil and corporate control of public utilities had proved unprogressive; the credit and banking structure was in need of some form of public control; there were several 'black spots' on the economy (e.g. agriculture and housing); and, finally, international markets were not functioning at all efficiently, owing to tariff barriers and foreign exchange complications.

The New Deal consisted of a series of empiric (not always very successful) answers to these problems, administered by innumerable more or less *ad hoc* agencies such as those previously adopted in World War I. For industry the National Industrial Recovery Act (1933) set up a National Recovery Administration (N.R.A.) to supervise the forming of 'code authorities' by individual branches of industry. The idea was very far from nationalization. It aimed to encourage industry to police itself through the code authorities which worked to ensure what was called 'fair competition'—the acceptance of a code of business practices. The Federal Trade Commission (under the Act of 1914, mentioned above in Chapter XII) had already come to terms with individual industries over the conference table concerning what constituted 'fair' and 'unfair' practices. The N.R.A. regularized these meetings and agreements and drafted a code for each branch (about 600 codes all told) which had precedence at law over the provisions of the Sherman Act, should they conflict. Many of the codes legalized practices previously regarded as monopolistic (e.g. 'open price filing'), and were thus in direct contradiction to the expressed anti-trust policy of the Democratic party.

In addition the codes gave protection to Labour, guaranteed freedom for collective bargaining and usually laid down maxima and minima respectively for hours and wages. Although in principle the representatives of Labour were to take part in the formulation of the codes, in practice their participation was rare, mainly because the Act did not specifically command it. In general however the codes did seek to establish a forty-hour week for manual labourers, minimum wages of $12 to $15 weekly, and the abolition of child labour.

Part II of the 1933 Act empowered the President to spend up to $3,300 million on public works. It was perhaps the most useful part of the measure, for the Act as a whole was not a thoroughgoing success. It helped in part to bring about an ephemeral recovery of sorts in the summer of 1933, but (as Professor W. A. Lewis points out) its two aims were contradictory: to create a prosperity atmosphere and stimulate investment by raising prices, and to expand purchasing power (and therefore consumption) by improving wages. As it was effective to about the same degree in both these goals, they effectively cancelled each other out.[1] To the complaints of small businessmen and consumers (who were totally ignored by the Act) and the disappointments of Labour (expressed in the textile strikes of September 1934) was soon added the overt hostility even of the larger industrial firms themselves which by the autumn were grumbling about too much government intervention. But in its decision on the Schechter case, in May 1935, the Supreme Court rapidly made this controversy a matter of interest chiefly for historians: it invalidated the National Industrial Recovery Act. This it did on two principal counts: that the Act authorized the use of delegated legislation, which was unconstitutional; and that it exceeded the limits of federal authority over interstate commerce.

New Dealers were not wholly sorry to see the N.R.A. safely out of the way, and soon after they began chasing the trust-busting hare with renewed enthusiasm. In his second term, Roosevelt enlarged the anti-trust investigating staff and gave it bigger funds; trust-busting hit the headlines once more, after a considerable armistice. But despite the flurry of activity little was done to reverse the trend towards oligopoly that the New Deal had itself encouraged earlier.[2] No 'return' was to be made to the semi-mythical pristine democracy of 'free competition'.[3] World War II was to reinforce the foundations of oligopoly in the United States, and the post-war prosperity of the late 1940's and 1950's—the most fabulous in American history—to dissolve, perhaps for ever, the rift between American economic

---

[1] W. A. Lewis, op. cit., pp. 107–8.

[2] Although in 1936 the Robinson-Patman Act aimed against chain stores, tried to check price-discrimination and undercutting in the retail trades, and in 1937 the Miller-Tydings Act legalized retail price maintenance in interstate commerce by public agreement between producer and retailer, in a similar attempt to prevent excessive price competition.

[3] For interesting *suggestions*, see J. K. Galbraith's *American Capitalism* (op. cit.), a most readable, deliberately provocative book which tries to restate the problem of competition, oligopoly and State intervention in the light of the author's theory of 'countervailing power'.

theory on the one hand and the facts of American economic organization on the other.[1]

As a general condition for recovery, prices had somehow to be stimulated. Roosevelt tried several devices besides the National Industrial Recovery Act. For instance he took the United States off the gold standard by executive orders in April 1933 forbidding the hoarding or export of gold, and by a joint resolution (June 1933) making all public and private debts payable only in legal tender, abrogating the gold clauses of contracts. The dollar depreciated on the foreign exchanges and the domestic price level rose. Gold was bought from abroad under the Gold Reserve Act (1934), which established what was virtually a 'managed' currency, but left gold available for payment of foreign balances.[2] The day after the Act was passed the President devalued the dollar to between 50 and 60 cents of its former worth in gold. This inflationary policy was not as successful as was expected, and the government shifted its attention from the currency itself to credit.

The outstanding problem in this sphere was the complete collapse of the banking system in 1933, a year in which, as we have seen, over 4,000 banks failed. On Roosevelt's inauguration day bank 'holidays' had to be declared in the two chief financial centres, Chicago and New York. The first action he took on coming to power was to complete and make official this tendency, by proclaiming a national banking moratorium (5 March). In addition other normal sources of credit, such as savings banks, insurance and trust companies, title and mortgage companies, had proved inadequate. It therefore proved necessary to expand the work of the R.F.C. (inherited by the Roosevelt administration, among other things, from Hoover), to reopen commercial banks and enable them to achieve liquidity rapidly. A special session of Congress was called to sanction the President's action, and was immediately presented with an Emergency Banking Act (9 March). This also gave him special powers to control monetary and foreign exchange transactions, and strengthened the hands of the R.F.C. by allowing it to buy up (or accept as collateral for loans) the preferred stock of banks in distress. Moreover, the Act permitted solvent and near-solvent Federal Reserve member banks to reopen under licence, and enlarged their note-issuing powers. A further Act augmenting the scope of the R.F.C. was the

[1] See Chapter XII, above, p. 195.

[2] A Silver Purchase Act was also passed in 1934, after agitation from the silver bloc, which remained influential in Congress. This purely national policy adopted by Roosevelt forced him to wreck the World Economic Conference of 1933 by refusing point-blank to co-operate in any way. The Conference aimed at currency stabilization on the basis of the gold standard and general tariff reductions.

Loans-to-Industry Act (June 1934) sanctioning direct industrial loans of up to $580 million.

Two Banking Acts were aimed more directly at reform of the banking structure, although the changes they achieved were not particularly radical or sweeping. The first Act (1933) introduced safeguards for depositors using Federal Reserve member banks, by creating a federal corporation to provide insurance on deposits. More than this, it prevented Federal Reserve banks from engaging in stock-market speculation either directly or through affiliated banks. The second Act (1935) tried to increase federal control of monetary affairs by giving the Federal Reserve Board (through an Open Market Committee) some supervisory authority over the credit policy of member banks, the right to vary their reserve requirements within certain limits, and the right to check their chief staff appointments. On the other hand nothing at all was done to give the Board authority over all commercial banks, including non-members, and this dichotomy remained the chief weakness in United States banking structure, especially in times of crisis.[1]

But the most important device for pushing up prices was neither currency nor banking reforms, but *pump-priming*—Federal Government lending and spending. After the failure of the N.R.A. the administration came to depend increasingly on the policy of deficit financing. The collegiate 'brain trust' (as it was called) that advised President Roosevelt was strongly influenced by the economic doctrines of John Maynard Keynes, whose *Treatise on Money* and *General Theory of Employment, Interest and Money* appeared in 1930 and in 1936 respectively. The notion that a cyclical fall in production and prices could be impeded by the deliberate use of deficit financing (government expenditure in excess of revenue) was thoroughly Keynesian. It was believed that the additional money being pumped into the economy (and into circulation) by such financing would increase consumption, thereby encourage investment, and thus lead to renewed economic growth.

What happened in practice? The theory—like most economic theories—was neither proved nor disproved by the facts. In the first place not all the money pumped into the economy by deficit spending was pumped thereby into circulation. This initial setback left the theory more or less intact; the question is, what were the effects of the money that did manage to get into circulation? This query must be preceded by another: which federal expenditures did and which did not get into circulation?

Government spending for the relief of debtors took two forms: that which operated through the strengthened R.F.C., and that which was administered by newly created agencies. Reconstruction Finance

[1] See Chapter XI, above, p. 186.

Corporation loans to bankers and industrialists were mainly used to pay off old debts, and as creditors remained wary to redeploy their repaid resources, which, like manna from Heaven, they had scarcely dared hope for, the money did not add directly to circulation or employment. Not all R.F.C. loans went in this way, and those used for investment did of course add to the total of money in circulation and to employment. The finances administered by special agencies, such as the Federal Farm Mortgage Corporation (dealt with later under agriculture) and the Home Owners' Loan Corporation, did not add directly to employment or circulation either. The Home Owners' Loan Corporation, set up in 1933, was an extension of a scheme that originated in the Home Loan Bank Act (1932) of the Hoover regime. The 1932 Act established federal banks to lend on real-estate mortgages to building and loan associations; the New Deal corporation (assimilated three years later by the Federal Housing Administration) was empowered to issue bonds up to $2,000 million to re-finance first mortgages on moderate and small-sized homes.

Money spent on the relief of debtors, however necessary and justifiable from other economic and social viewpoints, did not perform the functions hoped of it by the disciples of Keynes. Some federal expenditures did add to circulation: direct relief payments, such as those to farmers, the unemployed and war veterans, and expenditures on public works (which also added directly to employment). Farm and unemployment relief will be considered later; here we can take as an example of direct payments those to ex-servicemen ('veterans'). An Adjusted Compensation Act of 1924 gave every veteran an endowment and insurance policy valued according to length of service, with higher rates for service abroad, and averaging about $1,000 per policy.[1] When the depression struck, many veterans demanded immediate payment of the face value of these endowment policies, to be made in greenbacks. In 1931 Congress passed a Bill over President Hoover's veto allowing men to *borrow* up to one-half of the face value. This was not enough, and in June 1932 a 'Bonus Expeditionary Force' of impoverished veterans, about 20,000 in number, marched to Washington to present a 'petition on boots' and camped in hastily constructed ramshackle slum huts, on Anacostia Flats, in view of the Capitol itself. Hoover ordered the National Guard to drive them out and burn their shelters—a blunder that earned him much unpopularity. Under the New Deal in 1935 Roosevelt vetoed the Patman Bill for the payment of bonus certificates through currency inflation, but in January 1936 a new Bonus Act was forced through over his veto, by which the Federal Government had to pay out $1,500 million.

[1] This idea of a bonus is not to be confused with disability compensation, which was on the whole liberal, and about which there was little complaint.

Such relief payments, augmented by old age pensions (Social Security Act, 1935), subsidies, grants-in-aid and other devices, had a stimulating effect on the economy, as did public works schemes. The latter included shipbuilding, slum-clearance, construction of public buildings and roads, reafforestation and conservation, flood-control, dam-construction and even cultural projects.

Now we can revert to the original question: how effective was the money that did add to circulation? In 1930, with a balanced budget, federal expenditures totalled about $3,600 million; six year later there was a deficit of $5,000 million, and a total expenditure of about $9,000 million.[1] The national debt rose from $16,000 million to over $33,000 million, a *per capita* increase of from $131 to $263, and by 1939 it totalled over $40,000 million—or a figure per head of population of $309.[2] This was a 250 per cent rise in the total national debt (1930–9), and a 235 per cent increase in the *per capita debt*. After 1939 these figures are dwarfed by wartime finances[3] but they represent nevertheless a considerable increase in their day.

The results were, on the whole, not very startling. Consumption did increase slowly. Personal consumption expenditures began to creep up from the low level of $46,300 million (1933) to $56,200 million (1935), $62,500 million (1936) and a peak of $67,100 million (1937). Employment increased (according to National Industrial Conference Board figures) by 7,452,000 between 1933 and 1937, but population continued to grow, and although unemployment fell by 5,439,000 there was a continued average of 7,000,000 without work. The National Bureau of Economic Research index of physical output for all manufacturing industries (1929=100), which had fallen to 63 in 1933, was by 1937 three points above 1929. But private investment was still very sluggish. The figures (of gross private domestic investment) increased each year from 1933 to 1937, but apart from the boom that brought them up to $11,400 million in 1937, averaged well under 50 per cent of the 1929 total of $15,800 million. Prices were stimulated by New Deal policies. The wholesale price index which, as we have seen, had fallen to 64·8 in 1932, rose to 86·3 in 1937; farm wholesale prices, which had fallen more steeply then the general index, rose more steeply—from 48·2 (1932) to 86·4 (1937).[4]

Thus, *pump-priming* was neither a shattering failure nor a brilliant success. (A verdict one could safely pass on the New Deal as a whole.)

[1] See W. A. Lewis, op. cit., p. 112.

[2] *Historical Statistics of the United States*, op. cit., p. 305 (Series P 132–143).

[3] By 1945 total gross public debt was well over $258,000 million, an astonishing figure per head of population of $1,853. (Loc. cit.)

[4] Ibid., p. 12 (Series A 101–16), p. 65 (Series D 62–76), p. 180 (Series J 15–29), p. 233 (Series L 15–25).

What was especially disappointing was the continued high rate of unemployment, and the all too visible outward signs of national poverty and degradation it brought. Many of the more unfortunate and insalubrious aspects of American society which, mirrored or caricatured by the cinema, have left a lasting image with the people of other nations, grew up during this period of disillusionment, despair and crumbling values.

It was an extremely important part of the New Deal programme to introduce some degree of federal paternalism, of social security, into American life. For Labour, besides the provisions in the National Industrial Recovery Act of 1933 (which did survive), the administration formulated such measures as the National Labour Relations Act (1935) and the Fair Labour Standards Act (1938). The former (otherwise known as the Wagner-Connery Act) was introduced after a growing number of industrial conflicts of a violent nature (stoppages averaging 2,000 a year in 1934, 1935 and 1936) caused Congress to pass a Labour Disputes Joint Resolution (1934) authorizing the President to establish permanent machinery to deal with disputes. The Act set up a standing, independent National Labour Relations Board[1] to investigate complaints and proclaim 'cease and desist' orders against 'unfair practices' such as the coercion of workers in the exercise of their collective bargaining rights, discrimination against union members on the part of employers taking on men, and outright refusal of employers to bargain collectively. The Fair Labour Standards Act of 1938 came as the logical conclusion of a legislative movement that included the National Employment Service Act (1933) establishing a network of national employment exchanges, the Railroad Retirement Act (1934) whereby federal control was extended over the administration of pension schemes for railroad workers (judicially nullified 6 May 1935), and the Walsh-Healey (Government Contracts) Act (1936) which prohibited the offering of contracts for public work to any employer who did not meet certain minimum conditions regarding the hours and pay of his workers—the 8-hour day and 40-hour week, for instance, and no employment of lads of under 16 years old, or girls of under 18. The 1938 Act itself was first introduced by Senator Black of Alabama in the middle of 1937, a year of nearly 5,000 strikes involving about 2 million workers. Senator Black, who had introduced a surprisingly radical bill in 1933 demanding a national 6-hour day and 30-hour week to spread

[1] A board of the same name did in fact already exist, having replaced in June 1934 the National Labour Board set up in August 1933. Although the judicial invalidation of the N.I.R.A. did not specifically include its labour provisions, it was felt necessary to create a more permanent body under a new Act in 1935. The Act was accepted by the Supreme Court on 12 April 1937.

employment, wanted to place 'a ceiling over hours and a floor under wages'. While his Fair Labour Standards Act was not quite as momentous as the President described it ('the most far-sighted programme for the benefit of workers ever adopted in this or any other country'), it was nevertheless an important measure, ultimately giving protection to about 13 million workers. It established, for all labour engaged in interstate commerce or the production of goods for such commerce, a maximum working week of 40 hours and a minimum wage of 40 cents an hour, the time limit to be enforced after two years and the wage level after seven years. Meanwhile, transitional provisions were drawn up. Also the Act prohibited child labour in all industries connected with interstate commerce. The Supreme Court upheld the new law in a case in 1941 which overruled the case of 1918 which had invalidated the Keating-Owen Child Labour Act (1916).[1]

Before examining the Social Security Act of 1935 we should, at this convenient point, take up the thread of Labour history beyond the sphere of legislation.[2] The long decline in trade union influence and membership in the 1920's was reversed under the New Deal. Section 7(a) of the N.I.R.A. fully legalized unions and forbade employers' regulations forcing workers to join 'company unions', or to promise not to join a union at all, as a condition of being given work. A spate of enthusiastic labour organization ensued, also protected by the Norris-La Guardia Act passed in 1932 under Hoover, which built safeguards against the misuse of the injunction in labour disputes. Out of the resurgence of labour activity emerged one very important development: the C.I.O.

The drive to expand trade union membership after 1933 led to the acquiescence of the A.F.L. in the organization of so-called 'federal unions' on a basis of industry rather than craft. These unions, whose members were less experienced, more energetic and more radical than the A.F.L. leadership, forced through at the annual convention of 1934 a motion to promote industrial unionism in the mass-production industries—such as the automobile, steel, rubber, radio, aluminium, and in addition the textile industries and public utilities. The conservative leadership could not bring itself to execute this mandate, and the newer radical elements coalesced under John L. Lewis (President of United Mineworkers) and formed a Committee for Industrial Organization. Very soon the unions supporting Lewis were suspended from A.F.L. membership. What has been called 'Labour's Civil War' was on.

The C.I.O. (its name altered to Congress of Industrial Organizations in 1938, when it also adopted a constitution and a more per-

[1] The last was a measure in the New Freedom, See Chapter XII, above, p. 202.   [2] See Chapter IX, above, pp. 150–1.

manent form) aimed at uniting the skilled, unskilled and white-collar workers alike in the previously non-unionized industries. It represented a formidable resurrection of the industrial unionism of the 1880's and the Knights of Labour, but in a society dominated by huge oligopoly firms. These concerns, with their 'yellow dog' contracts (forbidding unionization) and 'company unions', their large armouries of tear and sickening gas, grenades, shells, sub-machine guns, rifles, revolvers, their industrial 'detectives' and spies,[1] had no intention of giving way easily. But on the other hand, many unions followed the lead of Lewis and left the A.F.L. for the C.I.O., and at first the latter body had much public sympathy, professional affiliated groups being formed by teachers, liberal journalists, and administrative workers. By mid-1937 the C.I.O. had captured 32 unions and almost 4 million members, while the A.F.L., with 100 affiliated unions, had under 3 million members.[2]

Lewis therefore determined to pursue a forceful strike policy, chiefly to assert C.I.O. hegemony, and began a new method: the 'sit-down' strike, in which workers refused to give up company machinery and property until they received satisfaction. The result was both highly successful and tragic. Many firms gave way—much to the surprise of everyone concerned—and the C.I.O. won several spectacular triumphs, culminating in the submission of United States Steel in March 1937. The last of the automobile firms to hold out against the C.I.O., Ford, acceded in 1941. But there was much violence. Firms like Republic Steel and General Motors denied the legality of the sit-down and went to court; when the courts issued injunctions that the unions flatly disobeyed, there was fighting. Perhaps the worst example was the 'Memorial Day Massacre' in South Chicago in June 1937. Police fought the strikers of the Republic Steel Corporation killing ten. Similarly, labour leaders were beaten up during a strike at Ford's River Rouge plant near Detroit. Although the report of a Senate committee on violence was not unfavourable to Labour, public opinion turned against the C.I.O. and the sit-down technique.

C.I.O. membership reached the 5 million mark in 1941, although the dynamic John L. Lewis resigned the previous year. By the end of World War II both A.F.L. and C.I.O. had over 6 million members. The chief trends since then are simply reviewed in the following

[1] The Senate Committee on Education and Labour (1936–40), found that the Republic Steel Corporation was the largest purchaser of tear and sickening gas in the U.S., that the arsenals of the Republic and the Youngstown Sheet and Tube Co. would equip a small war, and that the Republic in particular had an army of 400 armed 'police'.

[2] These figures can be checked in *Historical Statistics of the United States*, op. cit., p. 72 (Series D 218–23).

chapter; we must now return to a consideration of social security under the New Deal.

The central measure was the Social Security Act of 14 August 1935 (judicially validated 1937, amended 1939). This Act made more general the miscellaneous local provisions for unemployment and old-age pensions. In 1929 old-age pensions existed in only 29 of the 48 states; unemployment insurance schemes had been introduced in only one state (Wisconsin) by 1934. The federal system provided pensions for the needy, over 65 years old, the individual states who co-operated paying half the cost. Furthermore, an old-age insurance scheme gave benefits to members according to a complex structure of graduated premiums, paid by employer and worker. For unemployment insurance the plan was to tax employers (on the size of their pay-roll) and then give 90 per cent of this federal impost to those individual states whose unemployment schemes came up to the standards demanded by the Social Security Board. The Federal Government also gave the states $25 million for relief to dependent children and started annual appropriations of the same size to be used for maternal and child health, crippled children, the blind and vocational rehabilitation. The scope of American social security remains far behind that of the United Kingdom, or indeed of several European nations, but the Social Security Act was the first *national* attempt to insure the underprivileged in the United States.

Of the attempts to provide work, as opposed to federal charity, for the needy, the outstanding agencies and schemes worth mentioning here included the C.C.C., the P.W.A., the W.P.A., and the U.S.H.A. The first, the Civilian Conservation Corps, providing work-relief to young men, will be considered later with agriculture; the P.W.A. or Public Works Administration was set up under the National Industrial Recovery Act of 1933 with a capital of $3,300 million to promote construction in the public interest, and spent over $7,000 million during its existence; the W.P.A. or Works Progress Administration was established by executive order in 1935 after large appropriations for a second public works programme had been sanctioned by Congress, because the P.W.A.'s efforts had not appreciably reduced unemployment. The W.P.A. (later styled the Works *Projects* Administration) had the job of co-ordinating all public works schemes. Thus it was an important agency in the pump-priming operations. Given a capital of $4,880 million for relief, loans and grants to non-federal projects, roads, conservation, flood control, slum clearance, education, health and cultural work, it soon needed extra appropriations and spent altogether about $10,500 million and a further $2,700 million donated by state and local authorities, between 1935 and 1942, when it was dissolved. There was much waste and plenty of incompetence, but at the height of its career the W.P.A. found jobs for 3,800,000. It constructed 122,000 public buildings, 77,000 bridges, 285 airports, 664,000 miles of road, 24,000 miles of sewers, countless parks, playgrounds, reservoirs, and power plants—truly a gigantic prospectus, fit to bring tears to the eyes of a Louis Blanc.

The U.S.H.A.—United States Housing Authority[1]—served the dual purpose of providing low-cost housing and finding employment for workers. Although the housing boom had petered out after 1928-9 (see above, Chapter XIII), there still remained, as there still remains in many parts of the United States, an urgent demand for *cheap* housing. This demand was increased by depression conditions. The function of the U.S.H.A. was to assist local communities in slum clearance and the building of low-cost homes, for which it was given a capital of $500 million (later trebled). The private real-estate interests fought this idea bitterly and managed to hold up the programme so that by 1941 only 120,000 housing units had been actually completed.

New Deal policies have been illustrated in various fields: industry, credit and banking, pump-priming, labour and social security. The last major domestic[2] field of action to consider is agriculture.

In the last chapter the story of American agriculture was broken off at 1929, the year not only of the Crash but also of the Hoover Agricultural Marketing Act. This Act was principally concerned with the marketing of agricultural surpluses and with farm credit. The same two subjects were also dominant in the New Deal agricultural policy. As with industry (the N.I.R.A.) Roosevelt introduced a master measure, which did not live very long because it was judicially quashed and had to be replaced by several new Acts.

The master plan was the first Agricultural Adjustment Act (May 1933, otherwise known as the Farm Relief and Inflation Act). Its broad aim was to raise the status of agriculture within the economy, and it tried to effect this by stimulating the prices of farm goods and lightening the burden of farm debts and mortgages. An Agricultural Adjustment Administration (A.A.A.) was set up to super-

---

[1] Established by the Wagner-Steagall Housing Act (1937), and not to be confused with the Federal Housing Administration (set up in 1934), which assimilated the financial work of the Home Owners' Loan Corporation. (See above).

[2] In the international field (which cannot be considered more fully here) the New Deal administration established an Export-Import Bank to regulate American trade, and passed the Trade Agreements Act (12 May 1934), amending the highly protectionist Hawley-Smoot tariff of 1930 by allowing reciprocal trade agreements to be made with foreign nations. Twenty-six agreements were made up to 1941, but their effects on trade are not measurable in a period of such abnormal international conditions.

vice a system of agreements with farmers whereby production of the basic staples (cotton, wheat, corn, hogs and tobacco) was restricted deliberately, in return for government subsidies. In the following year the list of staples was enlarged to include beef and dairy cattle, rye, flax, barley, peanuts, sugar beet and cane and other products. Taxes on the processing of the goods concerned were to pay for the subsidies.

This recourse to 'planned scarcity' involved what Professor Broadus Mitchell has called the 'plow-up' and the 'kill': the ploughing back into the soil of 10 million acres of cotton and 12,000 acres of tobacco; the slaughter of over 6 million pigs; the abandonment of California fruit crops, left to rot on the trees and bushes. This incredible step, in a country where countless people were on the verge of starvation or at least utter destitution, was the logical conclusion pushed to its extreme, of a free-enterprise, profit-motive economy in which individual financial gain meant more than social production. More than this, it was a most extreme case of the dangers of taking a *theoretical* view and trying to enact it literally. Free-enterprise economists and (in less sophisticated form) politicians were constantly criticizing social reformers of all shades for their 'theories'; they were blithely unaware of the mote in their own eye. Nothing illustrates more clearly the fundamentally *conservative* nature of the New Deal than this manœuvre, supported by farmers and industrialists[1] but hated by the general public.

For reducing the cotton crop by about 4 million bales the planters receive $200 million from a grateful government; the average price of cotton almost doubled.[2] Wheat farmers received $100 million for taking about 8 million acres of land out of production; the price of wheat also doubled. Corn and pig producers received about $300 million for presenting a bewildered nation with the smallest corn crop since 1881 and tons of fertilizer instead of pork. Gross national farm income increased from $6,406 million (1932) to $11,265 million (1937).[3]

The Supreme Court declared the Agricultural Adjustment Act unconstitutional in January 1936, and Congress thereupon passed a conservation measure the underlying aim of which was in fact to curtail production, but which nevertheless proved to be helpful in the general progress of conservation. This was the Soil Conservation and Domestic Allotment Act (1936; technically an amendment to

[1] See B. Mitchell, op. cit., p. 190.
[2] The arrangements for limiting cotton output were strengthened by the Bankhead Cotton Control Act (April 1934). See M. R. Benedict, op. cit., p. 304.
[3] *Historical Statistics of the United States*, op. cit., p. 99 (Series E 88–104).

the Soil Erosion Act of April 1935). It proposed to spend $500 million for the improvement and preservation of soil fertility and to ensure safeguards against bad farming practices which lead to soil erosion and the depletion of its natural values. In his second term, however, Roosevelt had a more sympathetic Court, and the result was the second Agricultural Adjustment Act (February 1938) which authorized the limitation of acreage to be planted; established control over the marketing of surplus crops; began a system of 'parity price' payments (see Chapter XIII) to farmers who agreed to limit production; gave subsidies to those who planned production according to already approved soil-conservation practices; took over storage facilities for surpluses (the limited production of which was approved) in order to maintain an 'ever-normal granary' in case of drought or emergency; and introduced federal insurance for wheat.

Meanwhile, what of farm credit? The Hoover marketing Act had established the Federal Farm Board to make loans to agricultural co-operatives. The Board was abolished by order of President Roosevelt in May 1933, but its legislative authorization and remaining assets were useful in the creation of the Farm Credit Administration—a consolidation of the varied federal agricultural credit agencies, regularized by the Farm Credit Act (June 1933). In May, technically as Part II of the first Agricultural Adjustment Act, Congress had passed the Emergency Farm Mortgage Act, which empowered the Federal Land Banks (set up by the Act of 1916: see above, Chapter XII) to issue $2,000 million in 4 per cent bonds to refinance the thousands of farm mortgages that were being called by private lenders. Within three years more than 760,000 farms had been so saved.[1] In January 1934 the government also created the Federal Farm Mortgage Corporation, authorized to exchange private agricultural long-term paper for public guaranteed paper. It could issue fully guaranteed bonds up to a total of $2,000 million. Five months later Congress approved the Frazier-Lemke Amendment to the Federal Bankruptcy Act of 1898, allowing bankrupt farmers a five-year abeyance in which they could continue to inhabit their farms at a moderate rent; but in 1935 the Amendment was declared to violate the Fifth Amendment to the Constitution, and was accordingly revised as the Farm Mortgage Moratorium Act which gave farmers a respite of three, instead of five, years before seizure. The new version was upheld by the Supreme Court in March 1937 and continued in operation down to 1947.

Finally, no treatment of the New Deal for agriculture would be

[1] M. R. Benedict, op. cit., p. 282. Also the Federal Farm Loan Board, that had supervised the Land Banks under the Act of 1916, was abolished and its duties transferred to an official of the Farm Credit Administration.

adequate if it omitted to mention the tenancy laws. The Bankhead-Jones Farm Tenant Act (July 1937), besides providing for the retirement of submarginal lands, gave loans to tenant farmers and sharecroppers who wanted to own their farms. In September of the same year the Farm Security Administration was formed to advance small loans for agricultural rehabilitation, to maintain camps for migratory farm workers and to administer generally to the needs of the poorest and least protected members of rural society.

Closely connected with agricultural policy was the revived concern for conservation, which constituted in fact the second Conservation Movement (the first having been considered already in Chapter XII). During the depression years the physical results of over-exploitation of natural resources became increasingly visible, especially in the dreaded 'Dust Bowl' of the Southern Plains area of 1934–5. The immediate causes of the Dust Bowl were severe drought that withered the crops and dried to dust the exposed soil, and strong winds that gathered the dust up into immense, dark clouds. Its long-term causes were overcropping and overgrazing in parcels of land that were too small for the geographical conditions of the area, but were determined by the homestead legislation. The result was that Kansas farms were literally blown away, 9 million acres of land being destroyed by wind erosion and many humans and animals killed by dust pneumonia.

The predominant steps in New Deal conservation policy were: the relevant parts of the N.I.R.A. (public works provisions); the institution of the Civilian Conservation Corps; the Tennessee Valley scheme; the formation of the Federal Power Commission and the National Resources Board; the Taylor Grazing Act; the Soil Erosion Act and its later amendments; and of course, the conservation work of the W.P.A. already discussed. The C.C.C. was created in March 1933. In the years 1933 to 1941 it employed almost 3 million young men, supervised by army officers and foresters. Their main functions were to fight forest fires, investigate and check animal diseases and pests, gather tons of fish in hatcheries, add about 17 million acres of forest land to the nation's diminished reserves, build bridges and dams, prevent soil erosion by assuring water supplies and lay or suspend miles of telephone lines. The Federal Power Commission was set up by the Wheeler-Rayburn Act of August 1935, to regulate the public utility companies who provided electricity, but also was authorized to make a survey of national water-power resources; the National Resources Board (existing under various titles between June 1934 and June 1943) was expected to present the President with an over-all scheme for the utilization of land, water and other natural resources. About 142 million acres of Western grazing land were to be kept free of homesteaders by the Taylor Grazing Act of

June 1934.[1] The Soil Erosion Act (April 1935) gave sanction for a Soil Conservation Service to succeed the former Soil Erosion Service (created in 1933) and expand upon its work. The 1935 Act was amended by the Soil Conservation and Domestic Allotment Act of 1936, already mentioned above as a stop-gap after the invalidation of the first A.A.A.

But the most spectacular and internationally famous of all the conservation measures of Roosevelt was the Tennessee Valley Development Act (18 May 1933). The idea was, in simple terms, to dam the river and its tributaries, thus providing flood regulation, navigable reaches and an important source of power. The plan covered an area of about 40,000 square miles in seven states. Before long the T.V.A. assumed second place among American electrical supply systems; working hand in hand with state governments, the National Park Service, the National Resources Board, the Public Roads Administration, the U.S. Bureau of Fisheries (the largest fish hatchery in the world was established in the area) and the Biological Survey, the Authority not only embarked on a large-scale scheme of land reclamation but also opened huge sections to the tourist trade as recreational grounds and laid out five demonstration parks.[2] The T.V.A. carried out to the full its broad mandate to develop 'the economic and social well-being of the people living in the river basin'; it was a successful and courageous experiment in the rehabilitation of an area as a *geographical* entity.

'New Deal—evolution or revolution?' is perhaps not as barren a question as luckless examinees might be permitted to believe. From a study of precedents and consequences much that is instructive can emerge. At least two principal groups of precedents existed for the New Deal (its very name conjuring up memories of a *New* Freedom and a Square *Deal*). There was the federal legislation of the previous half-century: railroad regulation, farm relief, conservation, labour laws, monetary controls, banking acts, and the like. There was in addition the legislation of the individual states, especially the more progressive ones like Wisconsin, New York, and Massachusetts. Professor Brogan[3] has even made the interesting suggestion that it was not the New Deal, but the Harding-Coolidge era of legislative stagnation that was the interruption of a historical process. As for the consequences of the New Deal, these were far-reaching politically but essentially conservative economically. Even politically, the extension of federal control and authority entailed by the New Deal was clearly in the tradition of American historical developments,

[1] See Chapter XIII, above, pp. 223-4.
[2] For a full account see D. E. Lilienthal, *T.V.A.—Democracy on the March* (New York, 1944).   [3] Op cit., p. 238.

especially since the 1880's. This is abundantly clear if Chapter XII, XIII and XIV of this book are read (as they were meant to be) consecutively. Much of the 'revolutionary' character of the New Deal is derived from its breathtaking rapidity, and the scope and detail of its countless provisions; but this is easily understandable in the light of two factors—the severity of the Great Depression and the hiatus caused in the growing legislative reform movement by the abrupt intrusion of World War I.[1] In the United States as in Great Britain, the First World War cut across all lines of social development. The New Deal was an attack on a long-accumulated, miscellaneous heap of abuses, anachronisms, defects, malpractices—cracks in the body politic and economic—as well as a series of empiric answers to what were thought to be (perhaps sometimes mistakenly) the various causes of the depression itself. In other words it had a dual purpose: recovery and reform, and the long-term reform programme had to catch up on time lost through war and 'normalcy'. Here was no 'Five Year Plan' for radical economic reconstruction, but an attempt to continue a series of gradual revisions on several fronts which had suffered an untimely interruption, and which aimed at maintaining American capitalism by reforming it.

President Franklin D. Roosevelt's bold attempt to save American capitalism was brought to the verge of failure in 1937–8 by a new economic recession. The ship of state was undergoing heavy weather. Two years earlier, in 1936–7, there had been a 'boomlet' (a phrase coined by Dr. Broadus Mitchell)—a small-scale commodity boom, stimulated by several temporary factors, such as increases in deficit spending (e.g. the payment of the veterans' bonus under the Bill forced through in January 1936 and payments under the Social Security Act of 1935), and the Spanish war. The index of total manufacturing production (1935–9=100), which had fallen to 57 in 1932, rose to a peak of 113 in 1937; production of durables rose from 41 (1932) to 122 (1937), but remained 10 points *below* the 1929 level; output of non-durables rose from 70 to 106 (13 points above the 1929 figure); the agricultural production index was up to 106 in 1937, the highest level yet known; gross national product stood at $90,200 million, as compared with $55,800 million in 1933, and national income rose to $73,600 million from a 1933 figure of $39,600 million; the index of common stock prices (1926=100) climbed to 111·8 (1937) from a depth of 48·6 (1932); unemployment (N.I.C.B. data) fell from 11,842,000 (1933) to 6,403,000 (1937).[2]

[1] See Chapter XII, above, p. 206.
[2] *Historical Statistics of the United States*, op. cit., p. 180 (Series J 30–48), p. 98 (Series E 72–5), p. 12 (Series A 101–133), p. 281 (Series N 212–20) and p. 65 (Series D 62–76).

The possible flaws in this situation were: the short-lived nature of such stimuli as veterans' bonus payments; the continued existence of heavy unemployment (over 6 million); the failure of durable goods to recover sufficiently; a too rapid rise in costs, particularly of raw materials and labour, and a failure of profits to increase similarly; general overproduction in excess of increase in purchasing power; and stock-exchange speculation. Apparently, genuine recovery waited upon the restoration of long-term investment, which in turn waited upon profits, which depended on consumption and therefore, ultimately, on wages. This was a vicious circle, as wages were of course an important part of costs.

The so-called 'Roosevelt Depression' that began in August 1937 and continued until the early part of 1938 was perhaps chiefly the outcome of the above weaknesses. The government made cuts in deficit spending and there was a contraction of credit. The President thought prices were rising too much and took these two steps to check them. The reserve requirements of Federal Reserve member banks were raised 50 per cent. It is often claimed that the alienation of businessmen by the New Deal administration was a further complicating factor in the depression. This is a very doubtful notion however, not within the range of economic or historical investigation. What is more certain is that the situation was aggravated by drought which caused large agricultural losses and by a renewal of labour troubles. 1937, as we have seen, was a year of nearly 5,000 stoppages, and witnessed the Memorial Day Massacre at Chicago and the emergence of a full-scale programme of activity on the part of the newly founded C.I.O.

The trend of rising indices was instantly and steeply reversed. Total manufacturing production fell 26 points to 87 in 1938; durables fell more steeply than the general fall—44 points, to 78; non-durables fell 11 points, to 95; agricultural production fell only 3 points, to 103; gross national product fell by about 6 per cent to $84,700 million and national income decreased by a little over 8 per cent to $67,400 million. Unemployment rose by more than 50 per cent, to 9,796,000.[1] On the New York Stock Exchange the value of listed stocks dropped by about $20,000 million in the second half of 1937.

It was politically as well as economically imperative for the Democratic administration to do something as quickly as possible about this recession. New Dealers turned with relief to trust-busting agitation, but more constructive was the return to pump-priming in 1938: W.P.A. expenditures in the last half of 1938 were 50 per cent higher than in the last half of the previous year; A.A.A. expenditures were four times as high; the net deficit was almost six times as high. Yet even pump-priming was limited: gross capital formation fell by

[1] Loc. cit.

about $14,000 million between 1928 and 1932, whilst *total* spending by the Federal Government in the years of the pre-war New Deal (1933-8 inclusive) averaged $7,000 million. The gap could not be filled by government spending.

Pump-priming did bring a reversal of the recession in the last half of 1938, despite its long-term inadequacy. In Europe, which had also had a setback, large armaments orders were already coming in. The American economy faltered slightly in the spring of 1939; but by the spring of the following year the Second World War was beginning to make itself felt in the United States. From now on there could be little fear of economic contraction. Incidentally, the New Deal administration had been saved; but the task of Franklin D. Roosevelt had only just begun.

SUGGESTED FURTHER READING

BENEDICT, M. R. *Farm Policies of the United States, 1790-1950* (New York, 1953).
BROGAN, D. W. *Roosevelt and the New Deal* (London, 1952).
CLARK, J. M. *Strategic Factors in Business Cycles* (New York, 1934).
LEWIS, W. A. *Economic Survey, 1919-1939* (London, 1949).
MITCHELL, B. *Depression Decade, from New Era through New Deal* (Vol. IX of Rinehart & Co.'s *Economic History of the United States*, New York, 1947).

Epilogue

AMERICA AND WORLD POWER

World War II and the American economy – Post-war prosperity – Labour politics – International economic co-operation: U.N.R.R.A.; I.M.F. and World Bank; the Marshall Plan to 1949.

IT is still too early to attempt a treatment of the economic events since 1939 in the same fashion as those before that date have been treated in this book. On the other hand, it is interesting to take a rapid survey, although the selection of material may seem in future years to lack perspective. The aim of this chapter is therefore merely to follow up a few trends, which might serve to *illustrate* rather than give an integrated or balanced description of the economic development of the United States since 1939. The major part of the book ends with Chapter XIV; the following is but an epilogue.

The Second World War was a 'global', total, land, sea and air war, affecting every facet of national life. In the United States[1] in particular it implied: the rapid change-over from peacetime to wartime production; the raising, equipping and maintaining of armed services totalling about 15 million men; the transporting of men and materials to five continents and scores of sea islands; the maintenance of home production to safeguard the domestic population and supply the Allies; and the continuance of normal trade relations with Latin America and with neutral nations. A more complete mobilization the American people had never known. On the speed and efficiency of the industrial transformation of the United States depended the ultimate outcome of the war against the Nazis. The President promised that his country would become the 'arsenal of democracy'; this promise was entirely fulfilled.

The United States possessed many advantages over her Allies in the matter of mobilization, not the least of which were immunity from air raids, blackouts and food restrictions. Her huge industrial

[1] President Roosevelt delivered his war message to the country on 9 December 1941.

plant and labour force could work unhampered. Moreover, American industry was already on a partial war basis before she entered the battle, owing to Lend-Lease (sanctioned by Congress 11 March 1941) and the large defence commitments of 1940–1. Peacetime conscription through the Selective Service Act of 1940 laid the basis for the larger drafting of man-power that followed closely after the Japanese surprise attack on Pearl Harbour (7 December 1941). Already more than 6 million workers had been added to the labour force (by 1942 unemployment was liquidated), the index of manufacturing production was already twice the 1938 figure by 1941 (168) and gross national product increased 32 per cent rising in 1941 to $125,300 million.

Nevertheless, the general lack of urgency before Pearl Harbour, and the constant failure to understand how near America was to being forced into the international crisis, accounted for many serious shortages. The automobile industry long remained reluctant to turn over to military production; the steel industry's increase of 16 million tons was plainly insufficient; the armed services placed too few orders in the fear that rapid development in the technique of warfare would render the goods obsolete before delivery. There were critical shortages of machine tools and of medical products such as quinine, and inadequate stocks of copper, chrome, rubber and aluminium. Leading businessmen refused to co-operate with the New Deal government until they received heavy guarantees that the nation would take the financial risk; but this 'sit-down strike' of capital did not last long, as all the assurances were given.

Once the United States had entered the conflict and everyone knew exactly where they stood, production underwent an immense expansion. In 1942 the President set a target of 60,000 aircraft, 45,000 tanks and 8 million tons of merchant shipping—a target thought to be impossible by the War Production Board. To unify and co-ordinate the war machine on the domestic front, the Office of War Mobilization was set up, under ex-Supreme Court Justice James F. Byrnes (May 1943). The O.W.M. was meant to supervise the work of the War Production Board, the Oil Administration, the Office of Economic Stabilization, the War Labour Board and War Manpower Commission, and the Food Administration. The shock of Pearl Harbour effectively rid Americans of the idea that war production could continue alongside an unaltered or ever-increasing production of consumer goods; the latter was checked and in 1943 and 1944 the 'impossible' target of 60,000 military aircraft a year was surpassed by the totals 85,405 and 95,237. The fear of a shipping shortage was reduced in 1943 by production figures of a million tons a month. There was a need for more rubber however, and the Japanese victories cut off American imports; domestic production did not bridge the gap until 1944–5, and even then its total was 97,000 tons below the Baruch Committee's target of 1,037,000 tons, set in 1942. The steel industry did not expand phenomenally either, and was a constant headache to those concerned.

The contracts for increased wartime production went mainly to the largest corporations, both out of habit and for the sake of speed and efficiency. Ten corporations received one-third of all war orders, and General Motors itself accepted about $14,000 million of work. Despite the great deal of sub-contracting to smaller firms, one result of war production was thus the steady elimination of some 500,000 smaller businesses. During the war total industrial output almost doubled; but total productivity did not increase so rapidly because gains in such fields as shipbuilding and aircraft manufacture were offset by lower productivity elsewhere. The greater use of existing means and lengthened working hours accounted for much of the enlarged output rather than increase of productivity per man-hour. Whatever the causes, American industry produced enough for domestic and Allied needs; it equipped the French and Chinese armies; it built aerodromes and harbours the world over; it supplied Iran, Russia, Great Britain among others; it built highways in Burma and Alaska; and but twelve months after Pearl Harbour, outstripped the total production of the Axis powers combined.

The labour *shortage* during the war was indeed a new experience, not known for many decades. To meet the need there was an increase in young labour and over 5 million women went to work. Key workers were exempt, and retired men returned to their former jobs or new ones. By 1945 the total labour force (including the forces) totalled 65 million as compared with 56 million (employed and unemployed) in 1940.[1] The average working week had been extended from 40 to 48 hours, though the extra hours were normally counted as overtime. The trade unions made considerable progress in the war years (as in World War I), total membership rising to 14,796,000 (1945).[2]

The more or less normal migration of population from country to town was accentuated by the increased labour mobility, causing great urban housing, police, transportation and schooling problems. Urban population rose by almost 9 millions, and there was a noticeable tendency to move West and South-west with the shift of industry that was gradually taking place. Despite the growth of urban population there was an increase of farm output, perhaps to some extent the belated result of New Deal price subsidies, conservation and electrification schemes. The productivity of farm labour increased by 25 per cent and farm incomes doubled. There were large increases in the production of cereals, eggs and dairy goods, and meanwhile the Price Stabilization Act (1942) assured 'parity prices' for the farmer

[1] Ibid., p. 63 (Series D 11–31).   [2] Ibid., p. 72 (Series D 218–23).

until at least two years after the war's end. Agriculture profited even more than the large industrial corporations from the war.

The greatest fear was that of inflation. To avoid the tragedy of a price spiral the government took several steps. Price-regulation machinery was introduced in April 1941 (the Office of Price Administration—O.P.A.), but no general controls were exerted until January 1942 when prices had already risen 25 per cent. The Emergency Price Control Act of that month was soon supplemented by the General Maximum Price Regulation of the O.P.A., in April, and the Stabilization Act of October. The latter extended price and rent control to wages, and the law was stiffened again in April 1943. In addition restrictions were imposed by the mild rationing of goods and the prohibition of instalment buying. The assimilation of surplus income (which might have otherwise stimulated the Black Market or immediate post-war inflationary buying) was achieved by the sale of war bonds, and by a heavy taxation of the middle and upper income ranges through corporate, income, excise and inheritance taxes. Also there was a universal 5 per cent 'Victory Tax'. Taxation covered only 47 per cent of government expenditure in 1944, to select one year. The Second World War was financed in the United States like its predecessors: by borrowing. The national debt increased at the rate of $50,000 million yearly after 1941. In 1945 it totalled $258,682 million.[1] The tax burden of the American citizen thus never approached that of Great Britain.

Obviously 'total' war as experienced in Europe remains fortunately unknown on the American continent. The phenomenal all-out American economic effort was achieved without any definite control of man-power or direction of labour, for instance. It did not imply stringent rationing below normal food-consumption levels: meats, fats, sugar, coffee and canned goods were restricted to some extent; but motor-cars remained on the roads in thousands despite the rationing of petrol and tyres and the pressing rubber shortage. American living standards remained, as ever, generally high.

But the Second World War cost the United States eleven or twelve times as much as World War I—$360,000 million. This sum exceeded the *combined* total expended by Great Britain and the Soviet Union. Furthermore, it was American natural resources, wealth and engineering skill that enabled large-scale experimentation in atomic energy to be undertaken, a development that was to prove of such moment after 1945.

The Cold War brought with it an important social and political problem—the loyalty hysteria. But apart from this curious phenomenon (not by any means entirely new) American society showed no

[1] Ibid., p. 305 (Series P 132–43).

morbid traits in the post-war period. There was in fact a sharp contrast between the success story of internal affairs and the complexities and frustrations of external relations. This superabundant domestic prosperity, though not harmonious, served to underline the incredible nature of the external threats.

The United States emerged from the war as the political and military leader of the West, and the world's richest and most powerful nation. Economic reconstruction took place with few hitches: 12 million service people were absorbed into the economy; industry managed the change-over to peacetime activity with success; there was no post-war depression or unmanageable inflation. The Truman administration was committed to a continuation of the Roosevelt policy, with modifications, in the 'Fair Deal'. Gross national product, national income and productivity all continued to increase; the decade 1940-50 saw the largest population increase in United States history, achieved by the telling combination of a rising birth rate with a falling death rate; although there was a huge rise in the cost of living, there was also a leap in wages and salaries, and high employment; farm prices were maintained, as was the general prosperity of American agriculture, chiefly because of foreign demand, rising domestic living standards, and continued subsidies. Government spending continued to be heavy and was four times the size of expenditure at the depth of the Great Depression.

American labour politics continued to bewilder foreign observers, and shock the English by acts of violence. By the war's end the A.F.L. and C.I.O. had over 6 million members each; since then the A.F.L. has gained over its rival and is now (1955) almost twice as large.[1] The two groups have made arrangements to work more closely together. The year 1946 was one of great labour unrest throughout the nation; over 4,500,000 men took part in 5,000 disputes which affected all industries, particularly coal-mining, steel, automobile production and the electrical concerns. The government took over the mines when a bituminous coal strike threatened national and European recovery, and threatened to take over the railroads with Army help. On the whole, labour was successful in gaining wage increases, but managed to alienate large sections of public opinion. This made it possible for the Taft-Hartley Act to be re-enacted over President Truman's veto in 1947. The Act set up a new National Labour Relations Board, and added to the list of 'unfair practices' on the part of employers a formidable collection of such practices by labour. There was to be no 'closed shop' or discrimination by union members against non-union members; no

[1] H. Pelling, op. cit., p. 233. A useful account of contemporary unionism is C. E. Dankert, *Contemporary Unionism in the United States* (New York, 1948).

secondary boycotts (i.e. sympathetic action by non-strikers, such as refusing to handle material made by firms engaged in labour disputes); no 'featherbedding' (payment for work not in fact undertaken); and no strikes before a sixty-day 'cooling off' period had elapsed. An eighty-day injuction against strikes deemed prejudicial to national safety and health was introduced, as well as an *ad hoc* conciliation service outside the Department of Labour, which was believed to be too friendly to labour. Finally, all union leaders had to take a non-Communist oath. The Act was a major blow to the Labour Movement; but other legislation was not so unfriendly. A measure passed in October 1949 for instance extended protection to many classes of unorganized workers by setting a minimum wage of 75 cents an hour.

The principal theme of this chapter however is not domestic but foreign affairs. It concerns the most unusual economic experiments ever attempted by national governments in the field of international aid. The wave of Nazi nihilism and barbarism that swept over Europe left her helpless economically, though it never entirely sapped her moral resources. Food production was halved, cities and towns laid waste, transportation facilities dislocated and often gratuitously and senselessly destroyed, mines flooded, ports and harbours choked with debris, money reduced to worthless paper. Ten or twelve million displaced refugees wandered hopelessly or inhabited shanty camps over the face of the continent. The average nourishment of a European was 1,500 calories a day—often less. The American average was more than twice that amount (3,500 calories). Starvation, disease and anarchy typified the condition of the ancient centres of Western civilization. The heaviest burden of responsibility for relief devolved upon the United States, in view of her economic position as briefly illustrated above. The New World was to redress the balance of the Old in a manner and on a scale never envisaged by Canning.

As early as December 1942 Roosevelt had established an Office of Foreign Relief within the State Department, mainly for North Africa. In June 1943 the United States proposed an international relief organization which eventually formed the basis of the United Nations Relief and Rehabilitation Administration (U.N.R.R.A.). In this body 48 nations collaborated to provide direct relief in the form of food and clothing, seed, fertilizer and livestock, machinery and medical supplies. It spent $4,000 million, of which America gave $2,750 million. Furthermore the United States Army helped to feed much of occupied Europe.

But this programme was inadequate and well within the means of a nation that continued to feed cereals to cattle and had no post-war rationing of any kind. Lend-Lease was cut short rather abruptly in

August 1945 and U.N.R.R.A. was allowed to expire in 1947; Congressmen believed American supplies were being used to build up the strength of Communist areas, and there was a general feeling that the crisis was over. On the other hand the Reciprocal Trade Agreements of the 1930's were renewed in 1945 and in 1947 about 40 nations agreed at Geneva to lower tariffs on wool, lumber, copper, beef, sugar and other goods. Although American imports rose to over $7,000 million however, there was a persistent world 'dollar gap' of about $8,000 million. This problem had never been solved after 1919,[1] but after 1945 it was much more serious. Nothing could be sold by the United States to a bankrupt Europe. If trade were to flow, this gap must be closed.

Meanwhile, the Treasury Department had begun plans in 1943 for currency stabilization and in the summer days of 1944 the United Nations Monetary and Financial Conference (the Bretton Woods Conference) took place. It was agreed to set up two agencies: the International Monetary Fund to maintain stable exchange rates and move restrictions on the international transfer of funds (with a capital of $8,800 million, $2,600 million or so of which was subscribed by the United States), and the World Bank or International Bank for Reconstruction, to lend and borrow money and to underwrite private loans for productive uses.

The story of international aid had scarcely yet begun. Lend-Lease terminated in August 1945, as we have seen. Existing orders were delivered during 1946. The total of Lend-Lease grants was about $50,000 million and reverse Lend-Lease about $8,000 million. After World War I war debts had eventually been nullified (Congress having passed the Debt Default Act in 1934); after World War II there was a prompt and much less acrimonious settlement of Lend-Lease accounts by Great Britain, France, China and others—the Soviet Union refusing even to consider the matter. This settlement, though worthy from the international viewpoint, helped to precipitate a severe crisis in the United Kingdom.

Before the war the deficit of the U.K was made up by what are usually called economists 'invisible exports'—foreign investments, shipping banking and insurance services—at which Britain had become skilled over the years.' These assets were badly affected by the war: she lost investments abroad and incurred heavy debts in addition; she lost a third of her shipping and many foreign markets; she had part of her industrial plant at home destroyed by enemy action. She could neither recapture her export markets nor pay for imports with accumulated capital. Moreover she had large foreign commitments such as occupation costs in Germany and Austria, military expenses in Palestine, Greece and the Far East, colonial

[1] See Chapter XIII, above, pp. 216–18.

expenses, contributions to U.N.R.R.A., the Monetary Fund and the World Bank. Sir Stafford Cripps negotiated a loan of $3,750 million from the United States (having asked for $5,000 million) to run for 50 years at 2 per cent. Also he was given additional credit for the $650 million outstanding on Lend-Lease. Canada loaned the Mother Country $1,750 million as well. For her part, the United Kingdom had to abolish her exchange controls and blocked credits, and scale down her obligations to other countries.

Within two years the loans were used up, despite the maintenance of wartime rationing and a fierce struggle to recapture markets abroad, and Great Britain approached a new crisis in 1947. This fresh disaster, together with poor economic conditions in Italy, France and elsewhere and the fear of Communism, led to the drawing up of a more adequate United States plan for aid to Europe. On 5 June 1947, Secretary of State Marshall made his crucial speech at Harvard, suggesting what came to be called the 'Marshall Plan'. Its *motif* was that America would help those who helped themselves. Almost immediately the British and French governments invited 22 nations, including the Soviet Union, to a Paris meeting to implement the idea. Molotov dissociated himself and his satellites from the plan, and the final total of nations to co-operate was 16. With Sir Oliver Franks in the chair, an elaborate European Recovery Programme was drafted. If fixed new production targets, recommended free trade measures and the restoration of West German industries, promised monetary stability, and settled the total cost of the plan at $22,000 million. The United States was to pay the most, with help from Canada, Latin America, the World Bank and the International Monetary Fund.

In Congress opposition to the Marshall Plan was led by Senator Taft, who dubbed it 'Operation Rat-Hole'; support for it came from Senator Vandenberg (an internationally-minded Republican) and from liberals and labour organizations. The Marshall Plan Act was pushed through in April 1948, Congress being encouraged by the Communist manœuvre in Czechoslovakia. A sum of over $5,000 million was voted for the fifteen months up to the middle of 1949, it being stipulated that at least one-fifth of this should be a loan but the rest an outright gift to Europe. To administer the scheme a special agency was set up in Washington—the Economic Co-operation Administration—under Paul Hoffman. To ensure the very closest co-operation between the countries concerned, however, it was necessary to establish a permanent Organization for European Economic Co-operation (O.E.E.C.) in April 1948, barely a fortnight after the passing of the Marshall Plan Act. The work of O.E.E.C. in Paris involved annual discussions on the economic progress of member nations, recommendations to the E.C.A. on how best to distribute the aid, the submission by all members of long-term plans, and particular concentration on special empiric problems, such as manpower, intra-European payments, free trade and colonial development.

The underlying principle of all these arrangements was that Western Europe would make an all-out effort to restore its own trade and production. The effects of American aid were: to make good war losses in food, raw materials and machinery; to enable European factories, mines and farms to increase output; and to stimulate a revival of trade between O.E.E.C. nations. All over the face of Europe new steel plants, oil refineries and power stations were constructed. For every United States dollar that went into Europe there was (up to 1950) an increase in production worth six or seven dollars. Under the Marshall Plan the United States aid supplied Europe with $621 million worth of petroleum products, $607 million worth of cotton goods, $287 million worth of machinery, $273 million worth of coal, $117 million worth of motor vehicles, $150 million worth of iron and steel, $185 million worth of copper, and huge amounts of lead, zinc, aluminium, leather and other essential materials and goods. Industrial production in Europe rose 30 per cent in two years and in 1949 was 15 per cent higher than in 1938.

There remained the Dollar Gap. Imports by Europe from the New World were four times greater than exports in the opposite direction. Continued American aid was enabling this Gap to be closed, but not at the speed desired by many European statesmen. Marshall Aid was planned to come to an end in 1952. Would the Gap be closed in time?

Unfortunately, this must remain a rhetorical question.

Note

This book has tried to clear the undergrowth. It has tried to give, in as succinct and straightforward a way as possible, a *representative selection* of the events and ideas which go to make up the economic history of a great nation spanning a continent. It has been concerned primarily with the economic aspect of American life. But this by no means indicates the nature of the author's hierarchy of historical values; nor does it pass an implicit value-judgement on the materials of American history. For the study of the history of the United States must continue to grow and expand in Great Britain and in Europe— both as an academic discipline and as a subject of absorbing interest and primary significance for the general reading public—in all its aspects, economic, social, political and cultural.

INDEX

Abolitionism, 20, 81–3, 88–90, 99–100, 196
Acts of Congress, see under individual titles
Adams Act (1906), 134
Adams, John, 8, 65
Adams, John Q., 176
Adamson Eight Hour Act (1916), 202, 205
Addams, Jane, 197
Adjusted Compensation Act (1924), 241
Aetna Life Insurance Co., 225
Africa (as U.S. market), 174–5
Agricultural Adjustment Acts (1933 and 1938), 247–9
Agricultural Adjustment Administration, 247–8, 253
Agricultural co-operatives, 249
Agricultural education, 134, 136, 202, 226
'Agricultural industries', 109 n. 2, 131–3
Agricultural Marketing Act (1929), 227, 247, 249
Agricultural research stations, 134
Agricultural Wheel (Ark.), 139
Agriculture, 7–8, 14–27, 48, 110, 119–36, 141, 155, 161, 170, 171, 172, 181, 186, 190–3, 201, 202–4, 212–13, 214, 215–16, 217–18, 222–8, 230, 231, 236, 237, 241, 247–51, 252, 253, 257–9
Agriculture, Department of, 133–4, 136
Agrarian unrest, 136–41, 186–9, 225–8
Aircraft industry, 104, 215, 256
Air raids, 255
Alabama Midland Case (1897), 162
Alaska Railway Act (1914), 202
Aldrich Report (1893), 42–3

Aldrich-Vreeland Act (1908), 185, 192, 201, 206
Altgeld, J. P. (Governor), 145 n. 1
Aluminium industry, 104, 109, 165, 244, 256
Amalgated Association of Iron and Steel Workers, 146–7
Amalgamated Clothing Workers, 152
Amalgamated Society of Engineers (U.K.), 153
Amendments (to American Constitution), 5th (1791), 249; 14th (1868), 101 n. 1; 16th (1913), 171 n. 1, 201
American, The, 197
American Anti-slavery Society, 83
American Association for the Advancement of Science, 203
American Bankers' Association, 185
American Desert, 119 ff.
American Federation of Labour, 143, 144 n. 2, 145–6, 148, 150–1, 152, 153, 163, 181, 213, 228, 244–45, 259
American Forestry Association, 203
American Railway Union, 147–9
American Society of Equity, 225
American Sugar Refining Co., 113, 198
'American System', 69, 86
American Telephone and Telegraph Co., 234
American Tobacco Co., 114, 199
Ames, O., 159–60
Anaconda Copper Mining Co., 105–6
Anacostia Flats, 241
Anarchism, 142, 145, 147
Anglican Church, 4
Animal Husbandry, Bureau of, 133

Annapolis Convention, 63–4
Anti-Red hysteria, 150, 258–9
Apache Indians, 121
Appleby, J., 128
Arapaho Indians, 122
Armouries (of Corporations), 245, 245 n. 1
Army Appropriation Act (1916), 210
'Arsenal of Democracy', 255
Arthur, C. A., President, 169
Asia (as U.S. market), 174
Associated Pipe Works, 114
Associationists, 38
Atchison, Topeka and Sante Fe Railroad, 159, 160
Atlanta Cotton Exposition (1881), 110
Atlantic Monthly, 175, 197
Atlantic and Pacific Railroad, 159
Atomic energy, 258
Australian ballot, 140 n. 1
Automobile industry, 101, 108–9, 112, 165–6, 195, 209, 215, 219, 220–1, 229, 230, 245, 256, 259
Axis powers, 257

Back country, 4–7
Bacon's Rebellion (1765), 4
Baer, President (Reading Railroad), 161
Baltimore and Ohio Railroad, 52, 161
Bankhead Cotton Control Act (1934), 248 n. 2
Bankhead-Jones Farm Tenant Act (1937), 250
Banking, 9, 53, 63–74, 77–9, 81, 84, 85–6, 87, 99, 182–6, 190–3, 200–1, 206, 214, 224, 229–54
Banking Acts, 72 (1816), 99, 182–6, (1863), 184 n. 1 (1844, U.K.), 186 n. 1 (1946, U.K.), 240 (1933)
Banking consortium (China), 182
Banks: National, 99, 182–6, 192–3, 201; State, 68, 71–3, 77–9, 85–6, 99, 183; U.S., 63, 64, 65, 67–8, 69, 70, 71–4, 77, 78, 81, 84, 85–6, 87, 183. (See Federal Reserve System)
Bannock Indians, 121
Baruch, B., 210, 211, 257
Bauxite, 104
Bellamy, Edward, 197

'Belts' (agriculture), 129 (map), 130–1
Benedict, Prof. M. R., 227 n. 2
Benton, T. H. (Senator), 73–4
Bessemer process, 35, 102
Biddle, N., 72, 73–4, 77, 78
Bimetallism, 186–9, 191
Biological Survey, 251
Bitter Cry of the Children, 197
Black Friday (24 September 1869), 160
Black, H. (Senator), 243–4
Black Hills, 122
Black International, 145
Black Market, 258
Blackouts, 255
Black Thursday (24 October 1929), 234
Blaine, J. G. (Secretary of State), 170
Blanc, Louis, 247
Bland-Allison Act (1878), 187
Bliss, Rev. W. D. P., 197
Blueberry farms, 225
Boll-weevil, 19, 130, 130 n. 2
Bonds (Federal), 182, 192, 214–15, 232, 241, 249
Bonus Bill (1816), 86; (Veterans, 1936), 241, 252
Bonus Expeditionary Force (1932), 241
Booms, 41 (1835–7); 210 (1916); 218–22 (1920's); 220, 229 (Construction industries); 252 (1936–7)
Boone, Daniel, 16, 45
Borden, G., 132–3, 215
Boulton and Watt, 50
Boundary disputes (inter-state), 9
Boxer Rebellion (1900), 119, 181
'Brain trust' (F. D. Roosevelt), 240
Bretton Woods Conference (1944), 261
Brisbane, A., 196
'Broad-constructionists', 47, 64–5, 67–8
Brogan, Prof. D. W., 251
Brook Farm, 38
Brooks, J., 160
Bryan, William Jennings, 141, 188, 188 n. 2, 192, 196, 197
Bryan-Chamorro Treaty (1916), 178
Buchanan, J., President, 79
Buffalo herds, 119, 120–1, 203
Bureau of Labour Statistics, 145

INDEX

Burlingame Treaty (1868), 156, 156 n. 1
Byrnes, Justice J. F., 256

Calhoun, John C., 22, 60, 70, 71
Calumet and Hecla Mining Co., 105
Camden and Amboy Railroad, 53
Canada, 60–1, 164–5, 172, 174, 175, 179
Canals, 44–5, 48–50, 51, 55, 77, 86–7, 163–6, 190
Canning industry, 131, 132–3, 173, 180 n. 1, 195, 215
Canning, George, 260
Carey Act (1894), 123, 128–9, 203, 206, 223
Carnegie, A., 142
Carson, Kit, 121
Castlereagh, Viscount, 59
Cattle Kingdom, 124–5
Census of 1790, 222
Central Pacific Railroad Co., 121, 156, 159, 160
Century of Dishonour, 122, 197
Chain farms, 225
Chain stores, 238 n. 2
Charcoal (in iron industry), 34–5, 102
Charleston Courier (1855), 90
Charleston and Hamburg Railroad, 52
Chase, S. P., 98–9
Chemical industry, 102, 103, 171
Cheque payment system, 184, 184 n. 1, 192
Chesapeake incident (1807), 59
Chesapeake and Ohio Canal, 49
Cheves, L., 72, 73, 77
Cheyenne Indians, 122
Child Labour (Keating-Owen) Act (1916), 202, 206, 244
Children of the Poor, 197
Chile 179
China (as U.S. market), 181–2
Chinese coolies (Pacific coast), 156–7
Chinese Exclusion Acts (1879, 1882), 156–7
Chivington Massacre, 122 n. 1
Christensen, P. P., 228
Christian Socialism, 196–7, 205
Churchill, W. (novelist), 197
Cincinatti Convention (Populists), 140

City governments, 196, 197
Civilian Conservation Corps, 246, 250
Civil service reform, 196, 197
Clay, Henry, 23, 27, 60, 69, 70, 74, 86, 87
Clayton Anti-Trust Act (1914), 115 n. 1, 149, 198–200, 206
Clayton-Bulwer Treaty (1850), 177
Clermont, 50
Cleveland, G., President, 148, 149, 157, 169–70, 180, 188, 192, 203
Clipper ships, 62
Coal industry, 35, 100 ff., 106–8, 144 n. 1, 155, 191, 193, 204, 211–12, 218, 230, 231 n. 1, 233, 259
Code Authorities (New Deal), 211, 237 ff.
'Cold war', 258 ff.
Collier's, 197
Colombia, 177, 179
Colt six-shooter, 121
Combination, business, 102–3, 105, 106–7, 110–18, 128, 131, 133, 157, 170, 175, 196–7, 198–200, 220, 231, 257
Combine harvesters, 128, 131–2, 224
Commanche Indians, 122
Commerce, see Trade
Commerce Court (1910–13), 163
Commercial Conventions (Southern), 92
Committee on the Condition of the Indian Tribes (1865), 122
Commonweal, 145
Commonwealth v. Hunt (1842), 43
Commonwealth v. Pullis (1806), 40
Communitarians, 38–9, 196
'Company unions', 244, 245
Compromises: (1820), 20, 30, 84; (1850), 30, 84; (1860), 88, 92
Comptroller of the Currency, 182
Comstock Lode, 120, 139
Confederate Government, 91 (map), 97–9, 100
Confederation, Articles of (1777), 9–10
Congress of Industrial Organisations (C.I.O.), 151–2, 152 n. 2, 156, 244–6, 253, 259
Coniston, 197

Conservation, 126, 128–30, 196, 202–4, 206, 242, 246, 248–9, 250–1
Consolidation, see Combination
'Conspiracy' (legal doctrine), 39–40, 148
'Conspiracy Theory' (14th Amendment), 101 n. 1
Constitution: (U.S.), 3, 7, 11–12, 32, 101 n. 1, 152–3, 171 n. 1, 201, 249; (States), 6, 41, 41 n. 1, 113, 137
Constitutional Convention (1787), 10–11
Construction industries, 215, 219, 220, 221, 229, 230, 241, 247
Consumer demand, 101, 195, 221–2, 229, 230, 242, 256
Continental System, 33, 58–9, 61
Contract labour, 156–7
Cook, Captain, 179
Cooke, Jay, 99, 160, 190–1, 214
Coolidge, C., President, 171, 217, 227, 230, 251
Cooper, P., 138–9, 186
Co-operative Commonwealth, 197
Co-operative movement, 41–2, 137, 143, 145, 225, 225 n. 1
Copper industry, 100, 103, 105–6, 165, 169, 173, 179, 197, 209, 256
Cordwainers, Journeymen, 40
Corn Laws (U.K.), 33, 62, 78
Corn production, 130, 131–2, 140, 248 (Also see Grain)
Cornell, E., 134
Corporations, 157–8, 177, 215, 225, 257 (Also see Combination)
Cort process, 34–5, 106
Cotton, 7, 9, 17, 18–19, 34, 35–7, 69–70, 78–9, 82, 88, 90–2, 99–100, 109–10, 126, 130–1, 155, 170, 216, 225, 225 n. 1, 231 n. 1, 248, 248 n. 2
Cotton Futures Acts (1914, 1917), 133
Cotton Oil Trust, 115, 116
Cottonseed oil, 115, 116, 131, 139
Council of National Defence, 210, 211
Cowboys, 124–5
Cox, W. W., 228
Coxey, 'General' Jacob,' 192 n. 1, 228
Craft unions, 37–8, 39

Credit Mobilier, 159–60
'Crime of '73', 140, 187
Cripps, Sir Stafford, 262
Crises, economic:
1819, 61, 73, 76, 77, 190
1834, 74
1837, 41, 49, 50, 54, 62, 76, 77–8, 190
1857, 43, 48, 76, 77, 78–80, 92, 190
1873, 77, 136, 137, 143, 158, 160, 169, 184, 186, 190–1, 193, 194
1884, 184, 191, 194
1893, 77, 146, 147, 158, 161, 176, 184, 188–9, 190, 191–2, 193
1903, 184, 192
1907, 77, 184, 190, 192–3
1920, 218, 224
1927, 229–30
1929, 219, 229, 230–5
1937, 252–4
(Also see Depressions)
Critical Period, 7–9, 56–7, 63
Crocker Co., 160
Crop liens, 131
'Cross of Gold' speech, 188
Cuba, 176–7, 188, 213
Cumberland Road, 46–7
Currency, 8, 9, 11, 63, 67, 71–3, 77, 98–9, 136, 138–41, 143, 182, 183, 186–9, 190–3, 196, 200, 201, 214, 217–18, 231, 239, 261
Currency (Gold Standard) Act (1900), 141, 182, 184, 189, 206
Custer's 'Last Stand' (1876), 122
Czechoslovakia (Communist coup), 262

Dairying, 120, 130, 133, 170, 171, 248, 257
Danish West Indies (Virgin Islands), 178, 188
Darby, A., 106
Davis, Jefferson, 53
Dawes Severalty Act (1887), 122, 206
Dawes Plan (1924), 218
DeBow's Review, 82–3, 92
Debs, E. V., 147–9, 150, 228
Debt Default Act (1934), 261
Debt, National, 8, 63, 65, 67–8, 97–8, 242, 258

INDEX

Debtors, relief of (New Deal), 240–1
Debts, international, 216–18
Declaration of Independence, 64
Deficit financing, 235, 240 ff., 252, 253
Delegated legislation, 238
DeLeon, D., 150
Department of Agriculture (U.S.), 203
Department of Labour (U.S.), 260
Depressions:
  Post–1785, 7, 8, 9
  Post–1819, 69, 77
  Post–1837, 77–8
  Post–1857, 78–80
  Post–1873, 137, 138, 139, 140, 143, 191
  Post–1884, 144, 191
  1885–7, 124–5 (Ranching)
  Post–1893, 188–9, 191–2
  Post–1907, 193
  Post–1929 (Great Depression), 216, 219, 223, 229–35, 259
Desert Land Act (1877), 123, 128, 203, 206
'Detectives', 245, 245 n. 1
Diaz, P., 178
Digger Indians, 121
Dillon, Read and Co., 232
Dingley Tariff Act (1897), see Tariffs
Disraeli, B., 175
'Dollar diplomacy', 182
Dollar shortage, 217–18, 261–3
Douai, A., 197
Dry-farming, 223–4
'Dual' unionism, 152
'Dust Bowl', 250

Eaton, D., 196
Economic Co-operation Administration (E.C.A.), 262
Education, 134, 136, 195, 202, 206, 226, 246
Eight-hours movement, 142–3, 145, 146, 202, 213, 243
Eisenhower, D. D., President, 164
Elections:
  1860, 88–90, 188
  1872, 138, 143
  1876, 186–7
  1878 (Congressional), 187
  1880, 139, 160 n. 1, 187
  1888, 169, 187
  1890 (Congressional), 170
  1892, 141, 170, 188
  1896, 141, 182, 188, 192
  1904, 199
  1912, 200
  1920, 171, 228
  1924, 151, 197 n. 2
  1932, 236–7
Electrical industry, 101, 104, 105, 106, 111, 164–5, 195, 219, 221–2, 230, 250, 251, 259
Elevators (grain), 132, 137, 226, 227
Eliot, C. W. (President of Harvard), 204
Elkins Act (1903), 162, 205
Ely, Prof, R. T., 197
Embargo Act (1807), 33, 59, 60, 65
Emergency Banking Act (1933), 239
Emergency Credits Act (1921), 227
Emergency Farm Mortgage Act (1933), 249
Emergency Fleet Corporation, 168, 212
Emergency Price Control Act (1942), 258
Emergency Quota Act (1921), 157
'Empire-Builders', 159–61
Employers' Associations, 146 n. 2
Employment exchanges, 243
Empress of China, 57
Encyclopaedia of Social Reform (1897), 197
Enlarged Homestead Act (1909), 223
Erdman Act (1898), 149, 205
Erie Canal, 26, 48–9, 87, 117
Esch-Cummins (Transportation) Act (1920), 115 n. 1, 163
Estall, R. C., 165 n. 1
European Recovery Programme, 260–3
Evans, G. H., 196
Everybody's, 197
Expedition Act (1903), 162, 205
Export-Import Bank, 247 n. 2

Fabian Socialism, 141, 197
Factory system, 32–3, 35–7, 110
Fair Deal, 259
Fair Labour Standards Act (1938), 243–4
Far East (as U.S. market), 161, 179–82
Farm Bloc, 226–7

270 INDEX

Farm Bureau Federation, 226
Farm Credit Act (1933), 249
Farm Credit Administration, 249
Farm Loan Act (1921), 226–7
Farm Mortgage Moratorium Act (1935), 249
Farm Security Administration, 250
Farmer-Labour Party, 226, 227–8
Farmers, see Agriculture
Farmers' Alliances, 139–40, 225
Farmers' Alliance and Industrial Union, 139
Farmers' Declaration of Independence (1873), 138 n. 1
Farmers' National Council, 226
Farmers' Nonpartisan Political League, 226, 227–8, 227 n. 2
Farmers' Relief Association, 225
Farmers' Union, 139, 225, 226
Federal-Aid Road Act (1916), 133
Federal Board of Mediation, 163
Federal Farm Board, 227, 249
Federal Farm Land Bank Act (1916), 214
Federal Farm Loan Act (1916), 201
Federal Farm Loan Board, 201, 249 n. 1
Federal Farm Mortgage Corporation, 241, 249
Federal Housing Administration, 241, 247 n. 1
Federal Land Banks, 201, 214, 249
Federal Power Commission, 250
Federal Reserve Act (1913), 184–6, 201, 206
Federal Reserve Board, 231, 240
Federal Reserve System, 182, 185–186, 202, 214, 231, 232 n. 1, 239, 240, 253
Federal Trade Commission Act (1914), 199–200, 206, 237
Federal Warehouse Act (1916), 201 n. 3
Federation of Organised Trades and Labour Unions, 144
Feminism, 196
Fencing (Plains land), 120, 125
Filipino Revolution, 180
Film industry, 124, 195
Finance, 53–4, 62–75, 76, 78–80, 97–9, 100, 113, 157–61, 168, 175–6, 182–9, 190–3, 197, 201, 214–15, 216–18, 227, 229–54, 258

Fisher, Prof. I., 234
Fish hatcheries, 250–1
Fishing industry, 6, 8
Fisk, J., 160
Flagler, H. M., 118
Flour-milling, 26, 33, 34, 131, 133, 133 n. 2, 213
Food Administration, 211, 212–13, 256
Food and Fuel Control Act (1917), 211, 212
Foraker Act (1900), 177
Force Act (1833), 70
Ford, Henry, 108–9, 215, 245
Fordney Emergency Tariff Act (1921), see Tariffs
Fordney-McCumber Tariff Act (1922), see Tariffs
Forest Homestead Act (1906), 223
Forest lands, 202–4, 250–1
Forest Reserve Act (1891), 203, 206
Forestry, 133
Formosa, 181
Fort Laramie 'Entente' (1851), 122
Fort Lyon Treaty (1861), 122
Fort Sumner, 88, 121
Forty-Niners, 120, 121
Fourier, C., 38, 196
Franchise, 41, 41 n. 1
Franks, Sir O., 262
Frazier-Lemke Amendment (1934), 249
Free Silver movement, 138, 139, 140, 182, 187–9
Free-Soil movement, 196
French Revolution, 57
Frontier, 15, 28–9, 119–26, 127 (map), 135, 175
Fruit industry, 130, 131, 177, 180 n. 1, 225 n. 1, 248
Fuel Administration, 211–12
Fulton, R., 50
Funding Act (1790), 67

Gadsden Purchase (1853), 31, 53, 128
Galbraith, J. K., 238 n. 3
Gallatin, A., 71, 86
Garfield, J. A., President, 160 n. 1
Garrison, W. L., 82–3
Gas, natural, 204, 231 n. 1
General Electric Co., 234
General Motors, 245, 257
General Munitions Board, 211

INDEX

General Theory of Employment, Interest and Money (1936), 240
George, Henry, 28, 115, 196–7, 226
George, Lloyd, 211
George, Milton, 139
Ghent, Treaty of (1814), 61
Glass production, 221
Godkin, E. L., 196
Gold, 51, 62, 67, 79, 119, 120, 121–2, 139, 141, 160, 185, 186, 187–9, 191, 192, 201, 209, 217, 218, 239, 239 n. 2
Gold discoveries, 51, 62, 79
Gold Reserve Act (1934), 239
Gold Standard, 141, 187–9, 191, 217, 239, 239 n. 2
Gompers, S., 145–6, 148, 150, 200, 210
Gorman, Senator, 170
Gould, Jay, 144, 160
Grab for Africa, 175
Grain production, 50, 130, 131–2, 173, 209, 212–13, 224, 226, 227
Grain Futures Act (1922), 227
Grand Eight-Hour League of Massachusetts, 142
Granger Laws, 137–8, 161
Granger movement, 136–8, 139, 161, 225
Grant, U. S., President, 185 n. 2, 186, 191
'Great Abberation', 175–82
Great Lakes (traffic on), 164–5
Great Northern Railroad, 161
Greeley, H., 196
Gregg, W., 109–10
Greenback Labour Party, 139, 187
Greenback movement, 138–9, 141, 143, 182, 186–7
Gronlund, L., 197
Guam, 180, 180 n. 2

Haiti, 178
Hamilton, A., 10–11, 12, 35, 57, 63–4, 65–8, 71, 85
Handlooms, 36
Hansen, A., 42
Harding, W. G., President, 171, 228, 251
Harlan, Justice, 162
Harriman, E. H., 161, 182
Harrison, B., President, 60, 169–70, 187, 198, 203
Harvests, 191, 192, 193

Harvey, 'Coin', 196
Hatch Act (1887), 134
Hawaii (Sandwich Islands), 179–80, 188, 213
Hawley-Smoot Tariff Act (1930), see Tariffs
Hay, J., 181–2
Hay-Herran Treaty (1903), 177
Hay-Pauncefote Treaty (1901), 177
Hayes, R. B., President, 156, 186–7
Haymarket Riot (Chicago), 144–5
Haywood, W. D., 149–50
Hemp industry, 21, 23, 180
Hepburn Act (1906), 162, 205
Hessian labour, 8
Hildreth (*Despotism in America*, 1840), 82
Hill, J. J., 160–1
Hillman, S., 152
Hire-purchase, 222, 230, 230 n. 3, 231, 258
History of the Standard Oil Co., 197
Hoffman, P., 262
Holding companies, 114, 115–16, 192, 193, 198–9
Home Loan Bank Act (1932), 241
Home Owners' Loan Corporation, 241, 247 n. 1
Homestead Acts: (1862), 7, 17, 85, 123–4, 223, 250; (1906) 223, 250; (1909) 223, 250; (1912) 223; (1916) 223
Homestead Strike (1892), 146–7
Hoover, H., President, 164, 212, 227, 235–6, 239, 241, 244, 247, 249
'Hooverizing', 212
Hotchkiss rapid-fire gun, 122
Housing Corporation, 213
Hull House (Chicago), 197

If Christ Came to Chicago, 197
Illinois Central Railroad, 54, 88, 161
Immigration, 37–8, 101, 112, 130, 144, 150, 151–2, 154 7, 177, 181, 196, 213, 217
Imperialism, 175–82
'Implied powers', 68
Income tax, 140 n. 1, 145, 171 n. 1, 194–5, 201
Independent labour party, idea of, 146, 151–3
Independent National Party, 138, 186

INDEX

Independent Treasury, 78 n. 1, 98, 182, 185, 185 n. 1
Indians, American, 4, 7, 18, 60, 61, 119, 120–3, 124, 128, 197
Indian Wars, 120–2
Indigo production, 7, 18
Industrial Brotherhood, 143 n. 3
Industrial Commission (1900–2), 112, 112 n. 2, 113
Industrial Revolution, 32 ff., 100 ff; (in South), 109–10
Industrial Workers of the World (I.W.W.), 149–50
Industry, see Manufacturing, and individual industries
'Inevitability' (in history), 3–4, 80, 80 n. 1
Initiative and Referendum, 140 n. 1
Injunction, labour, 148–9, 148 n. 1, 244, 245, 260
Inland Waterways Commission, 164, 204
Instead of a Book, 197
Interlocking directorates, 115 n. 1, 201
Internal combustion engine, 158, 165
Internal Improvements, 44–55, 69, 81, 84, 86–8
International Cigar Makers' Union, 143, 146
International Harvester Co., 111, 128, 131
International Monetary Fund, 261, 262
International Securities Corporation, 232
International Trade Organisation, 261
Interstate Commerce Act (1887), 138, 148 n. 1, 161–2, 205
Interstate Commerce Commission, 115 n. 1, 161–3
Investment trusts, 232–3
Iron and steel industry, 8, 34–5, 100, 101–3, 108, 109, 169, 171, 190, 191, 192, 193, 204, 209, 215, 221, 244, 245, 256, 257, 259
Ironmoulders' Union, 142
Irrigation, 126, 128–30, 135, 177–8, 202–4, 223

Jackson, General A., President, 61, 70–1, 72–4, 77–8, 86, 87
Jackson, Helen H., 122, 197
Japan (as U.S. market), 181; (Pearl Harbour), 256
Jay, J., 58
Jay Treaty (1794), 58
Jefferson Territory, 120
Jefferson, T., President, 7, 27, 63, 64–5, 67–8, 71, 86, 176
Johnson, A., President, 143
Johnson, Tom, 196–7
Jones Act (Philippines, 1916), 181
Jones Act (Puerto Rico, 1917), 177
Jones, 'Golden Rule', 197
Jones Merchant Marine Act (1920), 168
Jungle, The, 197

Kearney, D., 156
Keating-Owen (Child Labour) Act (1916), 202, 204, 244
Kelley, O. H., 136–7
Kelly, W., 102
Kettell, T. P., 51, 90–2
Keynes, J. M., 234 n. 1, 240, 241
Kiowa Indians, 122
Kirkaid Act (1904), 223
Knickerbocker Trust Co., 193
Knights of Labour, 140, 143–5, 146, 153, 157, 187, 245
Knights of St. Crispin, 143 n. 3
Knox, P. C., 182
Korea, 181
Korean War, 186

Labour, 37–43, 101, 106, 107, 109, 110, 128, 130–1, 136, 141–53, 155–6, 158, 180, 191–3, 193–5, 196 ff., 202, 205, 211–12, 213–14, 216, 218–19, 221, 224, 225, 229–30, 231, 235, 237–8, 242, 243–6, 247, 251, 252–3, 256, 257, 259–60
Labour Disputes Joint Resolution (Congress, 1934), 243
Labrador mines, 165
LaFollette, R., 151, 197, 197 n. 2, 202, 206, 226, 228
LaFollette's Seamen's Act (1915), 168, 202, 206
LaFollette's Weekly, 197
Laissez-faire, 70, 73, 101, 101 n. 1, 142, 152–3, 196 ff., 202, 204–6
Lancaster Turnpike, 46
Land Office, 203

Land policy, 6–7, 14–31, 65, 66, 66 n. 2, 76, 77, 78–9, 81, 84–5, 87–8, 113, 122–4, 125, 131, 134, 139, 140, 158–9, 191, 196, 201, 202–4, 205, 223–4, 226
Laski, H., 153 n. 1
Latin Monetary Union, 187
Lawrence Strike (1912), 150
Lead industry, 100, 103, 104–5, 221
League for Progressive Political Action, 150
Leather industry, 34, 121, 171, 173, 218, 230
Legal Tender Act (1862), 99, 186
Leggett, W., 196
Lend-Lease, 256, 260–2
Lend-Lease Act (1941), 256
Lenin, 228
Lewis, John L., 244–5
Lewis, Prof. W. A., 219, 238
Liberator, 82, 83
Liberty Loans, 214 n. 1, 214–15, 232
Liliuokalani, Queen (Hawaii), 180
Limestone, 164
Limited liability, 111
Lincoln, A., President, 88–90, 98, 100, 188
Little Big Horn (Battle, 1876), 122
Livestock Corporations, 125
Living standards, 193–5
Lloyd, H. D., 115, 197
Loan Act (1862), 99
Loans, federal, 71–2, 98–9, 239–40
Loans, international (U.S.), 209–10, 231, 260–3
Loans-to-Industry Act (1934), 239–40
Lockner v. New York (1905), 153
London Stock Exchange, 233–4
Looking Backward, 197
Louisiana Purchase (1803), 5 (map), 17, 30, 61, 86
Lowell, F. C., 37
Lundy, B., 82

McAdoo, W. G., 163, 212, 214
Macauley, R. C., 228
McClure's Magazine, 197
McCormick, C., 27, 128, 131, 145
McCulloch v. Maryland (1819), 72
McDuffie, G., 70
Machinists' and Blacksmiths' Union, 142

McKinley Tariff Act (1890), see Tariffs
McKinley, W., President, 115, 141, 170, 180, 188, 192, 198, 203
McNary-Haugen scheme (1924–8), 227
Madero revolution (Mexico), 178
Madison, J., President, 59, 72, 86
Mahan, Capt. A. T., 175
Mail, federal, 167–8
Maine, 176
Malthus, Rev. T., 155
Manchuria, 182
'Manifest Destiny', 175
Mann-Elkins Act (1910), 162–3, 205
Manufacturing, 61, 69, 100–10, 126, 167, 172–5, 190–3, 211–12, 218–22, 229–54, 255 ff. See individual industries
Maritime rights, 58–61
Marsh brothers, 128
Marshall, Gen., G.C., 262, 263
Marshall Plan, 262–3
Marshall Plan Act (1948), 262
Martin, R. F., 194
Martineau, Harriet, 42, 47
Marx, Karl, 38, 196, 197
Mass media, 152
Mass production, 101, 108–9
Maximum Freight Case (1897), 162
Maysville Turnpike Bill (1831), 86–7, 88
Meat-packing industry, 26, 103 n. 2, 109 n. 2, 130, 131–3, 197, 215, 225, 226
Mechanics' Union of Trade Associations, 40–1
Mechanised agriculture, 131–3, 224
Memorial Day Massacre (1937), 245, 253
Mercantile National Bank, 193
Merchant marine, 57–9, 167–8, 217 n. 1, 226, 256
Merchant Marine Act (1936), 168
'Mergers', 114 n. 1, 192, 199, 200. See Combination
Mexican Constitution (1917), 179
Mexico (as U.S. market), 175, 178–9
Michigan Salt Association, 114
Military strategy (Civil War), 99–100
Miller-Tydings Act (1937), 238 n. 2
Miners (Far West), 119–20, 121
Mississippi river, 87, 164

Mississippi Territory (Act of 1803), 134
Mitchell, Prof. B., 248, 252
Model T, 108–9
Molly Maguires, 144 n. 1
Molotov, 262
Money, see Currency, Banking
Monoculture, 130, 135
Monopoly, 196–200, 227. See Combination
Monroe Doctrine, 178
Morgan, J. P., 193, 209, 234
Mormon settlements, 128
Morrill (Agricultural Colleges) Act (1862), 123–4, 134
Morrill (Agricultural Colleges) Act (1890), 134, 206
Morris, R., 8
Morris, William 145
Morrow, D. W., 179
Motor-car industry, see Automobile industry
Muckrakers, 197
Munitions, 8, 209, 254, 255–7
Munn v. Illinois (1876), 138

Napoleon (Berlin and Milan Decrees, 1806–7), 58–9
Napoleonic Wars, 58, 59, 60
National Association of Manufacturers, 146 n. 2
National Banks, and National Bank Act (1863), see Banking Acts and Banks
National Board of Farm Organisations, 226
National Conservation Commission, 204
National Debt, see Debt, National
National Defence Act (1916), 210
National Economist, 140
National Employment Service Act (1933), 143
National Farmers' Alliances, 139
National income, 190, 191, 193–5, 231, 236, 237, 242, 248, 252, 253, 259
National Industrial Recovery Act (1933), 237 ff.
Nationalization, 139, 140, 141, 145, 163, 186 n. 1, 197, 202, 226, 227, 237
National Labour Relations Act (1935), 243
National Labour Relations Board, 243, 243 n. 1
National Labour Union, 138, 142–3
National Lead Co., 105
National Metal Trades Association, 146 n. 2
National Monetary Commission, 185, 201
National Park Service, 251
'National Pike', 46–7, 86
National product, 235, 252, 253, 256, 259
National Recovery Administration, 237 ff.
National Refiners' Association, 117
National Resources Board, 250, 251
National Trades Union, 41
Nashville, 177
Navajo Indians, 121
Nazis, 255, 260
Negro, in U.S.A., 17–19, 20–2, 26, 28, 29–30, 80 ff., 90, 130–1, 134, 142, 143, 152 n. 2, 196, 197. See Slavery
New Deal, 150, 196, 202, 206, 210–11, 227, 235–54, 256
'New Era' (1920's), 230
New Freedom, 149, 171, 196, 198, 199–202, 214, 244 n. 1, 251
New Harmony, 39
New Imperialism, 175–82
Newlands Reclamation Act (1902), 203, 206, 223
Newlands Act (1913), 149, 205
New Model Unions (U.K.), 153
New Orleans, 51, 61
Newsprint, 174, 203 n. 1
New York Central Railroad, 52, 117
New York Stock Exchange, 190, 230, 231, 233, 234, 253
Nicaragua, 53, 178
Non-Intercourse Act (1809), 33, 59
'Normalcy', 252
Norris-LaGuardia Act (1932), 149, 200, 244
Norris, F., 197
Northern Pacific Railroad, 122, 159, 160–1, 190
Northern Securities Co. Case (1904), 199
North-West Ordinance (1787), 16, 24
Novelists, 197
Nullification Ordinance (1832), 70–1, 85

INDEX

Oberlin College, 83
Ocean Mail Act (1891), 167–8
Octopus, The, 197
Office of Economic Stabilization, 256
Office of Foreign Relief, 260
Office of Price Administration, 258
Office of War Mobilization, 256
Ohio Enabling Act (1802), 134
Ohio Life Insurance and Trust Co., 79
Oil Administration, 256
Oil and petroleum industry, 101, 103, 106, 107, 110, 116–18, 155, 164, 178–9, 199 n. 1, 203, 204, 215, 221, 231 n. 1
Oklahoma Indians, 123
Old age pensions, 242, 246
Old Northwest, 17, 19, 24–6, 47, 48
Old Southwest, 17–24
Olds, R. E., 108
Oligopoly, 200, 238, 238 n. 3, 245
Olmsted, F. L., 21
Omaha Platform (1892), 140–1, 188
Omnibus travel, 165–6
'Open Door' policy, 181–2
'Open price filing', 237
'Operation Rat-Hole', 262
Orders in Council, 56, 58–9
Organization for European Economic Co-operation (O.E.E.C.), 262–3
Oriental trade, 57, 161, 179–82
Owen, Robert, 38–9, 145–6

Packers' and Stockyards Act (1921) 227
Pakston Boys (1764), 6
Panama, 177
Panama Canal, 164, 177–8
Pan-American Airways, 180 n. 2
Panics, see Crises
Paper industry, 8, 109 n. 2, 174, 203 n. 1
Parity prices, 224, 249, 257–8
Parker, T., 82
Patent laws, 113 n. 2
Paterson Strikes (1912–13), 150
Patman Bill, 241
Patrons of Husbandry, see Granger movement
Payne-Aldrich Tariff Act (1909), see Tariffs
Peace of Paris (1898), 177, 180

Peace movement, 196
Pearl Harbour, 111, 256, 257
Peik v. Chicago and Northwestern Railroad (1876), 138
Pelling, H., 151–3
Pemmican, 121
Penal reform, 7
Pensions, Civil War, 97
People's Party, see Populism
People v. Melvin (1809–10), 40
Perlman, Prof. S., 39, 143, 153 n. 1
Perry, M. C., 179
Peru, 179
Petroleum, see Oil and Petroleum industry
Petrol-rationing, 158
Philadelphia Convention, 63–4
Philadelphia and Reading Railroad, 191
Philippine Islands, 180–1
Philippine Trade Act (1946), 181
Phillips, W., 82
Physical Valuation Act (1913), 163
Physiocrats, 64
Pierce, F., President, 53
Pigs, 132, 132 n. 1, 248
Pinchot, G., 203, 204
Pinkerton detectives, 146 n. 2, 147
Pit, The, 197
Pitt, William, 56
Plains, Great, 119 ff., 140, 223–4, 250
Plank roads, 48
Plantations, 17, 19, 20–1, 100, 130–1, 176, 177
Plastics, 204
Platt Amendment (Cuban Constitution, 1901), 176–7
Plough, steel, 120, 125, 128
Polk, J. K., President, 169, 176
Pools, 114–15
Poor, H. V., 48
Poor whites, 17, 19, 21
Population, 24–5, 81, 87, 120, 126, 132, 142, 151, 154–7, 158, 222–3, 231, 257, 259. See Immigration
Populism, 138, 139, 140–1, 188, 192 n. 1, 225
Postal Savings Act (1910), 206
Postal savings banks, 140 n. 1, 184, 206
Potato industry, 224
Potter, D. M., 195
Powderly, T. V., 144, 145

276 INDEX

Powder River Road, 122
Prairie Cattle Co., 125
Pre-emption Act (1841), 17, 17 n. 1, 84–5, 123
Prices, 71–2, 77, 78, 112, 127–8, 135, 139, 141, 147, 170, 183, 186–9, 190, 191, 192, 193–5, 200, 211, 212–15, 217–18, 220, 224, 227, 229–54, 257–8, 259
Price Stabilization Act (1942), 257–8
Primogeniture, 6–7
Privateering, 57
Processed foods, 131. See Canning industry
Progress and Poverty, 28, 196
Progressive movement, 115, 151, 171, 196 ff., 228
Progressive Party, 197–8, 228
Promontory Point, Utah, 121, 159
Publicity, 195, 222, 231, 232
Public Roads Administration, 251
Public utility companies, 233, 234, 237, 244, 250
Public Works Administration, 246
Puerto Rico, 177
Pujo Committee (1913), 115 n. 1, 201
Pullman's Palace Car Co., 147–9
Pullman Strike (1894), 147–9, 192
'Pump-priming', 240–3, 246–7, 253–4
Pure Food and Drugs Act (1906), 133
Pyrites, 103

Quebec Act (1774), 7
Quinine, 256
Quit-rents, 7
Quota system (immigration), 157, 217

Race riots (1871), 156
Radicalism, agrarian, 136–41, 196 ff., 225–8
Radio industry, 195, 221, 244
Railroads, 44–5, 48, 51–5, 78–9, 87, 88, 117, 121, 123, 124, 137, 138, 147–9, 155, 156, 157–63, 165, 166, 181, 182, 190, 191, 202, 205, 212, 218, 226, 230, 233, 234, 236, 243, 251
Railroad Administration, 211, 212
Railroad Brotherhoods, 149
Railroad Labour Board, 163

Railroad Retirement Act (1934), 243
Railroads' War Board, 212
Railway Mania (U.K., 1836–7), 78
Rainhill Trials, 52
Ranching, 119, 123, 124–5
Randolph, J., 61
Rationing, 158, 211, 255, 258, 262
Raw materials (trade in), 172–5
Rebates (railway), 117–18
Reciprocity, 170, 171, 247 n. 2, 261
Reclamation, 123, 202–4, 223–4, 250–1. Also see Conservation
Reclamation Act (1902), 123
'Reconstruction', 100, 100 n. 2
Reconstruction Finance Corporation (R.F.C.), 236, 239, 240, 241
Red River War (1874–5), 122
Refrigeration, 101, 132, 167 n. 2, 195, 221, 222
Refunding Agreements, 217–18
Regulator Movement (1768–9), 6
Reparations, 216–18
Report on the Establishment of a Mint (1791), 67
Report on Manufactures (1791), 65–6
Report on a National Bank (1790), 68
Report on the Public Credit (1790), 67
Republic Steel Corporation, 245, 245 n. 1
Reservations, Indian, 120, 121, 122, 123
Restrictive Acts (immigration), 157
Resumption Act (1875), 184
Revenue Act (1789), 67
Rice production, 7, 18, 21, 22, 155, 225
Riis, J., 197
Road system, 87, 163–4
Roads, 46–7, 86–7, 165–6, 202, 221, 251, 246–7
Robert E. Lee v. *Natchez* (Steamboat race), 50
Robinson-Patman Act (1936), 238 n. 2
Rochdale Pioneers, 137
Rockefeller, J. D., 116–18, 234
'Roosevelt Depression' (1937–8), 252–4
Roosevelt, F. D., President, 164, 196, 200, 204, 235–54, 255, 259, 260

INDEX

Roosevelt, T., President, 157, 162, 178, 192, 193, 197, 198–9, 200, 203–4
Rostow, E. V., 199 n. 1
Rubber industry, 173, 180, 221, 215, 244, 256–7, 258
Rule of 1756, 58
Rural Post Roads Act (1916), 202, 221
Russo-Japanese War (1904–5), 182
Rutgers v. *Waddington*, 63 n. 1

'Safety-valve' theory, 152
Sailing-ships, 62, 167, 167 n. 2
St. Lawrence Seaway and Power Project, 164–5, 165 n. 1
St. Louis Convention (1892), 140
Salt production, 103, 103 n. 2, 109
Samoa, 179, 179 n. 3
Sandalwood, 180
Santa Fe Trail, 45
Santo Domingo, 178
Savings banks, 140 n. 1, 145, 184, 206, 239
Schechter case (1935), 238
Schumpeter, J. A., 219
Scientific agriculture, 14, 27, 126 ff., 131–4, 224
Scientific management, 111–12
Seamen's Act (LaFollette, 1915), 168, 202, 206
Seamen's Union, 202
Secession, 60, 70–1, 80, 85, 92
Sectionalism, 3–6, 11, 14, 29–30, 80–92, 136, 151
Selective Service Acts:
(1917), 213
(1940), 256
Seligman, E. R. A., 214
Senate Committee on Education and Labour (1936–40), 245
Shame of the Cities, 197
Shannon, Prof. F. A., 225
Sharecropping, 131, 250
Shays' Rebellion, 9
Sheep rearing, 125
Sheffield, Lord John, 56–7
Sherman Anti-Trust Act (1890), 115, 148 n. 1, 162, 198–200, 206
Sherman Silver Purchase Act (1890) 187–8, 191, 192
Shipbuilding, 168, 212, 215, 218, 230, 242. See Merchant Marine
Shipping Act (1916), 168

Shipping Board, 211, 212
'Shun-pikes', 48
Silver, 67, 120, 138, 139, 186–9, 191, 192
Silver, G., 226
Silver Purchase Act (1934), 239 n. 2
Simpson, G., 196
Sinclair, Upton, 132 n. 2, 197
Singer, I. M., 19
Single Tax, 142, 226, 228
Sino-Japanese War, 181
Sioux Indian Wars, 122
Sitting Bull, Chief, 122
Skidmore, T., 196
Skunk farms, 225
Skyscrapers, 220
Slavery, 15–16, 19–22, 80–4, 90, 92, 100, 176
Slave-trading, 8, 11, 20, 21–2, 26
Slater, S., 36
Slum-clearance, 242, 246–7
Slump, World, 171 n. 1, 195, 219, 222, 224, 230–5. See Depressions
Smith-Hughes Act (1917), 134, 202, 206
Smith-Lever Act (1914), 134, 202, 206, 226
Snake Indians, 121
Socialism, 150, 151, 153, 185, 196–7, 205, 227 n. 2, 228
Socialist Labour Party, 197
Socialist Trade and Labour Alliance, 149
Social security, 243 ff.
Social Security Act (1935), 242, 244, 246, 252
Social settlements, 197
Soil Conservation and Domestic Allotment Act (1936), 248–9, 251
Soil erosion, 202–4, 249, 250–1
Soil Erosion Act (1935), 249, 250–1
South America (as U.S. market), 174, 179
South Improvement Co., 117
Southern Pacific Railroad, 159, 160, 161
'Southern rights', 85, 88–92
Southern Wealth and Northern Profits, 90–2
Southwest Ordinance (1790), 16
Sovereigns of Industry, 143 n. 3
Spain, 176–7, 184, 252
Spanish-American War (1898), 176–7, 184

Spanish Civil War, 252
Spargo, J., 197
Specie Circular (1836), 77–8
Specie Resumption Act (1875), 139, 186
Springfield armoury, 8
Square Deal, 198, 251
Standard Oil Co., 111, 114, 115, 116–18, 197, 199
States' rights, 65, 71, 74
Stead, W. T., 197
Steamboat Act (1852), 51
Steamboats, 44–5, 50–1
Steamship companies, 155
Steamships, 167, 167 n. 2
Steel industry, 146–7, 165, 167 n. 2. See Iron and Steel Industry
Steel-Rail Pool, 114
Steffens, L., 197
Stephens, U. S., 143
Steward, I., 142
Stock-raising Homestead Act (1916), 223
Stourbridge Lion, 52
Stove Founders' National Defence Association, 146 n. 2
Stove production, 35, 146
Stove Moulders' Union, 146
Stowe, Harriet B., 82
Street railways, 165
'Strict constructionists', 47, 64–5, 67–8
Strikes:
  1786, 40
  1790's and 1800's, 40
  1840's, 42
  1877, 142, 144, 156
  1885, 144–5
  1886, 142, 144–5
  1889 (U.K.), 150
  1892, 142, 146–7
  1894, 142, 147–9, 191–2
  1912, 150
  1913, 150
  1934, 228, 243
  1937, 243, 245, 253
  1946, 259–60
'Sub-Treasury' scheme, 140 n. 1
Sugar Bowl, 19
Sugar Equalization Board, 213, 227
Sugar production, 19, 21, 23, 58, 170, 171, 173, 176, 177, 180, 181, 198, 212–13, 243, 248

Suez Canal, 164, 175
Sulphur production, 103, 103 n. 1, 109
Summary View of the Rights of British America (1774), 64
Supreme Court (U.S.), 72, 118, 138, 149, 152–3, 162–3, 171 n. 1, 198–9, 202, 238, 243 n. 1, 244, 248–9
Sylvis, W. H., 142
Syndicalism, 149–50

Taft, W. H., President, 162, 171 n. 1, 182, 198, 199, 200, 213
Taft, Senator R. A., 262
Taft-Hartley Act (1947), 259–60
Tarbell, I. M., 115, 197
Tariffs, 23, 32, 34, 62, 63, 65–6, 68–71, 81, 84–5, 86, 87–8, 101, 102, 103, 109 n. 2, 111, 113, 139, 141, 162, 167, 168–72, 180–1, 188, 200–1, 205, 220, 225, 237, 239 n. 2
  1789, 59, 65
  1792, 66
  1828, 70–1, 85
  1857, 168, 201
  1861, 98, 168
  1864, 102, 168–9
  1867, 169
  1869, 169
  1872, 169
  1875, 169
  1883, 169
  1888, 169
  1890, 170, 176, 180, 187
  1894, 170, 171 n. 1, 176
  1897, 113, 115, 170
  1909, 170–1
  1913, 171, 200–1, 202
  1921, 171, 201
  1922, 171, 217, 236
  1930, 172, 236, 247 n. 2
Tariff Board (1909–12), 171, 171 n.1
Taxation, 66, 71, 98–9, 167, 169, 171, 171 n. 1, 183, 194–5, 196, 201, 205, 214, 215, 220, 226, 258
Taylor Grazing Act (1934), 223–4, 250–1
Tea production, 57
Tecumseh, 60
Telegraph, electric, 79 n. 3, 105
Telephone, 101, 250
Teller Resolution, 176

Temperance, 196
Tenancy laws, 249-50
Ten-Hours movement, 42
Tennessee Coal and Iron Co., 193
Tennessee Development Act (1933), 251
Tennessee Valley Scheme, 250-1
Territorial system, 16, 29-30
Texas, 30, 139
Texas and Pacific Railroad, 159, 160
Texas State Alliance, 139
Textile industry, 8, 69, 109-10, 150, 155, 218, 230, 231 n. 1, 238, 244
Thomas, Prof. B., 155-6
'Three-cornered' trade, 57
Three-Year Homestead Act (1912), 223
Tidewater aristocracy, 6, 26
Timber Culture Act (1873), 123
Timber and Stone Act (1878), 123
Tippecanoe, 60
Tobacco production, 7, 18, 21, 23, 177, 180, 181, 248
Tractors, 224, 231 n. 1
Trade, 8, 9, 56-62, 141, 163, 164, 167-82, 190, 191, 209-10, 216-18, 219-20, 225, 235, 247 n. 2
Trade Agreements Act (1934), 247 n. 2
Trade Disputes Act (U.K., 1927), 148 n. 1
Trade Unions, see Labour
Trade Union Congress (U.K.), 146
Trails, 15-16, 44-6
Transcontinental railroad, 53, 158-63
Transportation, 44-55, 101, 108-9, 132, 133, 137, 138, 139, 157-66, 175, 197, 212, 255
Transportation (Esch-Cummins) Act (1920), 115 n. 1, 163
Treasury Notes of 1890, 187-9
Treatise on Money (1930), 240
Treaty, Anglo-American (1846), 31
Treaty of Guadaloupe Hidalgo (1848), 30
Treaty of Paris (1783), 3, 6-7 8
Treaty of Titusville (1872), 117
Tripolitan pirates, 56, 57
Triumphant Democracy (1888), 142
Trolleys, electric, 165
Truck-farming, 26, 26 n. 2, 130

Truman, H., President, 164, 159
Trusts, 114 ff., 118, 136, 170, 192, 196, 197-200, 206, 237, 238-9, 238 n. 2, 253. See Combination
Tucker, B. R., 197
Turner, F. J., 15, 28
Turnpike Act (1817), 47
Turnpike roads, 44-5, 46-8. 165-6
Turnpike trusts, 46
Tutuila, 179 n. 3
Tydings-McDuffie Act (1934), 181
Tyler, J., President, 74
Typewriter, 101, 112, 112 n. 1
Typographical Society, 40

Uncle Tom's Cabin, 82, 122
Underwood-Simmons Tariff Act (1913), see Tariffs
Union Pacific Railroad, 121, 159-61
United Empire Loyalists, 6
United Garment Workers Union, 152
United Mineworkers of America, 149, 244
United Nations Relief and Rehabilitation Administration (U.N.R.R.A.), 260-2
United Shoe Machinery Co., 113, 199
United Shoe Machinery Co. case (1918), 199
U.S. Banks, see Banks, U.S.
U.S. Bureau of Fisheries, 251
U.S.—Dominican Treaty (1907), 178
United States v. E. C. Knight and Co. (1895), 198
U.S. and Foreign Securities Corportation, 232
U.S. Grain Corporation, 213, 227
U.S. Housing Authority, 246, 247, 247 n. 1
U.S. Maritime Commission, 168
U.S. Steel Corporation, 102-3, 111, 114, 115-16, 193, 199, 234, 245
U.S. Steel Corporation case (1920), 199
Up From Slavery, 197
Urban growth, 220, 221, 257
Ute Indians, 121

Van Buren, President, 42, 143
Vandenburg, Senator, 262

INDEX

Vanderbilt, W. H., 161
Venezuela, 179
Veterans, 120, 223, 241, 241 n. 1, 252, 253
Victory Tax, 258
Villard, H., 160
Virgin Islands (Danish West Indies), 178, 188

Wabash and Erie Canal, 49
Wabash, St. Louis and Pacific Railroad Co. v. *Illinois* (1886), 138
Wagner-Connery (National Labour Relations) Act (1933), 243
Wagner-Steagall Housing Act (1937), 247 n. 1
Walsh, F. P., 213
Walsh-Healey (Government Contracts) Act (1936), 243
'Waltham Plan', 37
War:
 Of Independence, 3, 4, 6, 7–8, 32
 1812, 17, 18, 32, 33, 35, 56–61, 71–2, 85, 171
 Civil, 3–4, 26, 32, 76–92, 97–9, 102, 111, 119, 136, 142, 157, 158, 167, 168, 171, 173, 182, 182 n. 1, 183, 186, 190, 194, 214, 219
 World War I, 150, 158, 163, 165, 167, 168, 171, 175–6, 182, 193, 199, 202, 206, 209–16, 225, 252, 257, 261
 World War II, 111, 146, 158, 164, 168, 173–4, 181, 211, 214, 232, 238, 242, 242 n. 3, 245, 254, 255–8, 261
 Russo-Japanese, 182
 Sino-Japanese, 181
 Korean, 186
'War Babies', 171
War Finance Corporation, 211, 214–15, 227
Warhawks, 60–1, 69, 70
War Industries Board, 211
War Labour Board, 211, 213, 256
War Manpower Commission, 256
War Production Board, 256
War Services Committee, 211
Washington, G., President, 27, 63, 64, 67
Wealth Against Commonwealth, 197
Weaver, J. B., 139, 141, 187, 188
Weeks Act (1911), 203, 204, 206
Weld, T., 82
Wells, D. A., 97, 169, 196
Western Federation of Miners, 149–50
Western Rural, 139
Westward movement, 14–31, 151, 152. (See Frontier)
Weydemeyer, J., 38
Wheat, 24–6, 78, 99, 120, 126, 128, 130, 131–2, 133, 139, 170, 171, 191–2, 212–13, 224, 225, 225 n. 1, 248, 249
Wheeler-Rayburn Act (1935), 250
Whisky Insurrection (1794), 6, 66
White-Jones Act (1928), 168
Whitney, E., 18–19, 36
Wilson-Gorman Tariff Act (1894), see Tariffs
Wilson, W., President, 157, 163, 171, 179, 182, 196, 198, 199–202, 209, 210, 211, 221
Withington, C. B., 128, 131
Woollen industry, 7, 8, 35–7, 131, 169, 170, 171–3
Works Progress Administration (W.P.A.), 246 ff.

Yellow dog contracts, 245
Yellow fever, 176
Young, A., 47
Youngstown Sheet and Tube Co., 245 n. 1

Zinc production, 104, 104 n. 1, 109